21世纪经济管理新形态教材 · 国际经济与贸易系列

国际货物运输与保险
（双语版）

崔　玮 ◎ 主编

清华大学出版社
北　京

内 容 简 介

本书阐述国际商品交换具体过程中运输与保险环节的基本知识、国际规则与惯例以及实际业务操作,具体包括:各种运输方式的特点、业务流程、运费计算及运输单据;保险的基本原则、货物运输保险条款、海运货物保险实务等。通过学习,学生能够较全面和熟练地掌握关于国际贸易运输与保险的基本知识与基础理论、法律规定和国际惯例,并具有处理具体国际货运与保险业务问题的能力及进行实际国际货运与保险业务操作的能力;同时,团队合作意识及商业伦理观念得以加强。

本书可作为高等院校经管类相关专业课或跨专业选修课使用的教材,特别适用于双语或全英语课程,也可作为国际贸易从业人员培训或自学的参考用书。

图书在版编目(CIP)数据

国际货物运输与保险 :双语版 :汉、英 / 崔玮主编. -- 北京 :清华大学出版社,2025.6.
(21世纪经济管理新形态教材). -- ISBN 978-7-302-69354-3

Ⅰ. F511.41;F840.63

中国国家版本馆 CIP 数据核字第 2025TP5185 号

责任编辑:张　伟
封面设计:汉风唐韵
责任校对:宋玉莲
责任印制:刘　菲

出版发行:清华大学出版社
　　　网　　　址:https://www.tup.com.cn,https://www.wqxuetang.com
　　　地　　　址:北京清华大学学研大厦 A 座　　　邮　　编:100084
　　　社 总 机:010-83470000　　　邮　　购:010-62786544
　　　投稿与读者服务:010-62776969,c-service@tup.tsinghua.edu.cn
　　　质量反馈:010-62772015,zhiliang@tup.tsinghua.edu.cn
　　　课件下载:https://www.tup.com.cn,010-83470332
印 装 者:小森印刷(天津)有限公司
经　　销:全国新华书店
开　　本:185mm×260mm　　印　张:21.5　　字　数:494 千字
版　　次:2025 年 7 月第 1 版　　印　次:2025 年 7 月第 1 次印刷
定　　价:69.00 元

产品编号:081397-01

前言

党的二十大报告指出："稳步扩大规则、规制、管理、标准等制度型开放。推动货物贸易优化升级，创新服务贸易发展机制，发展数字贸易，加快建设贸易强国。"在当前复杂多变的国际形势下，推动对外贸易的高质量发展不仅是经济高质量发展的内在需要，也是构建贸易强国的要求。外贸高质量发展对高质量外贸人才也提出了更高的要求，外贸从业人员应具备良好的国际视野以及海外营销、跨文化沟通和国际市场风险管理能力，熟悉国际贸易规则和惯例，了解国际贸易规则的最新变化，同时也应具备在复杂多变的环境下开展国际贸易业务的综合实践操作能力。这就要求高校在人才培养过程中强化国际贸易实务操作能力和国际商务拓展能力的培养，把分析和解决实际问题能力作为衡量培养质量的主要标准。

国际货物运输与保险是为国际贸易顺利开展保驾护航的两个关键环节。商品运输是外贸合同履行过程中标的交付的一项重要业务，国际货物运输不仅是国际贸易实现的必要条件，更是其发展的强大驱动力。它通过海、陆、空等多种方式，跨越国界将商品送达目的地，确保了商品与资源在全球范围内的流通与配置。高效、安全的运输体系能促进国际贸易的繁荣与发展；反之则可能成为贸易增长的瓶颈。同时，国际贸易的需求也推动着国际货物运输方式的创新与升级。两者相辅相成，共同推动全球经济的紧密连接与增长。因此，运输在国际贸易中的地位日益重要。但是，由于国际贸易运距长、涉及面广、中间环节多、情况复杂多变、时间性强，所以国际货物运输的风险比国内运输要大。国际贸易中的货物在运输过程中不可避免地会因国际形势变化、社会动乱、自然灾害和意外事故等而遭受损失。为运输途中的货物投保国际货运险是国际上普遍采用的行之有效的转嫁风险的对策，也是国际贸易活动中重要的一环。国际货物运输方式与运输线路的确定、运输流程的组织与管理、投保险别的选择、保险的理赔与索赔等都会直接影响进出口合同的顺利履行及买卖双方贸易利益的实现。

完成国际贸易运输与保险业务既需要熟悉相关的国际规则、国际公约、法律、法规与国际惯例，也需要具有较强的实践操作能力。同时，由于国际贸易运输与保险具有很强的涉外性，与国外客户沟通、向国外运输企业及保险公司办理业务、缮制及处理各种单据等都需要较强的英语运用能力。双语国际贸易运输与保险教材能够满足该课程双语或全英语教学的需要，同时也有利于学生更深入地理解国际规则、国际公约以及国内外保险条款等，使学生在专业课的学习过程中提高专业英语应用能力。

在本书编写过程中，编者将理论与实践相融合，力争体现以下特色：①保证在知识系统性的基础上突出重点。双语撰写使得教材的篇幅及内容受到一定的限制，但本书仍然对国际贸易运输与保险的理论与实践进行了系统梳理，在此基础上以与国际贸易关系最为密切的运输与保险内容及其最新发展作为重点进行阐述，如运输部分的海运、空运及集装箱运输，保险部分的海运保险，特别是主要保险条款的最新发展等。②注重应用性和操作性。本书更加注重实际工作的需要，对运输与保险的业务流程、各种运输方式运费及保险相关费用的核算、主要单据的缮制等都进行了阐述，并配有相关练习。③双语撰写并融入有关原文内容。将国际公约、伦敦保险人协会保险条款英文原文融入教材内容，并力求循序渐进、深入浅出。④注重编写体例的灵活性与多样性。每一章都设有学习目标、引导案例、扩展阅读、中英文对照专业术语、即测即练（英文）及解析、习题（英文）及参考答案等内容，增强导学导读的便利性。

本书旨在对国际贸易运输与保险的基本理论与操作实务以中英文对照的方式进行全面阐述。全书共有 13 章，其中，第 1 章至第 8 章为国际贸易运输部分，在对国际货物运输基本概念、发展、特性及作用进行概述的基础上，分别介绍国际海洋货物运输、国际集装箱运输、国际航空货物运输、国际铁路货物运输及国际多式联运等运输方式的基础理论与操作实务；第 9 章至第 13 章为国际运输保险部分，在介绍保险基础知识及保险原理的基础上，系统介绍国际运输保险保障的范围、保险条款以及投保与承保、索赔与理赔的实务操作。本书第 1 章至第 11 章由北京联合大学崔玮编写，第 12 章、13 章由北京联合大学赵绍全、崔玮编写。

本书编写过程中参考了众多专家、学者的著述，并得到了清华大学出版社的大力支持，在此一并表示诚挚的谢意！

由于作者水平有限，书中难免存在疏漏之处，衷心希望得到各位专家和广大读者的批评指正。

编　者

2024 年 9 月 4 日

目 录

第 1 章

Chapter 1

国际贸易运输概述
Overview of International Trade Transport

Learning Objectives：

1. Master basic modes and objects of international cargo transport；
2. Get to know the nature，roles and new development trends of international transport；
3. Master business scope of international freight agent and specify the roles of international freight agent for international trade，identify different types of freight forwarders and transport intermediaries；
4. Describe the strategic constraints on the choice of transport mode.

引导案例

苏伊士运河堵塞影响全球贸易

苏伊士运河建成于 1869 年，可连接地中海和红海，是欧洲到亚洲的最短航道，约 12％的世界贸易量都通过这条人造运河。2021 年 3 月 23 日，中国台湾长荣集团旗下巴拿马籍货轮"长赐号"在苏伊士运河搁浅，该船长达 400 米、宽近 60 米、排水量达 22 万吨，几乎完全侧着身子在运河中停了下来，而苏伊士运河在这一段只有 24 米深、205 米宽，实在没有太大操纵空间，因此导致欧亚之间最重要的航道之一——苏伊士运河被切断。运河两端停留了许多满载的油轮，船上装载着来自沙特阿拉伯、俄罗斯、阿曼和美国的石油。截至 2021 年 3 月 29 日，共有 450 艘船只因"长赐号"搁浅事故被卡住。其他船只则转向绕道非洲南端更长的路线。3 月 29 日，"长赐号"成功重新上浮，苏伊士运河货轮搁浅危机解除。"长赐号"搁浅 6 天，一度阻断约 12％的全球贸易流通，对运河管理部门、等待通航的船只、等待货物的零售商等而言，都意味着将面临巨额损失。德国保险公司安联的研究显示，搁浅导致的苏伊士运河封锁或使全球贸易每天损失 60 亿～100 亿美元，这次事件也反映了全球供应链的脆弱性。

资料来源：苏伊士运河［EB/OL］. (2024-07-18). https://baike. baidu. com/item/％E8％8B％8F％E4％BC％8A％E5％A3％AB％E8％BF％90％E6％B2％B3/312602? fromModule ＝ search-result _ lemma.

运输是人和物的载运与输送。运输是随着商品生产和商品交换而产生、发展的，没有运输，进行商品的交换是不可能的。按照运送对象，运输可分为货物运输与旅客运输。货物运输又可按照地域划分为国内货物运输与国际货物运输。

Transportation is the carrying and conveying of people and things. Transportation comes into being and develops with the production and exchange of goods. Without transportation, it is impossible to exchange goods. According to the object of transport, transportation can be divided into cargo transport and passenger transport. Cargo transport can also be divided into domestic cargo transport and international cargo transport according to the scope of transport.

1.1 国际贸易运输的概念及发展
(Concept and Development of International Trade Transport)

1.1.1 国际贸易运输的概念(Concept of International Trade Transport)

国际货物运输是货物在国家与国家、国家与地区之间的运输。从广义上讲,其泛指交通运输部门、外贸部门或其他货主和货运代理人办理的运输业务。(这三方面业务的工作性质是有区别的,但又是密不可分的。)通常其是指按照国际公约和国际惯例,遵照有关国家的法律规定,由货方与承运方签订并履行运输合同,将商品从出口国运送到进口国的经济行为。

International freight transport is the conveyance of goods between countries or regions. Broadly speaking, it refers to transport operations carried out by transport enterprises, foreign trade companies, or other cargo owners and freight forwarders. (The nature of work in these three areas of business is distinct but inseparable.) It is usually an economic activity in which goods are transported from the exporting country to the importing country in accordance with international conventions and practices, and in compliance with the legal provisions of the countries concerned, through the conclusion and fulfillment of a contract of carriage between the shipper and the carrier.

国际货物运输按照运输对象的性质可分为国际贸易物资运输和国际非贸易物资(如展览品、援外物资、个人行李、办公用品等)运输。由于国际货物运输主要是国际贸易物资运输,非贸易物资的运输往往只是贸易物资运输部门的附带业务,所以,国际货物运输通常又被称为国际贸易运输,对一个国家来说就是对外贸易运输。

International cargo transport can be divided into international trade goods transport and non-tradable goods (such as exhibits, foreign aid goods, personal baggage, and office supplies) transport according to the nature of the object of transport. Since international cargo transport is mainly the transport of goods for international trade, and the transport of non-tradable goods is often the incidental business of the transport company, international cargo transport is often referred to as international trade transport, which for a country is foreign trade transport.

在国际贸易中,进出口商品在空间上的流通范围更加广阔,运输工作更是不可缺少的重要环节。商品运输是合同履行过程中标的交付的一个重要环节。商品成交后,通过运输,按照约定的时间、地点和条件把商品交给对方,贸易的全过程才最后完成。

In international trade, the circulation scope of imported and exported commodities is wider in space, making transportation an indispensable and important link. Cargo transportation is an important part of contract performance. After the transaction of goods, they are delivered from the exporter to the importer through transportation according to the agreed time, place and conditions. Afterwards, the whole process of trade is finally completed.

国际贸易运输与进出口贸易相辅相成、互为促进。一方面,随着商品生产的不断发展和交换范围的日益扩大,进出口贸易不断增长,为国际贸易运输发展创造了更好的条件;另一方面,运输业的发展又为开拓越来越广阔的市场提供了可能性。这是因为运输业的发展加快了货运速度、增加了货物运载量、缩短了流通时间、节省了流通费用、扩大了各国对外贸易商品的流通量,从而推动了国际贸易的发展。因此,运输在国际贸易中所占的地位日益重要。

International trade transport is complementary to import and export trade, and they are mutually reinforcing. On the one hand, with the continuous development of commodity production and the expanding scope of exchange, import and export trade is growing, which creates better conditions for the development of international trade transportation; on the other hand, the development of transport industry provides the possibility to open up increasingly broad markets. This is because the development of the transport industry accelerates the speed of freight transport, increases cargo carrying capacity, shortens circulation time, saves circulation costs, and expands the flow of foreign trade commodities, thus promoting the development of international trade. Therefore, transportation plays an increasingly important role in international trade.

1.1.2 国际贸易运输的发展(Development of International Trade Transport)

自美国人富尔敦发明了轮船和英国人斯蒂芬孙发明了火车头之后,人类从事的运输活动就从利用自然动力和畜力进入机器动力时代。1807年,第一艘轮船"克莱蒙特"号在美国下水,1825年,第一条铁路在英国正式开通货运业务,标志着机械运输业的开端。在此之后,海洋运输与铁路运输飞速发展起来,20世纪30年代,汽车运输、航空运输和管道运输又相继迅猛发展。这样,就逐步形成了包括水、陆、空等多种运输方式的现代化运输体系。

第二次世界大战后,世界科学技术突飞猛进,人类开始进入一个原子、电子和宇航时代。科学技术的进步,进一步推动了运输业的发展,许多新的运输工具被发明并使用,其特点是向大型化、专业化、高速化和自动化发展。

(1)大型化。大型化指船舶向大型化方向发展。特别是油轮,最大的超级油轮达到80万吨,最大的超级大型矿砂轮已达40万吨,最大的集装箱船装载量超过24 000 TEU

（标准箱）①。

（2）专业化。专业化指为适应货运需要，提高装载能力，加速船舶周转，降低运费，船舶日趋专业化。如油轮、矿砂船、滚装滚卸船、载驳船、集装箱船等。尤其是集装箱船获得了迅速的发展。

世界各大航运国家的杂货船中有75%～90%使用集装箱船，而且世界各大港口中有相当一部分只允许集装箱船舶装卸。据统计，一艘集装箱船的运载量相当于七艘同样大小的普通型船舶，而且每载重吨营运成本比普通型船舶低约30%。此外，集装箱船又方便了进出口双方的运输，可进行"门到门"运输。

（3）高速化。高速化指当今世界船舶航速普遍提高，如集装箱船最高设计时速达到25节。从远东到欧洲，过去航行40～50天，现在需15～16天，从而大大缩短了时间，加速了船舶的周转。

（4）自动化。自动化指随着科学技术进一步发展，船舶自动化程度越来越高，船员人数显著减少，原来万吨轮需60人左右，现在大型的集装箱船仅需20名左右的船员。

Since Fulton invented the steamship and Stephenson invented the locomotive, transportation has entered the era of machine power from the use of natural power and animal power. The first steamship, Clermont, was launched in the United States in 1807; the first railway officially began freight service in Britain in 1825, marking the beginning of mechanical transportation. After that, maritime transport and railway transport developed rapidly, and in the 1930s, automobile transport, air transport and pipeline transport developed one after another rapidly, gradually forming a modern transport system including water, land and air transport.

After the Second World War, science and technology advanced rapidly, and mankind began to enter an era of atoms, electronics and astronautics. The progress of science and technology has further promoted the development of the transport industry. Many new means of transport have been invented and used, which are developing towards large scale, specialization, high speed and automation.

（1）Large scale. This refers to the fact that ships are moving towards larger sizes. Particularly for tankers, the largest supertanker has a load capacity of over 800 000 tons, 400 000 tons for the largest super-large ore carrier, and more than 24 000 TEU for the largest container ship.

（2）Specialization. This refers to the increasing specialization of vessels to meet the needs of freight transport, increase loading capacity, speed up vessel turnover and reduce freight rates. Vessels such as oil tankers, ore carriers, roll-on and roll-off ships, barges, container ships and other specialized ships emerged. In particular, container ships have developed rapidly.

---

① 世界上最大的集装箱船是地中海航运公司（MSC）旗下的"MSC Irina"和"MSC Tessa"，其最大装载量达到24 346 TEU和24 116 TEU。数据来源：交出实力｜连破世界纪录！交银金租为地中海航运订造的两艘超大型集装箱船同日命名交付［EB/OL］.（2023-03-22）. http://business. sohu. com/a/657486077_121123888.

75%-90% of the general cargo vessels in the world's major shipping countries are container ships, and a considerable part of the world's major ports only allow container ships to be loaded and unloaded. According to statistics, the carrying capacity of a container ship is equivalent to seven ordinary ships of the same size, and the operating cost per ton is about 30% lower than that of ordinary ships. In addition, container ships facilitate the transportation of both importers and exporters and can carry out "door-to-door" transportation.

(3) High speed. This refers to the general increase in the speed of ships nowadays, for example, container ships are designed to reach a maximum speed of 25 knots. It used to take 40-50 days to sail from the Far East to Europe, but now it takes 15-16 days, which greatly shortens the time and accelerates the turnover of ships.

(4) Automation. It means that with the further development of science and technology, the degree of ship automation is getting higher and higher, and the number of crew members is significantly reduced. It used to need about 60 crew members for a 10 000-ton ship, and now only about 20 crews are needed for a large container ship.

1.2 国际贸易运输的特点与作用
(Characteristics and Functions of International Trade Transport)

1.2.1 国际贸易运输的特点(Characteristics of International Trade Transport)

1. 国际贸易运输涉及国际关系问题,政策性强(International Trade Transport Involves Issues of International Relations and is Highly Policy-oriented)

国际货物运输是国际贸易的一个组成部分,在组织国际货物运输的过程中,需要经常与其他国家或地区发生直接或间接的广泛的业务联系,这种联系不仅是经济上的,而且常常涉及国际政治问题。因此,国际货物运输是一项政策性很强的涉外工作,我们在办理国际贸易运输业务时不仅要遵照相关国际贸易准则,还要严格按照有关国际公约、法律、法规和国际惯例以及我国对外政策的要求来进行工作。

International cargo transport is an integral part of international trade. In the process of organizing international cargo transport, it is necessary to have extensive direct or indirect business links with other countries or regions. Such links are not only economic, but also often involve international political issues. Therefore, international cargo transport is a highly policy-oriented foreign-related work, requiring us to not only comply with the relevant international trade rules, but also strictly comply with the relevant international conventions, laws, regulations and practices, as well as the requirements of China's foreign policies.

2. 国际贸易运输路线长,环节多(International Trade Transport Has Long Routes and Many Links)

国际贸易运输是国家与国家、国家与地区之间的运输。一般来说,其运输距离比较长，往往需要使用多种运输工具，通过多次装卸搬运，经过许多中间环节，如转船、变换运输方式等。如果其中一个环节出现问题，则会影响整个国际贸易运输过程。这就要求我们周密组织，注意各环节的衔接和配合，避免出现脱节现象。

International trade transport is transportation between countries and regions. Generally speaking, the transport distance of international cargo transportation is relatively long, which often requires the use of a variety of means of transport, going through multiple times of loading, unloading, and handling, through many intermediate links such as transferring ships and changing the mode of transport. If one of the links has problems, it will affect the whole process of international trade transport. It requires us to organize carefully and pay attention to the connection and cooperation of all links to avoid disconnection.

3. 国际贸易运输涉及面广，情况复杂多变（International Trade Transport Covers a Wide Range of Aspects and the Situation is Complex and Versatile）

国际贸易运输涉及国内外许多部门，需要和不同国家和地区的货主、交通运输部门、检验检疫部门、保险公司、银行或其他金融机构、海关、港口以及各种中间代理商打交道。同时，各国或地区的政治、法律、金融货币制度不同，政策、法令及规定不一，贸易、运输习惯和经营做法不同，加之政治、经济和自然条件的变化，都会对国际贸易运输产生较大的影响。

International trade shipments involve many sectors, both domestic and international. It requires dealing with cargo owners, transport enterprises, inspection and quarantine authorities, insurance companies, banks or other financial institutions, customs, ports and various intermediaries in different countries and regions. At the same time, different political, legal, financial and monetary systems, different policies, decrees and regulations, different trade and transport habits and business practices, as well as changes in political, economic and natural conditions in different countries or regions will have significant impacts on international trade transport.

4. 国际贸易运输的时间性强（International Trade Transport is Time-sensitive）

当前国际商品市场竞争十分激烈，不仅要求商品质量好，而且应适时供应市场。按时装运进出口货物，及时将货物运至目的地，对履行进出口合同、满足竞争市场的需求、提高市场竞争力、及时结汇都具有重要的意义。特别是一些鲜活商品、季节性商品和敏感性强的商品，更要求迅速运输，及时组织供应，才有利于提高其竞争力，巩固和扩大国外市场。

At present, international commodity markets are highly competitive and require not only the good quality of goods, but also timely supply to the market. The timely shipment of import and export goods and the timely delivery of goods to their destinations are of great significance for the fulfillment of import and export contracts, meeting the demands of competitive markets, improving market competitiveness and timely settlement of foreign exchange. In particular, some fresh commodities, seasonal commodities and sensitive commodities require fast transportation and timely organization of supply in order to improve their competitiveness and to consolidate and expand foreign markets.

5. 国际贸易运输风险较大（The Risk of International Trade Transport is Relatively High）

由于运距较长,涉及面广,中间环节多,沿途要经过许多国家和地区,情况复杂多变,加之时间性又很强,所以国际货物运输的风险比国内运输要大。运输沿途国际形势的变化、社会的动乱、各种自然灾害和意外事故的发生,以及战乱、封锁禁运或海盗活动等都可能直接或间接影响国际贸易运输,甚至造成严重后果。为了转嫁运输风险的损失,进出口货物和工具通常都要向保险人办理运输保险。

扩展阅读 1.1　IMB Piracy Report

The risks of international cargo transportation are greater than those of domestic transportation due to long distances, wide coverage, many intermediate links, passing through many countries and regions along the way, complex and changing situations, and the strong timeliness. Changes in the international situation, social unrest, various natural disasters and accidents, as well as wars, blockades and embargoes or piracy along the transport route may directly or indirectly affect international trade transport and may even lead to serious consequences. In order to pass on the loss of transport risk, imported and exported goods and conveyances are usually covered by transport insurance with an insurer.

1.2.2　国际贸易运输的作用（Functions of International Trade Transport）

1. 国际贸易运输是国际贸易的重要组成部分（International Trade Transport is an Important Part of International Trade）

国际贸易运输与国际贸易相互依存又相互促进。国际贸易运输是为适应国际贸易的需要而产生和发展的,它贯穿于国际贸易的整个过程。没有国际贸易运输,就不能实现货物由卖方向买方的跨国界移动,国际贸易也就无法实现和完成。因此,国际贸易依赖于国际贸易运输来最终完成贸易的全过程,它是国际贸易环节中不可缺少的重要组成部分。

International trade transport and international trade are interdependent and mutually reinforcing. International trade transport has emerged and developed in response to the needs of international trade, and it runs through the entire process of international trade. Without international trade transport, the cross-border movement of goods from the seller to the buyer cannot be realized, and international trade will not be achieved and completed. Therefore, international trade relies on international trade transport to complete the whole process of trade, which makes transport an important and indispensable part of international trade.

2. 国际贸易运输能够促进国际贸易的发展（International Trade Transport Can Promote the Development of International Trade）

随着世界各国生产的发展和世界贸易额的不断增长,国际贸易市场竞争越来越激烈。进口商对于交货时间、运输速度、运输质量、运输费用等越来越重视,从而对国际货物运输提出了更高的要求。为了满足这种不断提高的要求,通过改进现代化的运输工具、采用科学化的运输管理模式,国际运输体系、运输组织方法不断完善并日益成熟。运输能力的提高缩短了运输时间、加快了货物周转速度、增加了运载量、降低了运输成本、减少了货物损失,使得国际贸易中的货物运输质量不断提高,有力地促进了国际贸易的发展。

With the development of worldwide production and the increasing volume of world trade, the international trade market is becoming more and more competitive. Importers are paying more and more attention to delivery time, transport speed, quality, and costs, thus putting forward a higher demand on international cargo transportation. In order to meet this growing demand, international transport systems and transport organization methods improved and matured through the improvement of modern means of transport and the adoption of scientific modes of transport management. The improvement of transportation capacity shortens the transportation time, speeds up the turnover of goods, increases the carrying capacity, lowers the transportation cost, reduces the loss of goods, makes the quality of cargo transportation in international trade improve continuously, and strongly promotes the development of international trade.

3. 国际贸易运输能够平衡国际收支(International Trade Transport Can Help Achieving Favorable Balance of International Payments)

国际贸易运输是一种无形商品的国际贸易,它交换的是一种特殊的商品——运输服务。因此,对于一个国家而言,提供的运输服务越多,国际货运的规模越大,效益就越高,也就能获得越多的外汇收入,进而增加本国的外汇储备。

International trade transport is an international trade of intangible goods, which exchanges the special commodity of transport services. Therefore, for a country, the more transport services provided, the larger the scale of international shipments. It produces higher foreign exchange earning, which in turn increases the country's foreign exchange reserves.

4. 国际贸易运输能够促进国家间的经济与文化交流(International Trade Transport Can Facilitate Economic and Cultural Exchanges Among Countries)

发展对外贸易和对外贸易运输能促使国际商品流通日益频繁,国家间的经济分工与合作日益紧密,对全球经济一体化的形成也能起到积极的作用。同时,国际贸易运输促进了国际经济、贸易往来与交流合作,也促进了人员往来和各国科技、文化交流。

The development of foreign trade and foreign trade transport can promote the international circulation of goods, promote the economic division of labor and cooperation between countries, and also play a positive role in the formation of global economic integration. At the same time, it promotes international economic and trade exchanges and cooperation, as well as personnel exchanges and scientific, technological and cultural exchanges among countries.

1.3　国际贸易运输方式（Modes of International Trade Transport）

1.3.1　国际贸易运输的主要方式（Main Modes of International Trade Transport）

国际贸易运输的主要方式如图 1-1 所示。

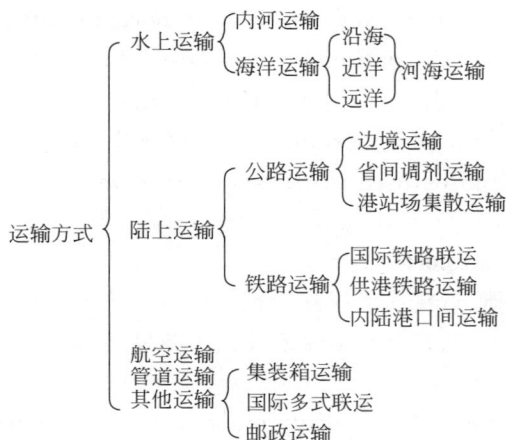

图 1-1　国际贸易运输的主要方式

1. 水上运输（Water Transport）

水上运输可分为海洋运输和内河运输。其中海洋运输又分为沿海运输、近洋运输和远洋运输。海洋运输是国际货物运输中最主要的运输方式。根据联合国贸易和发展会议（UNCTAD）的数据，超过 80％的国际贸易货物都是通过海洋运输的，我国进出口商品中 80％～90％的货物也是通过海洋运输的。内河运输则是连接内陆腹地与沿海地区的纽带，在运输和集散进出口货物中发挥着重要作用。

Water transport can be divided into marine transport and inland waterway transport. Among them, marine transport is divided into coastal transport, offshore transport and ocean transport. Marine transport is the most important mode of transport in international cargo transportation. According to the data of UNCTAD, more than 80％ of international trade goods are transported by sea, and 80％-90％ of China's import and export commodities are transported by sea. Inland waterway transport is the link between the inland hinterland and coastal areas, and plays an important role in the transportation and distribution of imported and exported goods.

2. 陆上运输（Land Transport）

陆上运输可分为铁路运输和公路运输。在国际贸易运输中，铁路运输是仅次于海洋运输的主要运输方式，海洋运输的进出口货物也大多是靠铁路运输进行集中和分拨的。铁路运输具有不受气候条件影响、可保障全年正常运输、运量较大、速度较快、连续性高、运转过程中遭遇风险的可能性较小、货运手续比海运简单等优点。公路运输是一种基础性的运输方式，它不仅可以直接运进或运出进出口货物，而且其他运输方式也需要公路运输的配合，是集散进出口货物的重要手段。

Land transport includes rail transport and road transport. In international trade transport, rail transport is the main mode of transport ranked only second to sea transport, and most of the imported and exported goods transported by sea are also centralized and allocated by rail transport. Rail transport has the advantages of being unaffected by climatic conditions and can be used normally all year round, with larger volume, faster speed, higher continuity, less possibility of encountering risks during operation, and simpler freight procedures than marine transport. Road transport is a basic mode of transport and an important means of collecting and distributing imported and exported goods. It can be used to transport imported and exported goods directly, and other modes of transport also need its cooperation.

3. 航空运输（Air Transport）

航空运输是一种快捷、运输质量很高的现代化运输方式，适宜运送急需物资、鲜活商品、精密仪器和贵重物品。随着航空运输事业的不断发展，采用航空运输的货物种类及其货运量也在不断增加。

Air transport is a fast, high quality, modern mode of transportation, suitable for transporting urgent supplies, fresh commodities, precision instruments, and valuables. With the continuous development of air transport, the types of cargo and the volume of cargo transported by air are also increasing.

4. 管道运输（Pipeline Transport）

管道运输是以铺设的管道作为运输工具和运输通路的一种长距离输送液体和气体物资的运输方式。管道运输具有运输量大、连续性高、运输速度快、安全可靠、投资少、费用低等优点。管道运输除广泛用于石油、天然气的长距离运输外，还可运输矿石、煤炭等粉末状、颗粒状固体。这种运输方式在俄罗斯、哈萨克斯坦等国家与中国的原油和天然气贸易中发挥着不可替代的作用。

Pipeline transport is a kind of long-distance transportation mode for liquid and gas materials, which takes pipeline as the transportation means and transportation channel. Pipeline transport has the advantages of large transportation volume, high continuity, fast speed, safety and reliability, less investment needed, and low cost. Pipeline transport is widely used not only for long-distance transportation of oil and natural gas, but also for transportation of powder and granular solids such as ore and coal. It plays an irreplaceable role in the oil and gas trade between Russia, Kazakhstan and China.

5. 其他运输（Other Transport）

在上述运输方式的基础上，随着运输包装工具的改进、运输组织方式的创新以及这两种因素的组合，又衍生出多种各具特色的组合运输方式，主要包括以下内容。

On the basis of the above modes of transport, with the improvement of transport packaging tools, the innovation of transport organizations and the combination of these two factors, a variety of combined transport modes with different characteristics has emerged, which mainly includes the following modes.

1) 集装箱运输(Container Transport)

集装箱运输是以集装箱这种新型的运输包装作为运输单元,将水上、陆上、航空等多种运输方式有机结合的一种现代化的、先进的运输方式。目前它已成为国际上普遍采用的一种重要的运输方式。它是件杂货运输的发展方向,是运输领域的重要变革。

Container transport is a modern and advanced mode of transport, which takes container, a new type of transport package as transport unit and combines water, land, aviation and other transportation modes. At present, it has become an important mode of transportation widely adopted in the world. It is the development direction of general cargo transportation and an important revolution to the field of transportation.

2) 国际多式联运(International Multimodal Transport)

国际多式联运是在集装箱运输的基础上产生和发展起来的一种综合性的连贯运输方式,它一般是以集装箱为媒介,将海、陆、空各种传统的单一运输方式有机结合起来,相互衔接,形成国际连贯运输。采用国际多式联运,货主只需要办理一次托运手续,一次支付全程运费,货物由承运人负责从发货人的仓库(工厂)直运到收货人的仓库(工厂),从而为货主提供经济、迅速、安全、便捷的运输服务。

International multimodal transport is a comprehensive and continuous mode of transport produced and developed on the basis of container transport. It generally takes containers as the medium and organically combines various singular traditional modes of transport, such as sea, land and air, so as to form a coherent international transport system. With international multimodal transport, the shipper only needs to go through consignment formality once and pay the whole freight at one time. The carrier is responsible for transporting goods directly from the shipper's warehouse (factory) to the consignee's warehouse (factory), so as to provide economic, rapid, safe, and convenient transport services for the shipper.

3) 邮政运输(Postal Transport)

邮政运输是以邮政部门作为货运代理人的运输服务形式,主要通过各种运输方式,尤其是航空运输的方式来完成。邮政部门类似于国际多式联运中的经营人,对邮包的递送负责。邮政运输具有手续简便、服务周到的特点,在小批量货物、样品的运送上具有优势。

Postal transport is a form of transportation service in which the postal department acts as freight forwarder. It is mainly accomplished by various modes of transportation, especially by air transportation. Postal departments are similar to operators in international multimodal transport and are responsible for the delivery of postal parcels. Postal transport is characterized by simple procedures and considerate service, and has advantages in the transport of small batches of goods and samples.

各种运输方式有其特点，对不同货物的运输具有不同的适应性。在国际货物运输中，应根据不同货物的性质、特点和对运输条件的要求选择适当的运输方式。

Each mode of transportation has its own characteristics，and it has different adaptability to the transportation of different goods. In international cargo transportation，appropriate modes of transport should be chosen according to the nature and characteristics of different goods and the requirements of transport conditions.

1.3.2　国际贸易运输方式的选择（The Choice of International Trade Transport Modes）

组织国际货物运输时，必须正确选择运输方式和管理组织方式。国际货物运输的方式除了一般的海洋运输、铁路运输、公路运输、航空运输、管道运输及邮政运输外，还有一些有特点的方式，如多式联合运输、大陆桥运输等。在组织国际货物运输时，对运输方式的选择主要从以下几个方面考虑。

When organizing international cargo transportation，it is necessary to correctly choose the mode of transportation and management organization. In addition to marine transport，railway transport，road transport，air transport，pipeline transport and postal transport，there are some other characteristic modes of international cargo transport，such as multimodal transport，continental bridge transport and so on. When organizing the international transport of goods，the choice of the means of transport is mainly based on the following considerations.

1. 运输成本（Transport Costs）

这是国际货物运输对运输方式选择首要考虑的因素，其原因是运距太长、运费负担较重。据统计，在外贸的价格中，货物运输费有时可占出口货价的 30%～70%，对于煤炭、矿石等低价值货物，这一比例或许更高。

在国际货物运输中，大型专用船舶的运输成本较低，定期班轮则较高，包轮则较低。一般而言，海运成本低于陆运成本，但如果海运有大迂回，则利用大陆桥运输在运载成本方面有一定的优势。

This is the primary consideration in the choice of mode of transport，due to the heavy freight burden caused by long distances. According to statistics，the cost of transporting goods can sometimes account for 30%-70% of the price of export goods. For coal，ore and other low-value goods，this ratio may be higher.

In international transport of goods，the transport cost of large specialized ships is lower，the cost of regular liner is higher，and the cost of chartered ships is lower than that of liner. Generally speaking，the cost of sea transport is lower than that of land transport，but if there is a large detour in sea transport，the use of the continental bridge transport has a certain advantage in terms of carrying costs.

2. 运输速度（Speed of Delivery）

国际货物运输速度也很重要，主要有两个原因：一是运距长，需时日较多，资金占用时间长,加快速度有利于解放占用的资金;二是运行速度慢,导致错过好的市场价位,使经济收益下降。所以缩短货物运输时间会有一系列的好处。

在各种货物运输方式中,航空货运有不容争议的高速度。在洲际运输中,用大陆桥运输取代海运,会获得提高货物运输速度的显著效果。

The speed of international cargo transportation is also important for two main reasons. One is that due to long transport distance, international carga transportation takes more time and the capital is occupied for a long time, so accelerating the speed is conducive to the liberation of occupied funds. The other reason is the market price, due to the slow speed, the good market conditions will be missed, which will make the revenue decrease. Therefore, shortening the transport time of goods will have a series of advantages.

Among the various modes of cargo transportation, air transport has an undisputed high speed. In intercontinental transportation, the replacement of sea transport by continental bridges has the significant effect of increasing the speed of cargo transport.

3. 货物的特点及性质(The Characteristics and Nature of Goods)

货物的特点及性质有时对货物运输方式选择起决定作用。经常是由于受到国际货物运输方式的限制,有些货物无法进行国际运输而失去市场时机。

一般来说,各种包装杂货可以选择各种货物运输方式,而诸如水泥、石油、沥青、危险品等,选择范围则较窄,如在国际货物运输中,选择汽车或飞机运输水泥显然是不恰当的。

The characteristics and nature of goods sometimes play a decisive role in the choice of modes of transport. Often, market opportunities are lost because some goods cannot be transported internationally due to restrictions on the mode of international cargo transport.

Generally speaking, all kinds of general goods can be transported by various means of transport, while the choice is narrower for cement, petroleum, asphalt, dangerous goods, etc. For example, in the international transport of goods, it is clearly inappropriate to choose to transport cement by car or air.

4. 货物数量(Quantity of Goods)

由于国际货物运输距离长,大数量货物运输受到了限制,因为国际货物运输距离往往超出了汽车等运输工具的经济里程,大数量货物也不可能选择航空运输,因为航空运输不具备那样大的运输能力,更不用讲价格了。

The long distances of international transport of goods limit the transport of large quantities of goods, because the distance of international transport of goods often exceeds the economic mileage of means of transport such as cars, and it is impossible to choose air transport for large quantities of goods, because air transport does not have such a large capacity, not to mention the price.

5. 运输基础设施条件(Transport Infrastructure Conditions)

由于国家之间运输基础设施发展的不平衡,一个国家中可以选择的货物运输方式,到另一个国家便不能采用,原因是另一个国家缺乏采用这种方式的必要基础设施。在选择运输方式时,如不考虑这个问题,是无法形成有效的货物运输系统的。最典型的例子是,大型船和集装箱船在缺乏必要的水域条件及港口条件时是无法作业的。因此不管运价如何便宜,在水域和港口条件不具备时,不能选择大型船;如果没有大型集装箱装运码头以及集装箱集疏的腹地条件,则也不可能大量选择集装箱运输方式。

Due to the unbalanced development of transport infrastructure among countries, a mode of transport that is available in one country may not be available in another because the other country lacks the necessary infrastructure to use it. Without taking this into account when choosing a mode of transport, it is not possible to develop an efficient cargo transport system. The most typical example is that large ships and container ships cannot operate in the absence of necessary water and port conditions. Therefore, no matter how cheap the freight rates may be, large ships cannot be selected when water and port conditions are not eligible, nor can container transport be selected in large number if large container loading terminals and hinterland conditions for container concentration and distribution are not eligible.

6. 清关(Customs Clearance)

不同的运输方式有不同的清关程序。这会影响转运时间。与海运相比,空运和邮运的海关手续简化,可以提高这些运输方式的竞争力。这也适用于某些公路运输和铁路运输。

Different transport modes have different customs clearance procedures, which can affect transit time. The simplified customs procedures for air and postal shipments, as compared to maritime transport, can increase the competitiveness of these modes of transportation. This also applies to certain road and rail shipments.

7. 支付方式(Payment Methods)

支付方式的选择会影响装运方式,反之亦然。例如,跟单信用证付款可能要求提示已装船海运提单。在这种情况下,空运将违反信用证条款,因为如果信用证要求提供海运提单,空运单将不被接受。

The choice of payment method can affect the mode of shipment, and vice versa. For example, payments by documentary letter of credit may require the presentation of an on board marine bill of lading(B/L). In such a case, air shipment will violate the terms of the L/C, because an air waybill will not be accepted if the L/C calls for a marine B/L.

1.4 国际贸易运输的组织
(Organizations Engaged in International Trade Transportation)

世界上从事国际贸易运输的组织可以归纳为三类:承运人、货主和运输代理人。这三类业务构成了国际货物运输工作的主要内容。它们之间虽然在工作性质上有区别,但在业务上却有密切的联系。

Organizations that engage in international trade transportation can be grouped into three categories: carriers, cargo owners and transport agents. The business of these three types of organizations constitutes the main content of international freight transport. Although there are differences in the nature of their business, there are also close links between them.

1.4.1　承运人（Carriers）

承运人是指专门经营水上、铁路、航空等客货运输业务的交通运输机构，它们一般拥有大量运输工具，为社会提供运输服务。各类中资、外资、中外合资运输公司，如中国远洋运输（集团）总公司、中国外运长航集团有限公司等，中国铁路集团有限公司及各地分局（分公司），各航空公司及中国邮政集团有限公司等都是我国国际贸易运输中的主要承运人。此外，无船公共承运人和多式联运经营人也是国际贸易运输的承运人。

Carriers are transportation enterprises that specialize in water, rail, air and other passenger and cargo transportation business, and they generally have a large number of conveyances to provide transportation services to the society. All kinds of Chinese-funded, foreign-funded and Sino-foreign joint venture transport companies, such as China Ocean Shipping (Group) Company, Sinotrans & CSC Holding Co. Ltd., as well as China Railway Corporation and its branches, airline companies and China Post Group are all main carriers in China's international trade transportation. In addition, NVOCC (non-vessel operating common carrier) and multimodal transport operators(CTOs) are also carriers of international trade transport.

1.4.2　货主（Cargo Owners）

货主是指从事国际贸易业务的进出口企业。它们为履行贸易合同必须组织进出口商品的运输，向承运人托运或收取货物。因此，货主多为国际贸易运输工作中的托运人或收货人。

Cargo owners refer to enterprises engaged in international trade. They must organize the transportation of import or export commodities, consign or collect goods from carriers in order to fulfill trade contracts. Therefore, cargo owners are mostly shippers (consignors)or consignees in international trade transportation.

1.4.3　运输代理人（Transport Agents）

1. 运输代理人的性质（Nature of Transport Agents）

国际运输业务遍布国内外广大地区，涉及面广，头绪多，而且情况复杂，任何一个运输承运人或货主都不可能亲自处理每一项业务，有些工作需要委托代理人办理，为了适应这种需要，在国际货物运输领域里就产生了从事代理业务的国际货运代理行或代理人。他们接受委托人的委托，代办各种运输业务并按其提供的劳务收取一定的报酬，即代理费、佣金或手续费。随着国际贸易和运输的发展，这种运输代理行业也就迅速广泛地发展起来。当前，代理行业已渗透到运输领域各个角落，成为运输业不可缺少的重要组成部分。在我国，中国租船有限公司、外轮代理公司及其他各种货运代理公司是国际贸易运输业务中常见的运输代理人。

The business scope of international transport covers a vast area at home and abroad, involving a wide range and links, and the situation is complex. Therefore, any carrier or cargo owner cannot personally handle every business, and some work need to be entrusted to an agent. In order to meet this need, in the field of international cargo transportation, there are international freight forwarding agents engaged in agency business. They are entrusted by the principal to handle all kinds of transport operations on behalf of the client, and receive a certain amount of remuneration for their services, namely agency fee, agency commission or charges. With the development of international trade and transportation, this kind of transport agency industry has developed rapidly and widely. At present, the agency industry has penetrated all corners of the transport field and has become an indispensable and important part of the transport industry. In China, China National Chartering Corporation, ocean shipping agencies, and other freight forwarders are common transport agents in international trade transport business.

2. 运输代理人的种类（Types of Transport Agents）

按照代理业务的性质和范围的不同，可将运输代理人分为租船代理、船务代理、货运代理和咨询代理四大类。

According to the nature and scope of agency business, transport agents can be divided into four categories: charter agent, shipping agent, freight forwarder and consulting agent.

1）租船代理（Charter Agent）

租船代理又称租船经纪人，它是以船舶为商业活动对象而进行船舶租赁业务的中间机构。它的业务活动是在市场上为租船人寻找合适的运输船舶或为船东寻找货运对象，它以中间人身份使船租双方达成租赁交易，从中赚取佣金。因此，其根据所代表的委托人身份的不同又分为船东代理人和租船人代理人。有些租船代理还兼办船舶买卖、船舶代理业务。

Charter agent, also known as ship broker, is an intermediary agency that engages in ship leasing business. Its business activities are to find suitable shipping vessels for charterers or freight objects for ship owners in the market, and it acts as an intermediary to enable charterers and ship owners to enter into lease transactions, from which it earns a commission. Therefore, according to the identity of the principal it represents, the agent can be categorized into the owner's agent and charterer's agent. Some charter agents also deal with the sale and purchase of ships and ship agency business.

2）船务代理（Shipping Agent）

船务代理是指接受承运人的委托，代办与船舶有关的一切业务的中间机构。船务代理业务范围很广,主要包括船舶进出港业务、货运业务、船舶供应和船舶服务等业务以及其他服务性业务等。

船务代理关系根据委托方式的不同,一般分为航运代理和长期代理两种。前者指委托人的委托和代理人的接受均以每船一次为限,后者则是指在船方和代理人之间签订有长期(1 年至 5 年或更长时间)代理协议的船务代理。

Shipping agent refers to an intermediary agency that accepts the entrustment of the carrier and undertakes all business related to the ship. The scope of business of shipping agency is very wide, mainly including ship inbound and outbound business, freight business, ship supply and ship services and other services, etc.

The shipping agency relationship is generally divided into agent on trip basis and agent on long-term basis according to the different entrustment methods. For the former, the entrustment of the principal and the acceptance of the agent shall be limited to one time per vessel; for the latter, a long-term (one year to five years or more) agency agreement is signed between the ship and the agent.

3)货运代理(Freight Forwarder)

货运代理是指接受货主的委托代表货主办理有关货物报关、交接、仓储、调拨、检验、包装、转运、订船业务的人,他与货主之间是委托和被委托关系,在办理代理业务时,他以货主的代理人身份对货主负责并按代理业务项目和提供的劳务向货主收取代理费。

A freight forwarder is a person entrusted by and on behalf of the consignor to handle the business of customs declaration, handover, warehousing, allocation, inspection, packaging, transshipment, chartering and booking. The relationship between him and the consignor is the relationship between trustor and trustee. In dealing with agency business, he is responsible for the consignor as the consignor's agent, and collects agency fees from the consignor according to the business items and services provided.

4)咨询代理(Consulting Agent)

咨询代理是专门从事咨询工作,按委托人的需要,以提供有关咨询情况、情报、资料、数据和信息服务而收取一定报酬的机构。这类代理人不仅拥有研究人员和机构,而且与世界各贸易运输研究中心有广泛的联系,所以信息十分灵通,例如设计经营方案、选择合理的经济运输方式和路线、核算运输成本、研究解释规章法律以及调查有关企业财务信誉等,均可根据委托,提供专题报告和资料情报。

Consulting agent is a kind of agency that specializes in consulting work and receives certain remuneration for providing relevant consulting, intelligence, data, and information service according to the needs of clients. Such agents are well informed because they not only have researchers and institutions, but also have extensive contacts with trade and transport research centres around the world. On request, they can provide reports and information on topics such as the design of business plans, the selection of rational and economical transport modes and routes, the calculation of transport costs，the interpretation of regulations and laws，and the investigation of the financial credibility of the enterprises concerned.

Words and Expressions

即测即练

习题

第 2 章

Chapter 2

国际海洋货物运输概述
Overview of International Marine Cargo Transport

Learning Objectives：

1. Understand the characteristics of international carriage of goods by sea；
2. Understand main international maritime organizations；
3. Obtain basic knowledge of maritime transport，including：knowledge about objects of international carriage of goods by sea，knowledge about merchant ships，etc.

引导案例

全球海运发展现状

据 UNCTAD 发布的《2023 全球海运发展评述报告》，截至 2023 年 1 月，世界船队由 105 493 艘 100 总吨及以上的船舶组成。2022 年，全球船舶运力以每年 3.2% 的速度增长，总吨位达到 22.7 亿载重吨。集装箱航运方面，据交通运输部发布的《2022 年水路运输市场发展情况和 2023 年市场展望》，截至 2022 年 12 月，全球集装箱船舶达到 5 690 艘、2 591 万 TEU，运力规模同比增长 4.15%。在全球集装箱运输需求总体下滑、有效运力持续增长等因素影响下，2022 年国际集装箱运价从高位持续回落。根据 UNCTAD 的数据，2023 年，集装箱船队的运力增长了 3.9%。干散货航运方面，2022 年，全球干散货海运贸易量 52.52 亿吨，同比下降 2.7%。运力方面，截至 2022 年底，全球干散货船队运力共计 13 113 艘、9.71 亿载重吨，较 2021 年底增长 2.86%，而 2023 年，散货船运力以 2.8% 的温和速度增长。全球原油运输需求改善，截至 2022 年 12 月，全球原油海运量约 19.53 亿吨，同比上升 5.1%，基本恢复至 2019 年水平。运力方面，2022 年底全球油轮（万吨以上）共 5 574 艘、6.34 亿载重吨，较年初下降 2.8%，而 2023 年增长 3.4%。随着全球石油供应风险的增加，同时受部分国家控制油价上涨抵抗通胀有关政策的影响，原油现货运输市场运价上涨明显。UNCTAD 指出，全球航运继续面临多重挑战，包括全球供应链危机的遗留问题、集装箱运输市场的疲软、贸易政策加剧和地缘政治紧张局势带来的航运和贸易模式的转变。2022 年，海运贸易量略微收缩了 0.4%，UNCTAD 预计，中期（2024—2028年）海运贸易量将继续增长，但增长放缓。

资料来源：联合国贸易和发展会议.2023 全球海运发展评述报告[R].2023；中华人民共和国交通运输部.2022 年水路运输市场发展情况和 2023 年市场展望[Z].2023.

海洋运输是历史悠久的国际贸易运输方式，也是国际物流中最重要的运输方式。它是指使用船舶通过海上航道在不同国家和地区的港口之间运送货物的一种方式，在国际贸易运输中使用最为广泛。科学技术的迅速发展也推动了海洋运输技术的发展，许多高精尖技术都被应用于海洋运输船舶上，从而促进了海洋运输在国际货物运输中的应用。海运承担了全球超过80%的商品运输量。① 近年来，随着全球贸易格局的变化和船舶技术的进步，海运行业呈现出大型化、自动化和环保化的趋势。

Maritime transport is a long-established mode of international trade transport and the most important mode of transport in international logistics. It refers to the use of ships to transport goods between ports in different countries and regions via sea lanes, and is most widely used in international trade transport. The rapid development of science and technology has also promoted the development of maritime transport technology, and many sophisticated technologies are applied to ships, thus promoting the application of maritime transport in the international cargo transport. Maritime transport carries more than 80 percent of the world's merchandise traffic. In recent years, with the changes in the pattern of global trade and the advancement of ship technology, the maritime transport industry has shown a trend towards large-scale, automation, and environmental protection.

2.1 海上货物运输的特点
（Characteristics of Carriage of Goods by Sea）

2.1.1 中国海洋运输的发展（The Development of China's Maritime Transport）

随着中国经济与对外贸易的快速发展，中国已经成为世界上最重要的海运大国之一。2023年，在外贸需求回暖、全球贸易体系重塑等因素推动下，中国外贸海运规模增长较快，全国沿海港口外贸吞吐量达49.6亿吨，同比增长9.6%。2023年，中国外贸海运量已占全球海运量的30.1%，较2022年上升2.2个百分点，凸显中国外贸大国的地位。② 我国海岸线长约18 000千米，沿海有许多优良的不冻港，具有发展海运的优良条件。我国港口与世界各国主要港口之间已开辟了许多定期或不定期的海上航线。海洋运输在我国对外经济贸易中起着越来越重要的作用，特别是集装箱运输发展迅猛，1973年9月，我国开始在天津、上海和日本神户、横滨之间开展集装箱运输。1978年9月，我国在上海和澳大利亚港口之间建立了第一条自己经营的集装箱班轮航线。目前，我国各大港口已形成了到达世界主要港口的国际集装箱运输网。

我国从事国际贸易运输的大型运输企业也逐渐成长壮大起来。1955年8月，成立中国对外贸易运输总公司，作为经营国际贸易运输的专业公司，同时仍然保留中国租船公

---

① 中国产业调研网.中国海运行业现状调研分析及发展趋势预测报告（2024版）[R]. 2024.
② 交通运输部规划研究院.中国港口运行分析报告（2024）[R]. 2024.

司,以适应对外开展租船业务的需要。为了发展我国的远洋运输事业,1961 年成立了中国远洋运输公司,并建立了我国自己的远洋船队,担负进出口货物运输任务,但成立之初仅有 4 艘船舶、2.26 万载重吨。2016 年 1 月,中远集团与中海集团重组成立中国远洋海运集团有限公司。截至 2023 年 12 月 31 日,中国远洋海运集团经营船队综合运力1.16 亿载重吨/1 417 艘,排名世界第一。其中,集装箱船队规模 305 万 TEU/504 艘,居世界前列;干散货船队运力 4 632 万载重吨/436 艘,油、气船队运力 2 858 万载重吨/229艘,杂货特种船队 620 万载重吨/180 艘,均居世界第一。[①]

With the rapid development of China's economy and foreign trade, China has become one of the most important shipping countries in the world. In 2023, driven by factors such as the rebound in demand for foreign trade and the reshaping of the global trade system, the scale of maritime transport for China's foreign trade grew relatively fast, with the throughput of foreign trade cargo at coastal ports reaching 4.96 billion tons, an year-on-year increase of 9.6%. In 2023, the maritime transport volume of China's foreign trade had already accounted for 30.1% of the world's maritime transport volume, an increase of 2.2% compared with the previous year, demonstrating the status of China as a major foreign trade country. China's coastline is about 18 000 kilometers long. There are many excellent non-freezing ports along the coast, which have good conditions for the development of maritime transport. Many regular or irregular sea routes have been opened up between China's ports and major ports in the world. Maritime transportation plays an increasingly significant role in China's foreign economy and trade. In particular, container transport has developed rapidly. Since September 1973, container transport has been carried out between Tianjin, Shanghai, Kobe and Yokohama, Japan. In September 1978, China established the first container liner route between Shanghai and Australian ports. At present, China has established an international container transport network between major ports and the world's major ports.

China's large transport enterprises engaged in international trade transportation are also gradually growing up. In August 1955, China National Foreign Trade Transportation Corporation (CNFTTC) was established as a professional company operating international trade transportation, while China National Chartering Corporation (CNCC) was retained to meet the needs of foreign chartering business. In order to develop China's ocean shipping business, China Ocean Shipping Company (COSCO) was established in 1961, and built its own ocean fleet to transport imported and exported goods. But at the beginning of its establishment, COSCO only had four ships with 22 600 deadweight tons. In January 2016, COSCO Group and China Shipping

---

① 中国远洋海运集团有限公司. 集团概况[EB/OL]. https://www.coscoshipping.com/col6858/art/2016/art_6858_45176.html.

Group reorganized to establish COSCO Shipping Lines Co. Ltd. As of December 31, 2023, the fleet operated by COSCO Shipping Lines has a combined capacity of 116 million DWT/1 417 vessels, ranking first in the world. Among them, the size of the container fleet is 3.05 million TEU/504 vessels, is in the front row in the world; the capacity of the dry bulk fleet is 46.32 million DWT/436 vessels, the capacity of the oil and gas fleet is 28.58 million DWT/229 vessels, and the capacity of the general cargo fleet and special fleet is 6.2 million DWT/180 vessels, all ranking first in the world.

2.1.2　海上货物运输的优点与缺点(Advantages and Disadvantages of Transport by Sea)

海上货物运输的优点包括以下几个方面。

The advantages of carriage of goods by sea include.

(1) 运输量大。船舶载运能力远远超过飞机、火车、汽车,是运载能力最大的运输工具,而且远洋运输船舶正在向大型化方向发展。如巨型油轮载货量为 50 万～80 万吨,散货船载货量在 15 万吨以上,而大型集装箱货船的载箱能力已达 21 000 个标准箱。

(1) Large transport capacity. Ships are the means of transport with the largest carrying capacity, and their carrying capacity is far greater than that of airplanes, trains, and cars. Moreover, ocean-going vessels are developing towards the direction of large scale. For example, the carrying capacity of supertankers reaches 500 000-800 000 tons, bulk carriers reaches 150 000 tons or more, while the carrying capacity of large container carriers has reached 21 000 TEU.

(2) 通过性强。海上运输的航道四通八达,不像公路运输、铁路运输和航空运输要受道路、轨道和航线的限制。此外,苏伊士运河、巴拿马运河等的开通,缩短了国际贸易运输的航程,使船舶的通过能力进一步得到提高。在遇到政治、经济、自然条件变化时,可以随时转换其他航线完成运输任务。

(2) Strong passability. The shipping lanes for maritime transportation are well-connected, unlike road, rail and air transportation, which are subject to the constraints of roads, tracks and routes. In addition, the opening of canals such as the Suez Canal and Panama Canal has shortened the voyage of international trade transport and further improved the passage capacity of ships. In the event of changes in political, economic and natural conditions, it is possible to switch to other routes at any time to complete transport tasks.

(3) 运费低廉。海洋水域、航道天然形成,不需花费投资,只需在港口建设和船舶购置上进行投资,港口设备一般均为政府修建;此外,船舶的动力燃油消耗少,再加上运量大、航程远,分摊于每吨的费用成本低,充分发挥了规模经济效益,因此,海上运输成本低,运费相对来说较低。据统计,海运费用一般为铁路运费的 1/5、公路运费的 1/10、航空运费的 1/30。这就为低值大宗货物提供了有利的运输条件。

(3) Low freight. Marine waterways are naturally formed and do not require costly

investment, except for investment in port construction and ship acquisition, and port equipment is generally built by the government. In addition, the low fuel consumption of ships, coupled with the low cost per ton due to the large volume and long voyage, gives full play to economies of scale, resulting in low maritime transportation costs and thus relatively low freight rates. According to statistics, sea freight is generally 1/5 of rail freight, 1/10 of road freight, and 1/30 of air freight, which provides favorable transportation conditions for low-value bulk cargoes.

（4）适货性强。海洋运输船舶种类繁多,能够适应液体、固体、气体等各种货物运输的需要。尤其是火车、汽车等无法运输的特种货物如石油井架、机车,以及超长、超大、超重货物均可利用海洋运输。

（4）Strong cargo adaptability. There are many kinds of marine transportation ships, which can adapt to the needs of transporting liquid, solid, gas and other cargoes. In particular, special cargoes such as oil derricks and locomotives that cannot be transported by trains and automobiles, as well as extra-long, extra-large and extra-heavy cargoes can be transported by sea.

海上货物运输的缺点包括以下两个方面。

The shortcomings of sea transport include the following two aspects.

（1）风险大。船舶在航行过程中受到气候和自然条件的影响较大,可能遭遇自然灾害和意外事故,以及海盗、恐怖袭击、罢工、禁运等社会风险,给船、货带来损失。因此,海运货物需要通过购买保险分散风险。

（1）High risk. Ships are greatly affected by climate and natural conditions during the voyage, and may encounter natural disasters and accidents, as well as social risks such as piracy, terrorist attacks, strikes and embargoes, which will bring losses to ships and goods. Therefore, marine cargoes need to be insured against losses caused by risks.

（2）送达速度慢。船舶行驶速度较慢,一般为15～20节,班轮航速较快,但也仅为30节左右。此外,海洋运输中换装、交接等环节较多,也会影响运送速度。

（2）Slow speed. The ship's travel speed is slow, generally between 15-20 knots, although the liner's speed is faster, but it is only about 30 knots. In addition, there are more links in ocean transportation such as transshipment and handover, which will also affect the delivery speed.

扩展阅读 2.1　联合国贸发会《全球海运评述报告》内容概述

2.2　国际海运组织（International Maritime Organization）

随着国际海运业的发展,各国政府和非政府组织相继成立了一些政府间国际组织和非政府间国际组织,海运企业间也成立了一些具有协作性质的国际组织。这些组织在保证海运安全、建立国际公约和提供海运服务等方面发挥着重要作用。

With the development of the international shipping industry, governments and nongovernmental organizations have established some intergovernmental and nongovernmental international organizations. Some international organizations with collaborative nature have also been established among shipping enterprises. These organizations play an important role in ensuring maritime safety, establishing international conventions, and providing maritime services.

2.2.1 国际海事组织（International Maritime Organization）

1959 年 1 月，"政府间海事协商组织"在伦敦正式成立，1982 年 5 月 22 日更名为"国际海事组织"。该组织是联合国在海事方面的一个技术咨询和海运立法机构，是政府间的国际组织，所有联合国成员国均可成为国际海事组织的会员国。中国于 1973 年正式恢复在国际海事组织中的合法席位，成为该组织的成员国，并于 1989 年首次当选为 A 类理事国并连任至今。

The Intergovernmental Maritime Consultative Organization (IMCO) was formally established in London in January 1959 and renamed the International Maritime Organization (IMO) on May 22, 1982. The organization is a technical advisory and maritime legislative body of the United Nations in maritime matters. It is an intergovernmental international organization. All United Nations member states can become members of the IMO. China formally resumed its legitimate seat in the IMO in 1973 and became a member of the organization. In 1989, China was elected as a Category A Council Member for the first time and has been re-elected consecutively ever since.

2.2.2 波罗的海国际海事协会（Baltic and International Maritime Council）

波罗的海国际海事协会属于非政府间国际组织，成立于 1905 年，总部设在哥本哈根。协会成员包括航运公司、经纪人公司以及保赔协会等团体或俱乐部组织。其宗旨是：保护会员的利益，为会员提供情报咨询服务；防止运价投机和不合理的收费与索赔；拟订和修改标准租船合同和其他货运单证；出版航运业务情报资料等。

The Baltic and International Maritime Council (BIMCO) is an international nongovernmental organization founded in 1905 and headquartered in Copenhagen. Its members include shipping companies, brokerage companies, Protection and Indemnity clubs(P&I), and other groups or club organizations. Its purpose is to protect the interests of its members and to provide them with information and consulting services; to prevent speculation in freight rates and unreasonable charges and claims; to prepare and amend standard charter parties and other freight documents; and to publish information materials on shipping operations, etc.

2.2.3 国际海事委员会（Comité Maritime International）

国际海事委员会于 1897 年成立于布鲁塞尔。其宗旨是促进海商法、海运关税和各种海运惯例的统一。它的主要工作是草拟各种有关海上运输的公约，如有关提单、责任制、海上避碰及救助等方面的国际公约草案。

Comité Maritime International(CMI) was established in Brussels in 1897. Its main purpose is to promote the unification of maritime law, customs and various maritime practices. Its main work is to draft various conventions on maritime transport, such as drafting international conventions on B/L, liability system, collision avoidance and salvage at sea.

2.2.4　联营体（Consortium）

联营体是由两家或两家以上航运公司为了共同开展一项业务而产生的临时性的、松散的自愿合作形式，通常是以航线为单位订立协议。其目的主要是通过共同经营、相互合作，从而节约成本，提高海运服务质量。

A consortium is a temporary, loose-form, voluntary cooperation between two or more shipping companies for the purpose of carrying on a business together, usually by entering into an agreement on a route-by-route basis. Its main purpose is to save costs and improve the quality of shipping services through joint operation and cooperation.

2.3　国际海上货物运输的对象（Objects of International Carriage of Goods by Sea）

海上运输对象——国际货物种类繁多，而且结构、形状、性质和包装千差万别，在搬运、积载、保管、装卸及运输过程中，必须根据货物的不同要求区别对待，才能做好国际运输工作。海上运输货物可以从不同的角度进行分类。

There are many kinds of international goods to be transported by sea, and their structure, shape, nature and packing vary greatly. In the process of handling, stowage, storage, loading, unloading, and transportation, it is necessary to treat them differently according to the different requirements of the goods in order to do a good job in international transportation. Goods transported by sea can be classified from different points of view.

2.3.1　按货物是否能分件划分（Classification According to Whether the Goods Can be Counted by Units）

按货物是否能分件，货物可分为件杂货和大宗货。件杂货是指有包装的、可分件点数的货物，约占世界海运总量的 25%，但其货价要占到 75%；大宗货一般是指数量较大、规格较统一的初级产品，如矿砂、煤炭、粮谷等。在运输时，它们大多是散装，故又称散装货。大宗货物约占世界海运总量的 75%~80%。

Cargo can be divided into general cargo and bulk cargo according to whether or not it can be divided into individual units. General cargo refers to packaged cargo that can be counted by units, accounting for about 25% of the world's total shipping volume, while its value accounts for 75% of the world's total. Bulk cargo generally refers to larger quantities of primary products with more uniform specifications, such as ore, coal, and grain, which accounts for about 75%-80% of the world's total shipping volume.

2.3.2 按货物含水量划分(Classification by Cargo Moisture Content)

按货物含水量,货物可分为干货和湿货。这种划分主要是为了租船订舱方便,因为不同类型的货物所需的船舶也不同。干货是指基本上不含水分或含水分很少的货物,件杂货大都属于此类。湿货是指散装液体货,如石油及其制品、植物油、化学品等。金属桶或塑料桶装运的流质以及半流质货物也都属于这种。

Cargo can be divided into dry cargo and wet cargo according to its moisture content. This division is mainly for the convenience of chartering a ship or booking shipping space, as different types of cargoes require different ships. Dry cargo refers to cargo that basically contains no water or little moisture, and general cargo mostly belongs to this category. Wet cargo refers to bulk liquid cargo, such as petroleum and its products, vegetable oil, and chemicals. Fluid and semi-fluid cargoes in metal or plastic drums also belong to this category.

2.3.3 按包装形式和有无包装划分(Classification by Packaging Form and With or Without Packaging)

按包装形式和有无包装,货物可分为:①包装货,如件杂货物;②裸装货,如钢板、钢材等;③散装货,如粮食、矿石、煤炭等。

According to the form of packaging and whether they are packaged or not, goods can be divided into:①packed cargo, such as general cargo;②no-packed cargo, such as steel plate and steel;③bulk cargo, such as grain, ore and coal.

2.3.4 按货物的理化性质划分(Classification by Physicochemical Properties of Goods)

按货物的理化性质,货物可分为普通货和特殊货。普通货包括清洁货物、液体货物和粗劣货物;特殊货包括:危险货物,易腐、冷藏货物;贵重货物;活的动植物等。其中,危险货物是指具有燃烧、爆炸、腐蚀、毒害、放射性、感染性等性质,在运输过程中可能会引起人身伤害和财产损失的货物。凡运输危险货物,必须严格遵照《国际海上危险货物运输规则》办理。

Cargo can be divided into ordinary cargo and special cargo according to its physicochemical properties. Ordinary cargo includes clean cargo, liquid cargo and crude cargo; Special cargo includes dangerous cargo, perishable and refrigerated cargo; precious goods; living animals and plants, etc. Among them, dangerous cargo refers to goods with the tendency of combustion, explosion, corrosion, poisoning, radioactivity, infection and so on, which may cause personal injury and property loss in the course of transportation. When transporting dangerous goods, *International Maritime Dangerous Goods Code* must be strictly followed.

2.3.5　按货物价值划分（Classification by Value of Goods）

按货物价值，货物可分为高值货物和低值货物。高值货物是指高价、贵重货物，如金、银、古董、艺术品、精密仪器等。低值货物是指价值较低的货物，大宗货物多数属于此类。

高值货物和低值货物并无严格界限，主要是根据货物运费率的高低决定，一般以班轮运价表中的货物分级为标准，1～8 级为低值货物，9～20 级为高值货物。

Goods can be divided into high-valued cargo and low-valued cargo according to their value. High-valued cargo refers to high-priced and valuable goods, such as gold, silver, antiques, works of art, and precision instruments. Low-valued cargo refers to goods of relatively low value, and most bulk cargo belongs to this category.

There is no strict boundary between high-valued cargo and low-valued cargo, which is mainly determined by the freight rate of the cargo. Generally, commodity classification in the liner tariff table is used as a criterion, with classes 1-8 being low-valued cargo and classes 9-20 being high-valued cargo.

2.3.6　按货物重量和体积的比率划分（Classification by the Ratio of Weight to Volume of Goods）

按货物重量和体积的比率，货物可分为重量货物和轻泡货物。重量货物简称重货，是指重量 1 公（长）吨的货物，其体积小于 1.328 立方米（40 立方英尺）。轻泡货物或称体积货物、尺码货物或轻货，是指重量 1 公（长）吨的货物，其体积大于 1.382 立方米（40 立方英尺）。

现行远洋运费制度以 1 立方米为计算标准，凡 1 公吨货物体积大于 1 立方米的，按货物体积计收运费；如小于 1 立方米，按货物重量计收运费。

Cargo is divided into weight cargo and measurement cargo according to the ratio of weight to volume. Weight cargo means cargo of 1 metric ton (or long ton) in weight and less than 1.328 cubic metres (or 40 cubic feet) in volume; measurement cargo means cargo of 1 metric ton (or long ton) in weight and greater than 1.382 cubic metres (or 40 cubic feet) in volume.

The current ocean-going freight system is calculated by the standard of 1 cubic metre, and where the volume of 1 metric ton of cargo is greater than 1 cubic metre, the freight shall be charged according to the volume of the cargo; if it is less than 1 cubic metre, the freight shall be charged according to the weight of the cargo.

2.3.7　按货物长度和重量划分（Classification by Length and Weight of Goods）

按货物长度和重量，货物可分为超长货物、超重货物和超重超长货物。超长货物、超重货物并无严格界限，一般超过 9 米的货物为超长货物，超过 2 公吨的货物为超重货物。对于超长、超重货物，运输中要收附加费。

According to the length and weight, cargo can be divided into lengthy cargo, heavy lift cargo, and heavy lift and lengthy cargo. There is no strict limit for lengthy and heavy lift cargo. Generally, cargo exceeding 9 meters is lengthy cargo, and cargo exceeding 2 metric tons is heavy lift cargo. Additional charges shall be levied for the transportation of lengthy cargo and heavy lift cargo.

2.3.8 按集装箱装箱类别划分(Classification by Container Loading Ways)

按集装箱装箱类别,货物可分为整箱货和拼箱货。整箱货是指托运人的货物能够装满一个整箱。拼箱货是指托运人的货物不能装满一个集装箱,须由承运人将其与其他货主的货物拼装于一个集装箱。

According to the type of container loading, cargo can be divided into Full Container Load (FCL) and Less than Container Load (LCL). FCL means the shipper's cargo can fill a full container. LCL means that the shipper's goods cannot fill a container and the carrier must assemble them into one container with the goods of other shippers.

2.4 国际海洋运输工具(International Maritime Conveyance)

在海运方式中,运载货物的船只类型很重要。海上航行的船舶种类很多,与国际货物运输有关的船舶主要是商船。商船是以商业行为为目的的船舶,是国际货物海洋运输的载体。

扩展阅读 2.2 商船的特征和规范

In maritime transport, the type of vessel carrying the cargo is important. There are many different types of ships that travel by sea, but the main types of ships associated with international carriage of goods are merchant ships. Merchant ships are ships that are used for commercial purposes and are carriers of international cargo transported by sea.

2.4.1 按运输对象不同划分(Classification by Transport Objects)

按运输对象不同划分,商船主要有以下几种。

According to the different objects of transport, merchant ships can be divided into the following categories.

1. 干货型船(Dry Cargo Ship)

(1) 杂货船。杂货船一般是指定期行驶于货运繁忙的航线,以装运带包装的零星杂货为主要业务的货船,其吨位大小视航线、港口及货源而不同。这种船本身有各种不同的货舱与装卸设备,能适应装载种类繁多的货物,而且航速较快,速度为 20 节左右。

(1) General cargo vessel. General cargo vessels generally sail on busy freight routes in designated periods, with the main business of shipping sporadic general cargoes with packages. Their tonnage varies according to route, port, and cargo source. The ship itself has a variety of cargo holds and loading and unloading equipment, can

accommodate a wide range of cargo, with a relatively fast speed of about 20 knots.

（2）干散船。干散船多用于装运煤炭、粮食、矿砂,这种船一般舱容较大,大都为单甲板。其舱内设有挡板,以防货物移动。船舶本身一般不带有装卸设备,机舱设于尾部,以便装卸操作。其航速为 15 节左右。

（2）Dry bulk cargo carrier. Dry bulk cargo carriers are mostly used to transport coal, grain, and ore. Generally, these vessels have larger holds and are mostly single deck. There are baffles in the cabin to prevent cargo from moving. Generally, the ship itself does not have loading and unloading equipment, and the engine room is located at the tail for loading and unloading operation. Its speed is about 15 knots.

2. 液体船（Wet Cargo Ship）

（1）油轮。油轮又称油槽船,是指以散装方式运输原油或燃料油的专用货船。油轮将船本身分隔成若干贮油舱。船上配有油管贯通各油舱。船上设有空气压缩设备,在装卸油料时,以空气压力将油料通过管道推送至各贮油舱。油轮载重最大在 80 万吨以上,航速约 16 节。

扩展阅读 2.3　世界能源运输线的咽喉要道

（1）Tanker. Tanker refers to a special cargo ship that transports crude oil or fuel oil in bulk. The tanker separates itself into several oil storage tanks, with oil pipes running through each tank. The ship is equipped with air compression equipment, which pushes the oil through pipes with air pressure to each tank when loading and unloading. The maximum load of the tanker is over 800 000 tons and the speed is about 16 knots.

（2）液化石油气船和液化天然气船。其用于运载液化石油气和天然气,船上配备现代化设备,货舱都是密封的气罐,采用管道装卸。

（2）Liquefied Petroleum Gas Carrier（LPGC）and Liquefied Natural Gas Carriers（LNGC）. LPGC and LNGC are used to carry liquefied petroleum gas and natural gas and are equipped with modern equipment. The cargo holds are all sealed gas tanks, using pipeline to load and unload.

（3）化工船。化工船是装载化学工业品的专用船舶。

（3）Chemical ship. Chemical ship is a special ship for loading chemical products.

3. 专用船（Special Cargo Ship）

（1）冷藏船。冷藏船是利用冷藏设备使货舱内保持一定的低温从事运输易腐货物的船舶,船上有冷冻系统,能调节多种温度,以适应各舱货物对不同温度的需要。冷藏船吨位不大,多为 2 000～6 000 吨,航速为 15 节左右。

（1）Refrigerated vessel. Refrigerated vessel is a ship that uses refrigeration equipment to keep a certain low temperature in the cargo hold to transport perishable goods. It has a refrigeration system on board, which can adjust to a variety of temperatures to meet the needs of cargo in different compartments at different temperatures. The tonnage of refrigerated vessels is not large, mostly between 2 000 tons and 6 000 tons, and the speed is about 15 knots.

（2）木材船。木材船是指专门用以运输木材或原木的货船，载重为 7 000～15 000 吨。

（2）Timber vessel. A timber vessel is a cargo ship designed to transport timber or logs with a deadweight of 7 000-15 000 tons.

（3）水果船。水果船通常装有保鲜设备，以防止水果腐烂。

（3）Fruit ship. Fruit ship is usually equipped with fresh-keeping equipment to prevent fruit decay.

4. 成组船（Unitized Vessel）

（1）集装箱船。集装箱船是专门用于装运标准集装箱货物的船舶，本身一般无装卸设备，装卸作业全凭码头专用设施。集装箱船的舱内有格槽和导轨，便于装载，又可防止集装箱倒塌，运载量大多为 3 000～15 000 TEU，航速为 20～30 节，最快可达 35 节。集装箱船运输能够限制和防止发生货损货差，有利于装卸货物和多式联运，船舶停港时间短，运输效率高。

（1）Container ship. Container ship is a ship specially designed to carry standard containerized cargoes. Generally, it does not have loading and unloading equipment, and the handling operation is entirely based on the special facilities （gantry crane） of the wharf. There are slots and guideway in the containers ship's holds to facilitate loading and prevent the collapse of the container. Most of the container ships carry between 3 000-15 000 TEUs and travel at speeds of 20-30 knots, with the fastest ones reaching 35 knots. Container ship transportation can limit and prevent the occurrence of cargo damage and cargo difference, is conducive to loading and unloading of goods and multimodal transport, and has the advantages of short berth time and high transport efficiency.

（2）滚装船。这种船可直接承接码头货物，不需吊车。船没有货舱，只有纵贯全船的甲板，船的一侧或船的首尾可以打开并有伸缩跳板，船本身无装卸设备，货车可直接进入船上甲板。滚装船最适合运载车辆和大型机械，也适于装载集装箱。装卸时，集装箱由拖车拖带，驶进驶出船舱，其装载速度要比集装箱船快。其优点是：不依赖码头机械，快速装卸，大大缩短装卸时间，灵活性大。但其存在亏舱较大的缺点。

（2）Roll on/Roll off ship （Ro-Ro ship）. Ro-Ro ships can directly take on wharf cargo without crane. The ship has no cargo hold, only the deck that runs through the whole ship. The side of the ship or the fore and aft of the ship can be opened and there are expansion springboards. The ship itself has no loading and unloading equipment, and the truck can drive directly onto the deck of the ship. Ro-Ro ships are most suitable for carrying vehicles and large machinery, as well as for loading containers. When loading and unloading, containers are towed by trailers and driven into and out of the cabin, and the speed is faster than that of container ships. The advantages of Ro-Ro ships are that it does not depend on wharf machinery and can be loaded and unloaded quickly, which greatly shortens the loading and unloading time and has great flexibility. But its biggest disadvantage is that it has a large broken stowage.

（3）载驳船。载驳船又称子母船,母船上搭载子船,子船上装载货物。每条母船可载子船 70～100 条不等,每条子船载重 300～600 吨不等。母船载重多为 5 万～6 万吨,最小的为 2 万余吨,最大的为 20 余万吨,船上设有巨型门吊或船尾升降平台,子船可以吊上吊下或驶进驶出。在港口设备不齐全,或港口拥挤,或港口与内地之间无合适的运输工具而需要依靠江河运输的情况下,可使用这种船。

（3）Lighter Aboard Ship（LASH）. Lighter Aboard Ship is also known as barge carrier. The mother ship carries the sub-ship and the sub-ship carries the cargo. Each mother ship can carry 70-100 sub-ships, and each sub-ship can carry 300-600 tons. The carrying capacity of the mother ship is mostly about 50 000-60 000 tons, the smallest is more than 20 000 tons and the largest is more than 200 000 tons. There are giant gantry cranes or lifting platforms on the stern of the ship, and the sub-ships can be lifted up and down, or drive in and out. Such vessels may be used in cases of incomplete port equipment, port congestion, or lack of suitable means of transport between ports and the inland where river transportation is required.

5. 多用途船（Multi-uses Ship）

这类货轮根据营运上的需要,可以改变运载功能。散货船、矿砂船、油轮等专用船舶的载重量虽然都很大,但由于所运载的货物种类单一,回航不能装运其他种类的货物,只好压载空放。而多用途船在往返航程中,可以装载不同种类的货物。例如,油/散货轮（O-B）:既可装运油类又可装运散装货物的船舶;油/矿货轮（O-O）:对油类与矿砂都可装运的两用船;油/散/矿货轮（O-B-O）:对油类、散货及矿砂都可装运的船。

This kind of cargo ships can change the carrying function according to the operational needs. Although the carrying capacity of bulk carriers, ore carriers, tankers and other specialized ships is very large, they have to be ballasted due to the fact that they carry a single type of cargo and cannot carry other types of cargo on the return voyage. In contrast, multi-purpose ships can carry different kinds of cargoes in the round-trip voyage. For example, Oil/Bulk carrier （O-B） can carry both oil and bulk cargoes; Oil/Ore carrier （O-O） is a dual-purpose ship that can carry both oil and ore; Oil/Bulk/Ore carrier （O-B-O） is a ship that can carry both oil, bulk cargoes and ore.

2.4.2　按货轮的载重量不同划分（Classification by Cargo Ship's Deadweight）

按货轮的载重量不同,商船可分为巴拿马型船、超巴拿马型船、灵便型船、好望角型船和巨型游轮或超巨型游轮等不同类型。

Merchant ships can be divided into types such as Panamanian ships, super Panamanian ships, handysize ships, Cape of Good Hope ships, and VLCC & ULCC. according to their different capacity tonnage.

1. 巴拿马型船(Panamanian Ships)

扩展阅读 2.4 巴拿马运河基本情况及其发展

这是一种专门设计的适合巴拿马运河船闸的大型船只,船宽和吃水受到巴拿马运河船闸闸室的严格限制。这类船一般载重为 65 000 吨,船长小于 294.1 米,船宽不超过 32.3 米,最大允许吃水 12.04 米,高不超过 57.91 米。

扩展阅读 2.5 巴拿马运河水位"新低"冲击国际贸易

随着巴拿马运河在 2016 年 6 月和 2018 年 6 月完成两次扩建,允许通过的集装箱船载重量得到了巨大的提升,2018 年 6 月后允许载货量 15 000 标准箱的集装箱船通过。也就是说,目前"新巴拿马型"可装载的箱数已经达到了"巴拿马型"的 3 倍。

It is a large ship specially designed for the Panama Canal lock. Its width and draft are strictly limited by the lock chamber of the Panama Canal. These ships generally have a deadweight of 65 000 tons, a length of less than 294.1 meters, a width of no more than 32.3 meters, a maximum allowable draft of 12.04 meters, and a height of no more than 57.91 meters.

With the two expansions of the Panama Canal completed in June 2016 and June 2018, the carrying capacity of container ships allowed to pass through has been greatly increased, and since June 2018, container ships with a capacity of 15 000 TEUs have been allowed to pass through. In other words, the number of containers that can be loaded on the "New Panamanian ship" is now three times that of the "Panamanian ship".

2. 超巴拿马型船(Super Panamanian Ships)

这是指那些因为船型过大无法通过巴拿马运河而需绕行合恩角的船舶,载重量为 90 000～99 000 吨,通常是船宽超过 32.2 米的大型集装箱船,如第五代集装箱船的宽为 39.8 米,第六代为 42.8 米。

It refers to ships that are too large to pass through the Panama Canal and have to bypass Cape Horn, with a deadweight tonnage of 90 000-99 000 tons, usually large container ships with a width of more than 32.2 m, such as the fifth-generation container ships with a width of 39.8 m and the sixth-generation container ships with a width of 42.8 m.

3. 灵便型船(Handysize Ships)

这类船的载重量为 3 万～5 万吨,可作为沿海、近洋和远洋运输谷物、煤炭、化肥及金属原料等散装货物的船。

The ship's carrying capacity is between 30 000 tons and 50 000 tons. It can be used as a ship for transporting bulk cargo such as grain, coal, fertilizer and metal raw materials along the coast, offshore and ocean.

4. 好望角型船(Cape of Good Hope Ships)

其原本指那些因为太大无法通过苏伊士运河和巴拿马运河的货船,当它们需要穿越大洋时就必须通过好望角或者合恩角,所以被称为好望角型船。好望角型干货船是市场上最常见的船型之一,载重量为 130 000～189 000 吨,一般用于运输大批量的原料,如煤炭、铁矿石等。

Originally, it refers to cargo ships that are too big to cross the Suez Canal and Panama Canal. When they need to cross the ocean, they must pass through Cape Good Hope or Cape Horn, so they are called Cape of Good Hope ships. Cape of Good Hope dry cargo vessels are one of the most common vessel types in the market, with a deadweight between 130 000-189 000 tons, and are generally used for transporting large quantities of raw materials, such as coal and iron ore.

5. 巨型油轮或超巨型油轮(VLCC&ULCC)

和好望角型干货船同样吨位的油轮称为巨型油轮或者超巨型油轮,载重量一般为 20 万～30 万吨。由于巨型油轮巨大的吨位和体积,所以它对港口的水深和基础设施要求非常高。

The tanker with the same tonnage as the Cape of Good Hope dry cargo ship is called VLCC(Very Large Crude Carrier) or ULCC(Ultra-Large Crude Carrier), and the tonnage of load is generally between 200 000 and 300 000 tons. Because of its huge tonnage and size, large tankers place very high demands on water depth and infrastructure of the ports.

2.4.3　按对货轮的经营方式不同划分(Classification According to Different Ways of Operation of Cargo Ship)

按对货轮的经营方式不同,货轮可分为班轮(又称定期船)和租船(又称不定期船)。

According to the different operation modes of freighters, freighters can be divided into liner (also known as regular ship) and charter (also known as irregular ship).

1. 班轮(Liner)

班轮运输是在一定航线上、在一定的停靠港口、定期开航的船舶运输,是国际海洋货物运输的主要方式,适用于零星成交、批次较多、到港分散的货物运输。

Liner transportation is a mode of ship transportation where ship sails regularly on certain routes and at certain ports of call, which is the main mode of international ocean cargo transportation, and is suitable for the transportation of goods with sporadic transactions, more batches and scattered ports of call.

2. 租船(Charter)

租船运输是租船人向船东租赁船舶用于运输货物的业务,又分为定程租船与定期租船。外贸企业使用较多的租船方式是定程租船,主要用于运输批量较大的大宗初级产品,如粮食、油料、矿产品和工业原料等。

Chartered shipping is the business in which the charterer leases the ship to the shipowner for the transport of goods. It is also divided into voyage charter and time charter. Foreign trade enterprises use voyage charter more frequently，mainly for transporting large quantities of primary products，such as grain，oil，mineral products and industrial raw materials.

Words and Expressions

即测即练

习题

Chapter 3

班轮运输与租船运输
Liner Transport and Charter Transport

Learning Objectives:

1. Master the characteristics of liner transportation and charter transportation;
2. Master the calculation method of liner freight skillfully;
3. Mater the forms of charter shipping and characteristics of various chartered modes of transport;
4. Understand the composition of the cost of charter shipping.

引导案例

美国港口工人罢工影响全球海运价格

2002 年 9 月 27 日至 10 月 9 日,代表美国各港口码头工人的劳工联盟与太平洋海洋运输协会之间的劳资纠纷谈判宣告破裂,美国西海岸 29 座主要港口 1 万多码头工人同时罢工,引发了 30 年来历时最长的封港事件。这次停工事件涉及美国西海岸加利福尼亚州、俄勒冈州和华盛顿州的 29 个主要港口,包括长滩港、奥克兰港、波特兰港和西雅图港。美国西海岸主要港口每年货物吞吐量总值超过 3 000 亿美元,占美国外贸总量的一半。据估计,每停工一天的直接损失为 10 亿美元,加上相关经济损失,每天超过 20 亿美元。事发后一个星期,就有 200 多艘大型集装箱运输船靠岸,价值数十亿美元的进口货物等待卸货,另有美国中西部大量农产品和肉类无法装船外运。来自亚洲的电脑、汽车零配件、电器、家具、成衣和玩具等日用品无法卸货,开始造成市场短缺。上海航运交易所 2002 年 12 月 12 日发布的《中国出口集装箱运输市场周度报告》指出,中国至美国东西海岸港口的运价,出现了较为明显的差异。"美西码头因劳资谈判始终悬而未决,口岸集输效率下降对于航商航班运营及航次成本的影响逐渐体现,为确保收益,本轮美西航线涨幅高于美东航线,部分航商涨幅达 800 美元/标准箱。12 月 12 日,上海出口至美西、美东基本港市场运价(海运及海运附加费)分别为 2 259 美元/标准箱、4 363 美元/标准箱,环比分别上升 23.8%、8.5%。"个别航线由于洛杉矶、长滩港口太拥挤,已经临时转移到美国其他港口,尽量避开拥堵点。美国南加州一家玩具和杂货进口商,正常年份从中国内地运抵洛杉矶、长滩港口的一个货柜,出关的物流成本是 265 美元,但由于码头工人罢工,为避免供应圣诞节的货物遥遥无期地抛在码头上,只能每个货柜多付工人 1 000 美元,该进口商运出 5 个货柜,多花了 5 000 美元。此次事件对我国和其他亚洲国家也造成很大损失,估计仅我国中远集团损失即达数亿元人民币。

资料来源:上海国际航运研究中心. 美国港口罢工影响中美航线运力[EB/OL]. (2014-12-22). http://www. sisi-smu. org/2014/1222/c8835a102918/page. htm;美国西海岸码头工人罢工事件[EB/OL]. (2023-08-04). https://wenku. baidu. com/view/7610d15929f90242a8956bec0975f46527d3a7c2. html? _wkts_=1724144144875&bdQuery.

海洋运输依照其经营方式的不同,可分为班轮运输和租船运输。班轮运输是在不定期船运输的基础上发展起来的,迄今已有 200 多年的历史,班轮航线已遍及世界各海域及主要港口,并分为件杂货班轮运输和集装箱班轮运输;租船运输是相对于班轮运输的另一种海运方式,在国际贸易运输中发挥着重要作用。两种运输方式能够适应不同货物和不同贸易对运输的不同需求,有利于合理利用海运船舶的运输能力,降低运输成本,提高运输效率。

Ocean transportation can be divided into liner transportation and charter transportation according to its different operation methods. Liner transportation is developed on the basis of tramp shipping, which has a history of more than 200 years, and the liner routes have spread to all seas and major ports in the world, and can be divided into liner shipping for general cargo and container liner shipping; charter transportation is an affernative shipping mode to liner shipping, which plays an important role in international trade transportation. The two modes of transportation can adapt to the different needs of different goods and different trade for transportation, which is conducive to the rational use of the transport capacity of marine vessels, reducing transport costs and improving transport efficiency.

3.1　班轮运输(Liner Transport)

班轮运输又称定期船运输,是指承运人接受众多托运人的委托,按事先公布的船期表,沿固定的航线,在各基本港口间从事杂货和集装箱货物运输业务,并按事先公布的费率收取运费的一种海运方式。由于班轮运输合同常以提单作为表现形式,因此又被称为提单运输。目前,班轮运输已成为海洋运输的重要经营方式之一,班轮航线已遍布世界各海域和主要港口。国际海洋货物运输中,除大宗商品外,零星成交、多批量且到港分散的货物大多采用班轮运输方式。

Liner transportation, also known as regular ship transportation, refers to a shipping method in which the carrier accepts the commission of many shippers and engages in the transportation of general cargoes and containerized cargoes between the basic ports along a fixed route according to the pre-announced sailing schedule, and collects freight according to the pre-announced tariff. As the liner contract of carriage is often in the form of Bill of Lading(B/L), it is also known as B/L shipments. At present, liner shipping has become one of the most important modes of operation for ocean transportation, and liner services are available in all seas and major ports around the world. In international maritime cargo transportation，except for bulk commodities，most of the cargoes with sporadic transactions，multiple lots，and scattered arrivals are transported by liner.

3.1.1　班轮运输的主要特点（Main Characteristics of Liner Transport）

（1）"四固定"。"四固定"即固定航线、固定停靠港口、固定船期和相对固定的费率。"四固定"有利于货主掌握船期，核算运输费用，组织货源，促进出口成交。

（1）"Four-fixed". That is，liner shipping has the characteristics of fixed routes，fixed ports of call，fixed sailing schedules，and relatively fixed rates. This feature of the liner is conducive to the cargo owners to master the ship schedule，account for transportation costs，organize sources of goods and promote export transactions.

（2）"一负责"。运价中已包括装卸、理舱、配载作业及相关费用。在使用班轮运输时，货物在港口的装卸及配载由承运人（班轮公司）负责，承、托双方之间不计算装卸货时间以及滞期费和速遣费。

（2）"One-Responsible". Stowage costs and related expenses are included in the tariff. In the case of liner transportation，the carrier（liner company）shall be responsible for the loading，unloading，and stowage of the cargo at the port. The laytime as well as demurrage charges and dispatch money are not calculated between the carrier and the shipper.

（3）在杂货班轮运输中，除非承、托双方另有协议，承运人通常采取"仓库收货，集中装船"以及"集中卸船，仓库交付"的方法办理货物交接。承运人对货物所承担的责任期间是"舷至舷"或"钩到钩"。在集装箱班轮运输中，承运人通常在集装箱堆场办理集装箱交接。拼箱货则由集拼经营人在集装箱货运站交接货物。承运人的责任期间通常为"堆场至堆场"或"门至门"。

（3）In the liner transportation of general cargo，unless otherwise agreed between the carrier and the consignor，the carrier usually adopts the method of "warehouse receipt，centralized loading" and "centralized unloading，warehouse delivery" for cargo handover. The carrier's period of responsibility for the goods is "side to side" or "hook to hook". In container liner shipping，the carrier usually handles the handover of FCL at the container yard（CY）. LCL is handed over by the carrier or its agent at the container freight station（CFS）. The carrier's period of responsibility is usually "yard to yard" or "door to door".

（4）承运人与托运人之间处理纠纷所依据的是班轮提单。班轮运输中，承运人和托运人之间并不签订运输合同，而是以签订装货单的方式订舱，并以提单作为承、托双方权利、义务和豁免的依据，该提单受国际公约和国内法的制约。

（4）The dispute between the carrier and the shipper is settled on the basis of liner B/L. In liner transportation，no contract of carriage is concluded between the carrier and the shipper，but rather a Shipping Order（S/O）is concluded for space booking，and the B/L is the basis for the rights, obligations and exemptions of both parties, which is governed by international conventions and domestic laws.

班轮船舶通常具有良好的技术质量,配备合格的船长、船员及船舶航运所需的供给品,且各班轮公司有着严格的管理制度,保证了货物运输的质量;班轮运输"四固定"的特点,使得航期和港口有保证、运价稳定,为进出口商订立买卖合同中的价格条款、交货条款,掌握交接货时间以及安排货物的运输提供了便利的条件;班轮船舶承运货物的种类、数量比较灵活,一般不作限制,因此,适用于零星成交、批次较多、到港分散的货物运输;班轮船舶负责办理货物的装卸及中途转运,且定期公布船期表,为货主提供了极大的方便。因而,班轮运输深受货主的欢迎,成为国际海洋货物运输的主要方式。

The liner ships are usually of good technical quality, with qualified captains, crews, and supplies for shipping, and the liner companies have a strict management system to ensure the quality of cargo transport. The "four-fixed" features of liner transportation makes the sailing time and ports guaranteed and the freight rate stable, and provides convenient conditions for importers and exporters to conclude price clauses and delivery clauses, to master delivery time and arrange the transportation of goods. The type and quantity of cargoes carried by liner ships are more flexible and generally not restricted. Therefore, liner ships are suitable for the transportation of cargoes with sporadic transactions, more batches, and scattered arrivals. The ship owners are responsible for loading, unloading and transshipment, and the schedule is regularly announced, which provides great convenience for cargo owners. As a result, liner shipping is very popular among cargo owners and has become the main mode of international maritime cargo transportation.

3.1.2　班轮运价与班轮运费(Liner Tariff and Liner Freight)

班轮运费是班轮公司为运输货物而向货主收取的费用。运费的单位价格称为运价。班轮运价并不仅仅是一个简单的价格金额,而是包括费率标准、计收标准、承托双方费用、风险及其划分等的综合概念。运费与运价的关系是:运费等于运价与运量之积。

Liner freight is the fee charged by liner companies from cargo owners for transporting goods. The unit price of the freight is called tariff. Liner tariff is not only a simple price amount, but also a comprehensive concept that includes rate standard, charging standard, costs for both carriers and shippers, risks, and their classification. The relationship between freight and tariff is that freight is equal to the product of tariff and quantity.

1. 班轮运价的特点(Characteristics of Liner Tariff)

由于班轮运输的特点,班轮运价与租船运输价格有所不同,具有以下特点。

Due to the characteristics of liner transportation, the tariff of liner differs from that of charter shipping and has the following characteristics.

1) 班轮运价高于租船运输价格(Liner Shipping Rates are Higher than Chartered Shipping Rates)

班轮经营人通常需要提高运输价格来保证正常的营运收入,主要的原因包括:①班轮运输船舶通常具有较高的技术性能,具备适宜装运各种货物的舱室与设备,因此船舶造价较高;②班轮挂靠港口多,为班轮运输设施服务的网络也多,使得营运成本较高;③班轮需按固定时间挂靠固定港口,难以保证船舶满舱满载,影响了航次运营收入。

Liner operators usually need to raise transportation prices to ensure normal operating income, mainly because: ① liner ships usually have higher technical performance, with holds and equipment suitable for loading various kinds of cargoes, so the building cost is higher; ② the large number of ports of call for liner and the networks serving liner transportation facilities make operating costs high; ③liner ships call at fixed ports at fixed times, making it difficult to ensure that the ships canbe fully loaded, which affects the voyage operation income.

2) 班轮货物有较强的运费承受力(Liner Shipment has Strong Freight Tolerance)

班轮货物通常是附加价值较高的、深加工的工业制成品,尤其是高科技产品,因此,运费在货物总价值中所占比重较小,对运价波动的承受力较强。通常来说,班轮货物的运费占商品价格的比例为 1%～30%,而大宗廉价货物这一比例为 30%～50%。

Liner shipments are usually high value-added, deep-processed manufactured goods, especially high-tech products, and freight accounts for a smaller portion of the total value of the goods, making them more resilient in freight. Generally speaking, liner freight accounts for 1%-30% of cargo prices, while for bulk cheap goods, the proportion is 30%-50%.

3) 班轮运价相对稳定(Liner Freight Rate is Relatively Stable)

班轮运价是以运价本的形式予以公布的。运价本包括的货物种类繁多,航线复杂,运价制定后,短期内相对稳定。联合国《班轮公会行动守则公约》也规定两次调整运价的间隔不得少于 15 个月。

The liner freight rates are published in the form of a Liner's Freight Tariff. They cover a wide variety of cargoes and complex routes, and are relatively stable in the short term after they are set. *Convention on a Code of Conduct for Liner Conferences* also stipulates that the interval between two tariff adjustments shall not be less than 15 months.

4) 班轮运价是垄断性的(Liner Freight Tariffs are Monopolistic)

世界上大部分班轮运输航线为少数大的班轮公司所垄断,且这些大的班轮公司还组成了若干行业组织——班轮公会来控制和协调班轮运输业务。班轮公会的主要任务之一就是统一航线运价。会员公司必须遵守公会的统一运价,不得自行调整。这也是当前国际班轮运输中存在的最不合理的现象。

扩展阅读 3.1　班轮公会的前世今生

Most of the world's liner shipping routes are monopolized by a few large liner companies，and these large liner companies have formed several industry organizations—liner conferences—to control and coordinate the liner shipping business. One of the main tasks of the liner conferences is to unify the tariffs of different shipping lines. The member companies must abide by the uniform tariffs of the liner conferences and are not allowed to adjust them on their own. This is also the most unreasonable phenomenon in international liner shipping at present.

2. 班轮运价的种类（Classification of Liner Tariff）

班轮运价一般是按照班轮运价表的规定计算的。运价表是船公司承运货物据以向托运人收取运费的费率汇总表，其内容通常包括说明及有关规定（运价表的适用范围、计价货币、计价单位及其他有关规定）、港口规定及条款、货物分级表、航线费率表、附加费率表以及冷藏货物及活畜费率表。

Liner freight is generally calculated in accordance with the liner tariff schedule. The tariff schedule is a summary of the rates charged by the shipping line to the shipper for the cargo carried and usually includes: instructions and relevant provisions (scope of application of the tariff schedule, currency, charge unit and other relevant provisions), port provisions and terms, classification of commodities, scale of rate for different sea routes, surcharge rate table, and freight rate for refrigerated goods and livestock.

1）按制定主体的不同划分（Division According to the Subject Who Set the Tariff）

按制定主体的不同，班轮运价可分为以下几种。

Liner tariffs are divided into the following categories according to the party who formulate the tariffs.

（1）班轮公会运价表。它即由班轮公会制定的运价表，为参加此公会的班轮公司所采用，是一种垄断性的运价表，所规定的运价较高，如远东水脚公会运价表。

（1）Liner conference tariff. That is, the tariff established by the liner conference and adopted by membership companies, which is a higher monopolistic tariff, such as Far Eastern Freight Conference tariff.

（2）班轮公司运价表。它是由班轮公司自行制定并负责调整或修改的运价表，如中远公司运价表。各班轮公司运价表不统一，但一般低于公会运价水平。

（2）Non-conference tariff. Non-conference tariff, such as COSCO tariff, is a tariff formulated，adjusted，or revised by the liner company itself. The tariffs are not uniform among liner companies，but are generally lower than conference tariffs.

（3）双边运价。双边运价是由船、货双方共同商议制定、共同遵守的运价。对运价的调整和修改必须经过双方协商，任何一方都无权单方面改变。承运人按照双方商定的运价表的费率和规定收取运费。中外运长航的运价表即属此类。

（3）Bilateral tariff. Bilateral tariff is a freight rate jointly negotiated，determined and observed by the carrier and the shipper. Adjustments and modifications to the tariff must be negotiated between the two parties，and neither party has the right to change it unilaterally. The carrier collects the freight according to the rates and provisions of the tariff schedule agreed between the two parties. This is the case with tariffs issued by Sinotrans&CSC.

（4）协议运价。20 世纪 70 年代以来,行驶美国航线的一些班轮公司与托运人签订了运价协议,并向美国联邦海事委员会申请登记,根据协议制定了统一的运价。一些掌握大数量货源的货主可以向船公司提出船方能够接受的运价,并在与船方协商的基础上对运价进行调整和修改。当货方对运价有较大决定权时,这种协议运价也称为货方运价。

（4）Freight agreement. Since the 1970s, a number of liner companies plying U. S. routes have entered tariff agreements with shippers and applied for registration with the Federal Maritime Commission（FMC）of the United States, under which uniform tariffs have been established. Cargo owners who have large quantities of cargo can propose a tariff acceptable to the shipping company, and adjust and modify the tariff on the basis of negotiations with the shipping company. When the shipper has a greater right to decide the tariff, it is also called shipper tariff.

2）按费率结构的不同划分（Division According to the Rate Structure）

按费率结构的不同,班轮运价表可分为以下几种。

According to the different rate structure, liner tariffs can be divided into the following kinds.

（1）等级运价表。此种运价表将全部商品分为若干等级（一般分为 20 个等级）,每一个等级对应一个基本费率。等级运价表前附有“商品分级表”,在计算运费时,首先根据商品名称在“商品分级表”中查找出该商品的等级,再从该商品的运输航线或运抵港口的“等级费率表”中查出该级货物的费率,才能进行具体的运费计算。在实际业务中,大都采用等级运价表。

（1）Classification rate freight tariff. This tariff divides all commodities into several classes（generally 20 classes）, and each class corresponds to a basic rate. A table named "classification of commodities" is attached to the front of the freight tariff. When calculating the freight, the commodity class is first found in the "classification of commodity" according to the name of the commodity, and then the freight rate of the commodity can be found in the "scale of class rate" of the shipping routes or arrival ports before the specific freight calculation can be carried out. In actual business, classification tariff is the most frequently used.

（2）单项费率运价表。此种运价表将每种商品及其基本费率一一列出,每种商品对应各自的费率。

（2）Commodity rate freight tariff. This tariff lists each commodity and its basic rate individually, with each commodity corresponding to its own rate.

（3）航线运价表。它是指按航线、商品名称或等级所制定的运价表。这种运价不考虑运输距离远近,只要起运港和目的港是同一航线上规定挂靠的基本港,就按货物等级收取同样的运价。

（3）Route tariff. It refers to the tariff set by route, commodity name or classification. This kind of freight rate does not take into account the distance of transport. As long as the port of departure and destination are the basic ports of call on the same route，the same tariff will be charged according to the classification of commodity.

3. 班轮运费的计算（Calculation of Liner Freight）

班轮运费的计算又分为件杂货与集装箱货物的运费计算。

件杂货采用班轮运输，其运费包括货物从装运港至目的港的海上运费以及货物的装卸费和附加费用。

班轮运费由基本运费和附加运费构成。

The calculation of liner freight is further divided into the calculation of freight of general cargo and containerized cargo.

When general cargo is transported by liner，its freight includes the sea freight from the port of shipment to the port of destination，as well as the loading and unloading charges and additional charges.

Liner freight consists of basic freight and additional freight.

1）基本运费（Basic Freight）

班轮运输航线上船舶定期或经常挂靠的港口称为基本港口。综合这些港口的基本情况，为在航线上基本港口间的运输而制定的运价称为基本运费或基本费率。它是计收班轮运输基本运费的基础。基本运费是班轮运输全程应收运费的主要部分。基本运费的计算标准主要有以下几种。

The ports where ships regularly or frequently call on liner shipping routes are known as basic ports. The freight rate established for transportation between the basic ports on the route，taking into account the basic conditions of these ports，is called the basic tariff or basic rate，which is the basis for charging the basic freight for liner transportation. The basic freight is the main part of the total freight chargeable for the liner transportation. The criteria for calculating the basic freight are as follows.

（1）按货物的毛重，即以重量吨为计算单位计收。1重量吨为1公吨或1长吨，视船公司是采用公制还是采用英制计量而定。按此方式计收运费者，班轮运价表中的货物名称后面均注有"W"字样。

（1）Gross weight of the goods. That is，the freight is charged in weight ton as a unit of calculation. 1 weight ton is 1 metric ton or 1 long ton，depending on whether the shipping company uses the metric or imperial system. If the freight is charged in this way，the name of the goods in the "classification of commodities" will be marked with "W".

（2）按货物的体积，即以尺码吨为计算单位计收。1尺码吨以1立方米或40立方英尺为计费单位，也视船公司是采用公制还是采用英制计量而定。按此方式计收运费者，运价表中均注有"M"字样。

（2）Measurement of the goods. That is，the freight is charged with measurement ton as a unit of calculation. A measurement ton shall be charged in units of one cubic meter or forty cubic feet, depending on whether the shipping company adopts the metric or imperial system. For those who collect freight this way, the name of the goods in the "classification of commodities" will be marked with "M".

以上两种计算运费的重量吨和尺码吨统称为运费吨。

The weight ton and measurement ton in the above two freight calculation methods are collectively referred to as freight ton.

（3）按货物重量或尺码从高计收，即在重量吨和尺码吨两种计算标准中选择其高者计收。按照惯例，凡重量 1 吨的货物，如果其体积超过 1 立方米或 40 立方英尺，则按其体积计收；相反，如果重量 1 吨的货物其体积不足 1 立方米或 40 立方英尺，则按其毛重计收。运价表中用"W/M"表示。

（3）The higher of weight or measurement of the goods. That is, the higher of the two calculation criteria, i. e. , weight ton and measurement ton, is used as the basis for calculation of freight. It is customary to charge freight by volume for goods weighing 1 ton if their volume exceeds 1 cubic meter or 40 cubic feet; conversely, to charge freight by gross weight for goods weighing 1 ton if their volume is less than 1 cubic meter or 40 cubic feet. "W/M" is marked in the freight tariff.

（4）按货物的 FOB(Free on Board,船上交货)价值的一定百分比计收，习惯称为从价运费。按此方式计收运费者，在运价表中注有"A. V. ""Val"或"Ad Val. "。

（4）A certain percentage of the FOB(Free on Board) value of the goods. It's customarily called ad valorem freight. When collecting freight in this way, the tariffs are marked "A. V. ", "Val", or "Ad Val. ".

（5）从货物重量、尺码和价值三者中选择一种最高的运费计收。运价表中用"W/M"或"Ad Val. "表示。

（5）Freight is charged on the basis of the highest of three options: weight, measurement, and value of the goods. In the tariff table, it is expressed as "W/M" or "Ad Val. ".

（6）按货物重量或尺码选择其高者，再加上从价运费计收。运价表中用"W/M plus ad val. "表示。

（6）Freight is charged on the basis of the higher of the weight or measurement of the goods, plus ad valorem freight charges. In the tariff table, it is expressed as "W/M plus ad val. ".

（7）按每件货物作为一个计费单位收费。如活牲畜按"每头"，车辆按"每辆"。

（7）Use each item as a charging unit. For example, live animals are charged "per head" and vehicles are charged "per unit".

（8）临时议定运价，即由货主和船公司临时协商议定。它通常适用于承运粮食、豆类、矿石、煤炭等运量较大、货值较低、装卸容易、装卸速度快的农副产品和矿产品。临时议定运价的运费率一般均较低。

（8）Open Rate. That is to say, the cargo owner and the shipping company shall negotiate the freight on an ad hoc basis. Usually it is suitable for carrying agricultural and sideline products and mineral products，such as grain，beans，ore，and coal，which have the characteristics of large quantity，low value，easy handling，and fast loading and unloading. Open rates are generally lower.

在实际业务中，基本运费的计算标准以按货物的毛重（"W"）、按货物的体积（"M"）、按重量、体积选择（"W/M"）三种方式居多。贵重物品如古玩、稀有金属、精密仪器等一般按货物的 FOB 价值的一定百分比（"A. V."）计收。各种计收方法的总结见表 3-1。

In actual business，the calculation criteria of basic freight is mostly based on gross weight（"W"），measurement（"M"）of the goods and on the higher of weight and measurement（"W/M"）. Valuables such as antiques，rare metals，and precision instruments are generally charged at a certain percentage of the FOB value of the goods （"A. V."）. Summary of various calculation criteria is showed in table 3-1.

表 3-1　各种计收方法的总结

计收方法	表示方法	计收标准	适用货物
重量法	W	按货物的毛重，即以重量吨（weight ton）为计算单位计收	建材、机械、钢材、水泥等实重货
体积法	M	按货物的体积，即以尺码吨（measurement ton）为计算单位计收	纺织品、日用百货等轻泡货
从价法	A. V.、Val 或 Ad Val.	按货物的 FOB 价值的一定百分比计收	贵重物品，如古玩、稀有金属、名贵药材、精密仪器等
选择法	W/M 或 Ad Val.	按货物重量或尺码从高计收。或按货物重量、尺码和价值三者从高计收	货物存在不确定因素，或不同货物混装在同一包装中
综合法			特殊商品
计件法	per head；per unit；per piece，etc.	按每件货物作为一个计费单位收费	活牲畜或活动物、车辆
议定法	open rate	由货主和船公司临时协商议定	粮食、煤炭、矿砂等大宗农副产品和矿产品
起码运费	minimum rate	Per B/L	每份提单上所列的货物重量或体积所计算出的运费不足运价表中规定的最低费率

2）附加运费（Additional Freight or Surcharge）

附加运费是承运人因某种特殊情况，在基本费率之外另行加收的一种临时性的费用。班轮附加费的名目繁多，主要包括以下几种。

（1）因货物自身因素而征收的附加费：超重附加费、超长附加费等。

（2）因市场因素而征收的附加费：燃油附加费、货币贬值附加费等。

（3）因港口因素而征收的附加费：港口拥挤附加费、港口附加费、选卸港附加费、变更卸货港附加费等。

（4）因航道因素而征收的附加费：直航附加费、绕航附加费等。

另外还有转船附加费、洗舱费等。班轮附加费通常以基本运费的一定百分率计收，也有以每运费吨若干金额计收的。

Additional freight is a temporary charge that is added to the basic rate by the carrier due to special circumstances. There are various types of liner surcharges, which mainly includes the following kinds.

（1）Surcharges imposed due to the goods' own factors. For example：over weight surcharge (heavy lift additional), over length surcharge (long length additional), etc.

（2）Surcharges imposed due to market factors. Such as the Bunker Adjustment Factor (BAF) or Bunker Surcharge, and Currency Adjustment Factor (CAF).

（3）Surcharge imposed due to port factors. Such as Port Congestion Surcharge, Port Surcharge, Surcharge for Optional Destination (Optional fees), and Surcharge for Alteration of Destination.

（4）Surcharge imposed due to channel factors, such as Deviation Surcharge and Direct Addition.

In addition, there are transshipment surcharges, cabin washing charges and so on. Liner surcharges are usually charged at a certain percentage of the basic freight rate, or at a certain amount per freight ton.

3）运费的具体计算方法（Specific Calculation Method of Freight）

班轮运费采用等级费率表的具体计算方法是：先根据货物的英文名称从班轮运价表中的货物分级表中查出有关货物的计费等级及其计算标准；再从航线费率表中查出有关货物的基本费率；然后查出各项须支付的附加费率，与基本费率相加，所得的总和就是有关货物的单位运费（每重量吨或每尺码吨的运费），再乘以计费重量吨或尺码吨，即得该批货物的运费总额。如果是从价运费，则按规定的百分率乘以货物的 FOB 价值即可。班轮运费采用单项费率运价表的货物按表列费率计算基本运费；采用临时议定运价的需由货方和船方协商确定。

The specific method of calculating liner freight by using classification rate freight tariff is as follows：First, using the name of the commodities, find out the charging class and calculation basis of the goods from the classification of commodities. Then find out the basic rates of the goods concerned from the scale of rates of specific routes, and then find out the additional rates to be paid and add them up with the basic rates, the sum of which is the freight rate (freight per weight ton or per measurement ton) of the goods concerned. Multiply the result by the chargeable weight ton or measurement ton to get the total freight of the cargo. In the case of ad valorem freight, multiply the FOB value of the goods by the prescribed percentage. When the liner freight rate adopts commodity rate freight tariff, the basic freight of the goods is calculated according to the rates listed in the fright tariff, and the open rate is determined by the shipper and the carrier through consultation.

根据一般运价表规定：不同货物混装在一个包装内，全部货物按费率中高的计收；同一提单内有两种以上不同计价标准的货物，托运时未分列货名和数量的，计收标准和运价全部按高者计；对于无商业价值的样品或体积小于0.2立方米或重量小于50千克的货物，可要求船公司免费运送；另外，一般运价表中还有起码运费的规定，起码运费是指按每份提单上所列的货物重量或体积所计算出的运费不足运价表中规定的最低费率时，则按起码运费计收，即对每一提单最低必须收取若干运费。

According to the stipulation of general freight tariff, when different goods are mixed in one package, all goods are charged at the highest of the rates. If there are two or more types of goods with different rates in the same B/L and the name and quantity of the goods are not specified at the time of consignment, the higher of the rates and basis shall be applied to all of them. For samples of no commercial value or cargo of less than 0.2 cubic metres in volume or less than 50 kilograms in weight, the shipping company may be requested to deliver free of charge. In addition, there is generally a minimum freight provision in the tariff, which is charged when the freight calculated on the basis of the weight or volume of the goods listed on each B/L is less than the minimum rate specified in the tariff. This means that a minimum freight must be charged for each B/L.

示例3.1 班轮运价表

示例3.2 班轮运费计算例题

3.2 租船运输(Charter Transport)

3.2.1 租船运输的基本特点(Basic Features of Charter Transport)

租船运输又称不定期船运输。在这种运输方式下，船舶所有人或出租人根据国际租船市场行情和租船人的需要，将整船或部分舱位出租给租船人使用，以完成特定的货物运输任务，租船人按照事先签订的租船合同中约定的运价或租金支付运费。

与班轮运输相比，租船运输具有以下特点。

Charter transport, also known as tramp transport. In this mode of transport, the ship owner or lessor leases the whole ship or part of the hold to the charterer for a specific cargo transportation task according to the international charter market situation and the charterer's needs, and the charterer pays the freight according to the tariff or rent agreed in the pre-signed charter party.

In comparison with liner transport, charter transport has the following characteristics.

(1)航线、装卸港口、船期均不固定。

(2)承租人和船舶所有人之间的权利、义务通过双方签订的租船合同来确定；没有固定的运价，运价按市场供求变化进行调整。

（3）租船运输单位成本较低,运费通常低于班轮运费。

（4）船舶出租人或承运人一般不承担货物装卸责任及费用,因此,租船人或托运人与船舶出租人或承运人之间可能要计算滞期费与速遣费。

（5）通常运输的是大宗的裸装或散装货物以及半成品货物等,如粮食、煤炭、矿砂、石油、木材、水泥等。货主或托运人通常为大贸易商、需要大宗原料的工厂或企业。

（1）The route, loading and unloading ports, and ship schedule are not fixed.

（2）The rights and obligations between the charterer and the ship owner are determined by the charter party signed by both parties. There is no fixed tariff and tariffs are adjusted according to changes in market supply and demand.

（3）The unit cost of chartered ship transportation is lower, so its freight rate is usually lower than that of liner shipping.

（4）The ship's lessor or carrier is generally not responsible for cargo handling and expenses, so demurrage charges and dispatch money may have to be calculated between the charterer or shipper and the ship's lessor or carrier.

（5）Chartering is usually used to transport large quantities of bare or bulk goods and semi-finished goods, such as grain, coal, ore, oil, wood, and cement. Cargo owners or shippers are usually large traders, factories, or enterprises that need bulk raw materials.

3.2.2　租船运输的方式（Modes of Charter Transport）

1. 定程租船（Voyage Charter）

定程租船简称程租,又称航次租船,是以航程为基础的一种租船方式。在这种租船方式下,船舶所有人向承租人提供船舶或船舶的部分舱位,在指定的两港或数港之间从事单向或往返的一个航次或几个航次运输。船方必须按时把船舶驶到装货港装货,再驶到卸货港卸货,完成合同规定的运输任务并负责船舶的经营管理以及航行中的一切费用开支。租船人按合同约定支付运费。

Voyage charter, also known as trip charter, is a way of chartering ships based on voyage. Under this type of charter, the ship owner provides the charterer with a ship or part of a ship's hold to engage in a one-way or round-trip voyage or voyages between two or more designated ports. The ship owner must drive the ship to the loading port for loading and then to the discharging port for discharging on time, complete the contracted transportation tasks and be responsible for the operation and management of the ship as well as all expenses during the voyage. The charterer pays the freight according to the charter party.

对承租人而言,这种租船方式简便易行,不必操心船舶的调度与管理,也易于根据运费估算每吨货物的运输费用。因此,在租船市场上,定程租船被广泛运用于大宗货物的运输,是租船的基本形式,租船市场行情也主要以程租运价来表现。

根据承租人的实际业务需要,定程租船主要分为单航次租船、来回程租船、连续单航次租船、连续往返航次租船四种形式。

This type of chartering is simple and easy for the charterer, as he does not have to be responsible for the scheduling and management of the vessel, and it is easy to estimate the transportation cost per ton of cargo based on freight. Therefore, in the ship chartering market, voyage charter is widely used in the transportation of bulk cargoes and is the basic form of chartering. Chartering market conditions are also mainly expressed in terms of freight rates of voyage charter.

According to the actual business needs of the charterer, the voyage charter is mainly divided into four forms: single-voyage charter, round-trip charter and consecutive single-voyage charter, and finally consecutive round-trip charter.

2. 定期租船（Time Charter）

定期租船简称期租,是以租赁期限为基础的租船方式。船舶出租人将船舶租给租船人使用一定期限,在期限内由租船人自行调度和经营管理。租期可长可短,短则几个月,长则几年,甚至直至船舶报废。期租租金一般按照每载重吨每月(或每日)若干金额计算,一般是预付。

Time charter is a kind of charter based on the term of charter. The ship's lessor charters the ship to the charterer for a certain period of time, during which the charterer is responsible for its own scheduling and management. The term of the lease can be as short as a few months or as long as a few years, even until the ship is scrapped. Rent for time charter is generally calculated on a monthly (or daily) basis in certain amounts per deadweight ton, usually paid in advance.

在期租情况下,承租人需要了解船舶的性能、质量、规范以及基本的航海知识和货物配载技术,以便做好货物的装载,保证船货运输的安全。此外,与程租方式相比,期租方式下的船舶完全由承租人控制和使用,船舶滞期风险由承租人承担,因此,承租人承担的风险比船舶所有人要大。基于以上原因,除非特别需要,货主一般不愿采用期租方式租船。

In the case of time charter, the charterer needs to know the ship's performance, quality, specifications, basic navigational knowledge and cargo stowage technology, so as to do a good job of cargo stowage and ensure the safety of cargo transportation. In addition, compared with voyage charter, the vessel under time charter is completely controlled and used by the charterer, and the risk of demurrage is borne by the charterer. Therefore, the charterer bears more risk than the vessel owner. Based on the above reasons, cargo owners are generally reluctant to use time charter unless they have special needs.

3. 光船租船（Bareboat Charter）

光船租船是期租的一种,所不同的是船东不提供船员,仅将船交给租方使用,由租方配备船员,并负责经营管理及船舶航行的各项事宜。光船租船实际上是一种财产租赁业务,而不完全是一种运输业务,租期一般较长且业务复杂,因此在国际租船市场上并不多见。

Bareboat charter is a kind of time charter, but the difference is that the owner does not provide the crew, but only gives the ship to the charterer to use. The charterer will provide the crew, and is responsible for the operation and management of the ship and all matters related to navigation. Bareboat charter is actually a property charter rather than a transportation business, and the leasing period is generally long and the business is complex, making it uncommon in the international charter market.

4. 包运租船(Contract of Affreightment)

包运租船是指船舶所有人提供给租船人一定运力,在确定的港口之间,以事先约定的期限、航次周期和每航次较为均等的货运量,完成运输合同规定的总运量的一种租船方式。由于这种方式的性质、费用和风险的划分基本与程租方式相同,因此,其通常被认为是定程租船派生出来的一种方式。

Contract of affreightment(COA) refers to a chartering method in which the shipowner provides the charterer with a certain amount of shipping capacity to complete the total volume of freight stipulated in the contract of carriage between the ports of destination for a pre-agreed period, voyage cycle and a basically equal amount of freight per voyage. As the nature, cost and risk allocation of this method is essentially the same as that of voyage charter, it is often assumed that COA is a method derived from voyage charter.

3.2.3　各种租船运输方式的特点(Characteristics of Various Modes of Charter Transport)

各种租船运输方式的特点如下。

(1) 定程租船方式简单易行,租船人不必操心船舶的调度、支配问题,而且容易估算出单位重量的运价。

(2) 在定期租船下,租船人须负责有关船舶管理的技术性工作,须具备基本的航海知识和配套技术等。

(3) 光船租船是一种特殊的期租方式,性质上实属财产租赁,租赁方要负责复杂的船员管理和雇佣工作。

(4) 包运租船类似于连续航次租船,两者的区别在于包运租船不固定船舶,一般仅规定船级、船龄和技术规范,因而,对船东在调度和安排船舶方面十分有利。

The characteristics of various modes of chartered ship transportation are as follows.

(1) Voyage charter is simple and feasible. The charterer does not have to worry about the scheduling and control of the ship, and it is easy to estimate the freight per unit weight.

(2) Under time charter, the charterer shall be responsible for the technical work related to ship management, and shall have basic navigational knowledge and other

supporting technologies.

（3）Bareboat charter is a special type of time charter，which is in the nature of a property lease，with the charterer being responsible for the complex management and employment of the crew.

（4）Contract of affreightment is similar to consecutive single-voyage charter，the difference between the two is that COA does not fix the vessel and generally only specifies the classification，age and technical specifications，thus providing a great advantage to the shipowner in scheduling and arranging the vessel.

3.2.4　租船运输的费用（Charter Transport Expenses）

1. 定程租船费用（Voyage Charter Expenses）

定程租船费用主要包括程租船运费和程租船装卸费、滞期费和速遣费等。

The expenses of voyage charter mainly include freight for voyage charter，loading and unloading charges for voyage charter，demurrage charges and dispatch money.

1）程租船运费（Freight for Voyage Charter）

程租船运费是指货物从装运港至目的港的海上运费。其计算方式主要有两种：一种是按运费率计算总运费，即规定每单位重量或单位体积的运费额，同时还要规定是按装船时的货物重量还是按卸船时的货物重量计算；另一种是整船包价，即规定整船运费，船东保证船舶能提供的载货重量和容积，不管租方实际装货多少，一律照整船包价计收。

Freight on voyage charter refers to the sea freight for goods from the port of shipment to the port of destination. There are two main ways to calculate the total freight：one is to calculate the total freight according to the freight rate，i. e. by specifying the amount of freight per unit of weight or volume，and also by specifying whether it is to be calculated on the basis of the weight of the goods at the time of loading (intaken quantity) or the weight of the goods at the time of unloading (delayed quantity). The other is charged by lump-sum freight，which only stipulates the whole ship's freight，and the ship owner guarantees the load capacity and volume of the ship. No matter how much the charterer actually loads，it will be charged according to the lump-sum freight.

2）程租船装卸费（Loading and Unloading Charges for Voyage Charter）

程租船运输情况下，有关货物的装卸费用由租船人和船东协商确定后在程租船合同中作出具体规定，具体做法主要有以下四种。

In the case of voyage charter，the cost of loading and unloading of the cargo is specified in the charter party after negotiation between the charterer and the shipowner，specific practices are as follows.

（1）船方承担装货费和卸货费。其又可称为"班轮条件"，即采用班轮运输的做法，将货物的装卸费用包括在程租船运费内。货方即租船人承担运费，装卸费由船方负责支付。在此条件下，船货双方一般以船边划分费用。其多用于木材和包装货物的运输。

（2）船方管装不管卸。船方承担装货费,但不承担卸货费。

（3）船方管卸不管装。船方承担卸货费,但不承担装货费。

（4）船方装和卸均不管。船方既不承担装货费,也不承担卸货费。这种条件一般适用于散装货。采用这一规定方法时,必要时还需明确规定理舱费和平舱费由谁承担。

（1）Loading and unloading charges are borne by the ship owner. It is also referred to as "liner terms"(gross terms or berth terms). That is, the loading and unloading costs are included in the freight of the voyage charter by using the practice of liner shipping. The shipper (the charterer) bears the freight, and the ship pays the loading and unloading charges.

（2）Free out (F. O.). That is, the ship bears the loading charge, but not the unloading charge.

（3）Free in (F. I.). That is, the ship bears the unloading charge, but not the loading charge.

（4）Free in and out (F. I. O.). That is, the ship is not responsible for either loading or unloading charges. This condition generally applies to bulk cargo. In adopting this method, it shall also specify, if necessary, who is to bear the stowage fee and trimming charge.

3）滞期费和速遣费（Demurrage Charges and Dispatch Money）

程租船运输情况下,装卸货时间的长短影响到船舶的使用周期和在港费用,直接关系到船方利益。因而,在程租船合同中,除需规定装卸货时间外,还需规定一种奖励和处罚措施,以督促租船人实现快装快卸。

如果租船人在规定的装卸期限内未能完成装卸作业,为了弥补船方的损失,租船人应向船方支付一定的罚款。这种罚款称为"滞期费"。相反,如果租船人提前完成装卸作业,则船方对所节省的时间要向租船人支付一定的奖金。这种奖金称为"速遣费"。后者一般为前者的二分之一。

In the case of trip charter transportation, the length of loading and unloading time influences the ship's service life and port expenses, and thus directly relates to the interests of the ship. Therefore, in the charter party, in addition to stipulating the loading and unloading time. Therefore, in the charter party, in addition to the need to stipulate loading and unloading time, it is also necessary to provide a kind of incentive and penalty measures, in order to urge the charterer to achieve fast loading and unloading.

If the charterer fails to complete loading and unloading within the stipulated period, in order to compensate for the ship's losses, the charterer shall pay a certain penalty to the ship. This penalty is called "demurrage charges". On the other hand, if the charterer completes the loading and unloading operation ahead of schedule, the ship has to pay a certain bonus to the charterer for the time saved. This bonus is called "dispatch money". The latter is generally one-half of the former.

2. 定期租船租金(Time Charter Rent)

在定期租船情况下,租船人为使用船舶而付给船舶所有人的费用称为租金。租金率取决于船舶的装载能力和租期的长短,通常规定为按月每载重吨若干金额或整船每天若干金额。

In the case of time charters, the fee paid by the charterer to the shipowner for the use of the ship is known as the rent. The rate of rent depends on the loading capacity of the ship and the length of the charter period, and is usually set at a certain amount based on dwt per month or per day for the whole ship.

Words and Expressions

即测即练

习题

第 4 章
Chapter 4

海 运 提 单
Ocean Bill of Lading

Learning Objectives：

1. Understand the concept and types of shipping documents；
2. Master the concept，nature and function of B/L；
3. Master the types of B/L，especially the concept of on board B/L，clean B/L，order B/L，original B/L，antedated B/L，etc.；
4. Know how to make a B/L.

📚 引导案例

倒签提单欺诈被起诉

2005 年,甲国 A 贸易公司与乙国 B 贸易公司签订了一项出口货物的合同。合同中,双方约定货物的装船日期为该年 11 月,以信用证方式结算货款。合同签订后,甲国 A 贸易公司委托甲国 C 运输公司运送货物到目的港乙国×市。但是,A 贸易公司没有很好地组织货源,直到第二年 2 月才将货物全部备妥,于第二年 2 月 15 日装船。甲国 A 贸易公司为了如期结汇取得货款,要求 C 运输公司按 2005 年 11 月的日期签发提单,并凭借提单和其他单据向银行办理了议付手续,收清了全部货款。但是,当货物运抵×港时,收货人 B 贸易公司对装船日期产生了怀疑,遂要求查阅航海日志,C 运输公司的船方被迫交出航海日志。B 贸易公司在审查航海日志之后,发现了该批货物真正的装船日期是 2006 年 2 月 15 日,比合同约定的装船日期要迟延 3 个多月,于是,B 贸易公司向当地法院起诉,控告甲国 A 贸易公司和 C 运输公司串谋伪造提单,进行欺诈,既违背了双方合同约定,也违反法律规定,要求法院扣留该 C 运输公司的运货船只。乙国当地法院受理了 B 贸易公司的起诉,并扣留了该运货船舶。在法院的审理过程中,A 贸易公司承认了其违约行为,C 运输公司亦意识到其失理之处,遂经多方努力,争取庭外和解,最后与乙国 B 贸易公司达成了协议,由 A 贸易公司和 C 运输公司支付乙国 B 贸易公司赔偿金,B 贸易公司方撤销了起诉。

资料来源：提单诈骗典型案例［EB/OL］.（2019-03-09）. https://www. lawtime. cn/info/baoguanshangjian/baoguanshouxu/201010272062.html.

在货物的运输委托中,出口商为托运人,船代、货代、外运为承运人或承运人的代理人。托运人出运货物时,首先向承运人或其代理人递交相应的单据,承运人或其代理人负责租船、订舱、配载。货物出运后,承运人或其代理人签发运输单据。因此,运输单据是承运人收到承运货物后签发给出口商的证明文件,具体反映了同货物运输有关的各种关系人(如发货人、承运人、收货人等)的责任和权益。运输单据是交接货物、处理索赔以及向银行结算货款或进行议付的重要单据。根据运输方式不同,运输单据主要包括海运提单、国际铁路运单、承运货物收据、航空运单以及国际多式联运单据等。由于海洋运输是国际贸易中最重要的运输方式,因此,海运提单在国际贸易运输中得到广泛运用,并经过几百年的时间和不断改善,成为国际贸易和海洋运输的基石。

In the consignment of cargoes, the exporter is the shipper, and the shipping agent, freight agent, and foreign trade transportation enterprise are the carrier or the agent of the carrier. When the shipper consigns the goods, it first submits the corresponding documents to the carrier or its agent, who is responsible for chartering, booking, and stowage. After the goods are shipped, the carrier or its agent issues the shipping document. Therefore, the shipping document is a certificate issued by the carrier to the exporter after receiving the cargoes, which specifically reflects the responsibilities and rights of various parties related to the carriage of goods (such as the consignor, the carrier, and the consignee). Shipping documents are important documents for handing over goods, processing claims and settling or negotiating payments to banks. According to the different modes of transportation, shipping documents mainly include ocean bill of lading, international through rail waybill, cargo receipt, air waybill and international multimodal transport document. As marine transport is the most important mode of transport in international trade, therefore, the ocean bill of lading is widely used in international trade transportation, and has become the corner stone of international trade and ocean transportation after centuries of practice and continuous improvement.

4.1　海运提单概述（Overview of Ocean Bill of Lading）

4.1.1　海运提单的概念［Concept of Ocean Bill of Lading(B/L)］

海运提单简称提单,是国际货物贸易和国际海上货物运输中的重要单据之一,它是随着国际贸易的不断发展而产生的。

提单是承运人或其代理人在收到有关承运货物时签发给托运人的一种收据。它是证明托运的货物已经收到,或已经装载到船上,并允诺将其运往指定目的地交付收货人的书面凭证。海运提单也是收货人在目的港据以向船公司或其代理人提取货物的凭证。

提单既是运输单据,又是贸易单据。作为运输单据,它既涉及货物的接收与交付,又涉及运输合同义务;作为贸易单据,它既涉及物权的转让,又涉及贸易支付。

Ocean B/L is one of the important documents in the international trade and the international carriage of goods by sea. It comes into being with the continuous development of international trade.

B/L is a receipt issued by the carrier or its agent to the shipper upon receipt of the consigned goods. It is a written proof that the consignment has been received or loaded on board on the vessel and that the carrier has promised to deliver it to the consignee at the named destination. The ocean B/L is also the document by which the consignee collects the goods from the shipping company or its agent at the port of destination.

B/L is both a transport document and a trade document. As a transport document, it involves not only the acceptance and delivery of goods, but also the obligations of the contract of carriage. As a trade document, it involves not only the transfer of real rights, but also the payment of trade.

4.1.2　海运提单的性质与作用(Nature and Function of Ocean B/L)

在国际海洋货物运输中,托运人与承运人之间一般需要订立运输合同和签发提单来确立双方的权利、义务及责任豁免。因此,提单是目前海运业务中使用最为广泛和重要的运输单据。

尽管目前国际上对提单的性质和作用存在争议,但大多数人认为提单具有以下性质和作用。

In international marine cargo transportation, it is generally necessary for shippers and carriers to conclude a contract of carriage and issue B/L to establish the rights, obligations, and exemptions from liability of both parties. Therefore, the B/L is currently the most widely used and important transportation document in the maritime transport business.

Although the nature and role of the B/L is currently disputed internationally, most people believe that the B/L has the following natures and roles.

1. 提单是承运人(或其代理)出具的货物收据[B/L is a Receipt for the Goods Issued by the Carrier (or its Agent)]

提单是由船长或船公司或其代理人签发给托运人的表明货物已经收讫的收据,它证明货物已运至承运人指定的仓库或地点,并置于承运人的有效监控之下,承运人许诺按收据内容将货物交付给收货人。因此,提单是托运人向银行结汇的主要单据之一。

B/L is a receipt issued to the shipper by the captain, the shipping company, or their agent indicating that the goods have been received. It certifies that the goods have been delivered to the warehouse or place designated by the carrier and are under the effective control of the carrier, and that the carrier promises to deliver the goods to the consignee in accordance with the contents of the receipt. Therefore, the B/L is one of the main documents used by the shipper to settle the foreign exchange with the bank.

对于提单作为货物收据的法律效力仍存在一定的分歧。《海牙规则》《维斯比规则》《汉堡规则》《鹿特丹规则》以及《中华人民共和国海商法》(以下简称《海商法》)规定,在承、托双方之间,提单是承运人收到货物的"推定证据""初步证据",即这种证据效力是相对的,如果承运人事后有证据证明提单记载的货物与实际不符,提单记载可被否定;但《维斯比规则》《汉堡规则》《鹿特丹规则》以及《海商法》都规定,提单证据对收货人则为"最终证据"或"绝对证据",即只要收货人等善意的第三者收到的货物与提单记载的状况不符,除不可抗力或其他可以免责的原因外,承运人则须对收货人等负责赔偿。

There are still some differences of opinion on the legal effect of the B/L as a receipt for the goods. *Hague Rules*, *Visby Rules*, *Hamburg Rules*, *Rotterdam Rules* and *Maritime Law of People's Republic of China* (hereinafter referred to as *Maritime Law*) stipulate that between the carrier and the shipper, the B/L is the "presumptive evidence" and "preliminary evidence" of the carrier's receipt of the goods. If the carrier has subsequent evidence to prove that the goods recorded in the B/L are inconsistent with the actual situation, the record of the B/L can be denied. However, *Visby Rules*, *Hamburg Rules*, *Rotterdam Rules*, and *Maritime Law* all stipulate that the evidence of bill of lading is "final evidence" or "absolute evidence" for the consignee. That is, as long as the goods received by the good-faith third party such as the consignee do not conform to the status recorded in the B/L, the carrier shall be liable for compensation to the consignee, except the case of force majeure or other exemptions.

2. 提单具有运输合同的属性①(B/L has the Property of Contract of Carriage)

对于提单作为运输合同的属性仍存在一定的争议。但将提单简单定义成"运输合同的证明"是不准确的。根据有关法律,提单运输合同关系有两种情况:第一种是建立在承运人和托运人之间的;第二种是在提单转让后建立在承运人和提单持有人之间的。

在第一种情况下,提单的运输合同属性在不同运输方式下的表现形式不同。我国法律界较普遍的观点是提单是运输合同的证明,这一观点体现在《海商法》关于提单的定义中,而英国提单法则承认提单具有运输合同的属性。

在班轮运输方式下,提单是运输合同的最重要的组成部分,运输合同的绝大部分条款都体现在提单中。从整体上看,订舱单、船期表、运价本、提单共同构成了班轮运输合同,其中提单是最重要的组成部分,因此有人称其为格式合同。在租船运输方式下,当承租人是发货人时(如在 CFR(Cost and Freight,成本加运费)、CIF(Cost, Insurance, and Freight,成本费加保险费加运费)条件下),承租人与托运人的权利与义务关系由租船合同约定,这时提单对于发货人而言不具有运输合同的属性;当承租人是贸易合同的买方时(如 FOB 条件下),提单对于该承租人不具有运输合同属性,但对于发货人而言具有特殊的运输合同属性,此时,提单有关条款和相关法律规定约束该实际托运人和承运人之间的权利与义务。

在第二种情况下,即提单转让之后,无论在什么运输方式下,提单都是约束承运人与提单持有人的运输合同。

正是由于上述提单运输合同的属性,提单条款的有关规定可以作为制约承运人与托运人或提单持有人等各方之间的权利与义务、责任与豁免,处理他们之间有关海洋运输方面争议的依据。

There is still controversy about the attributes of the B/L as a contract of carriage. However, it is not accurate to simply define the B/L as "evidence of the contract of

---

① 此处借鉴了李勤昌《国际货物运输》(东北财经大学出版社)中的部分观点。

carriage". According to relevant laws, there are two situations in the contractual relationship of the B/L: the first is between the carrier and the shipper; the second is between the carrier and the holder of the B/L after the transfer of the B/L.

In the first case, the manifestation of the property of the B/L as a contract of carriage is different in different modes of transport. The common view in China's legal circle is that the B/L is the evidence of the contract of carriage, which is embodied in the definition of the B/L in *Maritime Law*, while the British bill of lading law recognizes that the B/L has the nature of the contract of carriage.

In liner transportation, the B/L is the most important part of the transport contract, and most of the terms of the transportation contract are embodied in the B/L. From the overall point of view, booking note, shipping schedule, tariff schedule, and B/L constitute the liner transport contract, among which the B/L is the most important part, so it is called the format contract. Under charter shipping, when the lessee is the shipper [for example, under CFR(Cost and Freight) and CIF(Cost, Insurance, and Freight)], the rights and obligations between the lessee and the shipper are stipulated in the charter party, and the B/L does not have the attribute of the transport contract for the shipper; when the lessee is the buyer of the trade contract (for example, under FOB), the B/L does not have the attribute of the transport contract for the lessee, but for the shipper, it has a special nature of the contract of carriage. At this time, the relevant terms and relevant legal provisions of the B/L govern the rights and obligations between the actual shipper and the carrier.

In the second case, after the transfer of B/L, no matter the mode of transportation, B/L is the contract of carriage that binds the carrier and the holder of B/L.

It is because the B/L has the properties of the contract of carriage, the relevant provisions of the B/L can be used as the basis for governing the rights, obligations, liabilities, and immunities between the carrier and the shipper or holder of the B/L and dealing with disputes between them in relation to maritime transport.

3. 提单是物权凭证（B/L is a Document of Title）

提单是物权凭证、所有权凭证、抵押权凭证，还是债权凭证，目前仍存在争议。

运输单据在商业习惯或法律上一般不是物权凭证，但提单是一个例外。根据提单的含义，承运人要依据提单的规定凭单交货，在交付之前，货物是在承运人的保管或占有之下，指示提单和不记名提单可以转让，即在市场上同有价证券一样，善意受让提单的人即可凭以向承运人提货。因此，提单是根据习惯做法或制定法获得流通性，成为物权凭证。

中国司法界倾向于提单是债权凭证的观点，认为提单的持有和转让与货物所有权的拥有和转移是完全脱节的，提单的转让只是转让货物的推定占有，并不产生货物所有权的必然转移；即使在国际贸易中，提单也完全没有成为物权凭证的必要，它只能是一种可转让的权利或债权凭证，即据以向承运人提取货物的凭证。

《鹿特丹规则》规定提单仅表示对货物的"控制权"，而非"物权"凭证，这对平息提单究竟是物权凭证、所有权凭证、抵押权凭证还是债权凭证之争，可能具有一定的指导意义。

按照航运习惯，持有提单就意味着支配货物，这一效力包括货物在承运人掌管代运期间、运输途中和交付中的控制权，以及在目的地请求承运人交付货物的权利。在国际贸易中，正本提单作为钱与货的衔接点，是卖方凭以议付、买方凭以提货、承运人凭以交货的依据。此外，提单可以不经承运人的同意而转让的规定，体现了提单的可转让性。

提单可以通过背书进行转让，提单的转移就意味着提单所记载的货物占有权的转移。卖方将货物占有权（正本提单）转让给了银行，就可以得到相应的货款，买方只有将款项交付给银行，才能得到货物占有权（正本提单）并凭以提货。正因为提单具有此性质，所以提单的持有人可凭提单向银行办理抵押贷款或叙作押汇，从而获得银行的融资。

提单作为物权凭证或债权凭证的效力在国际货物买卖中发挥了重要作用：首先，它有效地维护了卖方的利益；其次，它有效地促进货物流通和转手买卖的进行；最后，它还可以作为预付货款的附加担保。

It remains controversial whether the B/L is a document of title, a document of ownership, a document of mortgage, or a document of creditor's rights.

Shipping documents are generally not documents of title in commercial practice or in law, but B/L is an exception. According to the meaning of the B/L, the carrier should deliver the goods on the basis of the stipulations of B/L. Before delivery, the goods are under the carrier's custody or possession. Order B/L and Bearer B/L can be transferred. That is to say, they are the same as securities in the market. Bona fide transferee of the B/L can pick up the goods from the carrier with it. Therefore, the B/L acquires negotiability and becomes a document of title according to customary practice or established law.

The Chinese judiciary favors the view that the B/L is a document of claim, and believes that the possession and transfer of the B/L and ownership of the goods is completely disconnected, the transfer of the B/L is only the transfer of the presumed possession of the goods, and does not produce the inevitable transfer of ownership of the goods. Even in international trade, there is no need for the B/L to serve as a document of title at all. It can only be a negotiable document of right or claim, i. e. a document by which the goods are collected from the carrier.

Rotterdam Rules, on the other hand, provides that the B/L expresses only the "right of control" over the goods, rather than a "document of title", which may be instructive in settling disputes as to whether the B/L is a document of title, a document of ownership, a document of mortgage or a document of claim.

According to shipping custom, holding a B/L means dominating the goods. This right includes the control of the goods during the carrier's administration of the consignment, in transit and in delivery, as well as the right to request the carrier to deliver the goods at the destination. In international trade, the original B/L, as the interface of money and goods, is the basis for the seller to negotiate payment, for the buyer to take delivery of the goods and the carrier to deliver goods. In addition, the provision that a B/L can be transferred without the consent of the carrier reflects its negotiability.

B/L can be transferred by endorsement. The transfer of the B/L implies the transfer of possession of the goods recorded in the B/L. The seller transfers possession of the goods (original B/L) to the bank and is paid for the goods; the buyer could obtain possession of the goods (original B/L) and take delivery of the goods only by delivering the money to the bank. Because of this nature of the B/L, the holder of the B/L can use it to apply for a mortgage loan or negotiation with the bank, so as to obtain bank financing.

扩展阅读 4.1　从历史发展角度再论海运提单的法律性质

The nature of the B/L as a document of title or creditor's right plays an important role in the international trade: first, it effectively safeguards the interests of the seller. Secondly, it effectively promotes the circulation of goods and switch trade. Finally, it can also be used as an additional guarantee for prepayment of goods.

4.1.3　海运提单的关系人(Parties to Ocean B/L)

（1）承运人。承运人是与托运人签订运输合同的关系人。根据不同情况,承运人可能是船舶所有人,也可能是租船人。

（1）Carrier. It is the party who signs the contract of carriage with the shipper. Depending on the circumstances, it may be the ship owner or the charterer.

（2）托运人。托运人是与承运人签订运输合同的关系人。根据情况不同,托运人可能是发货人,也可能是收货人。

（2）Shipper. It is the party who signs the contract of carriage with the carrier. Depending on the circumstances, it may be the consignor or the consignee.

（3）收货人。收货人是指有权在目的港凭提单向承运人提取货物的人。

（3）Consignee. It refers to the person entitled to take delivery of goods from the carrier by B/L at the port of destination.

（4）被通知方。被通知方是承运人在货物到港后通知的对象,一般是收货人的代理人,负责办理清关提货手续。提单上要详细列明被通知人的名称、地址,以及电话、传真号码和具体经办人等,以便货到目的港及时通知。

（4）Notify party. It is the person whom the carrier notifies upon the arrival of the cargo at the port, usually the consignee's agent, who is responsible for customs clearance and pick-up procedures. The B/L should specify the name and address, telephone number, fax number of the notify party and specific operator and so on, so that when the goods arrive at the destination port, it can get timely notification.

（5）受让人。受让人是指经过背书转让接受提单的人,也是提单的持有人。受让人有权向承运人提货,同时也承担了托运人在运输契约上的义务。比如,采用 FOB 术语时,提单显示"FREIGHT COLLECT",则受让人应支付运费。

（5）Transferee or assignee. It is the person who accepts the B/L by endorsement and is also the holder of the B/L. The transferee has the right to take delivery of the goods from the carrier and at the same time assumes the shipper's obligations under the contract of carriage. For example，when FOB terms are used，the B/L indicates "FREIGHT COLLECT"，and the transferee shall pay the freight.

（6）持单人。持单人是指经过正当手续持有提单的人。持单人可凭提单领取货物。

（6）Holder. It is the person who holds the B/L after due process. The holder may collect the goods against B/L.

4.1.4　提单的签发（Issuance of B/L）

1. 提单的签署（Signature of B/L）

提单必须经过签署才能产生效力。有权签署提单的人包括：承运人，即船东（也称轮船公司）；承运人的具名代理或代表；船长；船长的具名代理或代表。签署提单时必须加注承运人的名称，而且后两种签署人签署时还应加注船长的名称和身份。

B/L must be signed before it becomes effective. The persons entitled to sign the B/L include the carrier，i. e. the ship owner，the named agent or representative of the carrier，the captain，and the named agent or representative of the captain. The name of the carrier must be indicated when signing the B/L，and the name and identity of the captain of the ship should be added when the last two types of signatories sign.

2. 提单的签发地点和日期（Place and Date of Issuance of B/L）

提单的签发地点为货物的装船港，提单的签发日期应当是货物实际装船完毕的日期。在装运散装货物时，可按开装日期签发提单。

The place of issuance of the B/L is the port of loading of the goods. The date of issuance of the B/L shall be the date when the actual loading of the goods has been completed. When bulk cargo is shipped，B/L may be issued on the date of commencement of shipment.

3. 提单签发的份数（Number of Copies of B/L Issued）

提单是货物收据，最好签发一份正本，但实际业务中通常都签发三份正本，主要是防止提单遗失、被窃或延迟到达。每一份正本都必须正式签字，正本提单的正面印有正本份数，其中一份凭以提货后，其他两份就自动失效。根据信用证要求，可以签发若干份提单副本。信用证都要求受益人提交全套提单，即船公司签发的所有提单正本。

B/L is the cargo receipt. It is better to issue one original，but in practice，three original bills are usually issued，mainly to prevent the loss，theft or delay of arrival of the B/L. Each original B/L must be duly signed with the number of copies of the original printed on the front. After taking delivery of goods by one of the original Bs/L，the other two will automatically expire. According to the requirements of the L/C，several copies of B/L can be issued. The L/C requires the beneficiary to submit a full set of Bs/L，i. e. all original Bs/L issued by the shipping company.

4.2　海运提单的种类（Types of Ocean Bill of Lading）

国际海上运输存在不同的形式,国际贸易的做法也存在差异,因而就产生了不同种类的提单。常见的海运提单主要有如下几种。

There are different forms of international carriage by sea and different practices in international trade, so different kinds of Bs/L are produced. Common ocean Bs/L are as follows.

4.2.1　按签发人不同分类（Classification by Issuer）

1. 船东提单（Ship Owner's B/L）

船东提单是指由作为承运人的船东向托运人签发的提单。在不定期船运输中,作为承运人的船东可以向托运人签发提单,但随着班轮运输的发展,船东签发提单的情况越来越少见。各国法律承认的有权签发提单的"承运人"已经包括"无船承运人"等。

Ship owner's B/L refers to the B/L issued by the shipowner as the carrier to the shipper. In tramp transport, the shipowner as the carrier may issue a B/L to the shipper, but with the development of liner shipping, the issuance of a B/L by the shipowner is becoming less and less common. The carriers with the right to issue Bs/L recognized by the laws of various countries have included "NVOCC" and so on.

2. 租船人提单（Charterer's B/L）

租船人提单是由船东以外的租船人作为承运人向托运人签发的提单。在光船租船和定期租船情况下,与托运人订立运输合同的通常就是取得船舶运营权利的租船人,对托运人而言,他们承担承运人的责任,因此可以向托运人签发提单。

上述两种提单均可称为"承运人提单"。

Charterer's B/L is a B/L issued by a charterer other than the shipowner as the carrier to the shipper. In the case of bare boat charter and time charter, it is often the charterer who acquires the right to operate the ship that enters into the contract of carriage with the shipper. For the shipper, the charterer assumes the responsibility of the carrier and can therefore issue a B/L to the shipper.

Both Bs/L mentioned above can be called "carrier's bill of lading".

3. 货运代理提单（Freight Forwarder's B/L）

随着集装箱运输的不断发展,货运代理签发提单的情况越来越多。依据国际商会《跟单信用证统一惯例》(UCP600)的规定,只要货运代理承担承运人责任,其签发的提单就可以作为有效的结汇提单。

With the continuous development of container shipping, the issuance of Bs/L by freight forwarders is increasing. According to the *Uniform Customs and Practice for Documentary Credits* (UCP600) of the International Chamber of Commerce, as long as the freight forwarder assumes the responsibility of the carrier, the B/L issued by it can be used as a valid B/L for exchange settlement.

4.2.2 按货物是否已装船分类（Classification According to Whether the Goods Have Been Loaded on Board）

1. 已装船提单（On Board B/L or Shipped B/L）

已装船提单是指承运人在货物已经装上指定船舶后，船长或承运人或其代理人凭大副收据（收货单）向托运人签发的提单。其特点是提单上须以文字表明货物已经装上某具名船只、装船日期并签署。提单签发日期即视作装船日期或装运日期。在国际贸易中，一般都要求卖方提交"已装船提单"。根据 UCP600 第 20 条的规定，若信用证要求提单作为运输单据，银行将接受注明货物已装船或已装指定船舶的提单。

根据《海牙规则》等国际公约及各国海商法，在发货人（托运人）的要求下，承运人或船长必须在货物装船后签发已装船提单，不得推卸责任，这是强制性的要求。

It refers to the B/L issued by the captain or the carrier or their agents to the shipper on the basis of the mate's receipt after the goods have been loaded on board the designated ship(ON BOARD VESSEL _____ ON DATE _____). The B/L must indicate in writing that the goods have been loaded on board a named vessel, the date of loading, and be signed. The date of issuance of the B/L is regarded as the date of shipment. According to article 20 of UCP600, if the L/C requires a B/L as a transport document, the bank will accept a B/L indicating that the goods have been loaded on board or have been loaded on board a named ship. L/C usually stipulates the presentation of a Shipped B/L.

In accordance with international conventions such as *Hague Rules* and maritime laws of various countries, the carrier or the captain must issue the shipped B/L after the goods have been loaded on board the ship, and may not shirk their responsibility, which is a mandatory requirement.

2. 备运提单（Received for Shipment B/L）

备运提单又称收讫待运提单，是指承运人收到托运货物后等待装运期间所签发的提单。这种提单没有表明货物已装船，也没有装船日期，将来货物能否装运不确定，对提单受让人无保障，因此，买方和银行一般都不愿接受此种提单。在签发备运提单情况下，发货人可在货物装船后凭以调换已装船提单；也可经承运人或其代理人在备运提单上加注"货物已在某日装上某具名船舶"，并签署后使之成为已装船提单。

随着集装箱运输的发展，备运提单的使用日益增多，由于承运人在内陆收货，货运站无法签发已装船提单，且货物装入集装箱后，质量一般不会再受到影响，因此，除非信用证特别规定，银行可以接受集装箱备运提单。

It refers to the B/L issued by the carrier upon receipt of the consignment while awaiting shipment. This B/L does not indicate that the goods have been loaded on board the ship, nor the date of loading, the future shipment of the goods is uncertain, and there is no guarantee to the transferee of the B/L. Therefore, buyers and banks are generally reluctant to accept such B/L. In the case of issuance of received for shipment B/L, the consignor may exchange it for a shipped B/L after the goods have been loaded on board the ship. The carrier or its agent may also add "the goods have been loaded on a named ship on a certain day" on the received for shipment B/L and sign it to make it a shipped B/L.

With the development of container transport, the use of received for shipment B/L is increasing. This is because the carrier receives the goods inland, the freight station cannot issue the shipped B/L, and the quality of the goods will not be affected after they are loaded into the container. Therefore, banks may accept received for shipment B/L for container transportation unless otherwise specified in the L/C.

4.2.3　按提单上有无承运人对货物外表状况的不良批注分类（Classification According to the B/L With or Without the Carrier's Bad Comments on the Appearance of the Goods）

1. 清洁提单（Clean B/L）

在装船时货物外表状况良好,承运人或其代理人在签发提单时,未在提单上加注任何有关货物残损、包装不良的批注,或其他妨碍结汇的批注,这种提单称为清洁提单。按国际贸易惯例,除非另有约定,卖方有义务提交清洁提单。国际商会 UCP600 第 27 条规定,银行只接受清洁提单。清洁提单也是提单转让时必须具备的基本条件之一。

It is a B/L in which the carrier or its agent has not added any notations such as damage to the goods and/or poor packing, or other remarks that prevent the settlement of foreign exchange, because the goods are in apparent good condition when loaded on board the ship. According to international trade practice, unless otherwise agreed, the seller is obliged to submit a clean B/L. Article 27 of UCP600 stipulates that banks only accept clean B/L. Clean B/L is also one of the basic conditions for the transfer of B/L.

2. 不清洁提单（Unclean B/L or Foul B/L）

不清洁提单是指承运人加注明确宣称货物外表及/或包装状况不良、存在缺陷等的条款或批注的提单。由于承运人必须对承运货物的外表状况负责,因此,在装船时,若发现货物包装不牢、残损、渗漏、标志不清等现象,大副将在收货单上对此加以批注,并将其转移到提单上,这种提单称为不清洁提单。常见的不良批注有:货物表面有污渍,有渗漏,如 PACKAGING CONTAMINATED;包装标志不清,不牢固或不适当,如 PARTLY PROTECTED;货物包装残损,如 PACKAGING BROKEN/HOLD/TORN/DAMAGED;短量,如 20 CASES SHORT SHIPPED 等。不清洁提单是不能结汇的,因此在货物装船时,一旦发现存在问题,为保证安全收汇,托运人应及时整修或更换包装或表面状况有问题的货物。

It refers to a B/L endorsed by the carrier with a clause or notation that expressly declares the goods to be in poor condition or defective in appearance and/or packaging. Because the carrier must be responsible for the appearance of the cargo, the chief mate will annotate it on the mate's receipt and transfer it to the B/L. If the phenomenon of improper packing, damage, leakage, or unclear marking of the cargo is found during shipment, such B/L is called unclean B/L. Common negative comments include: PACKAGING CONTAMINATED, PARTLY PROTECTED, PACKAGING BROKEN/HOLD/TORN/DAMAGED, 20 CASES SHORT SHIPPED and so on. The unclean B/L cannot be used for exchange settlement. Therefore, once problems are found during the loading of the goods, the shipper should promptly repair or replace the goods with defective packaging or appearance in order to ensure the safe receipt of foreign exchange.

4.2.4　按提单收货人抬头方式分类（Classification by Mode of Consignee of B/L）

1. 记名提单（Straight B/L）

记名提单又称收货人抬头提单、直交提单，是指提单上的收货人栏内填明特定收货人名称的提单。记名提单只能由该特定收货人用以提货，而不能背书转让流通。记名提单使银行和托运人均无法控制物权，一旦遇到拒收货物，卖方须在买方所在地提货并就地转售或运回国内处理，将非常麻烦，所以进出口贸易中较少采用，一般只在价值贵重或展览品、援外物资等特殊货物交易时使用。

It refers to the B/L in which the name of a particular person or company is specified in the "consignee" column. A straight B/L may only be used by that particular consignee to take delivery of the goods, and cannot be transferred into circulation by endorsement. Straight B/L makes it impossible for both banks and shippers to control property rights. Once the buyer refuses to accept the goods, it will be very troublesome for the seller to resell the goods in the buyer's place or to ship them back to the exporting country. So straight Bs/L are seldom used in import and export trade, and are generally used only in the transaction of valuable or special goods such as exhibits and foreign aid materials.

2. 不记名提单（Bearer B/L）

不记名提单又称来人抬头提单，是指提单上的收货人栏内不写明具体收货人的名称，只写明"货交提单持有人"，或不填写任何内容的提单。不记名提单无须背书就可任意流通转让，且谁持有提单，谁就可以提货。一旦提单遗失或被盗，货物容易被人提走，引起纠纷，因此风险较大，在实务中极少使用。

It is also known as blank B/L or open B/L. It refers to a B/L in which the name of the consignee is not specified in the column of consignee, but only "to bearer" or no contents are filled in. The bearer B/L can be freely circulated and transferred without endorsement, and whoever holds the B/L, can take delivery of the goods. Once the B/L is lost or stolen, the goods can easily be taken away, thus causing disputes. As a result, bearer B/L is riskier and is rarely used in practice.

3. 指示提单（Order B/L）

指示提单是指提单上的收货人栏内填写"凭指示"或"凭某某人指示"字样的提单。在后一种方式下，必须明确指示人。常见的规定收货人的方式有以下几种。

It is a B/L in which "to order" or "to order of..." is filled in the column of consignee. Common ways of specifying a consignee include the following kinds.

（1）凭开证行指示。此种提单须经银行背书方可转让给买方，有利于银行在向买方收汇前牢牢掌握物权，在买方破产倒闭或拒绝付款赎单时，可凭提单提货并通过拍卖或转让自由处理货物，因而开证银行较乐于接受，但对议付行不能给予充分保证。

（1）To order of issuing bank. Such a B/L may be transferred to the buyer only with the issuing bank's endorsement. It facilitates the bank to hold on to the property rights until the buyer pays for the goods, and in the event of the buyer's bankruptcy or refusal to pay the B/L, the bank can take delivery of the goods with the B/L and dispose of them freely by auction or assignment, the issuing bank is thus more willing to accept such Bs/L. However, it does not give sufficient assurance to the negotiating bank.

（2）凭开证申请人指示。此种提单须经开证申请人背书才可转让，银行难以掌握物权，所以不乐于接受。

（2）To order of applicant. Such a B/L must be endorsed by the applicant before it can be transferred. Banks have difficulty holding real right and are therefore reluctant to accept them.

（3）凭托运人指示。这种提单等同于"凭指示"提单，由托运人押汇时将提单背书转让给议付行，议付行以提单为担保品对托运人支付款项，并将提单转给开证行索偿垫付款。这种提单对议付行和托运人都较为有利，在国际贸易中使用较为普遍。托运人在未背书前可掌握物权，如遇开证行或买方破产倒闭，卖方可行使收到货款前的停运权、留置权及对鲜活商品的再售权等。

（3）To order of shipper. Such B/L is equivalent to the "TO ORDER" B/L, which is endorsed and transferred to the negotiating bank by the shipper at the time of negotiation, and the negotiating bank uses the B/L as collateral for payment to the shipper and forwards the B/L to the issuing bank to claim advance payment. This B/L is more advantageous to both the negotiating bank and the shipper, and is more commonly used in international trade. The shipper may hold title in rem before endorsement and in the event of the bankruptcy of the issuing bank or the buyer, the seller may exercise suspension rights, lien rights and re-sale rights on fresh merchandise prior to receipt of payment.

背书的方式有"空白背书"和"记名背书"之分。"空白背书"是指背书人在提单背面签名，而不注明被背书人名称；经空白背书的提单再行转让时，仅凭交付即可转让，而不必再行背书。"记名背书"是指背书人除在提单背面签名外，还列明被背书人名称。记名背书的提单受让人（被背书人）如需再转让，必须再加背书。目前在实际业务中使用最多的是"凭指示"并经空白背书的提单，习惯上称其为"空白抬头、空白背书"（B/L MADE

OUT TO ORDER AND BLANK ENDORSED)提单。一般背书的基本格式如下（显示在提单背面）。

DELIVER TO（THE ORDER OF）

_____（被背书人名称）

FOR AND ON BEHALF OF

_____（背书人名称和签章）

（SIGNATURE）

There are two types of endorsement："blank endorsement" and "full endorsement"."Blank endorsement" means that the endorser signs on the back of the B/L without indicating the name of the endorsee；"full endorsement" means that the endorser not only signs on the back of the B/L，but also lists the name of the endorsee. Currently in the actual business，"to order" and blank endorsed B/L is commonly used (B/L MADE OUT TO ORDER AND BLANK ENDORSED). The basic format of the endorsement is generally as follows (shown on the back of the B/L).

DELIVER TO（THE ORDER OF）

_____（Name of the endorsee）

FOR AND ON BEHALF OF

_____（Endorser's name and signature）

（SIGNATURE）

> 扩展阅读 4.2 由一则案例引发的海运提单抬头的写法思考

4.2.5 按运输方式分类（Classification by Mode of Transport）

1. 直达提单（Direct B/L）

直达提单是指货物不经中转运输直接驶往目的港卸货的提单。提单上不得有"转船""在××港转船"字样。只要 L/C 规定不许转船或转运，受益人只能凭直达提单向银行交单议付。

It refers to the B/L for unloading goods directly to the destination port without transshipment. The words "transshipment" and "transshipment at port ××" are not allowed on the B/L. As long as L/C stipulates "TRANSSHIPMENT UNALLOWED"，the beneficiary can only negotiate with the bank by direct B/L.

2. 转船提单（Transshipment B/L）

转船提单是指货物在装运港装上某一海轮后，在航运的中途港要将货物卸入另一船舶再驶往目的港卸货的情况下所签发的包括运输全程的提单。转船会增加货物受损的风险、延误到货时间，所以一般应尽量采用直达运输方式。但有时遇到挂港船舶少、航次少的情形，转船反而能够加快货运，此时可以采用转船运输方式，出具转船提单。转船提单上一般由第一程船的承运人在全程提单上加注"在××港转船"字样即可。

It refers to the B/L issued when the goods are loaded on a ship at the port of shipment and unloaded at the port of transit to another ship and then to the port of destination, which includes the whole journey. Transshipment will increase the risk of damage to the goods and delay the arrival time, so direct transportation should be adopted as far as possible. However, sometimes when there are fewer ships hanging in port and fewer voyages, transshipment can speed up the transportation of goods. At this time, transshipment can be adopted, then transshipment B/L can be issued. Transshipment B/L is usually marked "transshipment at port ××" by the carrier of the first vessel.

3. 联运提单（Through B/L）

联运提单又称全程提单，主要适用于海/陆、海/陆/海、海/空等以海运为第一程运输的联合运输。它是指由第一程承运人（船公司）所签发的，包括全程运输并能在目的港或目的地凭以提货的提单，主要用于非成组化的杂货件的运输。

The through B/L is mainly applicable to the combined transportation of sea/land, sea/land/sea, sea/air, etc., which takes the sea as the first carriage. It is issued by the first carrier (shipping company), including the whole carriage and can take delivery of goods by it at the port or place of destination. It is mainly used for the transportation of non-containerized general cargo.

4. 联合运输单据（Multimodal Transport Documents）

联合运输单据又称多式联运提单。随着国际集装箱运输的发展，国际多式联运也得到了迅速发展。在国际多式联运中，多式联运经营人组织多式联运，负责全程运输并收取全程运费。多式联运经营人接管货物时，签发多式联运单据。它的特点是：①签发联合运输单据的联运经营人并不一定承担运输，但对货物负全程运输责任；②第一程运输不一定是海运，所以提单上不一定要注明第一程船的船名和装船日期。

It's also known as combined B/L. With the development of international container transport, international multimodal transport has also developed rapidly. In international multimodal transport, multimodal transport operator organizes multimodal transport, and is responsible for the whole transport and collects the through freight. When the multimodal transport operator takes over the goods, it issues the multimodal transport documents. It is characterized by two facts: ① the CTO issuing the CTO does not necessarily undertake the transportation, but is responsible for the entire transportation of the goods; ②the first leg of transportation does not have to be by sea, so the B/L does not have to indicate the name of the first vessel and the date of loading.

4.2.6　按船舶营运方式分类（Classification by Mode of Operation of Ships）

1. 班轮提单（Liner B/L）

采取班轮运输方式时，由经营班轮运输的承运人或其代理人签发的提单称为班轮提单。承运人与托运人、收货人之间的权利和义务以船公司签发的班轮提单条款为依据，不再另行签订租船合同。

When liner transportation is adopted，the B/L issued by the carrier（or its agent）operating liner transportation is called liner B/L. The rights and obligations of the carrier，the shipper，and the consignee shall be based on the terms of the liner B/L issued by the shipping company and no further charter party will be signed.

2. 租船提单（Charter Party B/L）

租船提单是承运人根据租船合同签发的提单。提单上通常注明"一切条件、条款和免责事项按照某某租船合同"字样。这种提单受租船合同条款的约束，银行或买方在接受这种提单时，往往要求卖方提供租船合同副本。

Charter party B/L is a B/L issued by the carrier under the charter party，on which "all conditions，terms and exemptions are in accordance with a charter party" is usually indicated. Such a B/L is subject to the terms of the charter party. When a bank or buyer accepts such a B/L，the seller is often required to provide a copy of the charter party.

3. 无船承运人提单（NVOCC B/L）

无船承运人提单指由无船承运人或其代理签发的提单。在集装箱班轮运输中，无船承运人通常为拼箱货签发提单，且因为拼箱货是在集装箱货运站内装箱或拆箱，而货运站又大多有仓库，因此又被称为仓至仓提单。当然，无船承运人也可为整箱货签发提单。

It refers to the B/L issued by the NVOCC or its agent. In container liner transportation，NVOCC usually issues Bs/L for LCL cargo. And because the LCL is packed or unpacked in the container freight station，and most of the freight stations have warehouses，it is also called house B/L. Of course，NVOCC can also issue Bs/L for FCL cargo.

4.2.7 按提单使用效力分类（Classification by Validity of B/L）

1. 正本提单（Original B/L）

正本提单是指提单上有承运人、船长或其代理人签名盖章并注明签发日期的提单。这种提单在法律上是有效的单据。正本提单上必须标明"正本"字样。正本提单一般签发一式两份或三份（个别也有只签发一份的），凭其中的任何一份提货后，其余的即作废。为防止他人冒领货物，买方与银行通常要求卖方提供船公司签发的全部正本提单，即所谓"全套提单"。

It refers to a B/L with the signature and seal of the carrier，the captain or their agents and the date of issuance. This B/L is legally valid. The original B/L must be marked with the word "original" and is usually issued in duplicate or in triplicate (occasionally only one). After picking up the goods with any one of the original Bs/L，the rest will be invalid. In order to prevent others from falsely claiming the goods，the buyer and the bank usually require the seller to provide all original Bs/L issued by the shipping company，namely the so-called "full set of Bs/L".

2. 副本提单（Copy B/L）

副本提单是指提单上没有承运人、船长或其代理人签字盖章，而仅供参考之用的提单。副本提单一般都标明"副本"或"不可转让"字样。

It refers to the B/L without the signature and seal of the carrier, captain, or his agent, and is for reference only. Copy Bs/L usually indicate "copy" or "non-negotiable".

4.2.8　按提单的签发时间分类（Classified by the Time of Issuance of Bs/L）

1. 倒签提单（Antedated B/L）

倒签提单是指承运人或其代理人应托运人的要求，在货物装船完毕后，以早于货物实际装船完毕的日期作为提单签发日期的提单。当货物的实际装船时间迟于信用证规定的装运期，托运人为了使提单日期与信用证的规定相符，可能会请求承运人按信用证日期签发提单，以便顺利结汇。承运人倒签提单的做法，掩盖了提单签发时的真实情况，将面临由此而引起的风险责任。

When issuing an antedated B/L, the carrier or its agent takes the date prior to the actual completion of loading of the goods as the date of issuance at the request of the shipper after the completion of the shipment. When the actual time of shipment of the goods is later than the time of shipment stipulated in the letter of credit, the shipper may request the carrier to issue the B/L on the date of the letter of credit in order to make the date of the B/L consistent with the stipulation of the letter of credit, so as to settle the foreign exchange smoothly. The carrier's practice of issuing antedated B/L conceals the real situation, and will face the risk liability arising therefrom.

2. 预借提单（Advanced B/L）

预借提单是指在信用证有效期即将届满，或交货期限已过，而货物尚未装船或尚未装船完毕的情况下，托运人为了及时结汇，而要求承运人提前签发的已装船清洁提单。其也即托运人为了及时结汇而从承运人那里借用的已装船清洁提单。

Advanced B/L is a clean on board B/L that the shipper requires the carrier to issue in advance in order to settle foreign exchange in time when the validity of the L/C is about to expire or the delivery period has passed, but the goods have not been loaded or shipped. That is to say, it is a clean on board B/L borrowed by the shipper from the carrier in order to settle exchange in time.

承运人签发预借提单时，不仅同样掩盖了签发提单时的真实情况，而且将面临比签发倒签提单更大的风险责任：一方面，货物尚未装船而签发提单，即货物还未经过大副的检验就签发清洁提单，有可能增加承运人的货损赔偿责任；另一方面，签发提单后，可能由于种种原因而改变原定的装运船舶，或发生货物灭失、损坏或退关，收货人便可凭借掌握预借提单的事实，以欺诈为由拒绝收货，并向承运人提出赔偿要求，甚至向法院起诉。

但与倒签提单一样，实务中为了经济利益，承运人得到托运人的保函后也可能签发这种提单。银行不接受倒签提单和预借提单。如果开证行发现提单倒签或预签，并有证据证实，可以伪造单据为由拒付。

When the carrier issues the advance B/L，it not only conceals the real situation when issuing it，but also faces greater risk liability than issuing the antedated B/L：on the one hand，it is possible to increase the carrier's liability for damage to goods by issuing clean Bs/L before the goods have been loaded on board and inspected by the mate；on the other hand，after issuing the B/L，if the original shipping vessel has been changed for various reasons，or if the goods have been lost，damaged or shut out，the consignee may refuse to accept the goods on the grounds of fraud，and make a claim for compensation from the carrier，or even sue in court relying on the fact that he has the advance B/L.

However，in practice，for the sake of economic benefit，the carrier may issue such a B/L after obtaining the shipper's guarantee，just like the antedated B/L. Banks do not accept antedated Bs/L or advanced bills of lading. If the issuing bank finds antedated or advanced B/L and has evidence to prove it，it may refuse payment on the grounds of forging documents.

3. 顺签提单(Postdated B/L)

顺签提单是指在货物装船完毕后,承运人或其代理人应托运人的要求,以晚于货物实际装船完毕的日期作为提单签发日期的提单,其目的是使其符合合同或信用证关于装运期的规定。

承运人签发顺签提单的做法同样掩盖了提单签发时的真实情况,也将面临由此而引发的风险责任。

It refers to the B/L issued by the carrier or his agent at the request of the shipper after the completion of the loading of the goods，taking the date later than the actual completion of the loading of the goods as the date of issuance of the B/L. The purpose is to make the date of B/L conform to the stipulations of the contract or letter of credit concerning the time of shipment. The carrier's practice of issuing postdated B/L also conceals the real situation of its issuance，and will also face the risk liability arising therefrom.

扩展阅读4.3 分析海运提单的风险及防范措施

4.2.9 按运费支付时间分类(Classified by Freight Payment Time)

1. 运费预付提单(Freight Prepaid B/L)

若贸易合同采用 CIF、CIP 或 CFR 等条件,按规定货物托运时,则必须预付运费。在运费预付情况下出具的提单称为运费预付提单。这种提单正面载明"运费预付"字样。付费后,若货物灭失,运费不退还。因此,这种提单对货主存在一定的风险。

If CIF，CIP or CFR are adopted in the trade contract，the freight must be paid in advance when the goods are consigned according to the stipulation. The B/L issued in the case of freight prepayment is called freight prepaid B/L. The word "freight prepaid" is stated on the front of this B/L. After payment，if the goods are lost，the freight will not be refunded. Therefore, this kind of B/L has certain risks for the shipper.

2. 运费到付提单(Freight to Collect B/L)

若贸易合同采用 FOB、FAS(Free Alongside Ship，船边交货)等条件，则无论是买方订舱还是买方委托卖方订舱，运费均为到付，并在提单上载明"运费到付"字样，这种提单称为运费到付提单。这种提单对承运人存在一定的风险。

If the terms of FOB and FAS(Free Alongside Ship) are adopted in the trade contract, the freight will be paid whether the buyer orders the shipping space or the buyer entrusts the seller to order the shipping space. The B/L contains the words "freight to collect". This kind of B/L is called freight to collect B/L. There are certain risks for the carrier when using this kind of B/L.

4.3　海运提单的缮制方法(Method of Making out Bill of Lading)

按照我国目前的操作习惯，海运提单通常由外贸企业自己或委托外运机构代为缮制，然后在货物装船后，再由外贸企业或外运机构将缮制好的海运提单送交船公司或其代理，请求签字。船长或承运人或其代理人在审核海运提单所载内容与大副收据内容相符后，正式签发提单，并加注"SHIPPED ON BOARD"字样，加盖装船日期印章。如果大副收据列有货物或包装的不良批注，船长或承运人或其代理人在签发提单时就要把所列批注照列于提单上，这种提单就是不清洁提单。如果要求签发的是运费预付提单，外贸企业或外运机构应向船公司或其代理缴付海运运费后，才能取得海运提单。

According to our current practices, the ocean B/L is usually made out by the foreign trade enterprise itself or entrusted to the foreign transport agency. After the goods are loaded on board, the B/L is sent to the shipping company or its agent by the foreign trade enterprise or foreign transport agency for signature. After examining and verifying that the contents of the B/L are in conformity with the contents of the mate's receipt, the captain or the carrier or their agent formally issues the B/L with the words "SHIPPED ON BOARD" and the date of shipment stamped. If the mate's receipt contains bad remarks on the goods or packaging, the master, carrier or their agents shall list the remarks on the B/L. Such B/L is an called unclean B/L. If freight prepaid B/L is required to be issued, the foreign trade enterprise or foreign transport agencies shall pay the freight to the shipping company or its agent before obtaining the B/L.

提单的基本缮制方法如下。

(1) 提单正面印明承运人的全名，最好还表明承运人的完整身份。

(2) 提单的名称。(见前面关于提单的介绍)

(3) 提单号码(B/L No.)。提单上必须注明承运人及其代理人规定的提单编号，以便核查，否则提单无效。

(4) 托运人(Shipper)。托运人即发货人，一般为 L/C 的受益人，也可是第三方。如发货人为出口商，此处缮打出口商名称、地址。

（5）收货人（Consignee）。收货人即提单抬头人，应严格按合同及 L/C 具体规定填写。一般填法有下面几种。

① 记名收货人：来证中有条款"Consigned to ×××"，则提单的"收货人"栏应照打"Consigned to ×××"，意为"交付×××"。

② 不记名式："收货人"一栏留空不填或填"To Bearer"。（极少采用）

③ 不记名指示：来证中有条款"Full set of B/L made out to order"，在提单的"收货人"栏中应缮打"To order"，意为凭指示。

④ 记名指示：来证中有条款"Full set of B/L made out to order of shipper"，则提单需经托运人背书进行转让，在提单的"收货人"栏中应缮打"To order of shipper"，意为凭托运人指示。

来证中有条款"Full set of B/L made out to order of Applicant"，则提单需经开证申请人背书进行转让，在提单的"收货人"栏中应缮打"To order of 开证申请人名称（完全照信用证中开证申请人名称缮制）"，意为凭开证申请人指示。

来证中有条款"Full set of B/L made out to order of Issuing Bank"，则提单需经开证行背书进行转让，在提单的"收货人"栏中应缮打"To order of 开证行名称"，意为凭开证行指示。

来证中有条款"Full set of B/L made out to order of Negotiation"，则提单需经议付行背书进行转让，在提单的"收货人"栏中应缮打"To order of 议付行名称"，意为凭议付行指示。

（6）被通知方（Notify Party）。一般应按 L/C 规定填写被通知方详细的名称、地址。若 L/C 中规定"NOTIFY…ONLY"（仅通知×××），则此栏中不可漏填"ONLY"。由于在指示性提单中无收货人的名址，因此须有被通知人来接受收货人的委托，通知收货人提货。被通知人通常为船运公司（收货人的代理人）或买方或其他与买方联系密切的人。我国一般为中外运长航或其代理公司或分公司。被通知人也可能是进口方或开证行，如信用证规定"Notify Party Applicant"，则只需将开证申请人的全称缮打在此栏即可；若信用证规定"Notify Party Applicant and us"，则缮打开证申请人的全称和开证行名称。若 L/C 未规定 Notify Party，提单正本中此栏可留空不填，但交给承运人随船带去的副本提单上必须缮打收货人详细的名称和地址，以便货物运抵目的港后联系被通知人做好报关提货准备。

（7）一程船名（Pre-carriage By）。如货物需要转运，在这一栏填写第一程船的船名；如果货物不需转运，此栏留空。

（8）收货地点（Place of Receipt）。收货地点指船方实际收货的地点（也可叫接受监管地）。如货物需要转运，在这一栏填写收货的港口名称或地点；如果货物不需转运，此栏留空。

（9）船名（Ocean Vessel）、航次（Voyage No.）。船名、航次均按配舱回单填写。没有航次的船舶可不填航次。货装直达船时，直接填写直达船名；货物需要转运，填写第二程船的船名；采用联合运输方式装运集装箱时，应注明海运船名和一种运输方式的运输工具的名称。

（10）装货港（Port of Loading）。填实际装运货物的港口的名称。若转运，应填写中转港名称；若不转运，则只填写起运港名称。应严格按照 L/C 的规定与要求。如果 L/C 中仅笼统规定，如"CHINA PORT"，或同时列有几个起运港，如"XINGANG/QINHUANGDAO/DALIAN"的，应根据实际情况填写具体港口名称。

（11）卸货港（Port of Discharge）。卸货港指海运承运人中止承运责任的港口，在直达运输情况下一般填目的港。对于 L/C 中尚未确定目的港的情形（如"ONE SUITABLE AMERICAN PORT AT OPENER'S OPTION"），提单上应按 L/C 规定照打。

（12）交货地（Place of Delivery）。交货地即最终目的地。如果货物目的地是目的港，这一栏可保持空白。

（13）封号、唛头及件号（Seal No.，Marks & Nos.）。如信用证中对唛头有明确规定，应按信用证缮制，每个字符和数字、图形的排列位置应与 L/C 完全一致，但箱数要明确，不能按 L/C 所写 1-UP 的形式，且提单上的唛头应与发票和装箱单上的完全一致。如果信用证中没有规定，则按买卖双方的约定，或由卖方决定缮制，并注意"单单一致"。如果没有唛头，填"N/M"。

（14）包装方式和件数（No. and Kind of Packages）。最大包装的方式和件数。若为散装货物，则件数栏内只填"In Bulk"，大写件数可不填。

（15）货名（Description of Goods）。货名与托运单内容完全一致。所使用文字按 L/C 要求。如无特殊说明，用英文填写。

（16）毛重（Gross Weight）。一般写货物的总毛重，以公吨表示。

（17）尺码（Measurement）。一般写货物的总尺码，以立方米表示。

（18）大写件数[Total Number of Containers or Packages(in words)]。用大写表示集装箱数或其他形式最大包装的件数，与 15 栏数字一致。在件数前须加上"SAY"字样，在件数后加上"ONLY"字样。如"SAY THREE HUNDRED FIFTY CARTONS ONLY"。

（19）提单签发的份数（Number of Original Bs/L）。一般地，一份 L/C 打一套提单，而不能两个 L/C 合打一套提单，否则结汇有困难。有时，L/C 中规定了许多商品、品种或数量，买方为了提货方便或须转让提单，要求每一种商品或每一定数量制一套提单，则将出现同一 L/C 项下的多套提单。提单正本一般一式两份或三份，当凭借其中任一份提货时，其余各份均告失效。副本非流通提单数量不限，除非信用证另有规定，签发的正本提单必须全套（"FULL SET"）提交。正本提单上应印有"ORIGINAL"字样，并须注明发单日和承运人、船长或其代理人的签章。对于未注明"ORIGINAL"字样，或标有"COPY"或"NON-NEGOTIABLE"（简称 N/N）字样的提单，只能是供参考用的副本提单，这种提单往往没有承运人、船长或其代理人的签章。

（20）运费（Freight and Charges）。除非 L/C 另有规定，提单上一般不必列出运费的具体金额。如可注明"FREIGHT PREPAID AS ARRANGED"字样。

（21）提单签发日期、地点（Place and Date of Issue）。提单签发日期不得迟于货物装运期。在备运提单下，提单签发日期为承运人收到货物的日期。在已装船提单下，提单签发日期与装船日期一致，为货物全部装上船的日期。提单签发地点指货物实际装运的港口或接受监管的地点。

| 单据 4.1 海运提单 | |

（22）承运人签章（Signed by the Carrier）。提单上必须有承运人本人或其代理的签章才能生效，签章的方式应按 L/C 的规定。

（23）如果信用证规定提供已装船提单，必须由船长签字并注明开船时间 Date：…和"LADEN ON BOARD"或"SHIPPED ON BOARD"字样。

Words and Expressions

即测即练

习题

实训操作

第 5 章
Chapter 5

国际集装箱运输
International Container Transport

Learning Objectives：

1. Understand the advantages of container transportation；
2. Understand the organizers of container transport；
3. Master the basic knowledge of containers，including container standard，types of container and container marking；
4. Master the forms，places and modes of handover of containerized goods；
5. Be able to skillfully calculate the freight of container liner；
6. Master the concept of dock receipt and container B/L，master the filling method of dock receipt.

引导案例

集装箱运输货物受损案

2022 年，发货人某海产品进出口公司委托对外贸易运输公司将 1 000 箱海产品从某港出口运往甲国，对外贸易运输公司接受委托后，向某远洋运输公司预约洽订舱位，该远洋运输公司指派了箱号为 CBHU3202732 等的三个满载集装箱，货物装船后，承运人签发了清洁提单，发货人在某保险公司投保了海洋货物运输保险条款中的一切险。货物运抵甲国港口后，收货人拆箱发现部分海产品因箱内不清洁而受污染，腐烂变质，即向某保险公司在甲国的代理人申请查验。检验表明，其中 300 箱海产品被污染。为此，某保险公司在甲国的代理人赔付了收货人的损失之后，向法院提起诉讼。根据国际惯例，该案例中远洋运输公司作为提供集装箱的承运人，应承担保持集装箱清洁、干燥、无残留物以及无前批货物留下的持久性气味的责任，因其未尽责，应对海产品的损失负责。对外贸易运输公司作为发货人的代理人应负有在装箱前检查箱体，保证集装箱适装的义务，而其未认真检查，主观上存在过失，同样应承担一定的货损赔偿责任。某保险公司在赔偿后取得代位求偿权，有权向远洋运输公司和对外贸易运输公司索赔。

资料来源：根据百度文库集装箱运输案例［EB/OL］.（2019-02-25）. https://wenku. baidu. com/view/a078e8ebb94ae45c3b3567ec102de2bd9605dea2. html. 改编。

集装箱运输是以集装箱为运输单元进行货物运输的一种现代化运输方式，它具有传统海运无法比拟的巨大优越性，是件杂货运输的发展方向。目前，集装箱运输已进入以国际远洋船舶运输为主，以铁路运输、公路运输、航空运输为辅的多式联运为特征的新时期。

Container transport is a modern mode of transport with containers as the transport unit for cargo transportation，which has great superiority unmatched by traditional sea transport，and is the development direction of general cargo transport. At present，container transport has entered a new period characterized by multimodal transport which is dominated by international ocean-going ship transport，supplemented by railway，road and air transport.

5.1　国际集装箱运输概述（Overview of International Container Transport）

5.1.1　集装箱运输的优点（Advantages of Container Transportation）

在国际海上货物运输中，散装货物和流体货物较早地完成了船舶专业化、大型化及装卸机械化，但传统的件杂货运输效率一直较低。杂货船在港停泊时间占总航次时间比例为 40%～50%，而大型散装货船这一比例仅为 10%～15%。这主要是件杂货品种繁多、包装方式与尺寸不统一、装卸工具效率低等原因造成的。为改变这一状况，20 世纪 50 年代，美国人开始试验集装箱海上运输，并取得了巨大的成功。20 世纪 60 年代中后期开始，一些发达国家也相继使用集装箱进行海上运输，开辟了北美—欧洲的大西洋航线、北美—日本/大洋洲的太平洋航线。目前，集装箱运输迅速发展，已经成为国际海上件杂货运输的主要方式，集装箱班轮航线连接世界各地。表 5-1 是 2023 年全球吞吐量前 20 名集装箱港口具体情况。

In international maritime cargo transportation，bulk cargo and fluid cargo have completed the specialization of vessels and mechanization of loading and unloading earlier，but the efficiency of traditional general cargo transportation has been low. The proportion of general cargo vessels' berthing time in port to total voyage time is as high as 40%-50%，while that of large bulk cargo carriers is only 10%-15%. This is mainly due to the wide variety of general cargo，inconsistent packaging methods and sizes，and inefficient loading and unloading tools. In order to change this situation，in the 1950s，Americans began to test container shipping，and achieved great success. Since the mid and late 1960s，some developed countries have also begun to use containers for maritime transport，opening up the North America-Europe Atlantic route，North America-Japan/Oceania Pacific route. At present，container transportation is developing rapidly and has become the main mode of international maritime general cargo transportation，with container liner routes connecting all over the world. Table 5-1 shows the details of the top 20 container ports of throughput in the world in 2023.

表 5-1　2023 年全球吞吐量前 20 名集装箱港口具体情况

排名	港口	国家	2023 年吞吐量/万 TEUs	2022 年吞吐量/万 TEUs	同比/%
1	上海港	中国	4 915.8	4 730.0	3.93
2	新加坡港	新加坡	3 901.3	3 730.0	4.59
3	宁波舟山港	中国	3 530.0	3 335.0	5.85
4	深圳港	中国	2 988.0	3 004.0	−0.53
5	青岛港	中国	2 875.0	2 567.0	12.00
6	广州港	中国	2 541.0	2 486.0	2.21
7	釜山港	韩国	2 275.0	2 207.8	3.04
8	天津港	中国	2 217.0	2 102.0	5.47
9	杰贝阿里港	阿联酋	1 447.2	1 400.0	3.37
10	香港港	中国	1 434.1	1 668.5	−14.05
11	巴生港	马来西亚	1 406.1	1 322.0	6.36
12	鹿特丹港	荷兰	1 344.7	1 445.5	−6.97
13	厦门港	中国	1 255.0	1 243.0	0.97
14	安特卫普-布鲁日港	比利时	1 252.8	1 350.0	−7.20
15	丹戎帕拉帕斯港	马来西亚	1 048.0	1 050.0	−0.19
16	盖梅-施威港	越南	975.0	500.0	95.00
17	林查班港	泰国	886.8	874.0	1.47
18	高雄港	中国	883.4	949.0	−6.91
19	洛杉矶	美国	863.0	991.0	−12.93
20	丹吉尔地中海港	摩洛哥	861.7	759.7	13.43

资料来源：美国交通杂志（AJOT）《2023 年全球 TOP100 集装箱港口排名》。

集装箱运输具有以下一些优点：

（1）无须开箱，可进行门到门的运输，从而加快货运速度；

（2）受天气限制小，可露天作业，露天存放，节省仓库；

（3）装卸速度快，提高了车船的周转率，减少港口拥挤，扩大港口吞吐量；

（4）提高货运质量，减少货损货差，提高了货物运输的安全与质量；

（5）节省了包装材料，简化了理货手续，减少了经营费用；

（6）简化货运手续，有利于开展多式联运。

Container transportation has the following advantages：

（1）No need to open containers during transportation，which enables door-to-door transportation，thus speeding up freight transportation；

（2）It is less restricted by the weather and can be operated and stored in the open air，thus saving the warehouse；

（3）Its fast loading and unloading speed improves the turnover rate of vehicles and vessels，reduces port congestion，and expands port throughput；

（4）It improves the quality of freight，reduces cargo damage and shortage，thus improving the safety and quality of cargo transportation；

（5）It saves packaging materials，simplifies handling procedures and reduces operating costs；

（6）It simplifies freight procedures and thus facilitates multimodal transport.

5.1.2 集装箱运输的组织者（Organizers of Container Transport）

集装箱运输涉及面广、环节多、影响大，是一个复杂的运输工程。集装箱运输系统包括海运、陆运、空运、港口、货运站以及与集装箱运输有关的海关、检验检疫、船舶代理、货运代理等企业或部门。它们相互配合，在整个运输过程中发挥着各自不同的作用。

Container transportation involves a wide range of aspects，links and impact. It is a complex transportation project. Container transportation system includes sea，land and air transportation，port，freight station，customs，inspection and quarantine department，ship agent，freight forwarder and other related enterprises or departments. They cooperate with each other and play different roles in the whole transportation process.

1. 经营集装箱货物运输的实际承运人（Actual Carrier Operating Container Cargo Transportation）

实际承运人是指拥有大量运输工具和一定数量的集装箱，直接为货主提供运输服务的机构，如船公司、铁路、公路、航空集装箱运输公司等。它们是集装箱运输的实际承运人，也是最重要的组织者。

It refers to an organization that owns a large number of means of transport and a certain number of containers and provides transport services directly to cargo owners，such as shipping companies，railways，highways and air container transport companies，etc. They are the actual carriers and the most important organizers of container transportation.

2. 无船公共承运人（Non-Vessel Operating Common Carrier）

集装箱运输大多是海、陆、空多种方式的联合运输，为了保证集装箱在各个环节顺利流转，通常有一个负责运输全过程的机构，一般称为"无船公共承运人"。该承运人一般不掌握运输工具，是集装箱货物运输的设计者和组织者。无船公共承运人是在国际集装箱运输这种特殊环境下产生的，它具有以下主要特征：①不是国际贸易合同的当事人；②在法律上有权订立运输合同，对货物全程运输负责；③本人一般不拥有运输工具；④有权签发提单，并受提单条款约束；⑤具有双重身份，对托运人来说，它是承运人或运输经营人，而对实际承运人而言，它又是货物托运人。

Container transport is mostly combined transportation by sea，land and air. In order to ensure the smooth flow of containers in all links，usually there is an organization responsible for the whole process of transportation，commonly known as "non-vessel operating common carrier" (NVOCC). The carrier generally does not own the means of transport and is the designer and organizer of containerized cargo transport. NVOCC is created in the special environment of international container transport，which has the following main characteristics：① it's not a party to an international trade contract；②it is legally entitled to conclude a contract of carriage，and is responsible for the entire carriage of the goods；③it generally does not own a means of transport；④it has the right to issue B/L and is bound by the terms of the B/L；⑤it has a dual identity，for the shipper，it is the carrier or transport operator，and for the actual carrier，it is the shipper of goods.

3. 集装箱租赁公司（Container Leasing Company）

它是指针对实际承运人、无船公共承运人和货主开展集装箱租赁业务的公司。

It is a company that leases containers for actual carriers，non-vessel common carriers and cargo owners.

4. 集装箱船舶出租公司（Container Vessel Leasing Company）

集装箱船舶租赁是随着集装箱运输的发展而兴起的行业。目前，国际租船市场上拥有相当数量的集装箱船舶，以满足贸易商或承运人的不同需求。

Container ship leasing is an industry that has emerged with the development of container transportation. At present，there are quite a number of container ships in the international charter market to meet the different needs of traders or carriers.

5. 国际货运代理人（International Freight Forwarder）

随着国际集装箱多式联运的发展，运送货物所涉及的范围越来越广，情况越来越复杂，货主和运输经营人不可能亲自处理每一项具体业务，而通过国际货运代理人则可以较好地解决集装箱运输中有关业务事项。

With the development of international container multimodal transport，the scope of transporting goods is more and more extensive and the situation is more and more complex. It is impossible for cargo owners and transport operators to handle each specific business in person，while the business matters related to container transport can be better solved through international freight forwarder.

6. 集装箱货运站（Container Freight Station）

集装箱货运站主要承担为货主办理托运、集装箱装卸及转运、空箱的发放和回收、拆装箱及集装箱维修、办理报关及报检等业务。

Container freight station（CFS）mainly undertakes the business of consignment，container loading and unloading and forwarding，issuance and recovery of empty containers，devanning，stuffing and container maintenance，inspection and customs declaration，etc. for shippers.

7. 集装箱码头经营人（Container Terminal Operator）

它是指拥有码头和集装箱堆场经营权（或所有权），从事集装箱交接、装卸、维修、清理、保管等业务的服务机构。

It is a service organization that has the right（or ownership）to operate the wharf and container yard，and engages in the business of container handover，loading and unloading，maintenance，cleaning and storage.

8. 货主（Cargo Owner）

货主是国际贸易中的买卖双方当事人，也是集装箱运输的服务对象。在集装箱运输中，货主可以成为运输的发货人（托运人）或收货人。

The cargo owner is both the buyer and the seller in international trade and the service object of container transport. In container transport，the cargo owner may become the shipper or consignee of the transport.

5.1.3　集装箱货物（**Containerized Cargoes**）

对于集装箱运输来说，国际运输货物可分为四类。

For container transport，international cargo can be classified into four categories.

（1）最适合集装箱化的货物：货价高、运费承受能力强且按其属性可有效通过集装箱运输的商品，如针织品、酒、医药品、各种小型电器、光学仪器、电视机、小五金等，约占国际贸易货物的 57%。

（1）The goods most suitable for containerization：goods with high price，strong freight bearing capacity and can be effectively loaded into containers for transportation according to their attributes. Goods such as knitwear，wine，pharmaceuticals，various small electrical appliances，optical instruments，television sets，and hardware，accounting for about 57% of international trade goods.

（2）适合集装箱化的货物：货价中等、运费承受能力适当，属性较适合集装箱装运的商品，如纸浆、天花板、电线、电缆、面粉、金属制品等，约占总数的 11%。

（2）The goods suitable for containerization：the commodities with moderate price，appropriate freight bearing capacity and suitable attributes for container shipment，such as pulp，ceiling，wire，cable，flour and metal products，accounting for about 11% of the total.

（3）边缘集装箱化的货物：可用集装箱装运，但因其货价较低，用集装箱运输不经济，且属性较难集装箱化的货物，如钢锭、生铁、原木等。

（3）The goods that can be containerized：goods that can be shipped in containers but are not economical to transport in containers as their lower prices and their properties make them less economical to be containerized，such as steel ingots，pig iron，and logs.

（4）不适合集装箱化的货物：不能装在集装箱运输的货物，使用专用船舶效率更高，如废钢铁、大型卡车、桥梁、铁塔、发电机等。

（4）The goods not suitable for containerization：goods that cannot be transported in containers，such as scrap steel，large trucks，bridges，towers，and generators. It is more efficient to use specialized ships to transport such cargoes.

5.2　集装箱基本知识(Basic Knowledge of Containers)

5.2.1　集装箱标准(Container Standard)

为了有效地开展集装箱多式联运,必须做好集装箱标准化工作。目前世界上通用的国际标准集装箱是根据国际标准化组织制定的国际标准来建造和使用的。其中,国际海上集装箱运输中采用最多的是 IA 型和 IC 型两种,其他规格的集装箱使用较少。IA 型集装箱即 40 英尺干货集装箱,高、宽为 8 英尺,长为 40 英尺,体积为 67.5 立方米,可装约 54 立方米或重 22～26 公吨的货物。IC 型即 20 英尺集装箱,高、宽为 8 英尺,长为 20 英尺,体积为 33 立方米,可装约 25 立方米或重 17.5 公吨的货物。因此,一般轻泡货均装 40 英尺柜,实重货装 20 英尺柜。

In order to effectively carry out container multimodal transport, it is necessary to do a good job of container standardization. At present, the international standard container in the world is built and used according to the international standard established by International Organization for Standardization (ISO). Among them, IA and IC are the two most widely used types in international maritime container transportation, while containers of other specifications are less used. Type IA container is a 40 ft dry cargo container, which is 8 feet high and wide, 40 feet long, 67.5 cubic meters in volume and can carry about 54 cubic meters or 22-26 metric tons of cargo. Type IC, or 20 ft container, is 8 feet in height and width, 20 feet in length, 33 cubic meters in volume, and can carry a load of about 25 cubic meters or 17.5 metric tons. As a result, measurement cargoes are generally packed in 40′ containers and weight cargoes in 20′ containers.

为了便于统计集装箱数量,国际上以 20 英尺标准集装箱作为计量单位,以 TEU (Twenty-foot Equivalent Unit) 表示,即"相当于 20 英尺单位"。它通常用来表示船舶装载集装箱的能力,也是集装箱港口吞吐量、集装箱保有量的重要统计单位。

In order to facilitate the statistics of the number of containers, 20-foot containers are used as measuring units in the world, expressed as TEU, which means "Twenty-foot Equivalent Unit". It is usually used to express the capacity of ships to load containers, and is also an important statistical unit of container port throughput and container holdings.

5.2.2　集装箱的种类(Types of Container)

1. 干货集装箱(Dry Container)

它也称杂货集装箱,是一种通用集装箱。其一般为封闭式,在一端或侧面设有箱门,可以用于装载除液体货、需要调节温度的货物及特种货物以外的一般件杂货,如日用百货、纺织品、五金、家电、日化产品、工艺品、化工产品等。这种集装箱使用最为广泛,占集装箱总数的 70%～80%。

It's also known as general cargo container, and is a general purpose container. Generally, it is enclosed and has a door at one end or side. It can be used to load general cargo except liquid cargo, cargo requiring temperature adjustment and special cargo, such as daily necessities, textiles, hardware, household appliances, daily chemical products, and handicrafts. This kind of container is the most widely used, accounting for 70%-80% of the total number of containers.

2. 通风集装箱（Air Ventilation Container）

这种集装箱一般在左侧壁或端壁上设有通风口，适用于装载不需要冷冻但需要通风、防潮的货物，如新鲜蔬菜、水果等，若将其通风孔关闭，则可作为杂货集装箱使用。

This kind of container is usually equipped with vents on the left side wall or end wall. It is suitable for loading goods that need ventilation and moisture-proof without freezing, such as fresh vegetables and fruits. If the vents are closed, it can be used as grocery containers.

3. 冷藏集装箱（Refrigerated Container）

它是一种附有冷冻设备，专门用于装载冷冻、保温货物的集装箱，适合运输冷冻鱼类、肉类、黄油、奶油等货物。

It is a container with refrigeration equipment, specially used for loading frozen and heat preservation goods. It is suitable for transporting frozen fish and meat, butter, cream and other goods.

4. 散货集装箱（Bulk Container）

这种集装箱除了箱门外，在顶部还设有 2～3 个装货口，底部有升降架，可升高呈 40 度的倾斜角以便卸货，主要用于运输谷物、豆类、硼砂等散装货物。

In addition to the container door, there are two to three loading hatches on the top of the container. There is a lifting frame at the bottom, which can be raised to a 40 degree inclination angle for unloading. It is mainly used to transport grain, beans, borax and other bulk cargo.

5. 开顶集装箱（Open Top Container）

它适用于装载较高的大型货物和须吊装的重货，如玻璃板、钢板、木材、机械等。

It is suitable for loading taller and larger cargoes and heavy cargoes that need to be lifted, such as glass plate, steel plate, wood, and machinery.

6. 框架集装箱（Frame Container）

它是没有箱顶和两侧，由箱底和四周金属框架构成的集装箱，用于装卸长大、超重、轻泡货物，还便于装载牲畜以及钢材、汽车、重型机械等裸装货物。其特点是可以从箱子侧面进行装卸。

It is also known as flat rack container. It is a container without the top and sides of the box and consists of the bottom and the metal frame around it. It is used to load large, overweight cargo or measurement cargo, but also easy to load livestock and no packed goods such as steel，automobiles，heavy machinery.

7. 罐式集装箱(Tank Container)

这是一种专门用于装运液体货的集装箱,如酒类、油类、药品及液状化工品等货物。

This is a container specially used for transporting liquid cargo，such as alcoholic drinks，oils，pharmaceuticals，and liquid chemicals.

5.2.3　集装箱的标记(Container Marking)

为了便于集装箱国际多式联运业务的管理与信息传递,国际标准化组织对集装箱的标记制定了标准。根据该标准,集装箱标记分为必备标记和自选标记两类,每一类标记中又分为识别标记和作业标记。

In order to facilitate the management and information transmission of container international multimodal transport business，the ISO has formulated standards for container marking. According to this standard，container markers can be divided into two categories：necessary markers and optional markers，each of which can be divided into identification markers and operation markers.

1. 必备标记(Necessary Markers)

必备标记中的识别标记包括箱主代号、顺序号和核对数字。其中,箱主代号通常为四个大写拉丁字母,如中国远洋运输(集团)公司的箱主代号为"COSU",美国总统轮船公司的箱主代号为"APLU"。顺序号为集装箱编号,由六位阿拉伯数字组成。核对数字是用来核对箱主代号和顺序号记录是否准确的依据。

必备标记中的作业标记主要包括额定重量和自重标记、空陆水联运集装箱标记(图 5-1)和登箱顶触电警告标记(图 5-2)。

The identification markers in the necessary markers include the container owner code，the sequence number，and the check number. Among them，container owner code is usually four uppercase Latin letters. For example，China Ocean Shipping（Group）Company's container owner code is "COSU" and American President Lines' container owner code is "APLU". The check number is used to check whether the record of the container owner code and the sequence number is accurate.

The operation markers in the necessary markers mainly include max gross and tare weight，Symbol to Denote Air/Surface Container（Figure 5-1）and warning signs for electric shock on the top of the container（Figure 5-2）.

图 5-1　空陆水联运集装箱标记

图 5-2　登箱顶触电警告标记

2. 自选标记（Optional Markers）

自选标记中的识别标记包括国籍代号、尺寸和类型代号（箱型代号）；作业标记包括超高标记和国际铁路联盟标记。

The identification markers in the optional markers include nationality code，size and container type code；operation markers include super high mark and mark of International Union of Railways（UIC）.

5.3 集装箱货物的装箱与交接（Container Cargo Stuffing and Handing Over）

5.3.1 集装箱货物的交接形态（Handover Form of Containerized Goods）

在集装箱运输中，货方与承运方货物交接的基本形态有两种：整箱交接与拼箱交接。

In container transportation，there are two basic forms of cargo handover between the cargo owner and the carrier：Full Container Load（FCL）handover and Less than Container Load（LCL）handover.

整箱交接是指发货人与承运人交接的是一个（或多个）装满货物的集装箱。当发货人的货物能装满一个（或多个）集装箱时，一般采用整箱交接方式。在整箱交接方式下，发货人自行装箱并办好海关加封等手续，承运人接收的是外表状态良好、铅封完整的集装箱。货物运抵目的地后，承运人将集装箱原封交付给收货人，收货人自行将货物从箱中取出。整箱交接情况下，集装箱中的货物一般只有一个发货人、一个收货人。

FCL handover refers to the handover of a container（or containers）filled up with goods between the shipper and the carrier. When the shipper's goods can fill up one or more containers，the FCL is generally adopted. Under the mode of delivery of FCL，the shipper packs the container by himself and completes the formalities of customs sealing，and the carrier receives the container with good appearance and intact seal. When the goods arrive at the destination，the carrier delivers the original container to the consignee，who takes the goods out of the container by himself. In the case of FCL handover，there is usually only one consignor and one consignee of the goods in the container.

拼箱交接是指发货人将各自小量的货物交给承运人，由承运人根据流向相同的原则将不同发货人的货物装入同一个集装箱进行运输的交接形式。在拼箱交接形式下，承运人或其代理人从发货人手中接收货物并组织装箱运输，运到目的地交货地点后，再负责将货物从箱中掏出，以原状态交付各收货人。在这种交接形态下，每个集装箱的货物有多个发货人、多个收货人。拼箱货物的交接和装箱要在码头集装箱货运站、内陆货运站、中转站和铁路办理站等地进行。

LCL handover refers to the form of handover in which the consignors hand over their respective small quantities of cargo to the carrier，and the carrier loads the goods belonging to different consignors but with the same destination into the same container for transportation. In the form of LCL, the carrier or its agent receives the goods from the consignors and organizes the container transport. After the goods arrive at the place of delivery at the destination, the carrier or its agent is then responsible for taking the goods out of the container and delivering them to the consignees as they are. In this handover form, each container has more than one shipper and more than one consignee. The handover and loading of LCL should be carried out at terminal container freight station, inland freight station, transfer station, and railway handling station.

在货物交接中,有时也会出现两种交接形态结合的情况,即承运人以整箱形态接收货物,而以拼箱形态交付货物,或者相反。

In the process of cargo handover, sometimes there is a combination of two handover modes, that is, the carrier receives the cargo in the form of FCL, and delivers the cargo in the form of LCL, or vice versa.

5.3.2　集装箱货物的交接地点(Place of Handover of Containerized Goods)

1. 集装箱堆场交接(Handover at Container Yard)

集装箱堆场交接包括集装箱码头堆场交接和集装箱内陆堆场交接。这两种方式都是整箱交接。

集装箱码头堆场交接是指发货人将在工厂、仓库装好货物的集装箱运到装运港码头集装箱堆场,承运人(集装箱运输经营人)或其代理人在集装箱码头堆场接收货物,运输责任开始。货物运达卸货港后,承运人在集装箱码头堆场向收货人整箱交付货物,运输责任终止。

集装箱内陆堆场交接是指在集装箱内陆货站堆场、中转站或办理站堆场的交接,这种交接方式适用于国际多式联运。在集装箱内陆堆场交接时,货主与多式联运经营人或其代理人在集装箱内陆堆场办理交接手续,货物交接后,由多式联运经营人或其代理人负责将货物从内陆堆场运到码头堆场。

Container yard (CY) handover includes terminal container yard handover and inland container yard handover. Both methods are FCL handover.

Terminal container yard handover means that the consignor ships the containers loaded in factories or warehouses to the container yard of the loading port, and the carrier (container transport operator) or its agent receives the goods at the terminal container yard, and its transportation responsibility will begin. After the cargo arrives at the port of discharge, the carrier delivers the cargo to the consignee as a whole at the terminal container yard, and the transportation liability terminates.

Inland container yard handover refers to the handover at container inland yard, transfer station or handling station, which is suitable for international multimodal transport. When handing over at an inland container yard, the cargo owner handles the handover formalities with the CTO or its agent at the inland container yard. After handover, the CTO or its agent is responsible for transporting the goods from the inland yard to the dock yard.

2. 集装箱货运站交接（Handover at Container Freight Station）

集装箱货运站一般包括集装箱码头货运站、集装箱内陆货运站、中转站和集装箱办理站。集装箱货运站交接一般是拼箱货交接。发货人自行将货物送到集装箱货运站，集装箱经营人或其他代理人在集装箱货运站以货物的原来形态接收货物并负责安排装箱，然后组织海上运输或陆海联运、陆空联运或海空联运等多式联运。货物运到目的地货运站后，多式联运经营人或其代理人负责拆箱并以货物的原来状态向收货人交付。

Container freight station (CFS) generally includes container terminal freight station, inland container freight station, transit station and container handling station. CFS handover is usually the handover of LCL. The consignor delivers the goods to the container terminal by himself, the container operator or other agent receives the goods in the original form at the container terminal and is responsible for arranging packing, then organizes maritime transport, or multimodal transport such as land-sea transport, land-air transport, and sea-air transport. When the goods arrive at the destination freight station, the CTO or its agent is responsible for unpacking and delivering the goods to the consignee in their original state.

3. 发货人或收货人的工厂或仓库交接（即门到门交接）[Handover in the Shipper or Consignee's Factory or Warehouse (i. e. Door-to-Door Handover)]

它是指多式联运经营人或集装箱运输经营人在发货人的工厂或仓库接收货物，在收货人的工厂或仓库交付货物。门到门交接都是整箱交接，由发货人或收货人自行装箱（拆箱）。运输经营人负责从接收货物地点到交付货物地点的全程运输。

It means that the CTO or container transport operator receives the goods in the shipper's factory or warehouse and delivers the goods in the consignee's factory or warehouse. The goods handed over from door to door are FCLs, which are packed (unpacked) by the consignor or consignee. The transport operator is responsible for the entire transport from the place of receipt of the goods to the place of delivery of the goods.

5.3.3　集装箱货物的交接方式（Handover Modes of Containerized Goods）

根据集装箱货物的交接地点不同，实际业务中，其主要的交接方式包括以下几种。

（1）门到门：从发货人工厂或仓库至收货人工厂或仓库。

（2）门到场：从发货人工厂或仓库至目的地或卸货港集装箱堆场。

（3）门到站：从发货人工厂或仓库至目的地或卸货港集装箱货运站。

（4）场到门：从起运地或装运港的集装箱堆场至收货人工厂或仓库。

（5）场到场：从起运地或装运港的堆场至目的地或卸货港的堆场，这是班轮公司通常采用的交接方式。

（6）场到站：从起运地或装运港的堆场至目的地或卸货港的集装箱货运站。

（7）站到门：从起运地或装运港的集装箱货运站至收货人工厂或仓库。

（8）站到场：从起运地或装运港的集装箱货运站至目的地或卸货港的堆场。

（9）站到站：从起运地或装运港的集装箱货运站至目的地或卸货港的集装箱货运站。

Depending on the place of delivery of containerized cargo, the main modes of handover in actual business include the following kincls.

（1）Door/Door：From the shipper's factory or warehouse to the consignee's factory or warehouse.

（2）Door/CY：From the shipper's factory or warehouse to the CY at destination or unloading port.

（3）Door/CFS：From the shipper's factory or warehouse to the CFS at destination or unloading port.

（4）CY/Door：From the CY at the place of departure or port of shipment to the consignee's factory or warehouse.

（5）CY/CY：From the CY at the place of departure or port of shipment to the CY at the destination or unloading port, this is the usual handover method used by liner companies.

（6）CY/CFS：From the CY at the place of departure or port of loading to the CFS at the destination or unloading port.

（7）CFS/Door：From the CFS at the place of departure or port of shipment to the consignee's factory or warehouse.

（8）CFS/CY：From the CFS at the place of departure or port of shipment to the CY at the destination or unloading port.

（9）CFS/CFS：From the CFS at the place of departure or port of shipment to the CFS at the destination or unloading port.

以上九种交接方式,进一步可归纳为以下四种方式。

（1）门到门。这种交接方式的基本特征是：在整个运输过程中完全是集装箱运输,没有货物运输,故最适宜整箱交、整箱接。

（2）门到场站。这种交接方式的基本特征是：由门到场站为集装箱运输,由场站到门是货物运输,故适宜于整箱交、拆箱接。

（3）场站到门。这种交接方式的基本特征是：由门到场站为货物运输,由场站到门是集装箱运输,故适宜于拼箱交、整箱接。

（4）场站到场站。这种交接方式的基本特征是：除中间一段为集装箱运输外,两端的内陆运输均为货物运输,故适宜于拼箱交、拆箱接。

The above nine modes of handover can be further summarized into the following four modes.

（1）Door/Door. The basic characteristics of this mode of handover are：the whole transportation process is completely container transportation, there is no cargo transportation, so it is suitable for receiving and delivering FCL.

(2) Door/CFS. The basic characteristics of this mode of handover are: container transportation from Door to CFS, and cargo transportation from CFS to Door. Therefore, it is suitable for receiving FCL and delivering it after devanning.

(3) CFS/Door. The basic characteristics of this mode of handover are as follows: cargo transportation from Door to CFS, and container transportation from CFS to Door, so it is suitable for receiving LCL and delivering FCL.

(4) CFS/CFS. The basic characteristics of this mode of handover are as follows: only the middle part involves container transportation, while inland transportation at both ends adopts cargo transportation, so it is suitable for receiving LCL and delivering it after devanning.

5.4 集装箱运费计算(Calculation of Container Freight)

5.4.1 集装箱运费的构成(Composition of Container Freight)

集装箱运输是以集装箱为运输单位进行运输的一种现代化的先进的运输方式,其运费的构成和计算方法与传统的运输方式不同。以海运为例,它包括内陆运输费或装运港市内运输费、拼箱服务费、堆场服务费、集装箱海运费、集装箱及其他设备使用费等。

Container transportation is a modern and advanced mode of transportation with container as transport unit. Its freight composition and calculation method are different from the traditional mode of transportation. Taking sea transportation as an example, it includes inland transport charge or intra-city transport charges at port of shipment, LCL service charge, yard service fee, container sea transportation fee, container and other equipment usage fee, etc.

内陆运输费或装运港市内运输费主要包括区域运费、无效拖运费、变更装箱地点费等。内陆或港口市内运输可以由承运人负责,也可以由货主自理。如由货主自理,有关费用负担和支付按买卖合同规定,由发货人或收货人负责。在通常情况下,在出口地发生的费用由发货人负责,在进口地发生的费用由收货人负责。

Inland transport charge or intra-city transport charges at port of shipment mainly include regional freight, invalid towage fee, and the cost of changing the place of packing. Intra-city transportation inland or at the port can be the responsibility of the carrier, or be undertaken by the cargo owner. If it is handled by the owner himself, the relevant expenses shall be borne and paid in accordance with the provisions of the sales contract, and the shipper or consignee shall be responsible for it. Usually, the consignor is responsible for the expenses incurred at the place of export and the consignee is responsible for the expenses incurred at the place of import.

拼箱服务费包括拼箱货在货运站至堆场之间空箱或重箱的运输、理货、货运站内的搬运、堆存、装拆箱以及签发场站收据、装箱单制作等各项服务费用。

The LCL service charge includes the service fee of tallying empty or heavy containers of LCL transportation between the freight terminal and the yard, removal, storage, packing, and unpacking in freight stations, as well as the issuance of dock receipts and the preparation of packing lists, etc.

堆场服务费也称码头服务费,包括在装船港堆场接收来自货主或集装箱货运站的整箱货和堆存、搬运至装卸桥下的费用,以及在卸货港的从装卸桥下接收进口箱,将箱子搬运到堆场和在堆场的堆存费用。堆场服务费还包括在装卸港的有关单证费用。

The yard service fee, also known as terminal handling charge, includes the cost of accepting FCL from the cargo owner or container terminal at the loading port yard and the cost of stockpiling, transporting it to the quay crane, as well as the cost of receiving containers from the crane at the discharging port and carrying them to the yard, and the storage cost at the yard. The yard service fee also includes the relevant document fee at the loading and unloading port.

集装箱海运费由船舶运费和有关杂费组成。

Container sea transportation fee consists of ship freight and related incidental charges.

集装箱及其他设备使用费是指当货主使用由承运人提供的集装箱及底盘车等设备时发生的费用。它还包括集装箱从底盘车吊上吊下的费用。

The container and other equipment usage fee is the cost incurred when the shipper uses the container, chassis car, and other equipment provided by the carrier. It also includes the cost of lifting containers from chassis vehicles.

5.4.2　集装箱海运费的计算(Calculation of Container Maritime Freight)

1. 集装箱包箱费率(Box-rate for Container Freight)

目前,集装箱海运费的计收方法基本上有两种:一种是按每运费吨计收运费,计算方法与传统件杂货相同,拼箱货常采用这种方法;另一种是以每个集装箱作为计费单位,按包箱费率计算运费,整箱货通常按一个货柜计收运费。

集装箱的包箱费率有三种规定方法。

At present, there are basically two methods of charging ocean freight for containers. One is to collect freight per freight ton, the calculation method of which is the same as that of traditional general cargo, and this method is often used for LCL. The other is to use each container as the unit of charge and calculate the freight according to box-rate. FCL usually charges freight on a container basis.

There are three methods of specifying the box-rate for container.

(1) FAK 包箱费率,既不分货物种类,也不计货量,只规定统一的每个集装箱收取的费率,其形式见示例 5.1 中表 1。

(1) FAK (freight for all kinds). It specifies a uniform rate for each container,

regardless of the type or volume of goods, as shown in table 1 in example 5.1.

（2）FCS 包箱费率，即按不同货物等级制定的包箱费率。货物等级也是 1～20 级，但级差较小。一般低价货费率高于传统运输费率，高价货费率则低于传统运输费率，同一等级货物，实重货运价高于体积货运价。其形式见示例 5.1 中表 2。

（2）FCS (freight for class). The rates are set according to different classes of goods. The cargo grade is also from 1 to 20, but the difference is smaller. Generally, the rates for low-priced cargoes are higher than the rates for conventional transportation, while the rates for high-priced cargoes are lower than the rates for conventional transportation, and for the same class of cargoes, the rates for weight cargoes are higher than that for measurement cargoes. The form of FCS is shown in table 2 in example 5.1.

（3）FCB 包箱费率，即按不同货物等级或货物类别以及计算标准制定的费率。同一级货物因计算标准不同，费率也不同。如 8～10 级，CY/CY 交接方式，20 英尺集装箱货物如按重量计费，费率为 1 500 美元；如按尺码计费，费率则为 1 450 美元。其形式见示例 5.1 中表 3。

（3）FCB (freight for class & basis). The rates are set by different classes or categories of goods and calculation basis. The rates will be different if the goods are of the same class but the calculation criteria are different. For example, for cargo of class 8-10, CY/CY handover mode, the rate for a 20-foot container shipment is ＄1 500 if billed by weight and ＄1 450 if billed by measurement. The form of FCB is shown in table 3 in example 5.1.

示例 5.1　集装箱费率表

2. 集装箱海运费的计算方法(Calculation Method of Container Shipping Freight)

集装箱海运费的具体计算方法如下。

首先通过查货物等级表得出货物的等级，然后查费率表，按航线和货物等级查出整箱或拼箱的基本费率。

The specific calculation of container ocean freight is as follows.

First, the cargo class is obtained by checking the cargo class table, and then the basic rate of FCL or LCL is found by checking the rate table according to the route and cargo class.

另外，还要确定所运输货物是整箱货还是拼箱货。若为拼箱货，应先算出所装箱的确切数量，再按件杂货的计算方法查费率表计算；若为整箱货，直接按表中给出的单箱运费计算即可。当托运的货物部分装整箱、部分以拼箱方式运输时，需混合这两种计算方式。

In addition, it is also necessary to determine whether the goods to be transported are FCL or LCL. If it is LCL, the exact quantity of goods loaded into containers should be calculated first, and then the freight calculation should be carried out through checking rate table according to the calculation method of general cargo. If it is FCL, the freight can be calculated directly according to the single container freight rate given in the table. When the consignment is transported partly in full containers and partly in LCL mode, it is necessary to combine these two calculation methods.

集装箱整箱货量的计算方式有两种:一种是用集装箱的长、宽、高分别除以单件货物的长、宽、高,得出一个集装箱可以容纳的最大货量。另一种是按经验值,仅考虑集装箱的有效容积。

There are two methods of calculating the amount of cargo that can be loaded in a full container: one is to divide the length, width and height of a container by the length, width and height of a single cargo to get the maximum amount of cargo that a container can hold. The other is to consider only the effective volume of the container according to the empirical value.

此外,同传统件杂货班轮运输相似,集装箱运价中也包括附加费。例如:变更目的港附加费、重件附加费、港口附加费、燃油附加费、季节附加费、汇率变动附加费、整体费率上调、目的地交货费、空箱调运费、原产地接货费、码头操作费等。这些名目繁多的附加费是集装箱运费的重要组成部分。

In addition, similar to the traditional liner transportation of general cargo, various surcharges are included in the container tariff, such as: surcharge for alteration of destination, over weight surcharge, port surcharge, bunker adjustment factor(BAF), peak season surcharge, currency adjustment factor(CAF), general rate increase(GRI), destination delivery charge (DDC), equipment reposition charge (ERC), original receiving charge (ORC), terminal handling charge (THC), etc. These various surcharges are an important part of container freight.

5.4.3　使用不同贸易术语下的集装箱运费(Container Freight Under Different Trade Terms)

由于集装箱运费计收与传统的海运费计收方法不同,贸易合同对双方费用划分的规定应当与运输合同中的运费支付条款协调一致,避免其中一方重复交费。

As the charging method of container freight is different from the traditional shipping, the provisions of the trade contract on the division of costs between the two parties should be harmonized with the freight payment terms in the contract of carriage to avoid double payment by one of the parties.

1. 使用 FOB、CFR、CIF 贸易术语的情况(The Situation When Using FOB, CFR and CIF Trade Terms)

集装箱运输中,发货人可以将集装箱直接发运至装货港码头堆场,收货人在目的港码头堆场提货,这实际采用的是港口至港口的运输方式。实际业务中,当采用 FOB、CFR、CIF 贸易术语时,一般是卖方支付装货港的装船费,买方支付卸货港的卸船费,而集装箱运价采用的是班轮运价计收方法,即运费中包含装船费和卸船费,此时,应当使用这三种价格术语的变形来协调,以免一方重复付费。

In the container transport, the consignor can ship the container directly to the loading port terminal yard, the consignee can pick up the goods in the destination port terminal yard, which is actually the port-to-port mode of transportation. In actual business, when FOB, CFR, CIF trade terms are used, the seller generally pays the loading charges at the port of loading and the buyer pays the unloading charges at the port of discharge, while the container tariff uses the collection method of liner tariff. That is, the freight includes the loading fee and unloading fee, in this case, a variation of these three trade terms should be used to coordinate so that one party does not pay twice.

2. 使用 FCA、CPT、CIP 贸易术语的情况（The Situation When Using FCA, CPT and CIP Trade Terms）

集装箱运输中，集装箱的交接地点大多是集装箱货运站或堆场，而不是码头。这时，贸易合同中不应采用传统的 FOB、CFR、CIF 贸易术语，而应使用 FCA（Free Carrier，货交承运人）、CPT（Carriage Paid To，运费付至）、CIP（Carriage and Insurance Paid To，运费和保险费付至）三种贸易术语。选用这三种贸易术语时，应考虑运输一方已支付了包括装卸费在内的运费，从而合理制定买卖价格。

In the container transport, the container handover location is mostly container freight station or yard, rather than the terminal. Therefore, not the traditional terms of FOB, CFR and CIF, but FCA, CPT and CIP should be used in trade contracts. When choosing these three trade terms, the buying and selling prices should be reasonably set after considering that the shipping party has paid for the freight, including handling charges.

5.5　集装箱运输单据（Container Transport Documents）

5.5.1　场站收据（Dock Receipt）

1. 场站收据的概念与作用（Conception and Function of Dock Receipt）

场站收据是由承运人或其代理人签发的证明已收到托运货物并开始对货物负责的凭证。广义上的场站收据是一套综合性单据，它把货物托运单、装货单、大副收据、理货单、配舱回单、运费通知等单据汇成一套，统称为场站收据联单，它有利于提高托运效率。

场站收据一般是在托运人与承运人达成运输协议后，由船舶代理人交给托运人或其代理人填制，承运人委托的码头堆场、集装箱货运站或内陆货运站在收到货物后签字生效。货物装船后，托运人或其代理人可凭场站收据向船舶代理人换取已装船提单。

Dock receipt is a document issued by the carrier or its agent certifying that the consignment has been received and its responsibility for the shipment has begun. Broadly speaking, dock receipt is a set of comprehensive documents, including cargo consignment note, shipping order, mate's receipt, tally sheet, booking receipt, freight notice and other documents, which is conducive to improving the efficiency of consignment.

Dock receipt is usually handed over by the ship's agent to the shipper or his agent to fill in after the shipper and the carrier have reached a transport agreement. It takes effect after the signature of the terminal yard, container freight station, or inland freight station upon receipt of goods. After loading, the shipper or his agent may exchange the dock receipt for the shipped bill of lading with the ship's agent.

场站收据的主要作用如下：

（1）它是运输合同的证明和货物收据；

（2）它是出口货物报关的凭证之一；

（3）它是换取提单的凭证；

（4）它是船公司、港口组织装卸、理货、配载的资料；

（5）它是运费结算的依据；

（6）如果信用证允许，可凭此向银行议付。

The main functions of dock receipt are as follows：

（1）It is the evidence of the contract of carriage and the receipt of goods；

（2）It is one of the documents for customs declaration of export goods；

（3）It is a voucher in exchange for a B/L；

（4）It is the information used by shipping companies and ports to organize loading and unloading, tallying and stowage；

（5）It is the basis of freight settlement；

（6）If L/C permits, it can be used for negotiation with the bank.

2. 场站收据的缮制（Preparation of Dock Receipt）

集装箱货物场站收据的缮制方法如下。

（1）编号（D/R No.）：这一栏填写将要签发的集装箱提单号码。

（2）发货人（Shipper）：托运人,指委托运输人,一般为出口方,填写卖方的名称,需与提单一致。

（3）收货人（Consignee）：具体填写方法见海运出口托运单。常采用指示收货人（TO ORDER 或 TO ORDER OF...）的填写方法。不标明具体收货人的名址,以方便单据的转让。

（4）通知人（Notify Party）：填制方法同散装运输托运单。在信用证支付方式下,按来证规定的通知人缮制。如来证不要求在提单上注明通知人,可提供目的港收货人的名称和地址,并注明仅缮制在副本提单上,以便船公司通知客户提货清关。

（5）集装箱号（Container No.）。

（6）铅封号、标记与号码（Seal No Marks & Nos.）：第五、第六栏的内容可以连在一起写。如果托运时已装好箱,即整箱货,则填集装箱号码及海关查验后作为封箱的铅封关封号；如果为拼箱货,可先填入货物具体唛头,在场站装箱完毕后,填集装箱号码。但如 L/C 有规定,则必须严格与信用证规定一致。在集装箱号和铅封号之后,还应加注货物的具体交接方式,如 FCL/FCL、CY/CY、LCL/LCL、CFS/CFS、CY/CFS、CFS/CY 等。

（7）箱数或件数（No. of Container or P'kgs）：如为托运人装箱的整箱货,可只注集装箱数量,如"3 container",只要海关已对集装箱封箱,承运人即对箱内的内容和数量不负责任。如需注明箱内小件数量,数量前应加"said to container...”。如果是拼箱货,该栏的填制可参照散装运输托运单相同栏目的填制方法,填写货物最大包装件数。

(8) 包装种类与货名(Kind of Packages; Description of Goods):①填写包装材料及形式,必须与合同及 L/C 要求一致;②货名可只填写统称,如同时出口两种及两种以上货物,需分别填写,不允许只填写其中一种数量较多或金额较大的商品。

(9) 毛重(Gross Weight):填写货物毛重,以千克计。

(10) 尺码(Measurements):此处为货物尺码总数,它不仅包括各种货物之和,还应包括堆放时件与件之间的空隙所占的体积。

(11) 集装箱数或件数合计(Total Number of Containers or Packages):用大写表示集装箱数(整箱托运时)或本托运单项下的商品总件数(拼箱托运时)。

(12)、(13)、(14) 由场站员或理货员(Terminal Clerk/Tally Clerk)于理货整箱后填写。

(15) Freight 由船方或其代理填写。正本提单份数(No. of Original B/L)按证中规定填写,若证中只规定"Full Set""Complete Set"等,未规定具体份数,可掌握两份到三份,提单份数通常用大写英文数字注明,有的在大写字母之后用括号或斜线隔开,注阿拉伯数字,如:"TWO/2"。

(16) 签单地点(Place of Issue):通常为承运人接收货物或装船地址,但有时也不一致,按实际情况填写即可。

(17)、(18) 货物交接方式一般有九种:

CY-CY   CY-DOOR   DOOR-CY

DOOR-DOOR   CY-CFS   CFS-CY

CFS-CFS   CFS-DOOR   DOOR-CFS

(19) 种类(Type of Goods):选择确认托运种类,打"√"。冷藏货物需填冷藏温度。危险品必须提供下列内容:危险品的化学成分、国际海运危险品法规号码、包装标志和使用鉴定、港监签证,外包装上注明危险品标志。

对于(20)~(24),分货物不需转运和需要转运两种情况讲解:

(20) 前程运输(Pre...Carriage by)。

① 空白。

② 填第一程船的船名或联合运输过程中在装货港装船前的运输工具。例如:从沈阳用火车将集装箱及货物运到大连新港,再运至目的港,此栏可填"Wagon No. ××××"。

(21) 收货地点(Place of Receipt)。

① 空白或场站。

② 指前段运输的收货地点,按上例情形,此栏应填沈阳(ShenYang)。

(22) 船名、航次(Ocean Vessel, Voy. No.):船名、第二程船名。

(23) 装货港(Port of Loading):装货港名称、中转港名称。

应按 L/C 规定填写。若证中只笼统规定装货港名称,如"Chinese main port",制单时应根据实际情况填具体港口名称,并加注"CHINA";如有重名,须加注地区名以资区别,如 XINGANG/DALIAN/CHINA 或 XINGANG/TIANJIN/CHINA；若证中同时列明几个起运港，如"XINGANG/ QINHUANGDAO/ TANGSHAN"，制单时只填实际装运港的名称。

（24）卸货港（Port of Discharge）：卸货港（目的港）名称、二程卸货港（目的港）名称。

（25）交货地点（Place of Delivery）：如为港至港运输，此栏填目的港；如为联合运输，此栏填最终将货物交与收货人的地点（城市）名称。除 FOB 术语外，目的港不能打笼统名称，如信用证规定目的港为"Negoya/Kobe/Yokohama"，表示由卖方选港，制单时根据实际只打一个即可，但若来证规定"Option Negoya/Kobe/Yokohama"，则表示由买方选港，制单时应按次序全部照打。

（26）目的地（Final Destination for the Merchant's Reference）：填货物实际到达的目的地，供货主参考。

对于（27）～（36），均用中文填写。

（27）、（28）、（29）分别为发货人或代理人地址、联系人、电话。

（30）可否转船：填 N/Y 或否/可，注意前后一致。

（31）可否分批：填 N/Y 或否/可，如为"Y"，则在备注栏内加以具体说明。

（32）装运期限（Time of Shipment）。装运期限严格按照信用证或合同规定填写，最好用英文书，例如，不迟于 2024 年 7 月 8 日，应写成 Not later than July 8, 2024。

装运期可表示为一段时间，例如 Month of Shipment：May, 2024；也可表示为不早于××日、不迟于××日，例如 Shipment not earlier than…and not later than…latest shipment be…

（33）有效期（Expiry Date）。在信用证支付条件下，有效期与运期有着较密切的关系。一般规定信用证至运输单据签发日后 21 天内有效。这一栏填写要参照信用证规定。如果装运期空白不填的话，这一栏也可空白。

（34）制单日期：它必须早于最迟装运期和有效期，可以是开立发票的日期，也可以早于发票日期。

（35）海运费由哪一方支付，如预付费用托收支付，填银行账号。

（36）备注：特别说明处。

（37）装箱场站名称。

（38）场站签章、日期：在货物入站 CY 或 CFS 后，由场站签收。

5.5.2 集装箱提单（Container B/L）

集装箱提单是集装箱运输方式下的主要运输单据，适用于集装箱运输的提单有两类：一类是港至港的海运提单，另一类是内陆至内陆的多式联运提单。此两类提单的法律效力和作用与传统提单基本相同。由于集装箱货物的交接一般都不在船边，因此，与普通船舶运输下签发的提单不同，集装箱提单一般是待装船提单。为了与信用证要求（已装船提单）一致，集装箱提单一般增加装船记录栏，以便必要时加上"已装船"批注，使之转变为已装船提单。

托运人通常在与集装箱运输经营人或其委托的堆场、货运站的业务人员交接货物后，用场站收据向运输经营人换取提单。

单据 5.1 场站收据

单据 5.2 集装箱货物托运单

单据 5.3 集装箱发放通知单

Container B/L is the main transport document under the mode of container transportation. There are two types of B/L applicable to container transport：one is port-to-port maritime B/L，the other is inland-to-inland combined transport B/L. The legal effect and role of these two types of Bs/L and the traditional B/L is basically the same. As the container cargo handover is generally not at the ship's side，therefore，unlike the B/L issued under ordinary shipping，the container B/L is generally received for shipment B/L. In order to be consistent with the requirements of the L/C（shipped B/L），container B/L usually adds the loading record column，so as to add the "on board" annotation when necessary，so that it can be converted into shipped B/L.

The shipper usually exchanges the dock receipt for a B/L from the transport operator after handing over the goods to the container transport operator or the operation staff of the yard or freight station entrusted by him.

Words and Expressions

即测即练

习题

Chapter 6

国际航空货物运输
International Air Cargo Transport

Learning Objectives：

1. Understand the characteristics and limitations of international air transport；
2. Be familiar with the major international air transport organizations and understand their aims and objectives；
3. Master the characteristics of main modes of international air cargo transport, including scheduled air line，chartered carrier transport，consolidation transport，air express service，and combined transport；
4. Understand the basic concept and composition of air freight and master the calculation method of international air freight；
5. Master the nature，functions，and types of air waybill；
6. Know how to make out an air waybill.

引导案例

航空货运遭拒付诉航空公司案

A 公司与 K 国 B 公司签订服装出口合同。B 公司于某年 5 月 7 日向 K 国中小企业银行申请开立以 A 公司为受益人的信用证，信用证中所需单据中关于空运单的要求是：收货人为 K 国中小企业银行、标明"运费预付""通知申请人"。C 航空在 6 月 4 日、6 日、7 日和 8 日签发了四份航空货运单，托运人为 A 公司、收货人为"凭 K 国中小企业银行指示"(to the Order of Industrial Bank of K××××)、运费预付、目的地机场为 J 国某市。B 公司于 7 月 21 日出具确认书，确认其已收到上述货物。A 公司在向 K 国中小企业银行主张支付信用证项下款项时，被以电汇余额后没有进行议付、透支、多次运输为由拒付。A 公司于 7 月 12 日接到 K 国中小企业银行有关其并未将提货单交给 B 公司，其仍持有正本单证的回函后，以承运人擅自放货为由诉至法院。法院认为，A 公司委托 C 航空承运货物时，所提示的贸易资料上明确载明买方、装运口岸、目的地、合同号、信用证号等信息，由于航空货运单不是通常意义上的有价证券或物权凭证，因而通常不应当将信用证开证行列为航空货运单的收货人。本案中航空货运单上收货人的这一写法仅是为了满足结算时单证相符、单单相符的要求。C 航空已将承运的货物交付给 A 公司提供的买卖合同的买方，且 A 公司业已收取买方的部分汇款，因此，C 航空在履行航空货物运输合同中没有过错。

随着全球性航空运输网的建立、飞机速度和运载能力的提升以及各国间经贸往来的不断加深，航空运输占国际货运的比重逐步增加。技术含量高的新兴产业，其产品通常具有体积小、附加价值高、运输时效性强等特点，对航空运输具有较强的依赖性；传统制造业的高级化也使得其产品对航空运输的需求越来越多。空运已成为国际货运特别是洲际货运的重要方式，也是目前最安全、迅速的运输方式。

With the establishment of a global air transport network，the increase in aircraft speed and capacity，and the deepening of economic and trade relations among countries，the proportion of air transport in international transport is gradually increasing. For emerging industries with high technological content，their products are usually characterized by small size，high added value，and strong transport timeliness，which have a strong dependence on air transport. The upgrading of traditional manufacturing industry has also led to an increasing demand for air transportation of its products. Air transportation has become an important mode of international freight transport，especially intercontinental freight transport，and is currently the safest and fastest mode of transportation.

改革开放后，中国民航业得到了迅速发展，目前我国民航业在旅客周转量、货邮周转量、运输总周转量等指标方面，均稳居世界第二，仅次于美国。中国航空市场成为除美国之外最大的民用航空市场。截至 2023 年底，我国共有运输航空公司 66 家，其中，全货运航空公司 13 家，民航全行业运输飞机期末在册架数 4 270 架。2023 年，我国共有定期航班航线 5 206 条，国内航线 4 583 条，其中，港澳台航线 65 条，国际航线 623 条。国内通航城市 255 个，国际通航 57 个国家的 127 个城市。全行业完成运输总周转量 1 188.34 亿吨公里，其中，国内航线完成运输总周转量 867.33 亿吨公里，国际航线完成运输总周转量 321.01 亿吨公里。[①]

After the reform and opening up，China's civil aviation industry has been developing rapidly. Currently，China's civil aviation industry ranks second in the world in terms of passenger turnover，cargo and mail turnover，and total transportation turnover，second only to the United States. The Chinese aviation market has become the second largest civil aviation market after the U. S. By the end of 2023，there were 66 transport airlines in China，including 13 all-cargo transport airlines，and 4 270 transport aircraft in the civil aviation industry as a whole. In 2023，there will be a total of 5 206 regular flight routes in China，including 4 583 domestic routes，of which 65 go through Hong Kong，Macao，and Taiwan，and 623 international routes. Domestic flights are available to 255 cities，and international flights are available to 127 cities in 57

---

① 中国民用航空局. 2023 年民航行业发展统计公报［Z］. 2023.

countries. The industry as a whole completed a total transport turnover of 118. 834 billion tons kilometers，of which 86. 733 billion tons kilometers were completed on domestic routes and 32. 101 billion tons kilometers on international routes.

6.1　国际航空货物运输概述（Overview of International Air Cargo Transport）

航空运输是指使用航空器运送人员、行李、货物和邮件的一种运输方式。国际航空货物运输即指一国的提供者向他国消费者提供运输服务并获取收益的活动。

Air transport is a mode of shipping that uses aircraft to transport personnel，baggage，goods and mail. International carriage of goods by air means the activity in which a provider of one country provides air transport services to consumers of another country for profits.

6.1.1　国际航空货物运输的特点（Characteristics of International Air Cargo Transport）

国际航空货物运输的发展虽然起步较晚，但极为迅速，这与它所具备的优点分不开，航空运输与其他运输方式相比，具有以下优势。

Although the development of international air cargo transport started late，it has developed extremely rapidly，which is inseparable from its advantages. Air transport has the following advantages compared to other modes of transport.

1. 运送速度快（Fast Delivery Speed）

飞机的飞行速度都在每小时 600～800 千米，比其他运输工具快得多。这种特点适应了一些特种货物的需求，例如，海鲜、水果等鲜活易腐的货物，由于货物本身的性质导致其对时间的要求特别高，只有采用航空运输方式。

The flight speed of aircraft is 600-800 km/h，which is much faster than other means of transport. This feature is adapted to the needs of some special cargoes such as fresh and perishable goods including seafood and fruits. The nature of these goods themselves leads to particularly high requirements for timeliness，which can only be met by air transport.

2. 安全性高，准确性好（High Security and Good Accuracy）

由于航空货物本身的价格比较高，其运输操作流程的环节比其他运输方式严格得多。使用航空运输，破损的情况大大减少。货物装上飞机后，在空中很难被损坏，因此在整个货物运输环节当中，货物的破损率低、安全性好。

As the price of air cargo itself is relatively high，the steps of operation process are much stricter than other transportation methods. The use of air transport significantly reduces the incidence of cargo breakage. After the cargo is loaded on the plane，it will hardly be damaged in the air，so the rate of damage to the cargo is low and the safety is good during the whole cargo transportation process.

3. 节省包装、保险、利息和储存费等费用(Save on Packaging，Insurance，Interest and Storage Fees，etc.)

由于采用航空运输方式,货物在途时间缩短,周转速度加快,企业存货可以相应地减少。一方面,这有利于资金的回收,减少利息支出;另一方面,企业仓储费用也可以降低。此外,由于航空货物运输安全、准确、货损货差少,保险费用也较低,与其他运输方式相比,航空运输的包装简单,降低了包装成本。

With the use of air transportation，the transit time of goods is shortened，the turnover speed is accelerated，and the enterprise inventory can be reduced accordingly，which on the one hand，is conducive to the recovery of funds and the reduction of interest expenses；on the other hand，it can also reduce the enterprise storage costs. In addition，insurance costs are also lower due to the safety and accuracy of air cargo transportation as well as less cargo damage and loss，for the more，compared to other modes of transport，the packaging of goods under air transport is simple，thus reducing packaging costs.

4. 不受地面条件影响(Unaffected by Ground Conditions)

航空运输利用天空这一自然通道,不受地理条件的限制,对于地面条件恶劣、交通不便的内陆地区非常合适,有利于当地资源的出口,促进当地经济的发展。

Using the sky as a natural channel，air transportation is not restricted by geographical conditions，which makes it very suitable for inland areas with poor ground conditions and inconvenient traffic，and is conducive to the export of local resources and the development of the local economy.

但航空运输也具有明显的局限性。

However，air transport also has obvious limitations.

1. 运量小、运价高(Small Volume and High Freight Rate)

航空货运的运费较其他运输方式更高,不适合低值货物;航空运载工具——飞机的舱容有限,对大件货物或大批量货物的运输有一定的限制。

Air freight is higher than other modes of transport，so it's not suitable for low-value goods. Air carriers—airplanes—have limited cabin capacity，thus limiting the transportation of large cargoes or large quantities of goods.

2. 易受天气影响(Susceptible to Weather)

飞机飞行容易受到恶劣天气的影响,如果遇到大雨、大风、雾等恶劣天气,航班得不到有效的保证,这对航空运输造成的影响较大。

Aircraft flight is vulnerable to bad weather. When encountering heavy rain, high winds，fog and other bad weather，flights are not effectively guaranteed，which will have a greater impact on air transport.

从以上对航空货运特点的分析可以看出,航空货运既有优势也有劣势,需要代理人在实际的操作当中充分发挥航空货运的优势、克服其劣势,才能更好地发挥航空货运在经济发展中的作用。

From the above analysis of the characteristics of air cargo transport，it can be seen that air transport has both advantages and disadvantages，so agents are needed to give full play to the advantages of air transport and overcome its disadvantages in the actual operation in order to better play the role of air transport in economic development.

6.1.2　国际航空运输组织（International Air Transport Organizations）

1. 国际民用航空组织（International Civil Aviation Organization）

国际民用航空组织是政府间的国际航空机构，它是根据 1944 年芝加哥《国际民用航空公约》设立的，是联合国所属专门机构之一，总部设在加拿大的蒙特利尔。中国于 2004 年首次当选为国际民用航空组织的一类理事国，并在此后历次选举中连任至今。

The International Civil Aviation Organization（ICAO）is an intergovernmental international aviation agency that was established under *Convention on International Civil Aviation* 1944（also known as Chicago Convention）and is one of the specialized agencies under the United Nations，with its headquarters in Montreal，Canada. China was first elected as a Category I Council Member State of the ICAO in 2004 and has been re-elected consecntively since then.

国际民用航空组织的宗旨和目的在于：发展国际航行的原则和技术，促进国际航空运输的规划和发展；保证全世界国际民用航空安全地和有秩序地发展；鼓励和平用途的航空器的设计和操作技术；鼓励发展国际民用航空应用的航路、机场和航行设施；满足世界人民对安全、正常、有效和经济的航空运输的需要。

The aims and purposes of ICAO are to develop the principles and techniques of international navigation and to promote the planning and development of international air transport；to ensure the safe and orderly development of international civil aviation throughout the world；to encourage the design and operation of aircraft technology for peaceful purposes；to encourage the development of airways，airports and navigational facilities for international civil aviation applications；and to meet the needs of the people of the world for safe，regular，efficient and economical air transport.

2. 国际航空运输协会（International Air Transport Association）

国际航空运输协会是各国航空运输企业之间的联合组织，会员必须是国际民用航空组织成员的空运企业。参加国际航空运输协会的航空公司所属国一般都是联合国成员。国际航空运输协会于 1945 年 4 月 16 日在哈瓦那（古巴）成立，总部设在加拿大蒙特利尔，执行机构在日内瓦。它是世界上有定期航班业务的航空公司（空运承运人）组成的国际民间组织，属非官方性质。1993 年，中国国际航空公司正式成为 IATA 会员，是中国首批加入该组织的航空公司。之后，东方航空公司、南方航空公司等也陆续加入。

International Air Transport Association（IATA）is a joint organization among air transport enterprises of various countries and its members must be air transport enterprises of ICAO member states. The countries of the airlines participating in IATA are generally members of the United Nations. IATA was established in Havana (Cuba) on 16 April 1945，with its headquarters in Montreal，Canada，and its executive body in Geneva. It is an international non-governmental organization of the world's airlines (air carriers) engaged in scheduled flight operations and is unofficial in its nature. In 1993，Air China officially became a member of IATA and was one of the first Chinese airlines to join the organization. Later，China Eastern Airlines and China Southern Airlines also joined.

协会的宗旨是：为了世界人民的利益，促进安全、正常和经济的航空运输，扶植发展航空运输业，并研究与此有关的问题；为直接或间接从事国际航空运输工作的各空运企业提供合作的途径；与国际民航组织及其他国际组织协力合作等。

The purpose of IATA is to promote safe，normal，and economical air transport for the benefit of the people of the world，to foster the development of the air transport industry，and to study issues related to it；to provide a means of cooperation for air transport enterprises directly or indirectly engaged in international air transport；to cooperate with ICAO and other international organizations，etc.

3. 国际货物运输代理协会联合会(International Federation of Freight Forwarders Association)

国际货物运输代理协会联合会是国际货运代理人的行业组织，于 1926 年 5 月 31 日在奥地利维也纳成立，总部设在瑞士苏黎世，是一个非营利性的国际货运代理行业组织。

该协会的宗旨是保障和提高国际货运代理在全球的利益，工作目标是团结全世界的货运代理行业；以顾问或者专家身份参加国际性组织，处理运输业务，代表、促进和保护运输业的利益；通过发布信息和出版物等方式，使贸易界、工业界和公众熟悉货运代理人提供的服务。

International Federation of Freight Forwarders Associations (FIATA) is a non-profit industrial organization for international freight forwarders. It was founded in Vienna，Austria，on May 31，1926，with headquarters in Zurich，Switzerland.

The purpose of FIATA is to safeguard and enhance the interests of international freight forwarders worldwide. The objectives of its work are to unite the freight forwarding industry worldwide；to participate in international organizations in an advisory or expert capacity in order to deal with transport operations and to represent，promote and protect the interests of the transport industry；to familiarize the trade circle，industry circle and the public with the services provided by freight forwarders by issuing information and publications，etc.

6.2　航空货物运输方式(Air Cargo Transport Mode)

航空货物运输方式主要有班机运输、包机运输、集中托运、航空快递和陆空联运等，不同的航空货运方式其运输程序、适用情况各有特点，贸易商可以根据具体情况选择。

The main modes of international air cargo transport are scheduled flight，chartered flight, consolidation transport, air express service, and land-air combined transport. Different air freight methods have their own characteristics in terms of transport procedures and applicability, so traders can choose according to the specific situation.

6.2.1　班机运输(Scheduled Flight)

班机运输是指在固定航线上飞行的航班运输,它有固定的始发站、途经站和目的站,按照业务对象不同,可分为客运航班和货运航班,但通常使用的是客货混合型飞机,其货舱容量小、运价较高。一些规模较大的航空公司也会在一些航线上开辟使用全货机运输的定期货运航班。

Scheduled flight refers to the transportation of flights flying on a fixed route, which has fixed departure, transit and destination airports. According to the different business objects, it can be divided into passenger flight and cargo flight, but the combination carrier is usually used, which has small loading capacity and higher freight rate. Some of the larger airlines also operate scheduled cargo flights on some routes using all-cargo aircraft.

班机运输具有以下特点。

Scheduled flight has the following characteristics.

(1) 迅速准确。班机固定航线、固定停靠站和定期开航的特点,可以迅速、安全地把空运货物运达全球各通航点。

(1) It is fast and accurate. The fixed routes, fixed terminals and regular schedules of the airliner make it possible to transport cargo quickly and safely to all airports around the world.

(2) 方便货方。它对市场上急需的商品、鲜活易腐货物以及贵重商品的运送非常有利。

(2) It's convenient to the consignor and consignee. It is very advantageous for the delivery of urgently needed goods, fresh and perishable goods, as well as valuable commodities.

(3) 舱位有限。班机运输一般是客货混载,不能使大批量的货物及时出运,往往需要分期分批运输。

(3) Its cabin space is limited. In general, scheduled flight carries passengers and goods together, so it cannot make the timely shipment of large quantities of goods, which often needs to be transported in stages and batches.

6.2.2　包机运输(Chartered Flight)

包机运输分为整包机与部分包机两种。

整包机是由航空公司或包租代理公司按照事先约定的条件和费用将整机租给租机人,从一个或几个航空港将货物运至指定目的地,适用于运输大批量货物。包机人一般要在货物装运前一个月与航空公司联系,以便航空公司安排运载和向起降机场及有关政府部门申请办理过境或入境的有关手续。

部分包机是由几家货运代理公司或发货人联合包租一架飞机,或者由包机公司把一架飞机的舱位分别租给几家空运代理公司。

包机运输适合于大宗货物运输,费率低于班机,但运送时间比班机要长些,且包机的活动范围比较狭窄,降落地点受到限制。

Chartered flight can be divided into two types: whole chartered flight and partial chartered flight.

whole chartered flight means that the whole aircraft is rented to the charterer by the airline or charter agent according to the pre-agreed conditions and fees to transport the cargoes from one or several airports to the designated destination. It is suitable for transporting large quantities of goods. The charterer usually contacts the airline one month before the cargo is shipped, so that the airline can arrange the transportation and apply to the landing airport and the relevant government departments for transit or entry formalities.

Partial chartered flight means that several freight forwarders or consignors charter an aircraft jointly, or the charter company leases the space of an aircraft to several air freight forwarders respectively.

Chartered flight is suitable for transporting bulk cargo and the rate is lower than that of scheduled flights, but the delivery time is longer, the range of activities is narrow, and the landing place is also restricted.

6.2.3　集中托运(Consolidation Transport)

集中托运是由空运货代公司(集中托运商)将若干单独发货人的货物集中起来组成一整批货物,由其向航空公司托运到同一到站,货到国外后由到站地的空运代理(分拨商)办理收货、报关并分拨给实际收货人。

集中托运方式具有以下优点。

(1) 节省运费。航空货运代理公司集中托运的运价一般都低于国际航空运输协会的运价,发货人可得到低于其他航空公司的运价,从而节省费用。

(2) 提供方便。将货物集中托运,可使货物到达航空公司到达地点以外的地方,从而延伸了航空公司的服务,给货主提供方便。

(3) 提早结汇。发货人将货物交给航空货运代理公司以后,即可取得货物分运单。这时,发货人就可以持分运单到银行办理结汇了。

Consolidation transport means that the air freight forwarder gathers the cargo of several individual shippers to form a whole batch of cargo, which are consigned to the same destination airport by the airline, and the air freight forwarder at the destination handles the receipt, customs declaration, and distribution to the actual consignees after the goods arrive abroad.

Consolidation transport has the following advantages.

（1）Save freight. Freight rates of consolidation transport offered by the air freight forwarder are generally lower than that of IATA，so the shippers can get lower rates than that of other airlines，thus saving costs.

（2）Provide convenience. Consolidation transport allows cargo to reach places other than where the airline arrives，thus extending the service of airlines and providing convenience to cargo owners.

（3）Earlier settlement of foreign exchange. The consignor can obtain the House Air Waybill after handing over the goods to the air freight agent. At this point，the consignor can take the House Air Waybill to the bank to settle the foreign exchange.

6.2.4　航空快递（Air Express Service）

航空快递也称急件传递、航空快件、快运。不同于一般的航空邮寄和航空货运，航空快递是由专门经营该项业务的航空货运代理公司，派专人以最快的速度，在货主、机场、客户之间运输和交接货物的运输服务业务，又被称为"桌至桌"的运输。其适用于急需的药品和医疗器械、贵重物品、图纸资料、货样、单证和书报杂志等小件物品的运输，是目前航空货物运输中最快捷的运输方式。

航空快递业务的形式包括：门/桌到门/桌、门/桌到机场和专人派送服务。航空快递业务的特点是：①快捷灵便；②安全可靠；③收件范围受限；④查询快。

Air express is also known as air courier. Different from the general air mail and air freight，air express is a transport service business in which the air freight forwarder specialized in this business sends specially-assigned person to transport and deliver goods between the cargo owner，the airport and the customer at the fastest possible speed，so it is also called "desk-to-desk" transportation. It is suitable for the transportation of urgently needed medicines and medical devices，valuables，drawings，samples，documents，newspapers and magazines，and other small items，and is the fastest mode of air cargo transportation at present.

The forms of air express service include "door/desk to door/desk"，"door/desk to airport" and personalized delivery service. The characteristics of air express service are：①fast and convenient；② safe and reliable；③ restricted scope of receipt；④ quick inquiry.

6.2.5　陆空联运（Land-air Combined Transport）

陆空联运是指包括空运在内的两种以上运输方式的联合运输。陆空联运的类型有三种：第一种是火车、飞机、卡车的联合运输；第二种是卡车、飞机的联合运输；第三种是火车-飞机的联合运输。

目前，我国长江以南的外运分公司办理陆空联运的具体做法是：用火车、卡车或船将货物运至香港，然后利用香港航班多、到欧美国家运价低的条件，把货物从香港运到目的地，或运到中转地，再通过当地代理用卡车送到目的地；我国长江以北的外运分公司多采用火车或卡车将货物送至北京、上海航空口岸出运。

Land-air intermodal transport refers to the combined transport of more than two modes of transport that include air transport. There are three types of land-air intermodal transport：Train-Air-Truck（TAT）, Truck-Air（TA）, and Train-Air（TA）.

Currently, the specific practice of handling land-air intermodal transport by branches of foreign trade transport companies located south of the Yangtze River is as follows：the goods are transported to Hong Kong by train, truck, or ship；then take advantage of the many flights from Hong Kong and low freight rates to Europe and the United States to transport the goods from Hong Kong to their destinations, or to a transit location, and then delivering them by truck to their destinations through local agents. The branches located north of the Yangtze River mostly use trains or trucks to send goods to Beijing and Shanghai air ports for shipment.

扩展阅读 6.1 国际著名的快递公司

6.3 国际航空运价与运费（International Air Freight Rate and Freight）

6.3.1 基本概念（Basic Concept）

1. 航空运价（Air Freight Rate）

航空运价又称费率，是指承运人对所运输的每一重量单位货物（千克或磅）所收取的自始发地机场至目的地机场的航空费用，不包括承运人、代理人或机场收取的其他费用。货物的航空运价通常以运输始发地的本国货币公布，有的国家以美元代替本国货币公布。

It refers to the air fee charged by the carrier for each unit weight of cargo（kilogram or pound）transported from the airport of origin to the airport of destination, excluding other fees charged by the carrier, agent or airport. The air freight rate is usually announced in the national currency of the place of origin of the carriage, and in some countries the US dollar is used instead of the national currency.

2. 航空运费（Air Freight）

航空运费是指航空公司将一票货物自始发站机场运至目的地机场所应收取的航空运输费用。这一费用根据每票货物所适用的运价和货物的计费重量计算而得。

Air freight is the air transportation fee charged by an airline for transporting a shipment from the airport of origin to the airport of destination, calculated on the basis of the applicable tariff to each shipment and the chargeable weight of the shipment.

3. 其他费用（Other Charges）

其他费用是指由承运人、代理人或其他部门收取的与航空公司货物运输有关的费用，如地面运输、仓储、制单、清关等环节所产生的费用。

Other charges are fees charged by carriers, agents, or other departments related to the carriage of cargo by airlines, such as those incurred for ground transportation, storage, documentation, and customs clearance.

6.3.2　计费重量与运价构成（Chargeable Weight and Freight Composition）

在计算一笔航空货物运费时,要考虑三个因素:计费重量、有关的运价和费用、货物的声明价值。

计费重量是指用以计算航空运费的重量。货物的计费重量是货物的实际毛重,或者是货物的体积重量,或者是较高重量分界点的重量。

There are three factors to consider when calculating the freight for an air shipment: the chargeable weight, the relevant tariffs and charges, and the declared value of the cargo.

Chargeable weight refers to the weight used to calculate air freight. The chargeable weight of the goods is its actual gross weight or the measurement weight, or the weight at the higher weight breakpoint.

1. 实际毛重（Actual Gross Weight）

实际毛重又称实际重量,指包括货物包装在内的货物重量。当实际毛重用千克表示时,计费重量最小单位为 0.5 千克,超过 0.5 千克按 1 千克计算。一般情况下,对于高密度混合物,应考虑货物实际毛重可能会成为计费重量。

Actual gross weight, also known as actual weight, refers to the weight of goods including the packaging. When the actual gross weight is expressed in kilograms, the minimum unit of chargeable weight is 0.5 kilograms, and more than 0.5 kilograms are calculated in terms of one kilogram. Generally speaking, for high density goods, the actual gross weight of the goods may be the chargeable weight.

2. 体积重量（Measurement Weight）

按照国际航空运输协会规则,将货物的体积按一定的比例折合成的重量,称为体积重量。由于货仓空间的限制,一般对于低密度的货物,即轻泡货物,考虑其体积重量可能成为计费重量。

体积重量的计算方法如下。

(1) 分别测出货物最长、最宽、最高的部分,尾数采用四舍五入法。三者相乘得出体积。

(2) 将体积折算成重量。换算标准是每 6 000 立方厘米或 336 立方英尺折合成 1 千克。

$$体积重量(千克,kg)=货物体积/6\,000\ 立方厘米$$

According to the rules of IATA, the weight that is calculated by converting the volume of goods into a certain proportion is called measurement weight. Due to the limitation of cargo space, generally for low density goods, i.e. measurement goods, the measurement weight is considered as the possible chargeable weight.

The calculation method of measurement weight is as follows.

（1）Measure the longest，widest and highest parts of the goods respectively，with the mantissa rounded off，and then multiply the three together to obtain the volume.

（2）Convert volume to weight. The conversion rate is 1 kilogram per 6 000 cubic centimeters or per 336 cubic feet. （Every 6 000 cubic centimeters or 336 cubic feet is converted to 1 kilogram. ）

$$\text{measurement weight （kg）} = \text{cargo volume}/6\,000\ \text{cm}^3$$

3. 计费重量（Chargeable weight）

确定计费重量的一般原则是：计费重量按实际毛重和体积重量相比较，选择较高者。但当货物按较高重量分界点的较低运价计算所得航空运费较低时，则以较高重量分界点的货物起始重量作为货物的计费重量。

国际航空运输协会规定，计费重量最小单位为 0.5 千克。尾数不足 0.5 千克按 0.5 千克计算，尾数为 0.5 千克以上不足 1 千克的，按 1 千克计算。如 100.1 千克按 100.5 千克计收，100.6 千克按 101.0 千克计收；以磅表示重量时，计费重量最小单位为 1 磅。

The general principle for determining the chargeable weight is to compare the actual gross weight with the volumetric weight and select the higher as the chargeable weight. However，when the air freight is lower based on the lower freight rate at the higher weight demarcation point （breakpoint），the initial weight of the higher weight demarcation point is used as the chargeable weight of the cargo.

示例 6.1 计费重量计算例题

IATA stipulates that the minimum unit of chargeable weight is 0. 5 kg. If the mantissa is less than 0. 5 kg, it is counted as 0. 5 kg, and if the mantissa is greater than 0. 5 kg but less than 1 kg, it is counted as 1 kg. For example，100. 1 kg is charged by 100. 5 kg, 100. 6 kg by 101. 0 kg, and the smallest unit of weight charged by pounds is 1 pound.

4. 集中托运货物的计费重量（Chargeable Weight of Consolidation Consignment）

在做集中托运时，一批货物由几件不同的货物组成，有轻泡货物也有重货，其计费重量则采用整批货物的总毛重，或总的体积重量，按两者之中较高的一个计算。

In consolidation transport，a batch of goods consists of several different pieces of goods，measurement goods and weight goods，and its chargeable weight is calculated by the higher of gross weight or measurement weight of the whole batch of goods.

5. 航空运价的构成（Composition of Air Freight Rates）

一般情况下，航空运价中通常包含以下几部分：

（1）运费（航空公司收取）；

（2）燃油附加费（根据机场和目的地价格不同）；

（3）安检费；

（4）机场操作费（机场负责运货上飞机）；

（5）终端费用；

（6）航空主运单出单费。

Generally speaking，air freight rates usually include the following parts：

(1) Freight (charged by airlines)；

(2) Fuel surcharge (prices vary according to airport and destination)；

(3) Security inspection fee；

(4) Airport operating fee (airport is responsible for cargo boarding)；

(5) Terminal charges；

(6) Document fee for master air waybill。

6.3.3　航空运费的计算（Calculation of Air Freight ）

1. 公布直达运价（Published Through Rates）

它是指航空公司在运价本上直接注明承运人对从甲地运至乙地的货物收取的一定金额。

It is the airline's tariff which directly indicates the air transport price of goods from the airport of departure to the airport of destination。

1）公布直达运价的种类（Types of Published Through Rates）

（1）普通货物运价。普通货物运价是使用最广泛的一种运价。当一批货物不能适用特种货物运价，也不属于等级货物时，就应该使用一般货物运价。

通常，各航空公司公布的普通货物运价，针对所承运货物数量的不同，规定几个计费重量分界点。

① 45 千克（100 磅）以下，运价类别代号为 N。

② 45 千克以上（含 45 千克），运价类别代号为 Q。

③ 45 千克以上的，可根据航线货流量的不同，再规定 100 千克、300 千克、500 千克、1 000 千克、2 000 千克等多个重量分界点，但运价类别代号仍以 Q 表示。

运价的数额随运输货量的增加而降低是航空运价的显著特征之一。

(1) General cargo rates (GCR). General cargo rates are one of the most widely used freight rates. When a batch of goods cannot be applied to the special commodity rates and the commodity classification rates，the general cargo rates should be used.

Usually，in the general cargo rates published by the airlines，several chargeable weight breakpoints are specified for the different quantities of cargo carried.

① Under 45 kg (100 pounds)：the rate category code is N (normal rate)。

② More than 45 kilograms (including 45 kilograms)：the rate category code is Q (quantity rate)。

③ For cargo more than 45 kg，multiple weight breakpoints such as 100 kg, 300 kg, 500 kg, 1 000 kg and 2 000 kg can be further specified according to the different cargo flow of the routes，but the rate category code is still indicated by Q。

One of the distinctive features of air freight rates is that they decrease as the volume of goods transported increases.

（2）等级货物运价。等级货物运价是对某些特定商品在普通货物运价基础上进行提价或优惠的价格,通常表示为在普通货物运价的基础上增加或减少一定的百分比。

适用等级货物运价的货物通常有:

① 活动物、活动物的集装箱和笼子;

② 贵重物品;

③ 尸体或骨灰;

④ 报纸、杂志、书籍、商品目录、盲人和聋哑人专用设备等;

⑤ 作为货物托运的行李。

注:①～③项通常在普通货物运价的基础上增加一定百分比,运价代号为 S。④、⑤项在普通货物运价的基础上减少一定百分比,运价代号为 R。

(2) Class rates or commodity classification rates (CCR)。Commodity classification rates is a price increase or concession for some specific commodities on the basis of general cargo rate, usually expressed as a certain percentage increase or decrease on the basis of general cargo rate.

The goods applicable to the commodity classification rates are usually:

① Live animals and containers and cages for live animals;

② Valuable articles;

③ Corpses or ashes;

④ Newspapers, magazines, books and catalogues, special equipment for the blind and deaf;

⑤ Luggage consigned as goods.

Note: ① to ③ usually increases by a certain percentage on the basis of general cargo rates, and the rate code is S (surcharged rate). ④ and ⑤ reduces a certain percentage on the basis of general cargo rates, the rate code is R (rebates rate).

(3) 特种货物运价。特种货物运价又称指定货物运价,是指自指定的始发地至指定的目的地而公布的适用于特定货物、特定品名的低于普通货物运价的某些指定货物运价。

对于一些批量大、季节性强、单位价值小的货物,航空公司可制定指定商品运价,运价优惠幅度不限,报民航管理部门批准执行(代号 C),目的是吸引客户,使运力得到充分利用。特种货物运价比普通货物运价低,且必须达到承运人所规定的起码运量(如 100 千克)。

特种货物运价的计算步骤如下。

① 确定货物所要求的航线上是否有适用的特种货物运价。

② 查《航空货物运价及规则手册》上的"特种商品分类表",找出指定商品编号。

③ 查《航空货物运价及规则手册》,选择合适的运价。

④ 计算计费重量。

⑤ 计算运费。

若计费重量>SCR 最低重量,则优先使用 SCR,运费=计费重量×SCR。

若计费重量< SCR 最低重量,则需要进行比较:

按 GCR 计算运费,运费=计费重量×GCR。

按 SCR 计算运费,运费＝SCR 最低重量×SCR。

取二者中低者为最后运费。

（3）Specific commodity rates（SCR）. Specific commodity rates, also known as designated commodity rates, refer to the published freight rates of certain specified goods delivered from the designated place of departure to the designated destination, which are applicable to specific cargoes and are lower than the general cargo tariffs.

For some large-volume, seasonal, and small unit value cargoes, airlines can set specific commodity rates with unlimited tariff concessions and report to the civil aviation authorities for approval and implementation, the purpose of which is to attract customers and make full use of the shipping capacity. The specific commodity rate is lower than general cargo rates, and must reach the minimum volume (e. g. 100 kg) stipulated by the carrier, and the rate code is C.

The steps for calculating specific commodity rates are as follows.

① Determine whether there is an applicable specific commodity rate on the route requested by the cargo.

② Look up "Special Commodity Classification" on *TACT* (The Air Cargo Tariff and Rules) *rates books* and find out the number of the special commodity.

③ Check *TACT rates books* and select the appropriate tariff.

④ Calculate the chargeable weight.

⑤ Calculate the freight.

If chargeable weight ＞ SCR minimum weight, SCR is preferred, Freight ＝ chargeable weight×SCR.

If chargeable weight is less than the SCR minimum weight, a comparison is needed：

Calculate freight according to GCR, freight ＝ chargeable weight×GCR.

Calculate freight according to SCR, freight ＝ SCR minimum weight×SCR.

Take the lower of the two as the final freight.

（4）起码运费。起码运费是航空公司办理一票货物所能接受的最低限额,是航空公司在考虑办理即使很小的一批货物也会产生的固定费用后制定的。

航空公司通常规定无论运送的货物适用哪一种航空运价,运费总额都不得低于起码运费。若计算出的数值低于起码运费,则以起码运费计收。

（4）Minimum charges（M）. The minimum charge is the minimum that an airline can accept to handle a shipment and is set by the airline after considering the fixed costs that would be incurred in handling even a small shipment.

Airlines normally require that regardless of the air tariff applied to the cargo being transported, the total amount of freight must not be less than the minimum charge. If the calculated value is less than the minimum freight, the minimum freight will be charged.

2）集中托运货物运价（Rate of Consolidation Transport）

集中托运货物也称混运货物，指使用同一份货运单运输的货物中包含不同运价、不同运输条件的货物。

运费计算要注意以下方面。

（1）申报整批货物的总重量或总体积。当使用同一份运单，运送两件或两件以上可以采用同样种类运价计算运费的货物时，计费重量为货物总的实际毛重与总的体积重量两者较高者。较高重量分界点重量也可能成为货物的计费重量。

（2）分别申报每一类货物的件数、重量、体积及货物品名。

（3）声明价值。混运货物只能按整批货物办理声明价值，声明价值费应按整票货物的总毛重计算。

（4）最低运费。混运货物的最低运费按整票货物计收，即无论是分别申报或不分别申报的混运货物，按其运费计算方法所得的运费与起止地点间的最低收费标准比较，取高者。

Consolidation transport goods, also known as centralized consignment, refer to the goods transported using the same waybill that contain goods with different freight rates and different transport conditions.

Freight calculation should pay attention to the following aspects.

（1）Declare the total weight or volume of the entire shipment. When two or more pieces of goods can be transported at the same freight rate using the same waybill, the chargeable weight is the higher of the total actual gross weight and the total volume weight of the goods. Weight at the higher weight breakpoint may also become the chargeable weight of goods.

（2）Declare the quantity, weight, volume, and name of each kind of goods respectively.

（3）Declared value. The declared value of centralized shipping goods can only be calculated according to the whole batch of goods. Declared value fee should be calculated according to the gross weight of the whole batch of goods.

（4）Minimum freight. The minimum freight for mixed shipments is charged on the basis of the entire shipment, i. e. , whether the mixed shipment is declared separately or not. The freight will be charged at the higher of the calculated freight and the lowest rate between the point of origin and departure.

3）公布的直达运价的使用及特点（Use and Characteristics of Published Through Rates）

（1）除起码运费外，公布的直达运价都以千克或磅为单位；

（2）运价选择顺序：特种货物运价、等级货物运价、普通货物运价；

（3）实际重量或体积重量从高计收，如有最低运量，以最低运量为计收重量；

（4）运费少于起码运费时，以起码运费计收；

（5）公布的直达运价是一个机场至另一个机场的运价，而且只适用于单一方向；

（6）公布的直达运费仅指基本运费，不包含仓储等附加费；

（7）运价货币单位一般以起运地当地货币单位为准。

（1）Except minimum charges，the published through rates are in kilograms or pounds.

（2）The order of freight rate selection is：specific commodity rates，commodity classification rates，general cargo rates.

（3）The freight should be calculated based on the higher of actual or volumetric weight. If there is a minimum freight volume，it shall be taken as chargeable weight.

（4）When the freight is less than the minimum charge，it shall be charged at the minimum charge.

（5）The published through rate is from one airport to another and only applies to a single direction.

（6）The published through freight only refers to basic freight，excluding warehousing and other surcharges.

（7）The currency unit of freight is generally the local currency unit at the place of dispatch.

2. 非公布直达运价（Non-published Through Rates）

1）比例运价（Constructive Rates）

《航空货物运价及规则手册》除公布直达运价外，还公布一种不能单独使用的附加数。当货物的始发地或目的地无

示例 6.2　航空运费计算例题

公布直达运价时，可采用比例运价与已知的公布直达运价相加，构成非公布直达运价。

In addition to the published through rates，the *TACT rates books* also publishes an additional number that cannot be used alone（Add-On Amount）. When there are no published through rates at the place of departure or destination of the goods，the constructive rates can be added to the known published through rates to constitute a non-published through rates.

2）分段相加运价［Combination of Rates（Segmental Additive Rates）］

两地间既没有直达运价也无法利用比例运价时，可以在始发地与目的地之间选择合适的计算点，分别找到始发地至该点、该点至目的地的运价，两段运价相加组成全程的最低运价。

When there are neither through rates nor constructive rates between the two places，the appropriate calculation point can be selected between the place of departure and the destination，and the tariff from the place of departure to the point and from the point to the destination can be found respectively，then the lowest tariff for the whole journey can be formed by adding the two tariffs.

6.3.4　航空附加费（Air Surcharge）

1. 声明价值附加费（Declared Value Surcharge）

航空运输的承运人需要对货主承担一定程度的责任。《华沙公约》第 22 条对承运人的责任限额作出了规定：承运人对货物灭失、损害或延迟交货的责任以每千克 250 金法

郎为限。《蒙特利尔公约》采用特别提款权作为承运人的责任限额计算单位，其规定的责任限额为 17 特别提款权，约合 23 美元。

如果发货人要求在发生货损货差时全部赔偿，则在交运货物时，应向承运人或其代理声明货物的价值，该价值称为"供运输用的声明价值"，该声明价值是承运人应负赔偿责任的限额，承运人或其代理根据货物的声明价值向托运人收取一定的费用，该费用即为"声明价值附加费"。若无声明价值，承运人的最高赔偿金额不超过责任限额。

声明价值附加费的计算方法如下：

$$声明价值附加费＝（整批货物的声明价值－货物毛重×责任限额/千克）×$$
$$声明价值附加费费率（费率通常为 0.5\%）$$

示例 6.3　声明价值附加费计算例题

Carriers of air transportation are subject to a certain level of liability to the cargo owner. The twenty-second article of the *Warsaw Convention* stipulates the limitation of liability for carriers：the carrier's liability for loss，damage or delay in delivery is limited to 250 gold francs per kilogram. *The Montreal Convention* uses special drawing rights （SDRs） as the unit of calculation for the carrier's limit of liability，which is set at SDR 17，or approximately US \$ 23.

If the consignor requests full compensation in case of damage or loss to the goods，it shall declare the value of the goods to the carrier or his agent at the time of delivery，which is called "declared value for carriage". The declared value is the limit of the carrier's liability. The carrier or his agent charges the shipper a certain fee according to the declared value of the goods，which is called "declared value surcharge". In the absence of declared value，the maximum amount of compensation of the carrier shall not exceed the limit of liability.

The calculation method of declared value surcharge is as follows：

$$declared\ value\ surcharge＝（declared\ value\ of\ whole\ goods\ －$$
$$gross\ weight\ of\ goods\ ×\ limit\ of\ liability\ /\ kg）×$$
$$declared\ value\ surcharge\ rate\ （usually\ 0.5\%）$$

2．其他附加费（Other Surcharges）

其他附加费包括货到付款附加费、货运单费即制单费、中转手续费、地面运输费等，一般只有在承运人或航空货运代理人提供服务时才收取。

Other surcharges include charges collect fee，air waybill fee，transit charge，surface charge，etc.，which are generally charged only when the carrier or air freight forwarder provides services.

6.4　国际航空运输单据（International Air Transport Documents）

航空运单是由航空公司或其代理人在接受托运人委托，并接运货物之后，向托运人签发的证明货物已接收的收据，同时也是托运人与航空公司之间的运输合同。

Air waybill (AWB) is a receipt issued by the airline or its agent to the shipper after accepting the shipper's commission and taking over the goods to prove that the goods have been received, and it is also the contract of carriage between the shipper and the airline.

6.4.1　航空运单的性质(Nature of Air Waybill)

　　航空运单是航空运输必不可少的单据,是由承运人或其代理出具的重要的货运单据及货物收据。航空运单是托运人与承运人之间的运输合同,不同于海运提单,不是物权凭证,不能背书转让,但可凭以办理议付结汇;不能凭以提货,收货人只能凭"到货通知"办理提货。

　　因此,在无收款保证的情况下,应慎重考虑是否接受空运交货方式,且为保障收汇,采用空运方式出运货物,应尽量采用 L/C 结汇方式。空运单抬头一般为买方(开证人)或托收行、开证行,并印有"Not Negotiable"字样以明确单据性质。

　　我国的航空运单由中国民用航空局印制,由承运的航空公司或其代理人签发。航空运单由一式十二联组成,包括三联正本、六联副本和三联额外副本。

Air waybill is an essential document for air transportation, and an important freight document and cargo receipt issued by the carrier or its agent. Air waybill is a contract of carriage between shipper and carrier, but different from ocean bill of lading, it is not a document of title and cannot be endorsed for transfer, but it can be used for negotiation and settlement of foreign exchange; it cannot be used to pick up the goods, and the consignee can only pick up the goods with the "Notice of Arrival".

Therefore, in the absence of guarantee of collection, careful consideration should be given to the acceptance of air delivery, and in order to protect the collection of foreign exchange, when using air transport, L/C should be used as much as possible to settle foreign exchange. The consignee of the air waybill is usually the buyer (issuer), the collection bank, or the issuing bank, and the words "Not Negotiable" are printed to clarify the nature of the documents.

The air waybill in China is printed by the Civil Aviation Administration of China (CAAC) and issued by the airline or its agent that carries the cargo. The air waybill consists of twelve copies in one, including three originals, six copies, and three additional copies.

6.4.2　航空运单的作用(The Functions of Air Waybill)

1. 运输合同(Contract of Carriage)

　　航空运单不仅证明航空运输合同的存在,而且其本身就是发货人与航空承运人之间缔结的货物运输合同,在双方共同签署后产生效力,并在货物到达目的地交付给运单上所记载的收货人后失效。

Air waybill not only proves the existence of the contract of carriage by air, but is also the contract of carriage of goods concluded between the consignor and the air carrier，which comes into effect after the joint signature of both parties，and expires after the goods arrive at the destination and are delivered to the consignee as stated on the waybill.

2. 接收货物的证明（Proof of Receipt of Goods）

航空运单也是货物收据，在发货人将货物发运后，承运人或其代理人就会将第一份运单的正本交给发货人（即托运人），作为已经接收货物的证明。

Air waybill is also the receipt of goods. After the consignor ships the goods，the carrier or its agent will hand over the first original waybill to the consignor（i. e. the shipper）as proof of having received the goods.

3. 核收运费的账单（Bill for Freight Collecting）

航空运单分别记载着属于收货人负担的费用、应支付给承运人的费用和应支付给代理人的费用，并详细列明费用的种类。

The air waybill respectively records the expenses to be borne by the consignee，the expenses to be paid to the carrier and the agent，and details the types of charges.

4. 收货人核收货物的依据（Basis for Consignee to Check and Accept Goods）

第二份航空运单正本由航空公司随航班带交收货人，收货人据此核收货物。

The second original air waybill shall be delivered to the consignee by the airline along with the flight，and the consignee shall check and accept the goods accordingly.

5. 报关单据（Customs Declaration Document）

在货物到达目的地机场进行进口报关时，航空运单也通常是办理清关手续和海关查验放行的基本凭证。

When the goods arrive at the destination airport for import customs declaration，the air waybill is usually the basic credential for customs clearance and customs inspection and release.

6. 保险证书（Insurance Certificate）

如果发货人要求承运人代办货物运输保险，则航空运单经适当签注后可用作保险证书。

If the consignor requires the carrier to arrange the cargo transportation insurance，the air waybill can be used as the insurance certificate after being properly signed.

7. 承运人内部业务的依据（Basis of Carrier's Internal Operations）

航空运单是承运人办理该运单项下货物装运、转运、交付的依据，承运人根据运单上所记载的有关内容办理相关事宜。

The air waybill is the basis for the carrier to handle the shipment，forwarding and delivery of the goods under the waybill，and the carrier handles related matters according to the relevant content recorded on the waybill.

6.4.3　航空运单的种类（Type of Air Waybill）

航空运输主要包括两类承运人。

　　（1）航空运输公司。它是航空货物运输业务中的实际承运人，负责办理货物从起运机场至到达机场的运输业务，并对全程运输负责。

　　（2）航空货运代理公司。它具有货主代理和航空公司代理的双重身份，既负责办理空运货物的订舱、起讫机场间货物交接及进出口报关等事宜，又可在办理接货过程中，以航空承运人的身份签发航空运单，对运输过程负责。中外运长航在实际业务中就承担了航空货运代理公司的职责，目前它已与世界上许多国家和地区的货运代理公司建立了航空货运代理业务。

　　There are two types of carriers in air transportation.

　　（1）Air transport company. It is the actual carrier in the air cargo transportation business, responsible for handling the transportation of goods from the airport of origin to the airport of arrival, and is responsible for the entire transport.

　　（2）Air freight forwarder. It has the dual roles of agent for the cargo owner and agent for the airline. It is not only responsible for the booking of space for air transportation, the handover of goods between origin and destination airports and import and export declaration, but also for issuing air waybill as an air carrier in the process of receiving cargo, and is responsible for the transportation process. Sinotrans & CSC acts as an air freight forwarder in the actual business, and now it has established air freight forwarding business with freight forwarders in many countries and regions in the world.

　　由于两类承运人的存在，航空运单也有两类。

　　（1）航空主运单。航空主运单是由航空公司签发给作为航空运输合同承运人的航空运输代理（集中托运人）的货物收据，如中国民用航空局签发的空运单。它是航空运输公司据以办理货物运输和交付的依据，是航空公司和托运人订立的运输合同。每一批航空运输的货物都有自己相对应的航空主运单。

　　（2）航空分运单。航空分运单是航空货运代理公司办理集中托运业务时签发的航空运单，如中外运长航签发的空运单。航空分运单一般标注主运单和分运单的编号。在集中托运情况下，除了航空运输公司签发的航空主运单外，集中托运人还要签发航空分运单。

　　两类运单的内容基本相同，法律效力相当，对于收货人和发货人而言，只是承担货物运输的当事人不同。航空主运单作为航空公司与集中托运人之间的货物运输合同，当事人为集中托运人和航空公司，实际货主与航空公司没有直接合同关系。航空分运单作为集中托运人与实际货主之间的货物运输合同，合同双方分别为实际货主和集中托运人。

　　Corresponding to these two types of carriers, there are also two types of air waybills.

　　（1）Master airway bill. The master air waybill is the cargo receipt issued by the airline to the freight forwarder（the consolidator）as the carrier of the air transport contract, such as an air waybill issued by CAAC. It is the basis on which air transport companies handle the transport and delivery of goods, and the transport contract concluded between airlines and shippers. Each shipment of air transportation has its own corresponding master air waybill.

(2) House air waybill. It is the air waybill issued by the air freight agency when handling consolidation transport business, such as the air waybill issued by Sinotrans & CSC. The house air waybill generally indicates the number of the master waybill and the house waybill. In the case of consolidation transport, in addition to the master waybill issued by the air transport company, the consolidator shall also issue the house air waybill.

The contents of the two kinds of waybills are basically the same, and the legal effect is equivalent for the consignee and consignor, only the party responsible for the transport of goods is different. As the contract of carriage of goods between the airline and the centralized shipper, the parties to the master air waybill are the consolidator and the airline, and the actual cargo owner has no direct contractual relationship with the airline. The house air waybill is the contract of goods transportation between the consolidator and the actual shipper. The two parties of the contract are the actual shipper and the consolidator respectively. The house air waybill is the contract of carriage of goods between the consolidator and the actual shipper, while the parties involved are the actual shipper and the consolidator.

6.4.4　航空运单的缮制（Method of Making out Air Waybill）

各航空公司所使用的航空运单大多借鉴国际航空运输协会所推荐的标准格式，差别不大。航空运单通常的内容及缮制方法如下。

（1）航空运单号。运单的右上角印有航空运单号码，其中前三位是航空公司的代号，如中国国际航空公司代号为999，东方航空公司代号为781，北方航空公司代号为782，南方航空公司代号为784，西南航空公司代号为785。后面的数码是由航空公司填入的该运单的编号，通常由七位数字组成，第八位是检查号。

（2）航空公司的名称。此栏印有航空公司的全称和简称，如中国民用航空局（Civil Aviation Administration of China），简称CAAC。除此以外，还印有"Not Negotiable"字样明确表示航空运单是不可转让的。

（3）托运人名称、地址（Shippers Name and Address）及账号（Shipper's Account Number）。应填托运人全称、国名及地址，需要时加注账号。托运人一般为信用证的受益人或合同卖方，但对其他人作为托运人的单据，银行无权拒收，除非L/C明确禁止。

（4）收货人姓名、住址（Consignee's Name and Address）。填写收货人姓名、地址所在国家及联络方法。与海运提单不同，因为航空运单不可转让，所以"凭指示"之类的字样不得出现。

（5）承运人的代理人名称及所在城市（Issuing Carrier's Agent Name and City）。它是指货运代理人的名称及所在城市。

（6）代理人的国际航空运输协会代号（Agent's IATA Code）。按实际情况填写，亦可不填。

（7）会计事项（Accounting Information）。填托运人账号、信用卡号、费用结算等有关会计事务方面的内容。只有在采用特殊付款方式时，才填写。

（8）始发站机场及所要求的航线（Airport of Departure and Requested Routing）。该栏填写始发站机场和预订的航空路线。始发站机场需填写国际航空运输协会统一制定的机场或城市的三字代码；实际运输时，承运人可改变航行路线，但运费按规定的路线收取。

（9）中转站及承运人。

9A（C、E）：去往（To）：分别填入第一（二、三）中转站机场的国际航空运输协会代码。

9B（D、F）：承运人（By）：分别填入第一（二、三）程运输的承运人。

（10）币别（Currency）。填写支付运费的 ISO 货币代号，如 RMB、USD 等。

（11）运费及声明价值费（Weight Charge/Valuation Charge，WT/VAL）。根据实际情况选项。其中，PPD＝prepaid，COLL＝collect，若为预付情况，则在"PPD"栏内注"×"号或填写"PP"；若属代付，则在"COLL"栏内注"×"号或填写"C"。需要注意的是，航空货物运输中的运费与声明价值费的支付方式必须一致，不能分别支付。

（12）其他费用支付方法栏（Other PPD or COLL）。其也有预付和到付两种支付方式，填具方法同（11）。

（13）运输声明价值（Declared Value for Carriage）。在此栏填入发货人要求的用于运输的声明价值。如果发货人不要求声明价值，则填入"NVD"（no value declared）。

（14）海关声明价值（Declared Value for Customs）。发货人在此栏填入对海关的声明价值，或者填入"NCV"（no customs valuation），表明没有声明价值。

（15）目的地机场（Airport of Destination）。填写最终目的地机场的全称。

（16）航班及日期（Flight/Date）。填入货物所搭乘航班及日期。

（17）保险金额（Amount Insured）。只有在航空公司提供代保险业务而客户也有此需要时，才填写。

（18）操作信息（Handling Information）。一般填入承运人对货物处理的有关注意事项，如"Shipper's Certification for Live Animals"（托运人提供活动物证明）等。

（19）19A～19I 项是货物运价和运费细节。

19A：货物件数和运价组成点（No. of Pieces RCP，Rate Combination Point）：填入货物包装件数，如 10 包即填"10"。当需要组成比例运价或分段相加运价时，在此栏填入运价组成点机场的国际航空运输协会代码。

19B：毛重（Gross Weight）：填入货物总毛重。

19C：重量单位：可选择千克（kg）或磅（lb）。

19D：运价等级（Rate Class），针对不同的航空运价共有六种代码，它们是 M（minimum，起码运费）、C（specific commodity rates，特种货物运价）、S（surcharge，高于普通货物运价的等级货物运价）、R（reduced，低于普通货物运价的等级货物运价）、N（normal，45 千克以下货物适用的普通货物运价）、Q（quantity，45 千克以上货物）。

19E：商品代码（Commodity Item No.），在使用特种货物运价时，填写国际航空运输协会制定的特种商品运价编号。按 45 千克以下普通货物运价的百分比收费的，则分别填

50％、100％或 200％字样。

19F：计费重量（Chargeable Weight）：此栏填入航空公司据以计算运费的计费重量。

19G：运价（Rate/Charge）：填入该货物适用的费率。

19H：运费总额（Total），此栏数值应为起码运费值或者运价与计费重量两栏数值的乘积。

19I：货物的品名、数量，含尺码或体积（Name and Quantity of Goods，Incl. Dimensions of Volume），货物的尺码应以厘米或英寸为单位，尺寸分别以货物最长、最宽、最高边为基础。体积则是上述三边的乘积，单位为立方厘米或立方英寸。

（20）预付费用（Prepaid）。预付费用指托运人在取得运单前已支付的各项费用，包括预付的重量运费（Weight Charges）、预付的价值运费（Valuation Charge）、预付的税款（Tax）、代理人要求预付的其他费用之和（Total Other Charges Due Carrier）、预付的费用总额（Total Pre-Paid）、货币兑换率（Currency Conversion Rates）等。

（21）到付费用（Collect）。到付费用指收货人在提货时支付的各项费用。

（22）其他费用（Other Charges）。这是指除运费和声明价值附加费以外的其他费用。根据国际航空运输协会的规则，各项费用分别用三个英文字母表示。其中，前两个字母是某项费用的代码，如运单费表示为 AW（airway bill fee）。第三个字母是 C 或 A，分别表示费用应支付给承运人（carrier）或货运代理人（agent）。

（23）签发日期和地点［Executed on（Date）at Place］。签发日期应与"起航日期"栏内容一致。若运单上未载明起航日期，则签发日期视为出口商交货日期，不得迟于合同或 L/C 的最迟交货期。签发地点为始发站所在地。

单据 6.1 航空托运单

单据 6.2 航空运单

（24）货币兑换汇率（Currency Conversion Rates）。

（25）到付货物运费（Charges in Des. Currency）（目的地机场收费记录）。

（26）发货人或其代理签字（Signature of Shipper or his Agent）。

以上内容不一定要全部填入空运单，国际航空运输协会也并未反对在运单中写入其他所需内容。但这种标准化的单证对提高航空货运经营人工作效率、促进航空货运业向电子商务的方向迈进有着积极的意义。

6.5　有关航空货运的国际公约（International Conventions Related to Air Transport）

航空货物运输的产生、发展伴随着调整这种运输方式的国际公约的产生与发展。由于航空业发展历史较短，其吸收了海运等其他运输方式有关国际公约、惯例的精神，并根据自身特点作出了修改。有影响力的国际航空运输公约包括《华沙公约》（1929 年）、《海牙议定书》（1955 年）、《瓜达拉哈拉公约》（1961 年）、《危地马拉议定书》（1971 年）、《蒙特利尔第一号-第四号附加议定书》（1975 年）等。其中《华沙公约》是最基本的，随后的各项议定书都是对《华沙公约》的补充或修改,所以,这几份文件又被合称为华沙体系。《华沙公约》和《海牙议定书》的适用范围最广,已经为世界大多数国家所认可。《华沙公约》和《海牙议定书》的有关规定如下。

The emergence and development of air cargo transportation was accompanied by the emergence and development of international conventions regulating this mode of transport. Due to the short history of the airline industry, it was able to absorb the spirit of international conventions and practices related to other modes of transport, such as maritime transport, and make modifications according to its own characteristics. Influential international air transport conventions include: *Warsaw Convention* (1929), *Hague Protocol* (1955), *Guadalajara Convention* (1961), *Guatemala Protocol* (1971), *Montreal Additional Protocol No.*1-4 (1975), etc. Of these, the *Warsaw Convention* is the most fundamental, and the subsequent protocols are the supplement or amendment to the *Warsaw Convention*. Thus, these documents are also collectively known as the Warsaw System. The relevant provisions of the *Warsaw Convention* and *Hague Protocol* are as follows.

6.5.1　公约的适用范围(Scope of Application of the Convention)

公约不仅适用于商业性的国际航空货物运输,还适用于包括旅客、行李在内的其他取酬和免费国际航空运输,但不适用于邮件和邮包运输。

The convention applies not only to commercial international air cargo transportation, but also to other paid and free international air transportation including passengers and baggage, but not to mail and parcel transportation.

6.5.2　航空货运单的性质(Nature of Air Waybill)

航空货运单是订立运输合同、接收货物和接受运输条件的初步证据。

AWB is the preliminary evidence for the conclusion of a contract of carriage, acceptance of goods and conditions of carriage.

6.5.3　航空运输期间(Period of Air Transportation)

《华沙公约》第18(1)条规定:"对于任何已登记的行李或货物因毁灭、遗失或损坏而产生的损失,如果造成这种损失的事故是发生在航空运输期间,承运人应负责任。"承运人的责任期间是"不论在航空站内,在航空器上或在航空站外降停的任何地点"。但对于在机场外陆运、海运或河运过程中发生的货物的灭失或损坏,只有当这种运输是为了履行航空运输合同,或者是为了装货、交货或转运时,承运人才予以负责。

Article 18(1) of the *Warsaw Convention* provides: "The carrier is liable for damage sustained in the event of the destruction or loss of, or damage to, any registered baggage, if the occurrence which caused the damage so sustained took place during the carriage by air." The period of responsibility of the carrier is "whether in the air terminal，on board the aircraft or at any place of landing outside the air terminal". However，the carrier is responsible for loss of or damage to the goods during land，sea，or river transportation outside the airport only if such transportation is for the purpose of fulfilling the contract of carriage by air，or for loading，delivery or transit.

6.5.4　承运人责任（Carrier's Liability）

采用推定过失原则，即一旦出现货物损失，首先假定承运人有过失，但如果承运人能够举证说明自己并无过失，则不必负责。与海运公约不同，《华沙公约》明确规定了承运人对货物运输过程中"因延迟而造成的损失应负责任"。

The principle of presumption of fault is adopted，that is，once the loss of goods occurs，the carrier is first assumed to be at fault，but if the carrier can prove that he is not at fault，he is not responsible. Unlike the maritime convention，*Warsaw Convention* clearly stipulates that the carrier is responsible for "losses caused by delay" in the course of the carriage of goods.

6.5.5　发货人、收货人的权利与义务（Rights and Obligations of the Consignor and Consignee）

《华沙公约》第 12 条规定："在履行运输合同规定的所有义务的前提下，发货人有权通过以下方式处置货物：在出发地或目的地机场提取货物，或在运输途中的任何着陆点截留货物，或要求在目的地或在运输途中将货物交付给航空货运单指定的收货人以外的人，或要求将货物运回始发机场。托运人在行使这一处置权时不得损害承运人或其他发货人的利益，且必须偿付因行使这一权利而产生的一切费用。"

扩展阅读 6.2 《华沙公约》

扩展阅读 6.3 《海牙议定书》

扩展阅读 6.4 《蒙特利尔公约(1999)》

扩展阅读 6.5 Montreal convention 4

Article 12 of the *Warsaw Convention* provides："subject to his liability to carry out all his obligations under the contract of carriage，the consignor has the right to dispose of the cargo by withdrawing it at the airport of departure or destination，or by stopping it in the course of the journey on any landing，or by calling for it to be delivered at the place of destination or in the course of the journey to a person other than the consignee originally designated，or by requiring it to be returned to the air port of departure. He must not exercise this right of disposition in such a way as to prejudice the carrier or other consignors and he must repay any expenses occasioned by the exercise of this right. "

6.5.6　索赔和诉讼时效（Statute of Limitations for Claims and Lawsuits）

对于货物损害，《华沙公约》规定索赔时效为 7 天；《海牙议定书》延长至 14 天。对于货物延迟,《华沙公约》规定索赔时效为 14 天;《海牙议定书》延长至 21 天。诉讼时效为两年。

For damage to goods, the *Warsaw Convention* provides a limitation period of 7 days for claims; the *Hague Protocol* extends it to 14 days. For delay of goods, the *Warsaw Convention* provides a time limitation of 14 days for claims; the *Hague Protocol* extends it to 21 days. The statute of limitations is two years.

Words and Expressions

即测即练

习题

实训操作

国际铁路货物运输
International Railroad Cargo Transport

Learning Objectives：

1. Know the overview and trends of international railroad transport development；
2. Know the main railroad lines and national border stations to neighboring countries in China；
3. Understand the characteristics and role of international railroad cargo through transport；
4. Master the relevant regulations of international railroad cargo through transport；
5. Master the calculation and collection of international railroad through transport costs；
6. Understand the characteristics of railroad cargo transportation from Chinese Mainland to Hong Kong，China.

引导案例

铁路运输在中欧贸易中的应用

在"一带一路"倡议的引领下，中国铁路依托新亚欧大陆桥和西伯利亚大陆桥两条重要通道，在早期尝试开通亚欧国际列车的基础上，逐步实现了中欧班列、中亚班列、中老班列等多条线路的常态化运营，为亚欧大陆的互联互通和"一带一路"建设的推进打开了新局面。中欧班列作为国际陆路运输的新型组织方式，为亚欧国际贸易提供了除海运、空运之外的跨境物流新选择。根据《中欧班列发展报告（2021）》，中欧班列运输费用约是空运的 1/5，运输时间约是海运的 1/4，综合考虑高附加值货物在途时间成本，中欧班列与传统的海铁联运相比可以节约 8%～20% 综合物流成本，且具有受自然环境影响小、稳定性高的特点，在满足高附加值、强时效性等特定物流需求方面具有比较优势。根据国铁集团发布的数据，2023 年，中欧班列开行超 1.75 万列、发送 190.1 万标箱，同比分别增长 6%、18%。从开行列数上看，中欧班列已经走过了头三四年不足 100 列的摸索期，经历了 2014—2021 年"狂飙式"的高速增长期，步入自 2022 年开始的平稳发展阶段。其中，2023 年去程 9 343 列、回程 8 180 列，去回程比为 1.142∶1，延续整体上的去回程基本平衡。俄乌冲突爆发以来，中欧班列在俄罗斯、白俄罗斯、波兰、德国等主要国家间的运行依然稳定。

由于欧洲制裁和俄罗斯提高北方走廊的过境费用,该走廊的铁路运输量急剧下滑,但仍有绕道、转港等措施,可以改用中间走廊的海铁联运路线或者从伊朗过境的中欧班列南线。俄乌冲突发生后,中间走廊和南线的运输量激增,中欧之间的贸易往来和投资协定合作没有遭受显著冲击。

资料来源:中欧班列 2023 年开行突破 1.7 万列　新年迎来新机遇[EB/OL]. (2024-03-05). https://baijiahao. baidu. com/s?id=1792678633890506837&wfr=spider&for=pc.

7.1　国际铁路货物运输概述(Overview of International Railroad Cargo Transport)

7.1.1　国际铁路运输发展概况(Overview of International Railroad Transport Development)

铁路运输是现代运输业的重要运输方式之一,在国际货物运输中,尤其是在陆上接壤的国家之间的贸易中起着无可替代的作用。根据国际铁路联盟的统计,2022 年全球铁路总里程数达 115.27 万公里,全球铁路货运量为 116 942.46 亿吨公里。[①] 世界铁路分布极不平衡,美洲约占 24%,欧洲约占 28%,亚洲和中东合占约 32%,非洲只占 7%。[②] 根据世界银行的数据,铁路里程最长的依次为美国、中国、俄罗斯、印度、加拿大等。[③]

Railroad transportation is one of the most important modes of modern transportation and plays an irreplaceable role in international cargo transportation, especially in trade between countries bordering on land. According to the International Union of Railways (UIC), in 2022, the total global railroad mileage reached 1 152 700 kilometers, and the global railroad freight volume was 11 694. 246 billion tons kilometers. The distribution of the world's railroads is highly unbalanced, with the Americas accounting for about 24 percent, Europe for about 28 percent, Asia and the Middle East together for about 32 percent, and Africa for only 7 percent. According to the World Bank, the countries with the longest railroad mileage are, in order: the United States, China, Russia, India, Canada, etc.

铁路货物运输的发展趋势是重载化、快捷化与物流化。重载运输已被国际公认为铁路货运发展的方向,成为世界铁路发展的重要趋势。在一些幅员辽阔、资源丰富、煤炭矿石等大宗货物运量大的国家,重载运输发展尤为迅速,如美国、加拿大、巴西、澳大利亚、南非等。由于采用长大列车和载重列车,运输效率大大提高,运输成本大大降低;同时,为满足货主对货物时效性越来越高的要求,发展快捷货物运输已成为世界铁路发展的必然趋势。如法国货运列车的最高设计速度可达 160 千米/小时;日本铁路货物列车全部实

---

① 2023 年全球铁路工程建设现状分析:铁路总里程约为 115.27 万公里[EB/OL]. (2023-04-07). https://www. gonyn. com/industry/1398864. html.

② 国际铁路联盟(UIC). Railway Statistics Synopsis 2024[Z]. 2024.

③ 世界银行. 铁路(总公里数)[EB/OL]. https://data. worldbank. org. cn/indicator/IS. RRS. TOTL. KM.

现了直达运输,开行直达货物列车和集装箱直达列车,直达列车的最高速度为 110 千米/小时以上;美国铁路快速运输系统中,部分路段的最高限速可达 129 千米/小时,特殊线路的最高限速可以达到 145 千米/小时。此外,为应对其他运输方式的竞争,国外铁路纷纷采取货运物流化战略,开展公铁联运,提供全程一站式物流服务。

The development trend of railroad freight transportation is heavy-haul, fast, and logistic. Heavy-haul transport has been internationally recognized as the direction of railroad freight development, becoming an important trend in the development of the world's railroads. In some countries with vast territory, rich resources, and large freight volume of coal, ore and other bulk cargo, heavy-haul transportation is developing especially rapidly, such as in the United States, Canada, Brazil, Australia, and South Africa. The transport efficiency is greatly improved and the transport costs are greatly reduced due to the use of long trains and load trains; at the same time, in order to meet the increasingly high requirements of cargo owners for transport timeliness, the development of fast cargo transportation has become an inevitable trend in the development of the world's railroads. For example, the maximum design speed of freight trains in French can reach 160 km/h; all Japanese railroad freight trains have realized direct transportation, running direct freight trains and direct container trains, with a maximum speed of 110 km/h or more; the maximum speed limit on some sections of the U. S. railway rapid transit system can be as high as 129 km/h, and the maximum speed limit on special railroad can be as high as 145 km/h. In addition, in order to cope with the competition of other modes of transport, foreign railroads have taken freight logistics strategy to carry out road-railway intermodal transport, to provide complete one-stop logistics services.

我国铁路事业发展迅速,1997—2007 年间实现 6 次大提速,时速 200 公里及以上的线路延展里程达 6 003 公里,时速 250 公里的线路延展里程达到 846 公里,标志着中国铁路已跻身世界先进铁路行列。[①] 2023 年,全国铁路货运总发送量完成 50.35 亿吨,比 2022 年增加 0.51 亿吨,增长 1.0%。全国铁路货运总周转量完成 36 460.39 亿吨公里,比上年增加 514.70 亿吨公里,增长 1.4%。截至 2023 年底,我国铁路营业里程已达到 15.9 万公里。其中,高速铁路营业里程达到 4.5 万公里,电气化率达到 73.8%。全国铁路路网密度 165.2 公里/万平方公里。[②]

In recent years, China's railroad business has achieved rapid development. Between 1997 and 2007, China realized six railroad speed-ups, with the mileage of lines with speeds of 200 kilometers per hour and above extending to 6 003 kilometers, and the mileage of lines with speeds of 250 kilometers per hour extending to 846 kilometers,

---

① 1997 年以来铁路六次大提速情况回顾［EB/OL］.（2011-08-11）. https://finance. sina. com. cn/roll/20110811/143710301174. shtml.

② 国家铁路局.2023 年铁道统计公报［Z］.2023.

marking that China's railroads have ranked among the world's advanced railroads. In 2023, the total volume of freight transported by China's railroads reached 5.035 billion tons, an increase of 0.051 billion tons, or 1.0%, over the previous year. The total turnover of railroad freight reached 3 646.039 billion tons kilometers, an increase of 51.47 billion tons kilometers, or 1.4%, over the previous year. By the end of 2023, the operating mileage of China's railroads had reached 159 000 km, of which the operating mileage of high-speed railroads had reached 45 000 km, with the electrification rate reaching 73.8%. The density of the national railroad network is 165.2 kilometers per 10 000 square kilometers.

我国拥有 2.2 万多千米的陆地边界,与 14 个国家接壤,其中有 8 个国家是没有出海口的内陆国家。我国与 6 个邻国有 14 个边界口岸可由国际铁路通道接轨:与俄罗斯接轨的满洲里、绥芬河、珲春、同江铁路口岸;与蒙古国接轨的二连浩特、策克口岸;与哈萨克斯坦接轨的阿拉山口、霍尔果斯口岸;与越南接轨的凭祥、河口口岸;与朝鲜接轨的丹东、集安、图们(暂停运营)口岸;与老挝接轨的磨憨口岸。我国与周边国家的货物进出口主要经由上述国际铁路通道进行。

With a land border of more than 22 000 kilometers, China shares borders with 14 countries, including 8 landlocked countries. China has 14 border railway ports connected via international railroad with six neighboring countries: the ports of Manzhouli, Suifenhe, Hunchun, and Tongjiang railway linked to Russia; Erenhot and Ceke ports connected to Mongolia; Alashankou and Khorgos ports interfacing with Kazakhstan; Pingxiang and Hekou ports adjoining Vietnam; Dandong, Jian, and Tumen ports (currently suspended) bordering Democratic People's Republic of korea; and the Mohan port integrated with Laos. The import and export of goods between China and neighboring countries are mainly carried out through the above-mentioned international railway lines.

7.1.2　国际货物铁路运输的特点(Characteristics of International Freight Rail Transport)

铁路运输的优点表现在:运行速度较快,载运量较大,运输成本低且在运输中遭受的风险较小,它一般能保持终年正常运行,受气候影响小,具有高度的连续性。

The advantages of railway transport are as follows: faster delivery, higher capacity, lower costs, and less risk in transit. It can generally maintain normal operation all year round, and is less affected by climate, with a high degree of continuity.

铁路运输的缺点则表现在:运费没有伸缩性;不能采取门对门服务;车站固定,不能随处停车;货物滞留时间长,不适宜紧急运输;机动性差,只能在固定线路上运行;初始投资成本远高于其他运输方式。

The disadvantages of railroad transportation are: no scalability of freight rates; no door-to-door service; fixed stations, unable to stop anywhere; long detention time of cargoes and therefore unsuitable for emergency transportation; poor mobility and operation only on fixed routes; much higher initial investment costs than other transport modes.

　　按照我国铁路技术条件，现行的铁路货物运输分为整车、零担和集装箱三种。整车适于运输大宗货物；零担适于运输少量的零星货物；集装箱适于运输精密、贵重、易损的货物。

　　According to the technical conditions of China's railroads, current kind of railroad freight transportation is divided into full-car-load(FCL), less-than-carload(LCL), and container. FCL is suitable for transporting bulk cargo; LCL is suitable for transporting small amount of sporadic cargo; container is suitable for transporting precise, valuable and fragile cargo.

7.1.3　中国通往邻国的铁路干线及国境车站（Railway Lines and Border Stations From China to Neighboring Countries）

　　目前，中国通往邻国的铁路干线主要包括滨洲线、滨绥线、集二线、沈丹线、长图线、梅集线、湘桂线、昆河线等，具体情况见表 7-1。中俄、中蒙铁路轨距不同，货物需换装。油罐车在蒙铁扎门乌德国境站换装。中朝铁路轨距相同，货车可以直接过轨。

　　At present, China's main railroad lines to neighboring countries mainly include: Binzhou line, Binsui line, Jier line, Shendan line, Changtu line, Meiji line, Xianggui line, Kunhe line, etc. Details are shown in table 7-1. China-Russia and China-Mongolia railroads have different gauges, and the cargoes need to be reloaded. The oil tank trains are changed at Zamen-Ude border station of Mongolian railway. The China-North Korea railway has the same gauge, and trains can pass through the tracks directly.

表 7-1　我国通往邻国的铁路干线、国境站站名、轨距及换装地点

中国与邻国	我国铁路干线	我国国境站站名	邻国国境站站名	我国轨距/毫米	邻国轨距/毫米	交接、换装地点	
						出口	进口
中俄	滨洲线	满洲里	后贝加尔	1 435	1 520	后贝加尔	满洲里
	滨绥线	绥芬河	格罗迭科沃	1 435	1 520	格罗迭科沃	绥芬河
	珲马线（珲春—马哈利诺）	珲春	卡梅绍瓦亚	1 435	1 520	卡梅绍瓦亚	珲春
	同江中俄黑龙江铁路大桥	同江北站	下列宁斯阔耶	1 435	1 520	下列宁斯阔耶	同江北站
中哈	北疆铁路	阿拉山口	多斯特克	1 435	1 520	多斯特克	阿拉山口
	精伊霍铁路	霍尔果斯	阿腾科里	1 435	1 520	阿腾科里	霍尔果斯
中蒙	集二线	二连浩特	扎门乌德	1 435	1 524	扎门乌德	二连浩特
	临策铁路	策克	西伯库伦	1 435	1 435	西伯库伦	策克
中朝	沈丹线	丹东	新义州	1 435	1 435	新义州	丹东
	长图线	图们	南阳	1 435	1 435	南阳	图们
	梅集线	集安	满浦	1 435	1 435	满浦	集安
中越	湘桂线	凭祥	同登	1 435	1 435/1 000	同登	凭祥
	昆河线	山腰	老街	1 000	1 000	老街	山腰
中老	中老铁路	磨憨	磨丁	1 435	1 435	磨丁	磨憨

7.2　国际铁路货物联运（International Railroad Through Transport of Goods）

国际铁路货物联运是指两个或两个以上不同国家铁路当局联合起来完成一票货物的铁路运送。它全程使用一份统一的国际联运单据,由铁路部门负责经过两国或两个以上国家铁路的全程运输,并且在由一国铁路向另一国铁路移交货物时不需发货人和收货人参加。

International rail freight intermodal transport means that railway authorities of two or more different countries jointly complete the rail transport of a shipment of goods. It uses a unified international intermodal transport document throughout the entire process, and the railroads are responsible for the entire transport through the railroads of two or more countries, and do not require the participation of the consignor and consignee when handing over the goods from one country's railroads to another.

7.2.1　国际铁路联运的特点（The Characteristics of International Railroad Through Transport）

1. 涉及面广（Involving a Wide Range of Areas）

按国际联运办理的货物运输,须经过发送国铁路发站、出口国境站、到达国的进口国境站和终点站,有时还要通过第三国过境站。此外,还要与海关、检验检疫、保险、银行、代理机构打交道,同时各国的规章制度又比较多,所以手续复杂。

International railroad through transport not only involves railways, stations, and border stations in several countries, but also involves foreign trade, customs, commodity inspection and quarantine, insurance, banking, agency, and other aspects. At the same time, there are different rules and regulations in various countries, so the procedures are complicated.

2. 标准较高（Higher Standards）

国际铁路联运参加国多,涉及多个国家的铁路、车站和过境站,这就要求每批货物的办理质量必须是高标准、严要求,符合有关规章和协议的规定,否则将造成货损、货差、延迟交货等运输事故。

As there are many countries participating in international railroad through transport, involving railroads, stations, and transit stations of many countries, it requires that the quality of handling each batch of goods must be of high standard and strict requirements, in line with relevant regulations and agreements, otherwise it will cause cargo damage, cargo loss, delayed delivery, and other transport accidents.

3. 运输时间短,成本低（Short Transportation Time and Low Cost）

由于国际铁路联运的始发站和最终目的站大多是内陆车站,使用发、收货人的铁路专用线,货物直接从发货人的专用线或就近车站出发,到达收货人的专用线或就近的车站,从而使运输时间比海运短、运输成本比海运低。这在从中国内陆发往伊朗、阿富汗、东欧、芬兰以及相反方向的货物运输上表现得特别明显。

As most of the departure and final destination stations of international railway through transport are inland stations, using the special railway lines of the consignor and consignee, the goods directly depart from the special line of the consignor or the nearest station and reach the special line of the consignee or the nearest station, thus making the transport time shorter than that of sea transport and the transport cost lower than that of sea transport. This is particularly evident for cargoes shipped from China's interior to Iran, Afghanistan, Eastern Europe, Finland and in the opposite direction.

4. 责任统一(Uniform Liability)

国际铁路联运仅使用铁路一种运输方式,使用一份铁路联运票据,运输责任采用统一责任制。

International railroad through transport uses only the mode of transport by rail, uses one railroad through transport document, and adopts unified liability system for transport responsibility.

7.2.2 国际铁路联运的作用(The Role of International Railroad Through Transport)

国际铁路联运的开办为参加国开辟了一条重要的国际贸易渠道,发挥了其应有的作用,具体表现如下:

(1) 免除了货物在过境站重新办理托运的手续,火车可以过轨运输;

(2) 减少了因换装所需的人力、物力、财力和时间;

(3) 减少了货损、货差,降低了运费;

(4) 欧亚各国(地区)铁路联运有利于各国(地区)经济交往。

The opening of international railroad through transport has opened up an important channel of international trade for the participating countries and plays its due role, which is manifested as follows:

(1) It eliminates the need to re-check the consignment of goods at the transit station, and the train can directly cross the track for transportation;

(2) It reduces the manpower, material resources, financial resources, and time required for changing;

(3) It reduces cargo losses and differences, and lowers freight costs;

(4) The through transport of railroads in Eurasian countries(regions) is beneficial to the economic interaction between countries (regions).

7.2.3 国际铁路货物联运的有关规章(Regulations Related to International Railroad Through Transport of Goods)

世界各国对铁路的客货运输组织非常重视,特别是在国际贸易中,通过国家之间的协商,订立了各种协定,建立了协约组织。各铁路局和国境站以及发货人、收货人在办理国际铁路货物联运业务时,必须遵循国际铁路货物运输的有关规章。

Countries of the world attach great importance to the organization of passenger and cargo transportation by railroads，especially in international trade，and through consultations between countries，various agreements have been concluded and concordant organizations have been established. The railroad bureaus and national border stations，as well as the consignor and consignee，must follow the relevant regulations on international railroad cargo transportation，when handling international railroad through transport of goods operations.

（1）《国际铁路货物联运协定》（简称《国际货协》）：对运输合同的缔结、履行和变更、铁路的责任、收发货人的权利与义务作出了规定。

（1）*Agreement on International Railroad Through Transport of Goods*（SMGS）：it regulates the conclusion，performance，and modification of the contract of carriage，the liability of the railroad，as well as the rights and obligations of the consignee and consignor.

（2）《国际货协统一过境运价规程》（简称《统一货价》）：规定了利用铁路运送过境货物时，办理货物运送的手续、过境运送费用的计算、货物品名分等表、过境里程表和货物运费计算表等内容，对铁路和发货人、收货人都适用。

（2）*Uniform Transit Tariff Regulations of* SMGS：it stipulates the procedures for handling cargo delivery，calculation of transit delivery charges，cargo classification tables，transit mileage tables，and cargo freight calculation tables when using railroads to deliver transit cargo，which are applicable to railroads，consignors，and consignees.

（3）《国境铁路协定》和《国境铁路会议议定书》：《国境铁路协定》是由相邻国家签订的，规定了办理联运货物交接的国境站、车站及货物交接条件和方法、交接列车和机车运行办法及服务方法等内容。根据该协定，两个相邻国家铁路定期召开国境铁路会议，对执行协定中的有关问题进行协商，签订《国境铁路会议议定书》。我国分别与俄罗斯、蒙古国、越南各铁路签订了国境铁路协定和议定书。

（3）*Agreement on Frontier Railroads* and *Protocol to the Conference on Frontier Railroads*：*Agreement on Frontier Railroads*，signed by neighboring countries，stipulates the conditions and methods of border stations and railway stations for the transfer of goods，and operation and service methods of trains and locomotives for the transfer of goods. According to the agreement，the two neighboring countries held a border railway conference regularly to discuss issues related to the implementation of the agreement，and signed the *Protocol to the Conference on Frontier Railroads*. China has signed frontier railroad agreements and protocols with Russia，Mongolia and Vietnam respectively.

7.2.4　国际铁路货物联运的范围（Scope of International Railroad Through Transport of Goods）

1. 同参加国际货协或未参加但采用"国际货协"规定的铁路间的货物运送（Freight Between Railways Participating in SMGS or not Participating but Using the Provisions of SMGS）

国际货协铁路间的货物运输使用一份运单，在发货站发运，由铁路在最终到达站将货物交付收货人。在同一铁路轨距国家间,用发送国原列车直接过轨;在不同轨距国家间,则在换装站或国境站进行换装或更换另一轨距的货车轮对或使用变距轮对。在铁路不连接的国际货协参加国铁路之间,其货物运送可通过参加国某一车站运用其他运输工具转运。

When cargo is transported between railroads participating in SMGS, it is shipped from the consignment station using one waybill, and delivered by the railroad to the consignee at the final arrival station. Between countries of the same railroad gauge, the original train of the sending country is used to cross the track directly; between countries of different gauges, the transshipment or replacement of wagon wheels of another gauge or the use of variable gauge wheels is carried out at the transfer station or border station. Between railroads of SMGS participating countries which are not connected by railroads, their cargo can be transferred by using other means of transport at one of the stations of the participating countries.

2. 同未参加国际货协铁路间的货物运送（Cargo Transportation Between Railroads of SMGS Participating Countries and Non-participating Countries）

发货人在发送路用国际货协运送票据办理至参加国际货协的最后一个过境路的出口国国境站的运输,由该站站长或收货人、发货人委托的收转人转运至最终到站。

The consignor uses the SMGS waybill to transport the goods via the sending country's railroad to the export border station of the last transit railroad participating in the SMGS, where the station master, the consignee, or the consignor's delegated forwarder will transfer the goods to the final arrival station.

3. 通过港口的货物运送（Delivery of Goods Through Ports）

通过过境铁路港口站的货物运送,从参加国际货协铁路的国家,通过参加国际货协的过境铁路港口,向其他国家运送货物时,用国际货协运送票据只能办理至过境铁路港口站,由港口站的收转人办理转发送。

In the case of cargo delivery through transit railroad port stations, when cargo is delivered from a country participating in SMGS to other countries through a transit railroad port participating in SMGS, the goods can only be transported to the transit railroad port station using SMGS waybill, and the forwarder at the port station will handle the forwarding and delivery.

7.2.5 国际铁路货物联运运单（International Railroad Through Transport Waybill）

国际铁路货物联运运单是参加联运发送国铁路部门与发货人之间缔结的运输合同,规定了参加联运各铁路和发、收货人在货物运送方面的权利、义务和责任。

国际铁路货物联运所使用的运单是铁路与货主间缔结的运输契约,也是货物收据。与海运提单不同,铁路运单不是物权凭证,但在托收或信用证支付方式下,托运人可凭运单副本办理托收或议付。运单正本从始发站随同货物附送至终点站并交给收货人,是铁路同货主之间交接货物、核收运杂费用和处理索赔与理赔的依据。运单副本是卖方凭以向银行结算货款的主要单据。

The international railroad through transport waybill is a contract of carriage concluded between the railroad of the country of shipment and the consignor，which stipulates the rights，obligations，and responsibilities of each railroad，consignor，and consignee in the delivery of goods.

扩展阅读 7.1　铁路提单能否成为信用证下的运输单据

The waybill used for international railroad through transport of goods is the contract of carriage concluded between the railroad and the owner of the goods，and is also the receipt for the goods. Unlike the maritime bill of lading，the railroad waybill is not a document of title，but under the payment method of collection or letter of credit，the shipper can handle the collection or negotiation with a copy of the waybill. The original waybill is sent from the originating station along with the goods to the terminal and handed over to the consignee，which is the basis for handing over the goods between the railroad and the cargo owner，collecting transportation and miscellaneous charges，and handling claims settlement. The copy of the waybill is the main document by which the seller settles the payment for the goods with the bank.

7.2.6　国际铁路货物联运运送费用的计算和核收（Calculation and Collection of Freight Charges for International Railway Combined Transport of Goods）

国际铁路货物联运运送费用包括货物运费、押运人乘车费、杂费和其他费用。运送费用核收的规定如下。

The freight for international railway through transport of goods shall include freight，supercargo fee，miscellaneous fees and other expenses. The provisions for the collection of transport charges are as follows.

1. 参加国际货协各铁路间运送费用核收的原则（Principles of Collecting Transportation Fees Between Railroads Participating in SMGS）

（1）发送路的运送费用按发送国国内运价规则以发送国的货币在发站向发货人或根据发送路国内现行规定核收。

（1）The delivery charges of the railroad sending the goods are levied on the consignor at the departure station in the currency of the sending country，in accordance with the domestic tariff rules of the country，or in accordance with the regulations in force in the country.

（2）到达路的运送费用按到达路国内运价规则以到达国的货币在到站向收货人或根据到达路国内现行规定核收。

（2）The delivery charges of the arriving railroad are charged to the consignee at the arrival station in the currency of the country of arrival in accordance with the domestic tariff rules of the arriving railroad or in accordance with the prevailing domestic regulations of the country.

（3）过境路的运送费用按《统一货价》在发站向发货人或在到站向收货人核收。

（3）The transit rail freight is charged to the consignor at the departure station or to the consignee at the arrival station according to *Uniform Transit Tariff Regulations of SMGS*.

2. 国际货协参加铁路与非国际货协铁路间运送费用核收的规定（Provisions on the Collection of Freight Charges Between SMGS and Non-SMGS Railways）

（1）发送铁路和到达铁路的运送费用与参加国际货协各铁路间收费标准相同。

（1）The freight charge between the railway where the goods are sent and the railway where the goods arrive is the same as that between the railways participating in the SMGS.

（2）过境铁路的运送费用：①参加国际货协并实行《统一货价》的各过境路的运送费用在发站向发货人核收，但办理转发送国家铁路的运送费用可以在发站向发货人或在到站向收货人核收；②过境非国际货协铁路的运送费用在到站向收货人核收。

（2）Transit rail freight：① The transportation expenses of the transit railways participating in the SMGS and implementing *Uniform Transit Tariff Regulations of SMGS* shall be collected from the consignor at the station that the goods are sent from；however，the transportation expenses of the transshipment railway may be collected from the consignor at the sending station or from the consignee at the arrival station. ②Transit charges for non-SMGS railways shall be collected from the consignee at the arrival station.

（3）通过过境铁路港口站货物运送费用核收的规定：从参加国际货协铁路发站至港口站的运送费用，在发站向发货人核收，反方向运送在到站向收货人核收。

（3）Provisions for the collection of charges for the delivery of goods through the port station of the transit railroad：the charges for the delivery from the consignment station of the participating SMGS railroad to the port station are collected from the consignor at the consignment station and from the consignee at the arrival station for delivery in the opposite direction.

（4）在港口站所发生的杂费和其他费用，在任何情况下都在港口车站向收转人核收。

（4）Miscellaneous and other charges incurred at the port station are in any case levied on the forwarder at the port station.

7.3　中国内地对中国香港铁路货物运输（Transportation of Goods by Rail from Chinese Mainland to Hong Kong，China）

7.3.1　中国内地对中国香港货物运输概况（General Situation of Cargo Transport Between Chinese Mainland and Hong Kong，China）

按照《中华人民共和国香港特别行政区基本法》的规定，中国内地与中国香港之间经贸活动参照国际惯例。中国香港作为单独关税区,实行独立税收制度,保持自由港的地位,实行自由贸易政策。双方商品、货物及相应物品往来进出都需要经过海关。

In accordance with the provisions of the *Basic Law of the Hong Kong Special Administrative Region of People's Republic of China*, economic and trade activities between Chinese Mainland and Hong Kong, China are governed by international practice. As a separate customs territory, Hong Kong, China implements an independent taxation system, maintains the status of a free port and implements a free trade policy. The import and export of commodities, goods and corresponding articles from both sides are subject to customs clearance.

中国内地不但是中国香港最大的进出口市场,而且是中国香港转口商品的最大来源地和最大的市场。在中国香港转口贸易总额中,约90%与中国内地有关。中国香港的九龙铁路从深圳车站至九龙车站,全长34千米。中国内地与中国香港之间旅客和货物铁路运输主要依靠这条铁路。其共有五个装卸点,其中九龙的红磡货场为港段最大的货场(杂货和果蔬)。中国内地与中国香港的公路运输主要有文锦渡、皇岗和沙头角三个口岸,可将货物用汽车运至中国香港。

Chinese Mainland is not only the largest import and export market for Hong Kong, China, but also the largest source and largest market for its re-exports. About 90% of the total re-export trade of Hong Kong, China is related to the Chinese Mainland. Hong Kong, China's Kowloon Railway runs 34 kilometers from Shenzhen Station to Kowloon Station. Rail transportation of passengers and goods between the Chinese Mainland and Hong Kong, China relies heavily on this railroad. There are five loading and unloading locations, with Hung Hom Yard in Kowloon being the largest yard in the Hong Kong, China section(for general cargo and fruits and vegetables). Road transportation between the Chinese Mainland and Hong Kong, China is mainly by three crossings at Man Kam To, Huanggang and Sha Tau Kok, where goods can be transported to Hong Kong, China by car.

7.3.2　中国内地对中国香港铁路运输的方式与特点(Mode and Characteristics of Rail Freight from Chinese Mainland to Hong Kong,China)

中国内地对中国香港铁路运输的方式与特点如下。

The mode and characteristics of rail freight from Chinese Mainland to Hong Kong, China are as follows.

1. 运输方式(Mode of Transportation)

对中国香港的铁路运输由内地段运输和港段运输两部分构成,它是一种特殊的租车方式的两票运输,由中外运长航各地分支机构和香港中国旅行社联合组织进行。

Railroad transportation to Hong Kong, China is composed of two parts: the mainland transportation section and the Hong Kong，China transportation section，which is a special kind of two-document transportation by renting a train. It is jointly organized by all branches of Sinotrans & CSC and China Travel Service(Hong Kong).

2. 运输单据(Transport Documents)

对中国香港的铁路两段运输分别由内地铁路部门与中国香港九龙铁路当局签发内地段铁路运单与广九铁路货物运单,再由各发货地的外运公司凭铁路运单以联运承运人的身份签发从起运地至中国香港的凭证,即承运货物收据。

For the two sections of rail transport to Hong Kong，China，the railroad waybill of the mainland section and the railroad waybill of Guangzhou-Kowloon section are issued respectively by the mainland railroad department and the Hong Kong，China's Kowloon railroad authorities，and then the cargo receipt is issued by the forwarding company of each place of shipment as an through carrier from the place of shipment to Hong Kong，China on the basis of the rail waybill.

3. 运输费用(Transportation Cost)

对中国香港铁路货物运输的费用,按内地段铁路运输和港段铁路运输分别计算,内地段按人民币计算,港段按港币计算。内地段运费包括铁路运费、深圳过轨租车费和深圳外运公司劳务费。港段运费包括铁路运费、港段终点站卸货费、港段调车费及劳务费等。

The cost of railroad cargo transportation to Hong Kong，China is calculated separately according to the railroad transportation of the mainland section and the railroad transportation of the Hong Kong section，with the mainland section calculated in RMB and the Hong Kong section calculated in HKD. The freight cost of the mainland section includes railway freight，Shenzhen over-rail rental fee，and the labor fee of Shenzhen foreign transportation company. The freight of the Hong Kong section includes railway freight，unloading fee at the terminal，shunting fee and labor fee of the Hong Kong section.

Words and Expressions

即测即练

习题

第 8 章
Chapter 8

国际多式联运
International Multimodal Transport

Learning Objectives：

1. Understand the concept and advantages of international multimodal transport；
2. Master the conditions that constitute international multimodal transport；
3. Master the differences between international multimodal transport and other modes of international cargo transport；
4. Master the scope of responsibility of CTO，especially the meaning， characteristics of uniform liability system，network liability system and modified uniform liability system.

引导案例

A 丝绸公司将装载布料的五个集装箱委托 B 集团承运，双方签订了国际多式联运合同，约定由 B 集团对全程运输负责，货交 C 服装公司。运输条款："FCL-FCL"，运单上同时记载"由货主装箱、计数"的批注。B 集团受理该票业务后，首先委托 D 物流公司公路运输到甲市，D 物流公司签发了以 B 集团为托运人的公路货运单。其后，货到甲市，B 集团又委托 E 船公司海运到乙市。集装箱在甲市装船后，E 船公司签发了以 B 集团为托运人的海运提单。集装箱在乙市港卸船后，五个集装箱中有三个外表严重破损。之后，B 集团又办理了由乙市到丙市的铁路运输。五个集装箱运抵 C 服装公司后，收货人开箱时发现：三个外表有破损的集装箱内布料已严重受损，另一个集装箱尽管外表状况良好、关封完整，但箱内布料也有受损，于是拒绝收货，并向发货人提出赔偿要求。发货人于是向 B 集团提出赔偿，并要求按最高货损限额的运输区段给予赔付。关于货损责任人、赔偿限额，B 集团与发货人、D 物流公司、E 船公司、铁路集团等涉案方产生了争议。本案中，A 丝绸公司将装载货物的集装箱交由 B 集团托运时，按照整箱货交接下的责任划分，B 集团只需对集装箱的外表状况负责，而无须对集装箱内的货物负责。因此，一个集装箱内部货损的责任应由发货人 A 丝绸公司自己承担；三个外表有破损的集装箱货损应由与 A 丝绸公司签订运输合同的 B 集团承担。由于三个外表有破损集装箱的受损区段发生在海运期间，因此 E 船公司应该承担与其有海运合同关系的 B 集团这三个集装箱的货损责任；D 物流公司（公路区段实际承运人）、乙市铁路集团没有造成货损，不承担货损责任。

资料来源：国际多式联运的案例［EB/OL］．（2019-03-02）．https://wenku.baidu.com/view/92c072f4f4335a8102d276a20029bd64793e62d0.

国际多式联运又称国际联合运输，是一种利用集装箱进行综合连贯运输的新型运输方式。集装箱的使用为国际多式联运的快速发展提供了更为有利的条件。多式联运一般以集装箱作为流通媒介，将海上运输、航空运输、铁路运输、公路运输和内河运输等传统的单一运输方式有机结合并有效地综合利用，构成连贯运输，为货主提供经济、迅速、安全、便捷的运输服务。采用多式联运，货主只需要办理一次托运手续、一次支付全程运费，承运人负责将货物从发货人的仓库（工厂）直接运到收货人的仓库（工厂），从而为国际贸易提供了极大的便利。如今，提供优质高效的国际多式联运服务已成为集装箱运输经营人增强竞争力的手段。

International multimodal transport, also known as international combined transport, is a new mode of transport using containers for integrated and coherent transport. The use of containers provides more favorable conditions for the rapid development of international multimodal transport. Multimodal transport usually uses containers as a circulation medium, which organically combines and effectively integrates traditional single modes of transport such as maritime transport, air transport, railway transport, road transport, and inland waterway transport to constitute continuous transport and provide economical, rapid, safe, and convenient transport services for cargo owners. Using multimodal transport, the shipper only needs to go through the consignment procedures once and pay the whole freight at one time, and the carrier is responsible for transporting the goods from the consignor's warehouse (factory) directly to the consignee's warehouse (factory), thus providing a great convenience for international trade. Nowadays, the provision of high-quality and efficient international multimodal transport services has become a means for container transport operators to enhance their competitiveness.

8.1 国际多式联运概述（Overview of International Multimodal Transport）

8.1.1 国际多式联运的概念（Concept of International Multimodal Transport）

国际多式联运是一种以实现货物整体运输的最优化效益为目标的联运组织形式。《联合国国际货物多式联运公约》对国际多式联运下的定义是：国际多式联运是指按照多式运输合同，以至少两种不同的运输方式，由多式运输经营人将货物从一国境内接管货物的地点运至另一国境内指定交付货物的地点的运输方式。

国际多式联运具有以下优点：责任统一，手续简便；中间环节减少，运输时间缩短，货运质量提高；节省运杂费，减少利息支出；实现门到门运输；提高运输组织水平，实现合理运输。

International multimodal transportation is a form of organizing intermodal transportations with the goal of achieving optimal efficiency of overall cargo transportation. The definition of international multimodal transport in *United Nations Convention on International Multimodal Transport of Goods*（UNCIMTG）is as follows："International multimodal transport means the carriage of goods by at least two different modes of transport on the basis of a multimodal transport contract from a place in one country at which the goods are taken in charge by the CTO to a place designated for delivery situated in a different country. The operations of pick-up and delivery of goods carried out in the performance of a unimodal transport contract, as defined in such contract, shall not be considered as international multimodal transport. "

International multimodal transport has the following advantages：it makes the responsibility unified and the formalities simple；it reduces the intermediate links, shortens the transportation time and improves the freight quality；saves the freight and miscellaneous expenses and reduces the interest expense；it realizes the door-to-door transportation；improves the transportation organization level and realizes the reasonable transportation.

8.1.2　国际多式联运经营人（Multimodal Transport Operator）

根据 1980 年《联合国国际货物多式联运公约》的定义，"多式联运经营人是指以自己的名义或通过代其行事的他人签订多式联运合同，以委托人身份而非发货人的代理人和参加多式联运的承运人的代理人或代表行事，并对合同的履行承担责任的任何人。"

As defined in the 1980 *United Nations Convention on International Multimodal Transport of Goods*，"Multimodal transport operator（combined transport operator, CTO）means any person who on his own behalf or through another person acting on his behalf concludes a multimodal transport contract and who acts as a principal, not as an agent or on behalf of the consignor or of the carriers participating in the multimodal transport operations, and who assumes responsibility for the performance of the contract. "

国际多式联运经营人既不是发货人的代理或代表，也不是承运人的代理或代表，它是一个独立的法律实体，具有双重身份，对于货主而言它是承运人，对于实际承运人而言它又是托运人。它一方面与货主签订多式联运合同，另一方面又与实际承运人签订运输合同，总承运人对全程运输负责，对货物灭失、损坏、延迟交付等均承担责任。

The international multimodal transport operator is neither the agent or representative of the consignor nor the agent or representative of the carrier, it is an independent legal entity with dual identity, it is the carrier for the cargo owner and the shipper for the actual carrier. It signs multimodal transport contract with cargo owner and contract of carriage with actual carrier, it is the general carrier responsible for the entire transportation and liable for loss，damage，and delay in delivery of goods.

8.1.3　国际多式联运的基本条件（Basic Conditions of International Multimodal Transport）

构成国际多式联运应具备下列条件。

（1）多式联运经营人与托运人之间必须签订多式联运合同，以明确承、托双方的权利、义务和豁免关系。

（2）国际多式联运必须使用一份全程多式联运单据，即证明多式联运合同及证明多式联运经营人已接管货物并负责按照合同条款交付货物所签发的单据。

（3）国际多式联运必须由一个多式联运经营人对全程运输负总责。由多式联运经营人去寻找分承运人实现分段运输。

（4）国际多式联运必须是两种或两种以上不同运输方式的连贯运输。这是确定一票货运是否属于多式联运的最重要的特征。

（5）国际多式联运必须是国际货物运输。这是区别于国内运输和是否符合国际法规的限制条件。

（6）国际多式联运必须对货主实行全程单一运费费率。多式联运经营人在对货主负全程运输责任的基础上，制定一个货物发运地至目的地全程单一费率并以包干形式一次向货主收取。

由此可见，国际多式联运的主要特点是：由多式联运经营人与托运人签订一个运输合同，统一组织全程运输，实行运输全程一次托运、一单到底、一次收费、统一理赔和全程负责。虽然它可能由各运输区段的承运人共同完成货物的全程运输，但它是将货物的全程运输作为一个完整的单一运输过程来安排。因此，它是一种以方便托运人和货主为目的的先进的货物运输组织形式。

The following conditions shall be met for international multimodal transportation.

（1）A multimodal transport contract must be signed between the multimodal transport operator and the shipper to clarify the rights，obligations，and exemptions of both parties.

（2）International multimodal transport must use a multimodal transport document covering the entire journey，which certifies the multimodal transport contract and proves that the CTO has taken over the goods and is responsible for the delivery of the goods in accordance with the terms of the contract.

（3）International multimodal transport must be carried out by a multimodal transport operator who has the overall responsibility for the whole transport. The CTO is responsible for finding sub-carriers to realize the sectional transport.

（4）International multimodal transport must be a coherent transport using two or more different modes of transport，which is the most important feature to determine whether a freight shipment is multimodal transport.

（5）International multimodal transport must be international transportation of goods, which is the restriction that distinguishes it from domestic transportation and judges its suitability for international regulations.

(6) International multimodal transport must implement a single freight rate for the whole journey to the shipper. The CTO shall, on the basis of taking responsibility of through carriage for the cargo owner, establish a single rate for the whole journey from the place of shipment to the place of destination and collect it from the cargo owner at one time.

It can be seen that the main characteristics of international multimodal transport are that the CTO signs a transport contract with the shipper to organize the entire process of transport in in a unified way, and implements "one consignment, one document, one charge, unified claim settlement and responsible for the entire process" for the whole process of transport. Although the multimodal transport may be completed by the carrier of each transportation section, it is arranged as a complete single transportation process. Therefore, it is an advanced form of cargo transportation organization for the convenience of shippers and consignees.

8.1.4 国际多式联运与一般国际货物运输的区别（The Difference Between International Multimodal Transport and General International Cargo Transport）

国际多式联运与一般国际货物运输的主要不同点有以下几个方面。

The main differences between international multimodal transport and general international cargo transport are as follows.

1. 货运单据的内容与制作方法不同（The Content and Making Method of the Shipping Documents are Different）

国际多式联运大都为"门到门"运输,故货物于装船或装车或装机后应同时由实际承运人签发提单或运单,多式联运经营人签发多式联运提单,这是多式联运与任何一种单一的国际货运方式的根本不同之处。在此情况下,海运提单或运单上的发货人应为多式联运经营人,收货人及通知方一般应为多式联运经营人的国外分支机构或其代理;多式联运提单上的收货人和发货人是真正的、实际的收货人和发货人,通知方则是目的港或最终交货地点的收货人或该收货人的代理人。

多式联运提单上除列明装货港、卸货港外,还要列明收货地、交货地或最终目的地的名称以及第一程运输工具的名称、航次或车次等。

Most of the international multimodal transport is "door-to-door" transport, so when the goods are loaded on the ship, truck or plane, the actual carriers should issue a bill of lading or waybill, while the CTO to issue a multimodal transport document, which is the fundamental difference between multimodal transport and any single mode of international freight. In this case, the consignor on the ocean bill of lading or waybill shall be the CTO, and the consignee and the notify party shall generally be the foreign branch or agent of the multimodal transport operator; the consignee and the consignor on the transport bill of lading shall be the real and actual consignee and consignor, and the notify party is the consignee or its agent at the port of destination or the final place of delivery.

In addition to the port of loading and unloading, the name of the place of receipt, delivery, or final destination as well as the name, voyage, or train number of the means of transport for the first journey shall also be listed on the combined transport bill of lading.

2. 多式联运提单的适用性与可转让性与一般海运提单不同(The Applicability and Transferability of Combined Transport Bill of Lading are Different from that of the Marine Bill of Lading)

一般海运提单只适用于海运,从这个意义上说,多式联运提单只有在海运与其他运输方式结合时才适用,但现在它也适用于除海运以外的其他两种或两种以上的不同运输方式的连贯的跨国运输(国外采用"国际多式联运单据"就可避免概念上的混淆)。

多式联运提单把海运提单的可转让性与其他运输方式下运单的不可转让性合二为一,因此多式联运经营人根据托运人的要求既可签发可转让的也可签发不可转让的多式联运提单。如属前者,收货人一栏应采用指示抬头;如属后者,收货人一栏应具体列明收货人名称,并在提单上注明不可转让。

General ocean bill of lading is only applicable to sea transport. In this sense, multimodal transport bill of lading is only applicable when sea transport is combined with other modes of transport. But now it is also applicable to the coherent cross-border transportation of two or more different modes of transport other than sea transport (the use of "international multimodal transport document" abroad can avoid the conceptual confusion).

Multimodal transport bill of lading combines the negotiability of ocean bill of lading with the non-negotiability of waybill under other modes of transport. Therefore, the CTO can issue both negotiable and non-

单据 8.1 多式联运单据

negotiable multimodal transport bill of lading according to the requirements of the shipper. In the case of the former, the consignee column shall be made "to the order of"; in the case of the latter, the consignee column shall specify the name of the consignee and indicate "Non-negotiable" on the bill of lading.

3. 信用证上的条款不同(The Terms on the Letter of Credit are Different)

根据多式联运的需要,信用证上的条款应有以下三点变动。

(1) 向银行议付时不能使用船公司签发的已装船清洁提单,而应凭多式联运经营人签发的多式联运提单,同时还应注明该提单的抬头如何制作,以明确可否转让。

(2) 多式联运一般采用集装箱运输(特殊情况除外,如在对外工程承包下运出机械设备则不一定采用集装箱),因此,应在信用证上增加指定采用集装箱运输条款。

（3）如不由银行转单，改由托运人或发货人或多式联运经营人直接寄单，以便收货人或代理尽早取得货运单证，加快在目的港（地）提货的速度，则应在信用证上加列"装船单据由发货人或由多式联运经营人直寄收货人或其代理"之条款。如由多式联运经营人寄单，出于发货人议付结汇的需要，应由多式联运经营人出具一份"收到货运单据并已寄出"的证明。

According to the needs of multimodal transport, the terms of the L/C should have the following three changes.

（1）When negotiating with the bank, the on board clean bill of lading issued by the shipping company cannot be used, but the multimodal transport bill of lading issued by the CTO should be used. At the same time, it should also indicate how consignee of the bill of lading is filled in to ascertain whether it can be transferred.

（2）Multimodal transport is generally carried out in containers (Except in special cases, such as under foreign engineering contracts, the transport of machinery and equipment is not necessarily using containers) and therefore, the provisions specifying the use of container transport should be added to the letter of credit.

（3）If it is not the bank that transfers the documents, but the shipper or the consignor or the CTO that sends them directly, so that the consignee or agent can obtain the shipping document as soon as possible and speed up the pick-up at the port (place) of destination, the term of "shipping documents are sent by the consignor or by the multimodal transport operator directly to the consignee or its agent" should be added on the letter of credit. If it is sent by the CTO, a certificate of "shipping documents received and shipped" shall be issued by the CTO for the consignor to negotiate and settle the foreign exchange.

4. 海关验放的手续不同（The Procedures for Customs Clearance are Different）

一般国际货物运输的交货地点大都在装货港，目的地大都在卸货港，因而办理报关和通关的手续都是在货物进出境的港口。而国际多式联运货物的起运地大都在内陆城市，因此，内陆海关只对货物办理转关监管手续，由出境地的海关进行查验放行。进口货物的最终目的地如为内陆城市，进境港口的海关一般不进行查验，只办理转关监管手续，待货物到达最终目的地时由当地海关查验放行。

Generally speaking, most of the delivery locations of international cargo transportation are at the loading port, and most of the destinations are at the discharge port, so the procedures for customs clearance are at the ports where goods enter and leave the country, while most of the international multimodal cargoes are shipped from inland cities, therefore, the inland customs will only carry out transit supervision procedures for the goods, and the customs at the place of departure will check and release them. If the final destination of the imported goods is an inland city, the customs at the port of entry will generally not conduct inspections, and only the transit supervision procedures will be carried out. When the goods arrive at the final destination，they will be checked and released by the local customs.

8.2　国际多式联运经营人的责任范围（Scope of Responsibility of CTO）

在多式联运情况下，多式联运经营人通常将全程或部分路程的货物运输委托给区段承运人去完成。在多式联运的两种或两种以上的不同运输方式中，每一种方式所在区段适用的法律对承运人责任的规定往往是不同的。当货物在运输过程中发生灭失、损坏或延迟时，应由何方来承担责任？如何确定货物损失的区段？是采用相同的标准还是区别对待？目前国际上对多式联运责任划分和赔偿限额有三种做法。

In the case of multimodal transport，the CTO usually entrusts the whole or part of the journey to the section carrier. In two or more different modes of transport in multimodal transport，the law applicable to the different transport section often provides for different carrier liability. When the goods are lost，damaged or delayed in the course of transportation，who shall bear the responsibility? How to determine where the loss of goods occurred? Should the same standard be applied to the compensation for the loss of goods，or should it be treated differently? There are currently three international approaches to the division of liability and limits of indemnity for multimodal transport.

8.2.1　国际多式联运责任制的类型（Types of International Multimodal Transport Liability System）

1. 统一责任制（ Uniform Liability System）

1）含义（Meaning）

多式联运经营人对货主负不分区段的统一原则责任，即货物若发生灭失、损坏，无论其发生在哪个区段，联运经营人都要按一个统一原则负责，并一律按一个约定的限额进行赔偿。

The multimodal transport operator shall be responsible for the cargo owner according to the uniform principle，regardless of the transport section. That is to say，in case of loss of or damage to the goods，the CTO is responsible for them according to a uniform principle，regardless of the section in which loss or damage occur，and should always compensate according to an agreed limit.

2）特点（Characteristics）

这种责任制下，在履行合同时一般不涉及其他运输公约或有关国家法律的赔偿规定，运输合同一经签订，托运人就清楚联运经营人对货损、货差或延期交付承担多大的责任，一旦发生损失，其所获赔偿不会因地而异。

Under this liability system，the performance of the contract does not generally involve the indemnification provisions of other transport conventions or relevant national laws. Once the contract of carriage is signed, the shipper is aware of the extent of the CTO's liability for damage, discrepancy or delay in delivery, and in the event of loss, the compensation he receives will not vary from place to place.

2. 网状责任制（Network Liability System）

1）含义（Meaning）

多式联运经营人的责任范围以各区段运输的原有责任为限,赔偿限额也分别按各区段的国际公约或国内法规进行赔偿,对不明区段的货物隐蔽损失按《海牙规则》办理,或按双方约定原则办理。

The scope of liability of CTOs is limited to the original liability of each section of transport, and the limit of compensation is also in accordance with the provisions of international conventions or domestic regulations of each section respectively, and the hidden loss of goods (unable to determine which section the cargo loss occurred in) is handled according to the *Hague Rules*, or according to the principles agreed by both parties.

2）特点（Characteristics）

这种责任制涉及的赔偿规则较多,差别也很大,事先不能知道依据哪个规则,托运人很难在合同中写明一个赔偿责任。但是,因为多式联运经营人对全程负责,发生损失时,托运人只找一个事主,得到单一运输方式的相同赔偿,因此,托运人乐意接受这种方式。

This liability system involves many and varied rules of indemnity, and it is not possible to know in advance which rules to rely on, so it is difficult for the shipper to specify a liability in the contract. Since the CTO is responsible for the entire transport and in case of loss, the shipper only has to claim from the CTO and receive the same compensation as for a single mode of transportation, the shipper is often willing to accept this approach.

3. 修正统一责任制（Modified Uniform Liability System）

1）含义（Meaning）

修正统一责任制是介于统一责任制和网状责任制之间的责任制,即责任范围方面与统一责任制相同,赔偿限额方面与网状责任制相同。

It is a liability system in between uniform liability system and network liability system. That is, the scope of liability is the same as uniform liability system, and the compensation limit is the same as network liability system.

2）特点（Characteristics）

知道货损发生区段时,若该区段运输公约的赔偿限额高于多式联运公约限额（如空运段）,则联运经营人按单一运输公约的限额赔偿;知道货损发生区段时,若该区段运输公约的赔偿限额低于多式联运公约限额（如海运段）,则联运经营人按多式联运公约的限额赔偿。这种规定对货主有利。

When the sector in which the cargo damage occurred is known, the CTO compensates the cargo owner in accordance with the limit of the convention for that single mode of transport if the limit of the convention for that sector is higher than the limit of the convention for multimodal transport (e. g. the air transport sector); when the segment of the damage is known, if the limit of compensation under the transport convention for that segment is lower than the limit of the multimodal transport convention (e. g. the sea section), the CTO shall compensate according to the limit of the multimodal transport convention. Such regulations are beneficial to the cargo owners.

8.2.2 《联合国国际货物多式联运公约》采用的责任形式(Forms of Liability Adopted in the UNCIMTG)

在《联合国国际货物多式联运公约》起草过程中,分歧最大的问题之一就是选择网状责任制还是统一责任制。

One of the most divisive issues during the drafting of *United Nations Convention on International Multimodal Transport of Goods* was the choice between network liability system or uniform liability system.

发展中国家主张采用统一责任制,认为其保证了货主的利益,简化货运事故的处理,也解决了整个运输过程中可能出现的"隐藏损害"的处理问题,是一种较为优越的责任制。

Developing countries advocate the use of a uniform liability system, which is considered to be a superior liability system as it guarantees the interests of cargo owners, simplifies the handling of freight accidents, and also solves the problem of "hidden damage" that may occur throughout the transport process.

发达国家则主张采用网状责任制,认为统一责任制有其优越性但并不完善,实际上是行不通的。这是由于各国及承运人早已接受了不同的国际公约,如果再接受统一责任制的多式联运公约,则会出现不能同时履行对每一公约义务的情况,这会给实际运作带来极大问题。并且目前与集装箱运输相关的人(如保险人等)的赔偿责任都是建立在单一运输法规的责任规定之上的,改为统一标准会给这些行业带来混乱。

Developed countries, on the other hand, favour the network liability system, arguing that the uniform liability system has its advantages but is imperfect and does not work in practice. This is due to the fact that countries and carriers have already accepted different international conventions and if they were to accept the uniform liability system for multimodal transport conventions, there would be a situation where they would not be able to fulfill their obligations to each convention at the same time, which would cause significant problems in practice. Furthermore, the liability of those associated with container transport (e. g. insurers) is currently based on the liability provisions of a single transport legislation and a change to a uniform standard would create confusion for these industries.

最终,分歧双方都做了让步,《联合国国际货物多式联运公约》采用了经修订的统一责任制。这种特殊规定使多式联运中出现了两层赔偿关系:第一层赔偿关系是多式联运经营人与货主间的赔偿关系;第二层赔偿关系是多式联运经营人与各区段实际承运人之间的赔偿责任。对于这一责任，公约中没作出任何规定，只能按目前各区段适用的法律处理。再者，想要使各种运输方式的实际承运人接受统一的责任限额也是很困难的。因此，经修订的统一责任制在目前确实难以实行。公约中出现的这种责任制问题在近期内也很难解决，只有当其他单一方式的运输公约、法律作出调整或出台新的规定后才能逐渐解决。

In the end，both parties to the disagreement made concessions and the UNCIMTG adopted a revised uniform liability system. This special provision allows for two levels of indemnity relationships in multimodal transport：the first level of indemnity is between the CTO and the cargo owner；the second level of indemnity is between the CTO and the actual carrier of each sector. There is no provision for this liability in the UNCIMTG and it can only be dealt with according to the law currently applicable in the various sectors. Furthermore，it would be difficult to try to get the actual carriers of the various modes of transport to accept a uniform limit of liability. Therefore，the revised uniform liability system is indeed difficult to implement at present. Such liability issues arising in the UNCIMTG will also be difficult to resolve in the near future and will only be resolved gradually when other single-mode transport conventions or laws are adjusted or new provisions are introduced.

扩展阅读8.1 《联合国国际货物多式联运公约》

8.3　国际多式联运业务（International Multimodal Transport Operations）

8.3.1　国际多式联运业务流程（Business Processes of International Multimodal Transport）

在组织国际多式联运时，其主要业务流程有以下几个环节。

When organising international multimodal transport，the main business processes are as follows.

1. 订立多式联运合同（Entering into Multimodal Transport Contracts）

国际多式联运经营人以契约承运人的名义与托运人签订国际多式联运合同。托运人应根据货物运输的需要及时备货并办理托运，申请出口检验，并制作贸易单证和运输单证。国际多式联运经营人接受托运后，就要对所托运的货物编制运输计划，运输计划的编制要符合运输线路的稳定性、经济性和合理性的要求。

The international CTO enters into international multimodal transport contract with the shipper in the name of the contract carrier. The shipper shall prepare and handle consignments in a timely manner according to the needs of the goods to be transported，apply for export inspection，and prepare trade and transport documents. After accepting a consignment，the international multimodal transport operator shall prepare a transport plan for the consignment，which shall be prepared in accordance with the requirements of stability，economy，and reasonableness of the transport route.

2. 空箱的发放、提运和运送（Provision，Pick-up，and Delivery of Empty Containers）

多式联运中使用的集装箱一般应由多式联运经营人提供。这些集装箱来源可能有三个：一是多式联运经营人自己购置；二是向租箱公司租用；三是由全程运输中的某一分运人提供。如果双方协议由发货人自行装箱，那么多式联运经营人应该签发空箱提运单（又称"集装箱发放通知单"，俗称提箱单），或者把租箱公司或分运人签发的提箱单交给发货人或其代理人，由他们在规定的时间内到指定的堆场提箱并自行将空箱运到装货地点，准备装货。

Containers used in multimodal transport shall normally be provided by the CTO. There are three possible sources of these containers：firstly，the CTO acquires the container himself；secondly，the operator hires the container from the leasing company；thirdly，provided by one of the sub-carriers in the full transport. If it is agreed that the consignor will load the container himself，then the CTO should either issue a container release order or hand over the container release order issued by the charterer or sub-carrier to the consignor or his agent，who will pick up the container at the designated yard at the specified time and transport the empty container to the loading place to prepare for loading.

3. 出口报关（Export Customs Declaration）

出口报关事宜一般由发货人或其代理人办理，也可委托多式联运经营人办理，但需要加收报关服务费和报关手续费。报关时应提供场站收据、装箱单和出口许可证等有关单证和文件。报关地随始发地而定，如果始发地在港口，就在港口报关；如果始发地在内陆地区，则应该在附近的内地海关办理报关。

Export customs declaration is generally handled by the consignor or his agent，or can be entrusted to the CTO，but additional customs service charges and customs clearance fees are required. Relevant documents and papers such as dock receipts，packing lists and export licences should be provided at the time of customs declaration. The place of customs declaration depends on the place of origin. If the place of origin is in a port，it will be declared at the port；if the place of origin is inland，the customs declaration should be made at the nearby mainland customs office.

4. 始发地的货物交接（Delivery of Goods at the Place of Departure）

托运人根据多式联运合同的规定将所托运的货物交至指定的地点。多式联运经营人对货物的状况进行检验，在确认无误后接收货物。随后，多式联运经营人根据具体的运输计划和所采用的运输方式签发多式联运单据。

The shipper delivers the consignment to the designated place in accordance with the provisions of the multimodal transport contract. The CTO inspects the condition of the goods and accepts them after confirming that they are correct. The CTO then issues the multimodal transport document according to the specific transport plan and the mode of transport used.

5. 多式联运经营人安排货物运输(Arrangement of Cargo Transportation by CTO)

国际多式联运经营人按托运人的要求安排运输线路、订舱配载、接货,安排内陆运输、仓储和装箱,将装好的集装箱送到实际承运人指定的堆场或港口进行装运。实际承运人向多式联运经营人签发多式联运提单或运单。

The international CTO arranges the transport route, booking and allocation, receiving cargo, as well as inland transportation, storage, and packing according to the shipper's requirements, and delivers the loaded containers to the yard or port designated by the actual carrier for shipment. The actual carrier issues a combined B/L or waybill to the CTO.

6. 办理运输过程中的海关业务(Handling Customs Business in the Process of Transportation)

国际多式联运的全程运输均为国际货物运输,因此需要办理货物所经过的国家的通关手续和进口国内路段保税运输手续等海关业务。这些涉及海关的业务一般由多式联运经营人的派出机构或代理人办理,也可由各区段的实际承运人作为多式联运经营人的代表代为办理,由此产生的全部费用应该由发货人或收货人负担。

The whole process of international multimodal transport is the transport of goods across national borders, so it is necessary to handle customs clearance procedures in the countries through which the goods pass and bonded transport procedures for the imported domestic section. These operations involving customs are generally carried out by a branch or agent of the CTO, or may be carried out by the actual carrier of each sector as a representative of the CTO, and all costs arising therefrom should be borne by the consignor or consignee.

7. 目的地交接货物(Delivery of Goods at Destination)

货物运达目的地后,由多式联运经营人或其代理人将货物交给收货人。多式联运经营人通常应该通知收货人做好提货准备,并办理货物的进口手续。当收货人出具多式联运单证或其他有效证明,并支付了到付的费用后,就可以办理货物的交接手续,将货物交给收货人。

Once the goods have arrived at their destination, the CTO or its agent will hand over the goods to the consignee. The CTO should normally notify the consignee of the readiness to collect the goods and carry out import formalities for the goods. Once the consignee has produced the multimodal transport document or other valid proof and paid the charges to be paid, the goods can be handed over to the consignee.

8. 货运事故处理(Handling of Freight Accidents)

如果全程运输中发生了货物灭失、损害和运输延误,无论是否能确定损害发生的区段,发货人均可向多式联运经营人提出索赔。多式联运经营人根据提单条款或双方协议确定责任并作出赔偿。

In the event of loss of, damage to the goods, and delay in transportation during the entire journey，the consignor may make a claim to the CTO whether or not the sector in which the damage occurred can be determined. The CTO will determine liability and make compensation in accordance with the terms of the B/L or by mutual agreement.

8.3.2　国际多式联运的组织形式（Organizational Forms of International Multimodal Transport）

由于国际多式联运具有其他运输组织形式无可比拟的优越性，因而这种新型国际运输方式已在世界各主要国家和地区得到广泛的推广和应用。目前，有代表的国际多式联运主要有远东/欧洲、远东/北美等海陆空联运，其组织形式包括以下几种。

As international multimodal transport has incomparable superiority to other forms of transport organization, this new mode of international transport has been widely promoted and applied in all major countries and regions in the world. At present，the representative international multimodal transport mainly includes Far East/Europe，Far East/North America and other sea-land-air intermodal transport，whose organizational forms include the following.

1．海陆联运（Sea-land Intermodal Transport）

海陆联运是国际多式联运的主要组织形式，也是远东/欧洲多式联运的主要组织形式之一。这种组织形式以航运公司为主体，签发联运提单，与航线两端的内陆运输部门开展联运业务，与大陆桥运输展开竞争。

Sea-land intermodal transport is the main form of organization of international multimodal transport and one of the main forms of the Far East/European multimodal transport. This form of organization is dominated by shipping companies，which issue combined B/L and carry out intermodal transport operations with the inland transport sector at both ends of the route，competing with the continental bridge transport.

2．大陆桥运输（Land Bridge Transport）

在国际多式联运中，大陆桥运输起着非常重要的作用。它是远东/欧洲国际多式联运的主要形式。所谓大陆桥运输是指采用集装箱专用列车或卡车，把横贯大陆的铁路或公路作为"桥梁"，使大陆两端的集装箱海运航线与专用列车或卡车连接起来的一种连贯运输方式。严格来讲，大陆桥运输也是一种海陆联运形式，只是因为其在国际多式联运中的独特地位，在此将其单独作为一种运输组织形式。目前，远东/欧洲的大陆桥运输线路主要有西伯利亚大陆桥、新亚欧大陆桥和北美大陆桥。

Land bridge transport plays a very important role in international multimodal transport. It is the main form of international multimodal transport from the Far East to Europe. The so-called land bridge transport is a continuous transport method using special container trains or trucks，and taking transcontinental railways or highways as "bridges" to connect container shipping lines at both ends of the continent with special trains or trucks. Strictly speaking，land bridge transport is also a form of sea-land combined transport，only because of its unique position in international multimodal transport, it is treated here as a separate organizational form of transport. At present, the main Far East/European land bridge routes are the Siberian Land Bridge, the New Eurasian Land Bridge and the North American Land Bridge.

1）西伯利亚大陆桥（Siberian Land Bridge）

西伯利亚大陆桥又称"第一亚欧大陆桥"，是指使用国际标准集装箱，将货物由远东海运到俄罗斯东部港口，再经跨越欧亚大陆的西伯利亚铁路运至波罗的海沿岸如爱沙尼亚的塔林或拉脱维亚的里加等港口，然后再采用铁路、公路或海运运到欧洲各地的国际多式联运的运输线路。西伯利亚大陆桥于 1971 年由原全苏对外贸易运输公司正式确立，是世界上最著名的国际集装箱多式联运线路之一。它通过苏联西伯利亚铁路，把远东、东南亚及澳大利亚地区与欧洲、中东地区联结起来，因此被称为亚欧大陆桥。

The Siberian Land Bridge, also known as the First Eurasian Land Bridge, is an international multimodal transport line that uses international standard containers to transport goods from the Far East to the eastern ports of Russia, and then to the ports of the Baltic Sea such as Tallinn in Estonia or Riga in Latvia via the trans-Eurasian railway, and then to Europe by rail, road, or sea. The Siberian Land Bridge, formally established in 1971 by the former All-Soviet Foreign Trade Transport Company, is one of the world's most famous international containerized multimodal transport routes. It connects the Far East, Southeast Asia, and Australia with Europe and the Middle East through the Soviet Siberian Railway, and is therefore known as the Asia-Europe Land Bridge.

西伯利亚大陆桥运输包括"海铁铁""海铁海""海铁公"和"海公空"四种运输方式。由俄罗斯的过境运输总公司担当总经营人，它拥有签发货物过境许可证的权利，并签发统一的全程联运提单，承担全程运输责任。至于参加联运的各运输区段，则采用"互为托、承运"的接力方式完成全程联运任务。可以说，西伯利亚大陆桥是较为典型的一条过境多式联运线路。

There are four modes of transportation on the Siberian Land bridge: sea-rail-rail, sea-rail-sea, sea-rail-road and sea-road-air. Sojuztransit of Russia acts as the general operator, which has the right to issue permits for the transit of goods, and issue unified combined transport bills of lading, and it assumes the responsibility for the entire transportation. As for the various transport sections participating in the multimodal transport, the relay mode of "mutual shipper and carrier" is adopted to complete the whole combined transport task. It can be said that the Siberian Land Bridge is a typical multimodal transit transport route.

西伯利亚大陆桥是目前世界上最长的一条大陆桥运输线。它大大缩短了从远东、东南亚及大洋洲到欧洲的运输距离，并因此而节省了运输时间。从远东经太平洋沿岸港口去欧洲的陆桥运输线全长 13 000 千米。而相应的全程水路运输距离（经苏伊士运河）约为 20 000 千米。从横滨到鹿特丹，采用陆桥运输不仅可使运距缩短 1/3，运输时间也可节省 1/2。此外，在一般情况下，运输费用还可节省 20%～30%，因而对货主有很大的吸引力。

The Siberian Land Bridge is currently the longest land bridge transport route in the world. It significantly reduces the transport distances from the Far East, South East Asia and Oceania to Europe and thus saves transport time. The total length of the land bridge route from the Far East to Europe via the Pacific ports is 13 000 km, while the corresponding distance by sea (via the Suez Canal) is approximately 20 000 km. From Yokohama to Rotterdam, the use of the land bridge can not only shorten the distance by 1/3, but also save the transport time by 1/2. In addition, transport costs can be saved by 20% to 30% in general, making it very attractive to shippers.

但是,西伯利亚大陆桥运输在经营管理上存在一定的问题,如港口装卸能力不足、铁路集装箱车辆不足、箱流严重不平衡以及严寒气候的影响等在一定程度上阻碍了它的发展。尤其是随着我国兰新铁路与中哈边境的土西铁路的接轨,一条新的"欧亚大陆桥"形成,为远东至欧洲的国际集装箱多式联运提供了又一条便捷路线,使西伯利亚大陆桥面临严峻的竞争形势。

However, there are certain problems with the management of the Siberian Land Bridge transport, for example, the lack of port handling capacity, the insufficient number of railway container vehicles, the severe imbalance of container flow and the influence of cold climate have hindered its development to some extent. Especially with the integration of China's Lanxin Railway and Turkmenistan-Siberian Railway on the border of China and Kazakhstan, a new Eurasian Land Bridge has been formed, which provides another convenient route for the international container multimodal transport from the Far East to Europe, making the Siberian Land Bridge face severe competition.

2)新亚欧大陆桥(New Eurasian Land Bridge)

新亚欧大陆桥又名"第二亚欧大陆桥",是从中国江苏连云港市开始,向西延伸,在中国西部边境阿拉山口与哈萨克斯坦的德鲁日巴站接轨,直到荷兰鹿特丹、比利时安特卫普等港口的国际化铁路交通干线,中国国内由陇海铁路和兰新铁路组成。

The New Eurasian Land Bridge, also known as the Second Eurasian Land Bridge, is an international transport arteries that starts from Lianyungang City in Jiangsu Province and extends westward, connects with Druzhba Station in Kazakhstan at Alashankou on the western border of China, and reaches Rotterdam in the Netherlands, Antwerp in Belgium and other ports. In China, it is composed of Longhai Railway and Lanxin Railway.

新亚欧大陆桥横贯亚欧两大洲中部地带,总长约 10 900 千米,连接着东亚、中亚、西亚、中东、东欧、中欧、南欧、西欧等地区 40 余国。

The New Eurasian Land Bridge stretches 10 900 kilometers across the central belt of the two continents, connecting more than 40 countries in East Asia, Central Asia, West Asia, the Middle East, Eastern Europe, Central Europe, Southern Europe, and

Western Europe.

新亚欧大陆桥运输与西伯利亚大陆桥运输相比有着较大的优势。

The transportation of the New Eurasian Land Bridge has greater advantages than that of the Siberian Land Bridge.

（1）它使亚欧之间的货运距离比西伯利亚大陆桥缩短得更为显著。从日本、韩国至欧洲，通过新亚欧大陆桥，水陆全程仅为 12 000 千米，比经苏伊士运河少 8 000 多千米，比经巴拿马运河少 11 000 多千米，比绕道好望角少 15 000 多千米。

（1）It shortens the freight distance between Asia and Europe more significantly than the Siberian Land Bridge. From Japan and the Republic of Korea to Europe through the New Eurasian Land Bridge，the whole land and sea transportation is only 12 000 kilometers，8 000 kilometers less than the Suez Canal route，11 000 kilometers less than the Panama Canal route, and 15 000 kilometers less than the detour through the Cape of Good Hope.

（2）它使东亚与中亚、西亚的货运距离大幅度缩短。如从日本神户、韩国釜山等港至伊朗德黑兰，经西伯利亚大陆桥，陆上距离达到 13 322 千米，走新亚欧大陆桥，陆上只有 9 977 千米，两者相差 3 345 千米。

（2）It has significantly reduced the freight distance between East Asia and Central and West Asia. For example，from the ports of Kobe in Japan and Pusan in the Republic of Korea to Iran and Tehran，the distance overland reached 13 322 km when transported via the Siberian Land Bridge，while only 9 977 km overland when transported via the New Eurasian Land Bridge，a difference of 3 345 km between the two routes.

（3）由于运距的缩短，它在运输时间和运费上将比西伯利亚大陆桥又有所减少，更有利于同海运的竞争。

（3）Due to the shortening of the transportation distance，it will reduce the transportation time and freight cost compared with the Siberian Land Bridge，which is more conducive to the competition with marine transportation.

（4）它的东端桥头堡连云港自然条件好，位置适中，气候温和，一年四季可不间断地作业。

（4）The bridgehead at its eastern end，Lianyungang，has good natural conditions，a moderate location，and a mild climate，allowing for uninterrupted operation throughout the year.

3）北美大陆桥（North American Land Bridge）

北美大陆桥是指利用北美的大铁路从远东到欧洲的"海陆海"联运，是世界上历史最悠久、影响最大、服务范围最广的陆桥运输线。该陆桥运输包括美国大陆桥运输和加拿大大陆桥运输。

The North American Land Bridge is the world's oldest，most influential，and most extensive land bridge transport route from the Far East to Europe using the Great North

American Railway. This land bridge transport is sea-land-sea combined transport and includes the US Continental Bridge transport and the Canadian Continental Bridge transport.

美国大陆桥有两条运输线路：一条是从西部太平洋沿岸至东部大西洋沿岸的铁路和公路运输线；另一条是从西部太平洋沿岸至东南部墨西哥湾沿岸的铁路和公路运输线。美国大陆桥于 1971 年底由经营远东/欧洲航线的船公司和铁路承运人联合开办"海陆海"多式联运线，后来美国几家班轮公司也投入营运。目前，主要有四个集团经营远东经美国大陆桥至欧洲的国际多式联运业务。这些集团均以经营人的身份签发多式联运单证，对全程运输负责。

The US Land Bridge has two transport routes: one is the rail and road transportation from the Pacific coast in the west to the Atlantic coast in the east; the other is the rail and road route from the Pacific coast in the west to the Gulf coast in the southeast. The US Land Bridge was launched at the end of 1971 as a joint venture between shipping companies and rail carriers operating Far East/Europe routes, and later several liner companies from the USA also entered into operation. There are currently four main groups operating international multimodal transport services from the Far East to Europe via the US Continental Bridge. Each of these groups issues multimodal transport documents as an operator and is responsible for the entire journey.

加拿大大陆桥与美国大陆桥相似，由船公司把货物海运至温哥华，经铁路运到蒙特利尔或哈利法克斯，再与大西洋海运相接。

The Canadian Land Bridge is similar to the US Land Bridge in that shipping companies transport goods by sea to Vancouver, by rail to Montreal or Halifax, and then by sea to the Atlantic Ocean.

据统计，从远东到北美东海岸的货物有 50% 以上是采用双层列车进行运输的，因为采用这种大陆桥运输方式比采用全程水运方式通常要快 1～2 周。例如，集装箱货从日本东京到欧洲鹿特丹港，采用全程水运(经巴拿马运河或苏伊士运河)通常需 5～6 周时间，而采用北美大陆桥运输需 3 周左右的时间。

According to statistics, 50% or more of the cargo from the Far East to the East Coast of North America is transported by double-decker trains, as it is usually 1 to 2 weeks faster by this land bridge method than by full water transport. For example, it usually takes about 5 to 6 weeks to transport container goods from Tokyo to Rotterdam via the Panama Canal or Suez Canal, while it takes about 3 weeks to transport by the North American Land Bridge.

随着美国和加拿大大陆桥运输的成功营运，北美其他地区也开展了大陆桥运输，墨西哥大陆桥就是其中之一。该大陆桥横跨特万特佩克地峡，连接太平洋沿岸的萨利纳克鲁斯港和墨西哥湾沿岸的夸察夸尔科斯港，陆上距离 182 海里。墨西哥大陆桥于 1982 年开始营运，目前其服务范围还很有限，对其他港口和大陆桥运输的影响还很小。

Following the successful operation of land bridge transportation in the United States and Canada, land bridge transportation in other parts of North America is also carried out, the Mexican Land Bridge is one of them. The land bridge crosses the Isthmus Tehuantepec and connects the port of Salina Cruz on the Pacific coast with the port of Quacha Cuarcos on the Gulf Coast, with a land distance of 182 nautical mile. The Mexican Land Bridge, which began operations in 1982, serves only a limited area and has had little impact on other ports and land bridge traffic.

4）其他大陆桥运输形式（Other Land Bridge Transportation Forms）

北美地区的大陆桥运输不仅包括上述大陆桥运输，而且包括小陆桥运输和微桥运输等运输组织形式。

The land bridge transportation in North America not only includes the above-mentioned land bridge transport, but also includes mini bridge and micro bridge transport and other transport organizations.

3. 海空联运（Sea-air Combined Transport）

海空联运又被称为空桥运输。在运输组织方式上，空桥运输与陆桥运输有所不同：陆桥运输在整个货运过程中使用的是同一个集装箱，不用换装，而空桥运输的货物通常要在航空港换入航空集装箱。但两者的目标是一致的，即以低费率提供快捷、可靠的运输服务。

Sea-air combined transport is also known as air-bridge transport. In the way transport is organised, air-bridge transport differs from land-bridge transport: land-bridge transport uses the same container throughout the freight transport process without changing, while air-bridge transport usually involves moving the cargo into an air container at the air port. However, the objective of both is the same, i.e. to provide fast and reliable transport services at low rates.

海空联运方式始于 20 世纪 60 年代，但到 80 年代才得以较快地发展。采用这种运输方式，运输时间比全程海运少，运输费用比全程空运便宜。20 世纪 60 年代，将远东船运至美国西海岸的货物，再通过航空运至美国内陆地区或美国东海岸，从而出现了海空联运。当然，这种联运组织形式是以海运为主，只是最终交货运输区段由空运承担。1960 年底，苏联航空公司开辟了经由西伯利亚至欧洲航空线。1968 年，加拿大航空公司参加了国际多式联运。20 世纪 80 年代，出现了经由新加坡、泰国等至欧洲的航空线。目前，国际海空联运线路主要有以下几种。

Sea and air combined transport started in the 1960s, but it was not developed until the 1980s. With this mode of transport, transport time is less than full sea transport and transport costs are cheaper than full air transport. In the 1960s, cargo shipped from the Far East to the West Coast of the United States was transported by air to the interior of the United States or to the East Coast of the United States, resulting in the emergence of sea-air multimodal transport. Of course, this kind of combined transportation is mainly organized by sea，but the final delivery transportation section is air. At the end of 1960，Soviet Airlines opened air routes to Europe via Siberia. In 1968. Air Canada joined the international multimodal transport，and in the 1980s，there were air routes to Europe via Singapore，Thailand，etc. Currently，the main international sea-air combines transport routes are as follows.

（1）远东—欧洲：目前，远东与欧洲间的航线有以温哥华、西雅图、洛杉矶为中转地，也有以香港、曼谷、符拉迪沃斯托克为中转地，此外还有以旧金山、新加坡为中转地。

（1）The Far East-Europe：at present，there are routes between the Far East and Europe with Vancouver，Seattle and Los Angeles as transit points，as well as Hong Kong，Bangkok and Vladivostok as transit points. In addition，there are also San Francisco and Singapore as transit points.

（2）远东—中南美：近年来，远东至中南美的海空联运发展较快，因为此处港口和内陆运输不稳定，所以对海空运输的需求很大。该联运线以迈阿密、洛杉矶、温哥华为中转地。

（2）The Far East-Central and South America：in recent years，air-sea multimodal transport from the Far East to Central and South America has developed rapidly，as there is a great demand for air-sea transport due to the instability of ports and inland transport here. This combined transport route takes Miami，Los Angeles and Vancouver as transit points.

（3）远东—中近东、非洲、澳大利亚：这是以香港、曼谷为中转地至中近东、非洲的运输服务。在特殊情况下，还有经马赛至非洲、经曼谷至印度、经香港至澳大利亚等联运线，但这些线路货运量较小。

（3）The Far East-Middle and Near East，Africa，Australia：these are transport services to the Middle East and Africa with Hong Kong and Bangkok as transshipment points. In exceptional cases，there are also multimodal transport routes to Africa via Marseille，to India via Bangkok，and to Australia via Hong Kong，but the freight volumes on these routes is small.

总体而言，运输距离越远，采用海空联运的优越性就越大，因为同完全采用海运相比，其运输时间更短；同直接采用空运相比，其费率更低。因此，从远东出发将欧洲、中南美以及非洲作为海空联运的主要市场是合适的。

Overall，the greater the distance travelled，the greater the advantages of using air-sea intermodal transport because of shorter transit time compared to full sea transport and lower rate compared to direct air transport. It is therefore appropriate to consider Europe，Central and South America，and Africa as the main markets for air-sea intermodal transport from the Far East.

Words and Expressions

即测即练

习题

第 9 章

Chapter 9

运输保险概论
General Introduction to Transport Insurance

Learning Objectives：
1. Master the concept and connotation of insurance；
2. Master the concept of international cargo insurance and its role；
3. Understand the types of insurance；
4. Focus on the basic principles of insurance，including principle of utmost good faith，principle of insurance interests，principle of proximate cause，principle of indemnity，principle of subrogation，and principle of repeated insurance apportionment.

引导案例

2022 年 6 月 1 日，甲国 A 茶叶进出口公司向乙国 B 公司出口一批乌龙茶，CIF 价格。A 公司向 C 保险公司投保了平安险，保险金额是 240 万元。运输途中船舶遭遇恶劣气候，暴风雨持续数日，致使船舶通风设备无法打开，导致货舱内湿度过高并形成舱汗，造成这批茶叶发霉变质、全部受损。乙国 B 公司遂向 C 保险公司提出索赔，要求赔偿全部损失。C 保险公司检查现场和了解情况后，认为该损失不属于平安险承保范围，因此拒绝赔偿。双方发生争议，并诉诸法院。法院在审理过程中，对 C 保险公司是否应承担赔偿责任有两种不同的处理意见：第一种意见是 C 保险公司应当拒赔。拒赔理由如下：本案中茶叶发霉变质是由于受潮和舱汗这两个原因引起的，而受潮和舱汗造成标的损失的责任分别由海上货运险的附加险中的受潮受热险和淡水雨淋险承保。A 进出口公司只投保了平安险，没有投保一般附加险或者附加受潮受热险和淡水雨淋险，所以本案中的货物损失不属于承保责任范围，C 保险公司应当拒绝赔偿。第二种意见是 C 保险公司应该给予赔偿。其理由是：本案茶叶受损之前，运输船舶首先碰到了持续数日的恶劣天气，恶劣天气与受潮和舱汗连续发生，恶劣天气是前因，受潮和舱汗是后果，即恶劣天气导致受潮和舱汗的发生，受潮和舱汗是恶劣天气的必然结果。因此，恶劣天气是茶叶受损的近因。根据保险的近因原则，保险人负责赔偿承保的风险为近因所引起的损失。本案中恶劣天气是平安险承保的风险。因此 C 保险公司应当赔偿 100 万元的茶叶损失。你认为哪种意见是合理的？

资料来源：近因原则在保险实践中的应用［EB/OL］. https://www.360docs.net/doc/83320204.html.

保险作为一种经济补偿手段，在国际贸易发展中发挥着重要作用，二者密不可分，相互作用，共同发展。本章主要学习保险，特别是国际货运保险的一些基本知识、世界各国保险法及海商法共同认可和遵循的保险基本原则。

Insurance, as a means of economic compensation, plays an important role in the development of international trade, and the two are inextricably linked, interacting and developing together. This chapter focuses on some of the basics of insurance, in particular international freight insurance, and the basic principles of insurance that are commonly accepted and followed by insurance laws and maritime laws throughout the world.

9.1　保险的概念、内涵及作用（Concept，Connotation and Function of Insurance）

从法律角度理解，保险是双方当事人的经济合同行为；从经济角度理解，保险是一种经济补偿手段，是对危险造成的损失进行补偿的制度。《中华人民共和国保险法》（以下简称《保险法》）第一章第二条对保险所下的定义是：投保人根据合同约定，向保险人支付保险费，保险人对于合同约定的可能发生的事故因其发生所造成的财产损失承担赔偿保险金责任，或者当被保险人死亡、伤残、疾病或者达到合同约定的年龄、期限等条件时承担给付保险金责任的商业保险行为。

From the legal point of view, insurance is the economic contractual act of both parties; from the economic point of view, insurance is a means of economic compensation, a system of compensation for losses caused by danger. Article 2, Chapter 1 of *Insurance Law of the People's Republic of China* (Hereinafter referred to as *Insurance Law*) defines insurance as a commercial insurance act whereby the policyholder pays insurance premiums to the insurer in accordance with the contract, and the insurer shall be liable for compensation for the property loss caused by the possible accident stipulated in the contract, or shall bear the liability to pay the premium when the insured dies, becomes disabled, falls ill, or reaches the age and time limit stipulated in the contract.

9.1.1　保险的内涵（Connotation of Insurance）

按照上述关于保险的定义，商业保险具有以下内涵。

According to the above definition of insurance, commercial insurance has the following connotations.

1. 保险是一种合同关系（Insurance is a Contractual Relationship）

通常所指的保险是一种商业保险关系，这种关系是以合同为基础的，有关保险人、被保险人等当事人之间的关系是一种合同关系。当事人的权利与义务以保险合同的具体规定为依据，因此，保险合同对合同当事人的权利与义务应有明确规定，且这些规定均具有法律约束力。保险合同作为一种损失补偿或履行保险金额给付义务的合同,要求投保人支付保险费,保险人在保险标的遭受承保责任范围内的风险损失时承担赔偿责任,或者在约定事故发生时和约定期限届满时履行给付保险金的义务。保险合同可分为两大类:一类是财产保险合同;另一类是人身保险合同。

What is commonly referred to as insurance is a commercial insurance relationship that is contract-based, the relationship between the parties involved, such as the insurer and the insured, is a contractual one. The rights and obligations of the parties are based on the specific provisions of the insurance contract, therefore, the insurance contract should have clear provisions on the rights and obligations of the parties to the contract, and these provisions should be legally binding. An insurance contract, as a contract for reimbursement of loss or fulfillment of the obligation to pay benefits, requires the policyholder to pay a premium and the insurer to assume liability in the event that the subject-matter insured suffers any losses within the scope of coverage, or to fulfill the obligation to pay benefits upon the occurrence of the agreed accident and the expiration of the agreed period of time. Insurance contracts can be divided into two main categories: one is property insurance contracts; the other is personal insurance contracts.

2. 保险承保的是一种不确定性风险(Insurance Covers an Uncertain Risk)

保险合同中约定承保的风险事故必须是不确定的。这是因为若约定的灾害事故肯定不会发生,则没有必要投保;相反,若约定的灾害事故一定会发生,则任何保险人都不会愿意承保。因此,只有在订立保险合同时,保险事故有可能发生,但究竟是否发生、何时发生、发生时会造成多大的损失都不确定的情况下,保险当事人之间的合同关系才能成立。保险承保的风险事故或事件的发生是投保人与保险人都无法预见或者难以控制的。

The risk or accident agreed to be covered in the insurance contract must be uncertain. This is because there is no need to insure if the agreed disaster or accident is certain not to occur; conversely, no insurer will be willing to insure if the agreed disaster or accident is certain to occur. Therefore, the contractual relationship between the insurance parties can only be established when there is a possibility of an insurance accident occurring at the time of the conclusion of the insurance contract, but there is uncertainty as to whether and when it will occur, and how much damage will be caused when it occurs. The occurrence of an accident or event covered by insurance is unforeseen or difficult to control by both the policyholder and the insurer.

3. 承保风险发生后,保险人承担赔偿或给付责任(The Insurer Assumes Liability to Indemnify or Pay Out After the Occurrence of an Insured Risk)

保险人对于被保险人因承保范围内的自然灾害、意外事故或外来原因造成的经济损失承担赔偿责任,或对人身伤亡、丧失工作能力承担给付保险金的责任。承担此项责任时,保险人通常支付相当于损失金额的货币。

The insurer is liable to pay compensation to the insured for economic loss caused by a covered natural disaster，accident，or external cause，or to pay insurance benefits for personal injury，death，or incapacity. When assuming this liability，the insurer usually pays a sum of money equivalent to the amount of the loss.

4. 保险具有互助的性质（Insurance has the Nature of Mutual Assistance）

从总体上看，一旦个别投保人遭受了风险损失，其他参与保险的投保人即以所缴纳的保险费共同承担其所遭受的经济损失，从而使保险具有互助的性质。保险使风险得以在参与保险的人之间进行分散，共同分摊损失。

From a general point of view，once an individual policyholder suffers the loss caused by the risk，the other policyholders who participate in the insurance will share the economic loss with the premium they pay，so that the insurance has the nature of mutual assistance. Insurance makes it possible to share the risks among those involved in the policy and share losses together.

9.1.2 国际货运保险的概念及其作用（The Concept and Function of International Cargo Transportation Insurance）

货物运输保险是指以海轮、火车、飞机、汽车、邮运和联运等各种运输工具承运的货物作为保险标的的一种保险，而国际货物运输保险是指对国家间运输的货物办理的保险。被保险人或称投保人在货物装运以前，估定一定的投保金额（即保险金额），向保险人或称承保人即保险公司投保货物运输险。国际贸易中的货运保险是涉外保险的重要险种之一，为国际贸易及其他经济交往活动中的货物运输提供保险保障，其作用主要体现在以下几个方面。

Cargo transportation insurance is a kind of insurance that takes the goods carried by various means of transportation such as sea vessels，trains，airplanes，automobiles，conveyance of mail and intermodal transportation as the subject of insurance，while international cargo transportation insurance refers to the insurance handled for the goods transported between countries. The insured or the applicant（policyholder）estimates a certain amount of insurance（i. e. insured amount）before the shipment of the goods，and insure against the risk of carriage of goods with the insurer(or underwriter)，i. e. the insurance company. Cargo transportation insurance in international trade is one of the important types of foreign-related insurance，providing insurance for the carriage of goods in international trade and other economic exchanges，and its role is mainly reflected in the following aspects.

1. 有利于企业经营的正常进行（Conducive to the Normal Operation of Enterprises）

企业投保国际货运保险，只需交付少量保险费，就可在遭遇保险事故损失时，按照保险合同约定条件得到保险赔偿，及时获得资金，从而使企业迅速恢复生产经营，减少经营损失，保障企业生产经营的正常进行。

When an enterprise is insured for international freight insurance，it only needs to pay a small amount of insurance premiums to get insurance compensation in accordance with the conditions agreed in the insurance contract in the event of an accidental loss, thus enabling timely access to funds, so that it can quickly resume production and operation, reduce operating losses, and ensure the normal production and operation.

2. 有利于促进国际贸易和国际经济交往的发展(Conducive to the Development of International Trade and International Economic Exchanges)

在国际贸易中,买卖双方往往相距遥远,进出口货物需经过长途运输才能到达目的地,在运输过程中容易因灾害事故的发生而遭受损失,阻碍国际贸易的顺利进行,因而,进出口货物均需投保国际货运保险,从而将不确定的风险损失转由保险公司承担。此外,在利用外资、引进技术、合作生产、合资经营、文化交流、国际服务贸易等国际经济交往活动中也常常会涉及国际货物运输。因此,国际货运保险是对外贸易及国际经济合作中不可缺少的重要环节,有助于促进国际贸易和其他国际经济交往的发展。

In international trade, buyers and sellers are often far away from each other, so imported and exported goods need to be transported over long distances to reach the destination, and thus they are prone to suffer losses in the process of transportation due to disasters or accidents, hindering the smooth implementation of international trade. Therefore, imported and exported goods are required to take out international freight insurance, thus the uncertain risks and losses are transferred to the insurance company. In addition, international transportation of goods is often involved in the utilization of foreign capital, the introduction of technology, cooperative production, joint ventures, cultural exchanges, international trade in services and other international economic exchanges. Therefore, international cargo insurance is an important and indispensable link in foreign trade and international economic cooperation, which helps to promote the development of international trade and other international economic exchanges.

3. 有利于加强风险管理,减少灾害损失(Conducive to the Strengthening of Risk Management and the Reduction of Disaster Losses)

保险公司是专门经营风险的企业,常年处理各种灾害事故的索赔案件,积累了丰富的风险管理经验,不仅可以向企业提供各种风险管理经验,而且通过承保时的风险调查分析、保险标的安全情况调查、承保期内风险核查和监督等环节,尽可能消除潜在的风险因素,并通过总结致损原因和规律,对投保人防灾防损措施提出改进建议,从而达到减少灾害事故发生的目的。此外,保险公司还可以在保险条款制定、费率核定、赔偿处理、安全优待等方面贯彻防灾防损精神,调动投保企业提高风险管理的积极性,从而减少灾害事故的发生及降低损害程度。

As an enterprise specializing in risk management, insurance companies have accumulated rich experience in risk management by handling claims of all kinds of catastrophes and accidents over the years. They can not only provide enterprises with various risk management experiences, but also eliminate potential risk factors as far as possible through risk investigation and analysis, safety investigation of the subject-matter insured at the time of underwriting, risk verification and supervision during the underwriting period, and make suggestions for improvement of the insured's disaster prevention and damage prevention measures by summarizing the causes and patterns of damage, so as to reduce the occurrence of disasters and accidents. In addition, insurance companies can also implement the spirit of disaster and loss prevention in the formulation of insurance clauses, the approval of premium rates, and the processing of compensation and preferential treatment of safety, so as to motivate insured enterprises to strengthen risk management and thus reduce the occurrence of disasters and accidents and the degree of damage.

4. 有利于增加外汇收入，增强国际支付能力（Conducive to Increasing Foreign Exchange Earnings and Enhancing International Payment Capacity）

保险费是进出口商品价格的构成要素之一，外汇保险费收入是一项重要的非贸易外汇收入。在出口贸易中，争取使用由卖方负责办理保险的贸易术语，则可赚取保险费外汇收入，增强出口创汇能力；在进口贸易中，争取由买方在本国自行办理保险，则可为国家节省外汇支出，对于增强国家的国际支付能力发挥积极作用。

Insurance premiums are one of the components of the price of imported and exported goods. Foreign exchange insurance premiums are an important source of non-traded foreign exchange income. In export trade, the seller should strive to use the trade terms for which he will be responsible for insurance, so as to earn foreign exchange income of insurance premium, increasing the ability to earn foreign exchange through export. In import trade, the buyer should strive to take out insurance in the country itself, which can save the country's foreign exchange expenditure and play a positive role in enhancing the country's international payment capacity.

9.2 保险的种类（Types of Insurance）

随着经济与科技的快速发展，人们的保险需求日益广泛，各国保险业得到迅速发展，保险的种类和业务范畴也不断扩展。目前，国际上还未形成统一的保险分类原则和分类标准，因此，保险的种类可从不同的角度划分，常见的类型主要有以下四种。

With the rapid development of economy and technology, people's demand for insurance is becoming more and more extensive, which makes the insurance industry in various countries develop rapidly, and the types of insurance and business scope are expanding. At present, there is no unified principle and standard of insurance classification at the international level. Thus, insurance can be categorized in different ways. There are four main common classifications.

9.2.1　按保险标的分类（Classification by Subject-matter Insured）

这是最基本的分类方法。保险标的又称保险对象，是指保险合同中所载明的投保对象。按照保险的标的或对象，保险可分为财产保险、人身保险、责任保险和信用保证保险四大类。

This is the most basic classification method. The subject-matter insured refers to the insured object specified in the insurance contract. According to the subject or object of insurance, it can be divided into four main categories: property insurance, personal insurance, liability insurance and credit & bond insurance.

1. 财产保险（Property Insurance）

财产保险是以物质财富以及相关利益作为标的的一种保险。财产保险主要有以下几种。

Property insurance is a type of insurance in which material wealth and related interests are the subject-matter. The main types of property insurance are as follows.

1）火灾保险（Fire Insurance）

火灾保险简称火险，是指保险人对于保险标的因火灾所导致的损失负责补偿的一种财产保险。火灾是财产面临的最基本和最主要的风险。火灾保险一般不作为单独的险别，而是被包括在综合性险别的责任范围内。

Fire insurance is a type of property insurance in which the insurer is responsible for compensating the subject-matter of the insurance for damage caused by fire. Fire is the most basic and primary risk to property. Fire insurance is generally not regarded as a separate type of insurance, but included in the scope of comprehensive insurance.

2）海上保险（Marine Insurance）

海上保险又称水险，是指保险人对海上标的因海上风险所导致的损失或赔偿责任提供经济保障的一种保险。海上保险主要包括海洋运输货物保险、船舶保险、海上石油开发保险、海上养殖业保险等。

Marine insurance is a type of insurance in which the insurer provides financial protection against loss or liability caused by marine risks to the subject-matter at sea. Marine insurance mainly includes marine transport cargo insurance, ship insurance, offshore petroleum development insurance, and marine aquaculture insurance.

3）货物运输保险（Cargo Transportation Insurance）

货物运输保险是指保险人对运输途中的货物因遭受保单承保的各类风险而导致的损失提供经济保障的一种保险。货物运输保险主要包括海洋运输货物保险、陆上运输货物保险、航空运输货物保险、邮政包裹运输货物保险等。

Cargo transportation insurance is a kind of insurance in which the insurer provides financial protection for loss caused by the various risks covered by the policy to goods in transit. Cargo transportation insurance mainly includes marine cargo insurance, land cargo insurance, air cargo insurance, and postal parcel cargo insurance.

4）运输工具保险（Conveyance Insurance）

运输工具保险是指承保海、陆、空、内河各类运输工具在行驶和停放过程中所发生的各种损失的保险，主要包括船舶保险、汽车保险、飞机保险、铁路车辆保险等。

Conveyance insurance refers to the insurance that covers all kinds of losses of various means of transport by sea，land，air and inland rivers in the process of driving and parking. It mainly includes ship insurance，automobile insurance，aircraft insurance，railway vehicle insurance，etc.

5）工程保险（Engineering Insurance）

工程保险是以各类建筑工程和机器安装过程中的财产为保险标的的保险。保险的责任除了包括自然灾害和意外事故所造成的财产损失外，还包括第三者人身伤害与财产损失的补偿。其主要包括建筑工程保险、安装工程保险等。

Engineering insurance is a kind of insurance that covers property in the course of various types of construction work and the installation of machinery. In addition to property damage caused by natural disasters and accidents，its insurance coverage also includes compensation for bodily injury and property damage to third parties. It mainly includes insurance for construction and installation works.

6）农业保险（Agricultural Insurance）

农业保险是指保险人为农业生产者在从事种植、养殖和捕捞生产过程中，因遭遇自然灾害或意外事故而导致的损失提供经济补偿的一种保险。其主要包括农作物保险、农产品保险、牲畜保险、家禽保险及其他养殖业保险等。

Agricultural insurance is an insurance in which the insurer provides economic compensation to agricultural producers for the losses caused by natural disasters or accidents in the process of planting，breeding and fishing. It mainly includes crop insurance，agricultural product insurance，livestock insurance，poultry insurance，and other aquaculture insurance.

7）盗窃保险（Burglary Insurance）

盗窃保险是指对财产因遭抢劫或者偷窃所造成的损失进行经济补偿的保险。盗窃保险一般包括在一揽子保险单中，包括商业盗窃保险、银行盗窃保险、个人盗窃保险等。

Burglary insurance is a kind of insurance that financially compensates for the loss of property due to robbery or theft. Burglary insurance is typically included in a package of policies，including commercial theft insurance，bank theft insurance，and personal theft insurance.

2. 人身保险（Personal Insurance）

人身保险是指以人的身体或生命为保险标的的保险。当投保人在保险期满继续生存或在保险期内死亡时，保险人应按保险合同约定承担给付保险金责任。人身保险可划分为人寿保险、人身意外伤害保险和健康保险。

Personal insurance refers to the insurance with human body or life as the subject-matter insured. When the policyholder continues to live at the end of the insurance period or dies during the insurance period，the insurer shall be liable for the payment of benefits in accordance with the insurance contract.

1）人寿保险（Life Insurance）

人寿保险简称寿险，是一种以人的生死为保险对象的保险，是投保人在保险责任期内生存或死亡，由保险人根据契约规定给付保险金的一种保险。人寿保险的业务范围包括生存保险、死亡保险、两全保险。

Life insurance is a kind of insurance that takes life and death as the insurance object. It is an insurance in which the insurer pays the insurance benefits according to the contract depending on whether the applicant survives or dies within the insurance liability period. It includes survival insurance，death insurance，and endowment insurance.

2）人身意外伤害保险（Personal Accident Insurance）

人身意外伤害保险是以人的身体遭受意外伤害为保险条件的保险。

Personal accident insurance is an insurance that takes the accidental injury of human body as the compensation condition.

3）健康保险（Health Insurance）

健康保险也叫疾病保险，是以非意外伤害而由投保人本身的疾病导致的伤残、死亡为保险条件的保险。

Health insurance，also known as disease insurance，is a type of insurance that compensates the insured when disability or death occurs due to the insured's own illness rather than an accident.

3. 责任保险（Liability Insurance）

责任保险是以投保人依法应负的民事损害赔偿责任或经过特别约定的合同责任作为保险标的的保险。按照承保责任的不同，其可分为公众责任保险、产品责任保险、职业责任保险和雇主责任保险。

Liability insurance is an insurance that takes the civil liability for damages to which the policyholder is legally liable or contractual liability specifically agreed upon as the subject-matter insured. According to the scope of coverage，it can be divided into public liability insurance，product liability insurance，professional liability insurance，and employer's liability insurance.

4. 信用保证保险（Credit & Bond Insurance）

信用保证保险，是一种以经济合同所规定的预期应得的有形财产或预期应得的经济利益为保险标的的保险。按照担保对象的不同，信用保证保险可分为信用保险和保证保险。

Credit & bond insurance is a kind of insurance which takes the expected tangible property or expected economic benefits stipulated in the economic contract as the subject-matter insured. According to the different warrant objects of guarantee，it can be divided into credit insurance and bond insurance.

1）信用保险（Credit Insurance）

信用保险是权利人要求保险人担保对方（被保证人）的信用的保险。

Credit insurance is a kind of insurance in which the obligee requires the insurer to guarantee the credit of the other party（the insured）.

2）保证保险（Bond Insurance）

保证保险是被保证人根据权利人的要求，要求保险人担保自己信用的保险。保证保险的主要险别有忠诚保证保险和履约保证保险。

Bond insurance is an insurance in which the insured requires the insurer to guarantee his own credit according to the requirements of the obligee. The main types of bond insurance are loyalty bond insurance and performance bond insurance.

9.2.2　按保险的性质分类（Classification According to the Nature of Insurance）

1. 商业保险（Commercial Insurance）

商业保险是指投保人和保险人订立保险合同，根据保险合同约定，投保人向保险人支付保险费，保险人对可能发生的事故，因其发生所造成的损失承担赔偿责任，或者当投保人死亡、疾病、伤残或者达到约定的年龄期限时承担给付保险金责任的保险。

Commercial insurance refers to the insurance contract concluded between the policyholder and the insurer，according to which the policyholder pays the premium to the insurer and the insurer assumes the liability for the loss caused by the accident that may occur，or the liability to pay the premium when the insured is dead，disabled，sick，or reaches the agreed age or time limit.

2. 社会保险（Social Insurance）

社会保险是指国家通过立法对社会劳动者在暂时或永久丧失劳动能力或失业时，提供一定的物质帮助，以保证其基本生活的社会保障制度。社会保险是强制性的，凡符合法律规定条件的成员，不论愿意与否，都要参加社会保险；而商业保险出于自愿。

Social insurance refers to the social security system whereby the state provides certain material assistance to social workers when they are temporarily or permanently incapacitated or unemployed through legislation，so as to ensure their basic livelihood. Social insurance is compulsory for all members who meet the conditions established by law，whether they wish to join or not，while commercial insurance is voluntary.

3. 政策保险（Policy Insurance）

政策保险是政府由于某个特定的政策目的，以商业保险的一般做法而举办的保险。比如，为促进进出口贸易的出口信用保险。政策保险通常由国家设立专门机构，或者委托官方或者半官方的保险公司具体承办。比如，我国的出口信用保险是由国家政策性保险公司——中国出口信用保险公司专门为出口企业提供政策性保险产品。

Policy insurance is a kind of insurance which is organized by the government according to the general practice of commercial insurance for a specific policy purpose. For example，export credit insurance to facilitate import and export trade. Policy insurance is usually provided by specialized institutions set up by the state, or by official or semi-official insurance companies. For example, China's export credit insurance is provided specifically by the state policy-based insurance company, China Export & Credit Insurance Corporation, to support export enterprises.

9.2.3　按保险的实施方式分类(Classification According to the Implementation Mode of Insurance)

1. 强制保险(Compulsory Insurance)

强制保险又称法定保险,是指国家对一定的对象,以法律或者行政法规的形式规定必须参加的保险。这种保险关系的建立是依据国家立法,而不是投保人和保险人的意愿与合同行为。强制保险又有两种实施形式:一是通过立法规定,在特定范围建立保险人与被保险人的关系,如飞机、铁路、轮船的旅客意外伤害险;二是有关法律、法规规定一定范围内的人或物必须参加保险,否则不允许从事法律所许可的业务或活动,如许多国家的劳工法规定,雇主必须为其雇员投保人身意外伤害险。

Compulsory insurance, also known as statutory insurance, is the insurance that is required by the state for a certain object, in the form of a law or administrative regulation. The establishment of this insurance relationship is based on national legislation, not on the will and contractual actions of the insured and the insurer. Compulsory insurance has two further forms of implementation: the first is to establish the relationship between the insurer and the insured in a specific scope through legislation, such as the accidental injury insurance for passengers of aircraft, railways, and ships; second, the relevant laws and regulations stipulate that persons or things within a certain scope must be insured, otherwise they are not allowed to engage in business or activities permitted by law, for example, labour laws in many countries require employers to insure their employees against bodily injury.

2. 自愿保险(Voluntary Insurance)

自愿保险又称任意保险,是指投保人与保险人在平等、自愿的基础上,通过签订保险合同而成立的保险关系。自愿保险其实就是投保人有权决定是否投保、向谁投保、投保险别、投保金额、保险期限以及是否退保等事项。至于保险人,也有权选择被保险人,决定承保金额和保险期限等保险条件。自愿保险是商业保险的基本形式。

Voluntary insurance, also known as arbitrary insurance, is an insurance relationship between the policyholder and the insurer established through an insurance contract on an equal and voluntary basis. In fact, voluntary insurance means that the applicant has the right to decide whether to insure, from whom to insure, the type of insurance, the amount of insurance, the period of insurance, and whether to surrender the insurance. As for the insurer, he also has the right to choose the insurant, and to determine insured amount, insurance period, and other insurance conditions. Voluntary insurance is the basic form of commercial insurance.

9.2.4 按承担责任次序的不同和承保方式的不同分类(Classified According to the Order of Responsibility and the Way of Underwriting)

1. 原保险(Original Insurance)

原保险又称第一次保险,是指投保人与保险人直接订立保险合同、建立保险关系的保险形式。保险人对被保险人因事故所导致的损害承担直接原始的赔偿责任。我们一般所说的保险大多指的是原保险。

Original insurance refers to the form of insurance in which the policyholder and the insurer directly enter into an insurance contract and establish an insurance relationship. The insurer assumes direct original liability to pay compensation for damage caused by the accident of the insured. Most of what we generally refer to as insurance is original insurance.

2. 再保险(Reinsurance)

再保险又称分保,是指将原保险责任的一部分或者全部转让给另一个保险人承保的保险形式。《保险法》第二章第二十八条对再保险作出了如下定义:保险人将其承担的保险业务,以分保形式部分转移给其他保险人的,为再保险。最初承保业务的公司称为分出公司或者原保险人;接受分出公司保险的公司称为再保险人。再保险是保险业务不可缺少的组成部分,国际上已经出现了不少专门经营再保险业务的再保险公司和再保险集团,如慕尼黑再保险公司、瑞士再保险公司等。中国再保险(集团)有限责任公司成立于1996年,专门经营国内、国际再保险业务。

Reinsurance refers to the transfer of part or all of the original insurance liability to another insurer for coverage. Article 28 of chapter 2 of *Insurance Law* defines reinsurance as follows: reinsurance is the assignment of some or all of the original insurance liability to another insurer for coverage. Reinsurance is an indispensable part of the insurance business, and there are many specialized reinsurance companies and reinsurance groups in the world, such as Munich Re and Swiss Re, etc. China Reinsurance (Group) Co. , Ltd. was established in 1996, specializing in domestic and international reinsurance business.

3. 共同保险(Coinsurance)

共同保险简称共保,是指由两个或者两个以上保险人,在相同的保险期限和范围内,承保同一风险的保险形式。当发生赔偿责任时,其赔偿按照保险人各自承保的金额比例分摊。

Coinsurance is a form of insurance in which two or more insurers, for the same period and scope of coverage, cover the same risk. When liability arises, the compensation shall be apportioned according to the proportion of the amount insured by each insurer.

4. 重复保险(Double Insurance)

《保险法》第二章第五十六条对重复保险作出了如下定义:重复保险是指投保人对同

一保险标的、同一保险利益、同一保险事故分别与两个以上保险人订立保险合同,且保险金额总和超过保险价值的保险。《保险法》进一步规定:各保险人赔偿保险金的总和不得超过保险价值。除合同另有约定外,各保险人按照其保险金额与保险金额总和的比例承担赔偿保险金的责任。此外,重复保险的投保人可以就保险金额总和超过保险价值的部分,请求各保险人按比例返还保险费。在重复保险中,根据保险的补偿原则,为了防止被保险人获得双重赔偿,需要将保险标的的实际损失在各保险人之间分摊。

Article 56 of chapter 2 of the *Insurance Law* defines double insurance as follows: double insurance refers to the insurance in which the applicant has entered into insurance contracts with more than two insurers for the same subject-matter, the same insurable interest, and the same insured accident, and the sum of the insured amount exceeds the insurable value. The *Insurance Law* further stipulates that the sum of the indemnities of the insurers may not exceed the insured value. Unless otherwise stipulated in the contract, each insurer is liable for compensation in the proportion of its insurance value to the sum of the insured values. In addition, the policyholder of a double insurance may request a pro-rata refund of the premium from each insurer for the portion of the total insured amount that exceeds the insured value. In double insurance, according to the compensation principle of insurance, in order to prevent the insured from receiving double compensation, it is necessary to apportion the actual loss of the subject-matter insured among the insurers.

9.3 保险的基本原则(Basic Principles of Insurance)

9.3.1 最大诚信原则(Principle of Utmost Good Faith)

1. 最大诚信原则的含义(Meaning of the Principle of Utmost Good Faith)

最大诚信原则起源于海上保险,现在已成为所有保险合同中各方需遵循的基本原则。国际货物海上运输需跨越国界,作为保险标的的船舶或货物与保险人相距甚远,保险人对承保标的实际情况一无所知,对承保风险难以控制,只能依据投保人的申报内容判断风险情况,决定是否承保及保险费率的高低,因此,投保人的告知是否真实、全面,对保险人极为重要,最大诚信原则逐渐成为保险业务活动的基本原则之一。很多国家还将其以法律形式加以确认,如英国 1906 年《海上保险法》第十七条规定,海上保险契约以最大诚信为基础,倘若任何一方不遵守最大诚信原则,另一方必须声明此项契约无效。《中华人民共和国民法典》第一章第七条规定,民事主体从事民事活动,应当遵循诚信原则,秉持诚实,恪守承诺。《保险法》第一章第五条规定,保险活动当事人行使权利、履行义务应当遵循诚实信用原则。

所谓最大诚信原则,就是指保险双方当事人在签订和履行保险合同的过程中,都能做到最大限度的诚实和守信,不隐瞒与保险相关的重要事实,不逃避或减少按合同规定对另一方所应承担的责任。

The principle of utmost good faith originated in marine insurance and is now a fundamental principle to be followed by all parties in all insurance contracts. International maritime transportation of goods needs to cross the national border, and the insured ship or cargo is far away from the insurer, so the insurer knows nothing about the actual situation of the insured object and can hardly control the insured risk. The insurer can only judge the risk situation based on the declaration of the policyholder and decide whether to insure and the premium rate, therefore, whether the information of the policyholder is true and comprehensive is very important to the insurer, and the principle of utmost good faith is becoming one of the basic principles of insurance business activities. In many countries, this principle is also recognized by law. For example, article 17 of the *Maritime Insurance Act* 1906 provides that marine insurance contracts should be based on utmost good faith, and if either party fails to observe the principle of the utmost good faith, the other party must declare the contract void. Chapter 1, article 7 of *Civil Code of the People's Republic of China* stipulates that the parties to civil legal relations shall conduct civil activities under the principle of good faith, adhere to honesty, and fulfill their promises. Chapter 1, article 5 of *Insurance Law* stipulates that parties to insurance activities shall exercise their powers and perform their obligations in accordance with the principle of honesty and trustworthiness.

The principle of utmost good faith means that both parties to an insurance contract will act with utmost honesty and trustworthiness in the conclusion and performance of the insurance contract, will not conceal material facts relating to the insurance, and will not evade or reduce their liability to the other party under the contract.

2. 最大诚信原则的基本内容（Basic Content of the Principle of Utmost Good Faith）

最大诚信原则主要涉及两个方面的问题，即告知（说明）和保证。

The principle of utmost good faith mainly involves two aspects, namely disclosure and warranty.

1）告知（Disclosure）

所谓告知，就是指在订立保险合同时，投保人应将有关保险标的的重要事实如实告知保险人，以使保险人了解保险标的的真实情况，最终决定是否承保和费率的大小；而保险人也应当向投保人说明保险合同的条款内容，使投保人决定是否投保。

Disclosure refers to that the policyholder should truthfully inform the insurer of the important facts about the subject matter of the insurance when concluding the insurance contract, so that the insurer can understand the real situation of the subject matter insured and decide whether to underwrite the insurance and the level of the premium rate. The insurer should also explain the terms and conditions of the insurance contract to the policyholder so that the policyholder can decide whether or not to take out insurance.

（1）保险人的告知。

（1）Disclosure by the insurer.

① 保险人告知的内容。保险人告知的内容主要有：一般说明的义务，即在订立保险合同时，要主动向投保人说明保险合同的条款内容；明确说明义务，即向投保人明确说明保险人责任免除条款，未明确说明的，该条款不产生效力。

① Content of the insurer's disclosure. The contents of the insurer's disclosure mainly include: the duty of general explanation, i. e. when concluding the insurance contract, the insurer should take the initiative to explain the terms and conditions of the insurance contract to the policyholder; the duty of explicit explanation, i. e. exemption clause of insurer's liability should be clearly explained to the policyholder, if it is not explicitly stated, the clause will not be effective.

② 保险人告知的方式。保险人告知的方式一般分为明确列明与明确说明两种。

② Ways of disclosure by insurer. There are two ways of disclosure by the insurer, which are explicitly listed and explicitly stated.

（i）明确列明。明确列明是指保险人只需将保险的主要内容明确列明在保险合同当中，即视为已告知投保人。

（ii）明确说明。明确说明是指不仅应将保险的主要内容列明在保险合同中，还需对投保人进行明确提示，并加以适当、正确的解释。

（i）Explicitly listed. It means that the insurer is deemed to have informed the policyholder as long as the main contents of the insurance are clearly stated in the insurance contract.

（ii）Explicitly stated. It means that not only should the main elements of the insurance be set out in the insurance contract, but also that the policyholder should be given a clear prompting and a proper and correct explanation.

国际上通常只要求保险人做到明确列明保险的主要内容，而我国为了更好地保护投保人的利益，要求保险人向投保人明确说明保险的主要条款和责任免除内容。

Internationally, the insurer is usually only required to clearly specify the main contents of the insurance, while in China, in order to better protect the interests of the insured, the insurer is required to clearly explain the main provisions of the insurance and the exemption of liability to the insured.

（2）投保人的告知。投保人的告知是指投保人在投保时，应把他所知的有关保险标的的重要事实全部告诉保险人，而且投保人所作的每次陈述都必须是真实的。

（2）Disclosure by the policyholder. The policyholder's disclosure refers to that the applicant should tell the insurer all the material facts about the subject-matter insured that he knows, and every statement made by the policyholder must be true.

① 投保人告知的内容。投保人告知的内容包括：保险合同签订时，投保人应将已知或应知的与保险标的及其危险有关的重要事实如实告知保险人；保险合同订立后，保险标的的风险情况发生变化应及时通知保险人；保险事故发生后，应及时通知保险人，并提

供保险人所要求的各种真实证明;保险标的的权益发生变化,放置地点发生转移,应及时通知保险人,经保险人同意变更合同后继续承保。

① Content of disclosure by the policyholder. The contents of the policyholder's disclosure include that, at the time of the conclusion of the insurance contract, the policyholder shall truthfully inform the insurer of material facts known or to be known about the subject-matter of the insurance and its perils; after the conclusion of the insurance contract, changes in the risk profile of the subject-matter insured should be notified to the insurer promptly; after the occurrence of an insurance accident, the insurer shall be notified promptly and all true proofs required by the insurer shall be provided; any change in the interest of the subject-matter insured and any transfer of the place of placement shall be notified to the insurer in time, and coverage shall continue after the insurer agrees to change the contract.

② 投保人告知的形式。从各国保险立法来看,投保人告知的形式一般分为无限告知和询问告知两种。

② Ways of disclosure by the policyholder. From the insurance legislation of various countries, the way of notification of policyholders is generally divided into two types: by unlimited notification and by inquiry.

(ⅰ) 无限告知又称客观告知,是指法律或保险人对告知的内容没有明确性的规定,投保人应主动将其所知的与保险标的危险状况有关的任何重要事实告知保险人,而其所做的陈述必须与客观事实相符。目前,法国、比利时以及英美法系国家的保险立法均采用无限告知制度。《海商法》也规定采用无限告知制度。

(ⅱ) 询问告知又称主观告知,是指投保人对保险人询问的问题作出如实回答,即已履行告知义务,若保险人没有询问,则投保人无须告知。在具体实务中,保险人询问的方式包括要求投保人填写投保单、告知书以及口头询问等,投保人只要逐项如实填报或口头回答,即已履行告知义务。目前世界上大多数国家,包括《保险法》在内的保险立法都采用询问告知形式。

(ⅰ) Unlimited notification, also known as objective notification, means that the law or the insurer does not specify the content of the disclosure, and the policyholder shall voluntarily inform the insurer of any material facts known to him that are relevant to the perilous condition of the subject-matter insured, and the statements he makes must be consistent with the objective facts. At present, France, Belgium, and common law countries have adopted an unlimited notification system in their insurance legislation. *Maritime Law* also provides for the adoption of an unlimited notification system.

(ⅱ) Inquiry and notification, also known as subjective notification, means that the policyholder has fulfilled his obligation to inform by answering truthfully to the questions asked by the insurer, and if the insurer does not ask, the policyholder is not required to inform. In specific practice, the insurer may ask the policyholder to fill in the insurance application, or ask the policyholder orally. The policyholder has fulfilled the obligation to inform as long as he/she truthfully fills in each item or answers orally. Insurance legislation in most countries around the world，including *Insurance Law*，now takes the form of inquiry and notification.

（3）违反告知义务的法律后果。

（3）Legal consequences of violating the duty of disclosure.

① 保险人违反告知义务的法律后果。根据《保险法》的规定，如果保险人没有向投保人明确说明责任免除条款，则该条款无效。

① Legal consequences of the insurer's breach of the duty of disclosure. According to *Insurance Law*，if the insurer does not clearly state the exclusion clause to the policyholder，the clause is invalid.

② 投保人违反告知义务的法律后果。《保险法》规定，投保人故意隐瞒事实，不履行如实告知义务的，或者因过失未履行告知义务的，足以影响保险人决定是否同意或者提高保险费率的，保险人有权解除保险合同；投保人故意不履行如实告知义务，保险人对于保险合同解除前发生的保险事故，不承担赔偿或者给付保险金的责任，并不退还保险费；投保人因过失未履行如实告知义务，对保险事故的发生有严重影响的，保险人对于保险合同解除前发生的保险事故不承担赔偿或者给付保险金的责任，但可以退还保险费。

② Legal consequences of the policyholder's breach of the duty of disclosure. *Insurance Law* stipulates that if the insured intentionally conceals the facts and fails to fulfill the obligation of truthful disclosure，or negligently fails to fulfill the obligation of disclosure，which is sufficient to influence the insurer's decision on whether to agree or increase the premium rate，the insurer has the right to terminate the insurance contract；if the insured deliberately fails to perform his duty of truthful disclosure，the insurer shall not be liable to compensate or pay the insurance money for the insurance accident occurring before the termination of the insurance contract，and shall not refund the premium；if the policyholder fails to perform the duty of truthful notification due to negligence，which has a serious impact on the occurrence of the insurance accident，the insurer is not liable to compensate or pay the insurance money for the insurance accident that occurred before the termination of the insurance contract，but can refund the insurance premium.

2）保证（Warranty）

保证是指保险人要求投保人或被保险人对某一事项的作为或不作为、履行某项条件以及某种事态的存在或不存在等作出承诺。保证的内容是保险合同的重要条款之一。保险人要求投保人作出某种保证，其目的在于控制风险，确保保险标的及其周围环境处于良好的状态中。

The warranty means a promissory engagement，that the insured undertakes that some particular thing shall or shall not be done，or that some condition shall be fulfilled，or whereby he affirms or negatives the existence of a particular state of facts. The content of a warranty is one of the key terms of an insurance contract. The purpose of an insurer requiring a policyholder to commit certain warranties is to control risks and ensure that the subject-matter insured and its surroundings are in good condition.

(1) 保证的形式。根据保证存在的形式不同,保证分为明示保证和默示保证两种。

(1) Form of warranty. Depending on the form of the warranty, there are two types of warranties: express warranties and implied warranties.

① 明示保证。明示保证是指以文字或者书面的形式载明于保险合同中约定的事项或保险合同的保证条款。例如,船舶保险单中附有"投保人保证船舶不去南极、北极、大湖区、波罗的海"的条款,就是投保人对船舶航行区域所做的明示保证。

① Express warranties. An express warranty is something that is set out in writing in an insurance contract or a warranty clause in an insurance contract. For example, the clause "the policyholder warrants that the ship will not travel to the Antarctic, the Arctic, the Great Lakes or the Baltic Sea" in the ship insurance policy is an express warranty by the policyholder for the sailing area of the ship.

② 默示保证。默示保证是指根据有关法律或国际惯例产生的,不载明于保险合同中,习惯上或社会公认的投保人必须遵守的保证。海上保险的默示保证有三项:船舶必须适航;船舶需按预定航线航行,不得绕行;船舶必须从事合法的运输。

② Implied warranties. An implied warranty is a warranty that arises under the relevant law or international practice and is not contained in an insurance contract but is customarily or socially accepted to be observed by the policyholder. There are three implied warranties of marine insurance: seaworthiness; non-deviation; legality of the voyage.

(2) 违反保证的法律后果。各国立法一般均规定被保险人若违反保证,不论其是否有过失,保险人均有权自被保险人违反保证之时解除合同,不承担保险赔偿责任。但在被保险人违反保证之前,其并未损害保险人的利益,此时若保险事故已发生,造成保险标的损失,保险人须负责赔偿。若被保险人自订立合同之时即已违反保证,则保险合同无效,保险人对损失一概不承担责任。但随着保险实践的发展,在保险合同纠纷案审判中,越来越趋向于被保险人违反保证与保险事故的发生有关联时,保险人方可拒赔,否则仍应承担保险责任。

(2) Legal consequences of a breach of a warranty. The legislation of each country generally provides that if the insured breaches the warranty, the insurer has the right to terminate the contract without liability from the moment the insured breaches the warranty, regardless of whether the insured is at fault. If the insured has not harmed the interests of the insurer prior to the breach of warranty, the insurer is liable for the loss of the subject-matter insured if an insured event has occurred. If the insured has breached the warranty at the time of conclusion of the contract, the insurance contract is void and the insurer is not liable for any loss. However, with the development of insurance practice, in the trial of insurance contract disputes, there is an increasing tendency that the insurer can refuse to pay compensation only when the insured's breach

of warranty is related to the occurrence of an insurance accident, otherwise the insurer should still bear the insurance liability.

9.3.2　保险利益原则（Principle of Insurable Interest）

1. 保险利益及保险利益原则的含义（Meaning of Insurable Interest and Insurable Interest Principle）

保险利益又称可保利益、可保权益,是指投保人对保险标的具有的法律上承认的经济利益。保险利益体现为投保人和保险标的之间的利益关系。保险人所承保的标的是保险所要保障的对象,但被保险人投保的并不是保险标的本身,而是被保险人对保险标的所具有的利益,这个利益叫作保险利益。保险标的因保险事故而致损或伤亡时,保险人赔偿或给付的是被保险人因此而遭受的经济损失,即被保险人对该保险标的所具有的保险利益而非保险标的本身,即保险合同真正保障的是保险利益。

保险利益是保险合同的效力要件。世界各国的保险法都规定投保人或被保险人必须对保险标的具有保险利益,才能同保险人订立有效的保险合同。如果投保人或被保险人对保险标的不具有保险利益或超越保险利益的范围,则他们同保险人所签订的保险合同无效。因此,保险利益原则可以表述为:在订立和履行保险合同的过程中,投保人或被保险人对保险标的必须具有保险利益,如果投保人或被保险人对保险标的不具有保险利益,签订的保险合同无效;保险合同生效后,如果投保人或被保险人失去了对保险标的的保险利益,则保险合同随之失效(人身保险合同除外)。保险标的发生保险责任事故,只有对该标的具有保险利益的人才具有索赔资格。

Insurable interest, also known as insurance interest, is a legally recognized economic interest that the policyholder has in the subject-matter insured. An insurable interest is a relationship of interest between the policyholder and the subject-matter insured. The subject-matter insured by the insurer is the object to be covered by the insurance, but it is not the subject matter itself that is insured, but the interest that the insured has in the subject-matter insured, and this interest is called the insurable interest. In the event of loss or casualty to the subject-matter insured, the insurer indemnifies or pays for the economic loss suffered by the insured as a result, i. e., the insured's insurance interest in the subject-matter insured, rather than the subject-matter insured itself, so that what the insurance contract really protects is the insurance interest.

Insurable interest is an essential element of the validity of an insurance contract. Insurance laws around the world require that the policyholder or the insured must have an insurable interest in the subject-matter insured in order to enter into a valid insurance contract with the insurer. If the policyholder or the insured does not have an insurable interest in the subject-matter insured or exceeds the scope of the insurance interest, the insurance contract concluded between the insured and the insurer is void. Therefore, the insurable interest principle can be expressed as follows: in the process of concluding and performing an insurance contract, the policyholder or insured must have an insurable interest in the subject-matter insured, and if the policyholder or insured does not have an insurable interest in the subject-matter insured, the insurance contract is invalid; after the insurance contract comes into effect, if the policyholder or insured loses the insurable interest in the subject-matter insured, the insurance contract is invalidated (except for personal insurance contracts). In the event of an insured liability incident on the subject-matter insured, only persons with an insurable interest in that subject-matter are eligible to claim.

2. 保险利益原则在国际贸易中的应用(Application of Insurable Interest Principle in International Trade)

国际货运保险实践中,货物所有权并非保险利益的来源,承担货物灭失或损坏风险的一方才具有保险利益。不同贸易术语对风险转移的规定不同,而风险转移的时间又决定对货物保险利益转移的时间,因此货物自起运地卖方仓库运至目的地买方仓库的过程中,何方具有保险利益、享有在事故发生时向保险人索赔的权利,取决于买卖双方在贸易合同中所采用的贸易术语。国际商会制定的 2020 年《国际贸易术语解释通则》所解释的 11 种贸易术语的风险转移时间,以及由此决定的保险利益转移时间具体如下。

In the practice of international freight insurance, the ownership of goods is not the source of insurable interest, but the party who bears the risk of loss of or damage to the goods has the insurable interest. Different trade terms have different provisions on the transfer of risk, and the time of the transfer of risk determines the time of the transfer of the insurable interest in the goods, so that during the transport of the goods from the seller's warehouse at the place of departure to the buyer's warehouse at the place of destination, who has the insurable interest and the right to claim compensation from the insurer in the event of an accident depends on the trade terms used by the buyer and the seller in the trade contract. The risk transfer times for the 11 trade terms explained in the *Incoterms*® *2020* developed by the International Chamber of Commerce (ICC), and the resulting insurable interest transfer times, are specified below.

1) EXW

在 EXW(Ex Works,工厂交货)贸易术语项下,卖方在其所在地或其他指定地点(如工厂、仓库等)将货物交给买方处置时即完成交货,货物灭失或损坏的风险自交货时起由卖方转移给买方承担。因此,对货物的保险利益也于此时转移给买方。

Under EXW (Ex Works) term, delivery of the goods is completed when the seller places them at the buyer's disposal at his place of business or other designated place (e. g. factory, warehouse, etc.) and the risk of loss or damage passes from the seller to the buyer from the time of delivery. Thus, the insurable interest of the goods passes to the buyer at that time as well.

2）FAS

在此贸易术语下，卖方将已办理出口清关手续的货物运至指定的装运港船边，即完成交货。货物损坏或灭失的风险于此时转移至买方，买方从受领货物时起具有保险利益，可通过办理国际货运保险转嫁风险。由于卖方承担船边交货之前的风险，享有货物的保险利益，因此卖方一般应投保内陆运输险。

Under FAS term，delivery is completed when the seller brings the goods，which have been cleared for export，alongside the ship at the designated port of shipment. The risk of damage to or loss of the goods passes to the buyer at that point and the buyer has the insurable interest from the time of taking delivery of the goods and can transfer the risk by taking out international cargo insurance. Since the seller has the insurable interest for the goods by assuming the risk until delivery alongside the ship，the seller should normally take out inland transport insurance.

3）FOB、CFR 和 CIF

在 FOB、CFR 和 CIF 术语下，卖方承担货物在装运港装上船舶之前的风险，享有货物的保险利益；货物装上船舶后，风险由卖方转移给买方，此时买方享有保险利益。

Under FOB，CFR and CIF terms，the seller has an insurable interest in the goods by assuming the risk of the goods until they are loaded on a ship at the port of shipment，while the buyer has an insurable interest when the risk passes from the seller to the buyer after the goods are loaded on the ship.

在 FOB、CFR 术语下，卖方无投保国际货运保险的义务，由买方自行办理保险。若货物损失发生在装运港装船之前，风险尚未转移，买方不具有保险利益，尽管运输保险责任期限是仓至仓条款，买方也无权就此项损失向保险人索赔。卖方若未办理货物自发运地仓库至装运港船舶之间的保险，卖方也无权向保险人索赔。卖方若希望得到保险保障，需自行办理这一段运输的保险。若货物损失发生在装运港装船之后，且买方已投保国际货运险，则可向保险公司索赔。

Under FOB，CFR terms，the seller is not obligated to take out international freight insurance，but the buyer to handle the insurance. If the loss of the goods occurs before the goods are loaded on board the ship at the port of shipment and the risk has not been transferred，the buyer has no insurable interest，nor is he entitled to claim against the insurer for such loss，notwithstanding the fact that the period of liability for transport insurance is a warehouse-to-warehouse clause. The seller is also not entitled to claim from the insurer if the goods are not insured from the warehouse at the place of shipment to the ship at the port of shipment. Sellers who wish to obtain insurance coverage needs to obtain their own insurance for this leg of the shipment. If the loss of the goods occurs after they have been loaded on board the vessel at the port of shipment，and the buyer may claim compensation from the insurance company if he has taken out international cargo insurance.

在 CIF 术语下，卖方自付费用办理国际货运保险。当货物在装运港装船前发生损失,卖方承担风险并享有保险利益,有权向保险人索赔;货物在装船后发生损失,买方具有保险利益,可凭卖方背书转让的保险单向保险人索赔。由此可见,CIF术语下,保险人承担责任的期限包括货物由起运地发货人仓库至目的地收货人仓库的整个运输过程。

Under CIF term, the seller insures the international carriage of goods at its own expense. When a loss occurs before the goods are loaded on board the vessel at the port of shipment, the seller bears the risk and therefore has the benefit of insurance and is entitled to claim compensation from the insurer. If the goods are lost after shipment, the buyer has an insurable interest and may claim against the insurer on the basis of an insurance policy endorsed by the seller. Thus, under the CIF term, the insurer's period of liability covers the entire transport of the goods from the shipper's warehouse at the place of origin to the consignee's warehouse at the place of destination.

4) FCA、CPT和CIP

采用FCA、CPT和CIP贸易术语订立贸易合同,卖方将经过出口清关手续的货物在指定地点交给指定承运人,即完成交货,货物风险自交货时起转移给买方承担,对货物的保险利益也于此时转移给买方。

For a trade contract using FCA, CPT or CIP terms, the seller completes delivery of the goods at the designated place by handing them over to the designated carrier after completion of export customs clearance, and the risk of the goods passes to the buyer from the time of delivery, at which time the insurable interest on the goods also passes to the buyer.

在FCA和CPT贸易术语项下,卖方无办理国际货运保险的义务。如果买方已投保货运保险,且货损发生在承运人接管货物之前,由于买方不具有保险利益,无权向保险人索赔;若货损发生在承运人接管货物之后,买方具有保险利益,可作为被保险人向保险人索赔。

Under FCA and CPT trade terms, the seller has no obligation to take out international freight insurance. Where the buyer has taken out cargo insurance, and the damage occurs before the carrier takes over the goods, the buyer is not entitled to claim compensation from the insurer because he does not have an insurance interest; if the damage occurs after the carrier takes over the goods, the buyer has an insurance interest and may claim compensation from the insurer as an insured.

在CIP术语项下,卖方负有订立保险合同并支付保险费的义务。卖方办理货运保险后,若货物在承运人接管前发生损失,卖方承担风险,享有该货物的保险利益,可向保险人索赔;若损失发生在承运人接管货物后,买方承担风险,具有该货物的保险利益。由于货运保单可通过卖方背书转让给买方,买方可凭已转让的保险单向保险人索赔。

Under CIP term, the seller is obliged to conclude a contract of insurance and pay the premium. After the seller takes out cargo insurance, if the goods are lost before they are taken over by the carrier, the seller assumes the risk and has the insurable interest of the goods and may claim compensation from the insurer; if the loss occurs after the carrier has taken over the goods, the buyer assumes the risk and has the insurable interest of the goods. Since the insurance policy could be transferred to the buyer by endorsement of the seller, the buyer could claim against the insurer on the basis of the assigned policy.

5) DAP、DPU 和 DDP

在 DAP(Delivered at Place,目的地交货)、DPU(Delivered at Place Unloaded,卸货地交易)和 DDP(Delivered Duty Paid,完税后交货)术语下,卖方在规定日期或期限内,在指定目的地的约定地点,将货物置于买方支配下,风险即转移至买方。在此之前的风险由卖方承担,因此,卖方应自付费用投保国际货运险。若在交货前发生货损,只有卖方享有可保利益,所以只能由卖方向保险人索赔。货物置于买方支配后的风险,应由买方办理保险,此时所发生的货损,只有买方有权向保险人索赔。

Under this set of terms, the risk passes to the buyer when the seller places the goods at the buyer's disposal at the named place of destination on a specified date or within a specified period of time. The seller bears the risk up to that point, and shall therefore take out international cargo insurance at its own expense. If the damage occurs prior to delivery, only the seller has an insurable interest and therefore can only claim against the insurer at the seller's expense. The risk of the goods at the buyer's disposal shall be insured by the buyer. Only the buyer has the right to claim against the insurer for the damage of the goods.

9.3.3　近因原则(Proximate Cause Principle)

1. 近因及近因原则的含义(Meaning of Proximate Cause and the Proximate Cause Principle)

保险人依照保险合同中规定的保险责任承担保险赔偿责任,即保险人对其承保的风险所引起的保险标的的损失承担责任。然而,造成保险标的损失的原因是多种多样的,并非任何原因造成的损失保险人都予以赔偿。对保险人而言,风险一般可分为三类:一是承保风险,即在保险合同中明确规定属于保险人承保责任范围内的风险;二是除外风险,这类风险是在保险合同中明确列明保险人不予承担的,其造成的损失,保险人不予赔偿;三是不保风险,或称非承保风险,即在保险合同中既未列明承保风险也未列明除外风险。也就是说,除第一类承保风险和第二类除外风险之外,其他导致损失的风险均为不保风险。由于导致损害事故的原因有时是单独发生的,有时是多个同时发生或连续发生或交叉发生的,关系错综复杂,而且,这些原因有的属于承保风险,有的属于除外风险,还有的属于不保风险,因此,判断保险公司是否对损失承担保险责任的关键是保险标的的损失是否与承保风险之间存在直接的因果关系。这就涉及保险理赔的一个重要原则——近因原则。

The insurer assumes insurance liability in accordance with the insurance contract, i. e., the insurer is liable for the loss of the subject-matter insured caused by the risks insured. However, the causes of loss of the subject-matter insured are varied and not all losses caused by any cause will be compensated by the insurer. For the insurer, risks generally fall into three categories: the first is insured risks, i. e., risks that are expressly stated in the insurance contract to be within the scope of the insurer's covered liability; the second is excluded risks, which are expressly excluded in the insurance contract and the insurer will not pay for the loss caused by it; the third is uninsured risks, or non-covered risks, which are risks that are neither covered nor excluded in the insurance contract. In other words, risks other than the first type of insured risks and the second type of excluded risks that result in a loss are uninsured risks. Since sometimes a single cause causes the occurrence of the damage, and sometimes multiple causes act simultaneously or successively or intersectingly, the relationship is complicated. Moreover, some of these causes belong to insured risks, some belong to excluded risks, and some belong to uninsured risks; therefore, the key to determine whether the insurance company is liable for the loss is whether there is a direct causal relationship between the loss of the subject-matter insured and the insured risks. This involves an important principle of insurance claims—the principle of proximate cause.

所谓近因原则是指在多个原因导致保险标的损失的情况下,只有导致保险标的损失的近因在保险责任范围之内,保险人才对保险标的的损失负赔偿责任。这里的近因并不是指时间或空间上最接近的原因,而是指导致保险事故发生的最有效、最直接、最主要的或起决定作用的原因。

The principle of proximate cause means that when multiple causes lead to the loss of the subject-matter insured, the insurer is liable for the loss of the subject matter only if the proximate cause of the loss is within the scope of insurance liability. Proximate cause here does not refer to the closest cause in time or space, but the most efficient, direct, primary, or decisive cause of the insured accident.

2. 近因原则的应用(Application of Proximate Cause Principle)

1) 单一原因致损(A Situation in Which a Single Cause Results in a Loss)

如果造成保险标的损失的原因只有一个,情况相对简单,这个单一的原因就是近因。若该原因属于承保风险,保险人承担保险责任;否则,保险人不承担保险责任。

The situation is relatively simple if there is only one cause for the loss of the subject-matter insured, and that single cause is the proximate cause. If the cause is a insured risk, the insurer assumes liability, otherwise the insurer is not liable.

2) 数个原因同时致损(A Situation in Which Damage is Caused by Several Reasons at the Same Time)

数个原因同时发生作用,是指无法严格区分不同原因在发生时间上的先后顺序。由于各原因的发生无先后之分,而且对损害结果的形成均有直接的、有效的影响,原则上它们都是损失的近因。

The simultaneous action of several causes means that it is impossible to strictly distinguish the order of occurrence of different causes. Since there is no sequence of occurrence of each cause and they all have a direct and effective influence on the formation of the damage result, in principle, they are all proximate causes of the loss.

（1）当各个原因所致的损失结果可以划分时，保险人对所有承保危险引起的损失均需负责，但对不保风险和除外风险所致的损失不需负责。

（1）The insurer is liable for losses arising from all insured risks, but not for losses arising from excluded and uninsured risks, when the result of the loss from each cause is divisible.

（2）当各个原因所致的损失结果无法划分时，保险人按下面两种情况处理。

（2）When the result of loss caused by various reasons cannot be divided, the insurer shall deal with it according to the following two situations.

① 数个原因之中既有承保风险，又有不保风险，保险人对全部损失予以负责，即承保风险优于不保风险。

② 数个原因中既有承保风险，又有除外风险，保险人对损失都不负责，即除外风险优于承保风险。

① Where there are both insured and uninsured risks among several causes, the insurer is liable for the entire loss, i.e. the insured risk has priority over the uninsured risk.

② Where there are several causes with both insured and excluded risks, the insurer is not liable for the loss, i.e. the excluded risk takes precedence over the insured risk.

3）数个原因先后发生致损（A Situation in Which the Loss Arose From Several Successive Causes）

在此情况下，两个或两个以上的危险事故连续发生作用造成损失。由于各原因依次发生，在时间上可进行明显的区分，而且前后因之间不断地存在因果关系，此时，最先发生并导致一连串事故的原因即为近因。

In this case, two or more incidents occur consecutively and cause losses. Because the causes occur in sequence, there is a clear temporal distinction and a continuous causal relationship between the preceding and following causes; thus, the cause that first occurred and led to the chain of accidents is the proximate cause.

（1）前因为承保风险，即近因为承保风险，保险人应承担赔偿责任。

（2）前因为除外风险，即近因为除外风险，保险人不承担赔偿责任。

（3）前因为保单不保风险，而后引起的原因属保单承保风险，保险公司应承担赔偿责任。

（4）前因为保单不保风险，而后引起的原因属保单除外风险，保险公司不承担赔偿责任。

（1）If the preceding cause is an insured risk, that is, the proximate cause is an insured risk, the insurer shall be liable for compensation.

（2）If the preceding cause is an excluded risk, that is, the proximate cause is an excluded risk, the insurer shall not be liable.

（3）If the preceding cause is an uninsured risk and the subsequent cause is an insured risk under the policy, the insurance company shall be liable for compensation.

(4) If the preceding cause is an uninsured risk and the subsequent cause is an excluded risk under the policy, the insurer shall not be liable.

4) 数个原因先后间断发生致损(A Situation in Which the Loss Arose as a Result of the Interrupted Occurrence of Several Causes)

数个原因先后间断发生致损,是指造成损失的各原因在发生时间上存在先后顺序,但相互之间不存在直接的、必然的联系,即各原因之间不存在因果关系,是完全独立的。

A loss resulting from the interrupted occurrence of several causes means that the causes of the loss are sequential in their occurrence, but there is no direct and necessary connection between them, i. e. , there is no causal relationship between the causes and they are completely independent.

(1) 如果数个原因对损害结果的形成均有直接的、实质的影响,即它们均为近因。在这种情形下,判定保险人如何承担责任与数个原因同时发生致损基本一致。

(1) If several causes have a direct and substantial influence on the outcome of the damage, they are all proximate causes. In this case, the determination of the insurer's liability is essentially the same as if several causes had contributed to the damage simultaneously.

(2) 如果新出现的原因具有现实性、支配性和有效性,那么在此之前发生的原因就被新的原因所取代,可以不予考虑。此时,新的原因即为近因,当其为承保风险时,保险人对损失承担责任;当其为除外风险时,保险人对损失不承担责任。

扩展阅读 9.1 近因原则的应用

(2) If the new cause is realistic, dominant, and valid, the cause that occurred before is superseded by the new cause and may be disregarded. In this case, the new cause is the proximate cause, and the insurer is liable for the loss when it is a insured risk, but not when it is an excluded risk.

9.3.4 补偿原则(Principle of Indemnity)

1. 补偿原则的含义(Implications of the Principle of Indemnity)

补偿原则又称损害赔偿原则,是保险人计算保险赔偿金额时所运用的重要原则。其基本含义是:当保险事故发生时,被保险人有权按照保险合同的约定得到充分的赔偿,但同时赔偿金额受到限制,被保险人不能由此而额外获利。其具体体现在:①被保险人只有受到约定的保险事故所造成的损失,才能得到补偿;②补偿的数额必须等于损失,被保险人不能获得多于损失的补偿。

The principle of indemnity is an important principle used by insurers to calculate insurance benefits. The basic meaning is that when an insurance accident occurs, the insured is entitled to full compensation as agreed in the insurance contract, but at the same time the amount of compensation is limited so that the insured cannot make additional profits. This is reflected in the following: ①the insured can be compensated only for the loss caused by the agreed insurance accident; ②the amount of compensation must be equal to the loss, and the insured cannot be compensated for more than the loss.

2. 补偿原则的限制（The Limitation in the Principle of Indemnity）

保险人履行补偿原则时通常以实际损失、保险金额和保险价值作为限制，既保证被保险人能恢复失去的经济利益，又保证其不会因保险补偿而获得额外利益。在这三者中，应以金额最小的限额作为保险补偿的额度。

The insurer's fulfilment of the principle of indemnity is usually limited by the actual loss, the insured amount, and the insurable value, in order to ensure that the insured can recover the lost financial benefit without gaining additional benefits from the insurance coverage. Among the three, the minimum amount should be taken as the limit of insurance compensation.

（1）以实际损失为限。实际损失是指保险事故发生所致保险标的损失的实际现金价值，即以损失当时保险标的的市场价为准，计算损失金额（定值保险、重置价值、人身保险和施救费用的赔偿除外）。

（1）Limited to the actual loss. Actual loss means the actual cash value of the loss of the subject-matter insured resulting from the occurrence of the insured event, i. e., the amount of loss is calculated based on the market value of the subject-matter insured at the time of the loss (except for fixed value insurance, replacement value, life insurance, and compensation for sue and labour charges).

（2）以保险金额为限。保险金额是保险双方事先约定的、记载于保险单上的保险人承担赔偿责任的最高限额。因此，无论保险标的发生全损或部分损失，保险人的最高赔付责任都不能超过合同规定的保险金额。

（2）Limited to the insured amount. The sum insured is the maximum amount of the insurer's liability as agreed in advance between the insurance parties and recorded in the insurance policy. Therefore, the insurer's maximum liability cannot exceed the amount insured under the contract, regardless of whether the subject-matter insured has suffered a total or partial loss.

（3）以保险价值为限。保险价值可能在订立保险合同时即已确定，也可能在保险标的发生保险事故后才予以确定。保险价值的金额因被保险人与保险人约定的不同而不同，双方可以约定以保险标的的重置价值作为保险价值，也可以约定以保险事故发生时保险标的的实际价值作为保险价值。《保险法》第二章第五十五条规定，保险金额不得超过保险价值。超过保险价值的，超过部分无效，保险人应当退还相应的保险费。因此，如果保险金额超过保险价值，即使保险标的发生全损，保险人的赔偿责任也只能以保险价值为限，而不是以保险金额为限。

（3）Limited to the insurable value. The insurance value may be determined at the time of the conclusion of the insurance contract, or it may be determined after the occurrence of an insured event in the subject-matter insured. The amount of the insurance value varies depending on the different agreements between the insured and the insurer，and the parties may agree to take the replacement value of the subject-matter insured or the actual value of the subject-matter insured at the time of the insurance accident. Chapter 2，article 55 of the *Insurance Law* stipulates that the amount of insurance shall not exceed the insurable value. If it exceeds the insurable value，the excess shall be null and void and the insurer shall refund the corresponding premium. Therefore，if the insured amount exceeds the insurable value，the insurer's liability is limited to the insurable value，even if the subject-matter insured has suffered a total loss.

9.3.5　代位追偿原则(Principle of Subrogation)

1. 代位追偿原则的含义和作用(Meaning and Function of Principle of Subrogation)

代位追偿原则是指当保险标的发生了在保险责任范围内的、由第三者责任造成的损失时,保险人向被保险人履行了赔偿责任之后,在其已赔偿金额的限度内,享有以被保险人的地位向在该项损失中的第三者责任方索赔的权利,保险人享有的这种权利称为代位追偿权。例如,在海运货物保险中,由于承运人的管理失误造成火灾,导致货物被焚毁,火灾造成的损失在保险人承保责任范围内,因此,保险人按照保险合同赔偿被保险人之后,有权向该损失的责任方,即承运人进行追偿。

The principle of subrogation means that when the subject matter insured has suffered a loss within the scope of the insurance liability and caused by a third party's liability，the insurer，after fulfilling its liability to the insured，has the right to claim compensation from the third party liable for the loss in the position of the insured to the extent of the amount of the compensation paid by the insurer. This right of the insurer is called subrogation. For example，in marine cargo insurance，the cargo is incinerated due to a fire caused by the carrier's management error. Since the loss caused by the fire is within the scope of the insurer's coverage，the insurer has the right to recover the loss from the responsible party，which is the carrier，after compensating the insured in accordance with the insurance contract.

代位追偿原则是补偿原则的派生原则,其目的是防止被保险人由于保险事故的发生而获得超过其实际损失的经济利益,同时也维护了社会公共利益和保险人的合法权益。保险人在履行赔偿义务后才取得代位追偿权,追偿金额不超过其赔偿额。

The principle of subrogation is a derivative of the principle of indemnity，the purpose of which is to prevent the insured from gaining economic benefits that exceed their actual losses due to the occurrence of an insurance accident，and also to safeguard the public interests of society and the legitimate rights and interests of the insurer. The insurer acquires the right of subrogation only after the obligation to indemnify has been fulfilled，and the amount of the claim does not exceed the amount of its indemnity.

2. 代位追偿原则的主要内容（Main Elements of Principle of Subrogation）

1）代位追偿产生的条件（Conditions Under Which Subrogation Arises）

代位追偿的产生必须具备以下四个条件：①保险合同具有补偿性；②保险标的的损害由保险事故所致；③保险事故的发生是由第三者责任方造成的；④保险人先履行赔偿义务。

The following four conditions must be present for a subrogation to arise：① the insurance contract is compensatory；② the damage to the subject-matter insured is caused by an insurance accident；③ the occurrence of the insurance accident is caused by the liability of a third party；④ the insurer shall first perform its obligation to indemnify.

2）代位追偿产生的时间（Time When Subrogation Arises）

根据《保险法》的规定，代位追偿权产生于保险人支付赔款之后。保险事故发生后，被保险人将其与第三者之间产生的损害赔偿的权利转让给保险人，从而使保险人取得代位追偿权。因此，代位追偿产生于保险人支付赔款之后。在实际业务中，保险人支付保险赔款后，通常要求被保险人签署"权益转让书"，明确表示将向第三者请求赔偿的权利转让给保险人。"权益转让书"可以确认保险赔偿的全额和赔偿的时间，进而确认保险人取得代位追偿权的时间和代位追偿的范围。

According to the *Insurance Law*, the right of subrogation arises after the insurer pays the indemnity. After the occurrence of an insurance accident，the insured assigns to the insurer the right to recover damages arising between him and a third party，thereby giving the insurer the right of subrogation. The right of subrogation therefore arises after the insurer has paid the claim. In practice，the insurer usually requires the insured to sign a "letter of subrogation" after paying the insurance claim，expressly assigning the right to claim compensation from a third party to the insurer. A "letter of subrogation" confirms the full amount and timing of the insurance recovery and，consequently，the timing and extent of the insurer's right of subrogation.

3）代位追偿的范围（Scope of Subrogation）

保险人所获得的代位追偿范围，以其对被保险人赔付的金额为限。如果保险人从第三者责任方追偿的余额大于其对被保险人的赔偿，超过部分应归被保险人所有，以避免保险人因代位追偿权而额外获利，损害被保险人的利益。

The extent of the subrogation recovery obtained by the insurer is limited to the amount it has paid out to the insured. If the balance of the insurer's recovery from the third party responsible for the damage is greater than its compensation to the insured，the excess part shall be owned by the insured，so as to avoid the insurer making additional profits due to the right of subrogation，which damages the interests of the insured.

由于有些保险合同属于不足额保险或规定有免赔额等原因，保险事故发生后被保险人获得的保险赔款往往低于其实际遭受的经济损失，此时被保险人有权就未取得保险赔偿的部分向第三者请求赔偿。

For some insurance contracts that are underinsured or have a deductible，the insured will often receive less than the actual economic loss it suffered after an insurance accident. In this case，the insured has the right to claim compensation from a third party for the unearned portion of the insurance claim.

由于代位追偿是保险人履行赔偿责任之后才产生的,此前被保险人与第三者之间债务关系如何,即被保险人是否保留对第三者追偿的权利,直接影响保险人能否顺利行使其代位追偿权。对此,《保险法》第二章第六十一条第一款规定:保险事故发生后,保险人未赔偿保险金之前,被保险人放弃对第三者请求赔偿的权利的,保险人不承担赔偿保险金的责任;第三款规定:被保险人故意或者因重大过失致使保险人不能行使代位请求赔偿的权利的,保险人可以扣减或者要求返还相应的保险金。

Since subrogation arises after the insurer performs the liability，the debt relationship between the insured and the third party，that is，whether the insured retains the right to recover the third party，directly affects whether the insurer can successfully exercise its right of subrogation. In this regard，article 61（1）of chapter 2 of the *Insurance Law* stipulates that after the occurrence of an insured accident，if the insured waives the right to claim compensation from a third party before the insurer fails to pay the insurance premium，the insurer shall not be liable to pay the premium；article 61（3）provides that if the insurer is unable to exercise the right of subrogation due to the insured's intent or gross negligence，the insurer may deduct or demand the return of the corresponding premium.

9.3.6　重复保险的分摊原则（Principle of Double Insurance）

1. 重复保险的分摊原则的含义（Meaning of Principle of Double Insurance）

重复保险的分摊原则也是补偿原则的派生原则,是指当投保人就同一保险标的向两个或两个以上保险人投保相同的保险,即重复投保时,如果保险标的发生损失,各保险人应采取适当的分摊方法分配赔偿责任,使被保险人既能得到充分的补偿,又不会超过实际损失而获得额外的利益。

The principle of double insurance，which is also a derivative of the principle of indemnity，means that when an insured takes out the same insurance with two or more insurers in respect of the same subject-matter insured，i. e.，when the insurance is carried out repeatedly，in the event of a loss of the subject-matter insured，the insurers shall adopt an appropriate method of apportionment for the allocation of liability，so as to make sure that the insured can receive adequate indemnification without obtaining additional benefits in excess of the actual loss.

2. 重复保险的分摊方式（Method of Apportionment of Duplicate Insurance）

1）比例责任分摊（Apportionment of Proportional Liability）

比例责任分摊是最常见的重复保险损失分摊方式。根据《保险法》的规定,除非保险

合同另有规定,各保险人按照其保险金额占保险金额总和的比例承担赔偿责任。其计算公式为

$$各保险人的损失分摊额＝损失金额×\frac{该保险人承保的保险金额}{各保险人承保的保险金额总和}$$

Apportionment of proportional liability is the most common way of apportioning losses of duplicate insurance. According to *Insurance Law*, unless otherwise provided in the insurance contract，each insurer bears the liability in proportion to the sum of its insured amount. The formula for its calculation is：

apportionment of each insurer ＝ amount of loss×(insured amount underwritten by this insurer/total insured amount underwritten by each insurer)

2) 限额责任分摊(Apportionment of Limits of Liability)

限额责任分摊是指以各保险人在没有其他保险人重复保险的情况下,按对某次保险事故损失单独应负的最高赔偿限额与各保险人应负的最高赔偿限额总和的比例,承担赔偿责任。其计算公式为

$$各保险人的损失分摊额＝损失金额×\frac{该保险人的赔偿限额}{各保险人的赔偿限额总和}$$

Apportionment of limits of liability means that each insurer，in the absence of duplicate coverage by other insurers，assumes liability in the proportion of the maximum limit of indemnity payable individually in respect of an insured loss to the aggregate of the maximum limits of indemnity payable by the insurers. The formula for its calculation is：

apportionment of each insurer ＝ amount of loss × (limit of indemnity of this insurer/total limits of compensation for each insurer)

3) 顺序责任分摊(Apportionment of Sequential Liability)

顺序责任分摊是指按各保险人出立保险单的先后顺序分摊损失,当发生保险事故时,最先出立保险单的保险人先负责赔偿,若保险标的的损失超过其赔偿责任限额,超过部分依次由之后出立保险单的保险人负责赔偿。

Apportionment of sequential liability means that losses are apportioned according to the order in which the insurance policies are issued by each insurer. In the event of an insurance accident，the first insurer to issue an insurance policy will be responsible for compensation first，and if the loss of the subject-matter insured exceeds the limit of its liability，the excess will be compensated by the insurer that issues the insurance policy after it.

4) 相同份额责任分摊(Apportionment of Responsibility in Equal Shares)

相同份额责任分摊是指不管各保险人的责任限额为多少,保险标的损失均按相同份额分摊。如果分摊后的损失金额超过某保险人的责任限额,超过部分由其他保险人继续按相同份额分摊,以此类推,直至损失全部分摊完毕或各保险人承担的赔偿金额均已达到

其责任限额。

Apportionment of responsibility in equal shares means that the loss of the subject-matter insured is apportioned on the basis of equal shares, irrespective of the limit of liability of each insurer. If the amount of loss after apportionment exceeds the limit of liability of one insurer, the other insurers will continue to apportion the excess on an equal share basis, and so on, until the loss has been fully apportioned or the amount of compensation to be borne by each insurer has reached its limit of liability.

Words and Expressions

即测即练

习题

第 10 章

Chapter 10

海洋运输货物保险的保障范围
Coverage of Marine Cargo Transportation Insurance

Learning Objectives：

1. Master the types of risks covered by marine cargo insurance，the classification of perils of the sea and extraneous risks，and their respective meanings；

2. Master the classification of losses covered by marine cargo insurance，the classification of total loss and partial loss，and their respective meanings；

3. Master the concepts of actual and constructive total loss，and the difference between actual and constructive total loss；

4. Master the concept of general average and particular average，the conditions for constituting general average，and its contribution principle；understand the difference and connection between general average and particular average；

5. Master the concept and distinction between sue and labour charges and salvage charges；understand the differences between the insurer's compensation for sue and labour charges and salvage charges.

引导案例

2021 年 10 月 20 日，甲国 A 公司与乙国 B 公司签订了购买 52 500 吨化肥的 CFR 合同。A 公司开出的信用证规定装运期为 2022 年 1 月 1 日至 1 月 10 日。由于 B 公司租用的"顺风号"在前往乙国港口的途中遭遇飓风，直到 2022 年 1 月 20 日才完成装运。1 月 21 日，承运人根据 B 公司出具的保函，按照信用证条款签发了提单，并离开了装货港。A 公司已为货物投保水渍险。2022 年 1 月 30 日，"顺风号"船在通过巴拿马运河时起火，导致一些化肥燃烧。在命令灭火的过程中，船长弄湿并销毁了一些化肥。由于船在装货港延误，这艘船到达目的地时，化肥价格下跌，A 公司不得不大幅度降低剩余化肥的价格，这对 A 公司造成了巨大的损失。该案例中的损失具有不同的性质：①途中燃烧的化肥损失属于单独海损，根据 CFR 条款，风险由 A 公司即买方承担，而 A 公司已购买了水渍险，赔偿范围包括单独海损，因此该损失应由保险公司承担。②淋湿及销毁化肥的损失属于共同海损。由于船舶和货物处于共同的危险之中，船长出于共同的安全考虑，故意合理地采取措施而造成化肥的淋湿及销毁，因此该损失属于共同海损，应由 A 公司和船运公司按受益比例分摊。③如果承运人延迟装运并签发提单，则承运人应对延迟交货负责。

资料来源：共同海损案件［EB/OL］.（2022-05-30）. https://www. lawpa. cn/changshi/10122360. html.

海洋货物运输保险是最早形成的运输险种，陆运、空运、邮包运输等其他形式的运输保险都是以它为基础的。海洋货物运输保险是指以海上运输有关的财产（货物或船舶）、利益或责任作为保险标的的一种保险，其属于财产保险的范畴，是一种特殊形式的财产保险。保险人对保险标的在海上所遭遇的风险、损失和相关费用负赔偿责任。

Marine cargo transport insurance is the earliest form of transport insurance, on which other forms of transport insurance such as land, air, and parcel transport are based. Marine cargo transportation insurance is a kind of insurance in which the property (cargo or ship), interest, or liability related to marine transportation is the subject-matter insured. It belongs to the category of property insurance, and is a special form of property insurance. The insurer is liable for the risks, losses, and related expenses incurred by the subject-matter insured at sea.

由于海洋运输具有运费低、运量大、可以到达世界各主要港口等优点，因此其成为国际贸易中货物运输的最主要方式。但是海洋运输货物容易遭遇各种海上风险的侵袭和威胁，从而导致货物的灭失和损害，还可能产生有关费用的支出。为了保证货物受损后能够获得经济补偿，买方或卖方通常需要对海运货物办理运输保险。海上保险主要是以货物和船舶作为保险标的，把货物和船舶在运输中可能遭受的风险、损失及费用作为保障范围的一种保险。然而，由于货物的性质、船舶的用途、运输的路线及区域、海上自然条件等因素的不同，需要保险人提供的风险保障也不同。为了适应被保险人不同的需要，保险公司制定了不同的保险条款。在保险业务中，风险、损失、费用和险别之间具有密切的联系，风险是导致货物和船舶损失及费用支出的原因，险别是具体规定保险人对风险、损失和费用予以承保的责任范围。

Due to the advantages of low freight, large volume, and being able to reach major ports in the world, maritime transportation has become the most important mode of cargo transportation in international trade. However, the goods transported by sea are vulnerable to the invasion and threat of various maritime perils, which may lead to the loss of and damage to the goods, and may also produce the expenditure of related costs. In order to secure financial compensation for damaged goods, it is often necessary for the buyer or seller to take out transport insurance for goods shipped by sea. Marine insurance is a type of insurance that covers cargo and ships against the risks, losses, and expenses that they may suffer during transportation. However, different factors such as the nature of the cargo, the purpose of the ship, the route and area of transport, and the natural conditions at sea require different risk cover from the insurer. In order to accommodate the different needs of the insured, insurance companies have developed different insurance clauses. In the insurance business, there is a close link between risk, loss, expense, and insurance coverage, with risk being the cause of loss and expense of cargo and ships, and insurance coverage specifying the extent of the insurer's liability to cover risks, losses, and expenses.

10.1　海洋货物运输保险保障的风险（Risks Covered by Marine Cargo Insurance）

海洋货物运输保险保障的风险可以分为两大类,即海上风险和其他外来原因引起的外来风险。

The risks covered by marine cargo insurance can be divided into two categories, namely perils of the sea and extraneous risks.

10.1.1　海上风险（Perils of the Sea）

海上风险一般是指船舶或货物在海上运输过程中发生的或随附海上运输所发生的风险。海上风险有其特定的含义和范围,一方面,它并不包括所有发生在海上的风险,另一方面它又不局限于航海中所发生的风险。现代海上保险将与海运相连的包括陆上、内河、驳船运输过程中的风险包含在海上风险中予以承保。

Perils of the sea generally refer to the risks of ship or cargo occurred in the process of or accompanied by maritime transportation. Maritime peril has a specific meaning and scope which, on the one hand, does not cover all risks occurring at sea and, on the other hand, is not limited to risks occurring at sea. Modern marine insurance covers the risks associated with maritime transport, including land, inland waterways, and barge transportation, under marine risks.

保险人承保的各种海上风险来源于英国劳合社的船、货保险单中的风险条款。按照发生性质,海上风险可以分为自然灾害和意外事故两大类。

The various perils of the sea covered by insurers derive from the risk clauses in Lloyd's S. G. Policy. Marine risks can be divided into two main categories, natural calamities and fortuitous accidents.

1. 自然灾害（Natural Calamities）

自然灾害,一般是指不以人的意志为转移的自然界力量所引起的灾害。但在海运货物保险中,它并不是泛指一切由于自然界力量所引起的灾害,而且不同国家、不同时期对自然灾害的解释也不同。我国 1981 年 1 月 1 日修订的《海洋运输货物保险条款》规定:所谓自然灾害仅指恶劣气候、雷电、海啸、地震、洪水等人力不可抗拒的灾害。而 1982 年 1 月 1 日开始实施的英国《协会货物条款》规定属于自然灾害性质的风险有:雷电、地震、火山爆发、浪击落海,以及海水、湖水、河水进入船舶、驳船、运输工具、集装箱、大型海运箱或储存处所等。

Natural calamities generally refer to disasters caused by the forces of nature that are not subject to the will of man. In the context of marine cargo insurance, however, it does not generally refer to all disasters caused by the forces of nature. And natural calamities are interpreted differently in different countries at different times. China's *Ocean Marine Cargo Clauses*, revised on 1 January 1981, stipulates that the term "natural calamity" refers only to disasters beyond human control, such as heavy weather, lightning, tsunami, earthquake and flood. In contrast, *Institute Cargo Clauses*, which came into effect on 1 January 1982, provides that natural calamities include not only lightning, earthquakes, volcanic eruptions, but also washing overboard, and the entry of sea, lake, or river water into vessel craft, hold, conveyance, container, liftvan, or place of storage.

上述各种风险的主要含义如下。

The main implications of the various disasters mentioned above are as follows.

1）恶劣气候（Heavy Weather）

恶劣气候一般指海上飓风、大浪引起船舶颠簸、倾斜，造成船体破裂、机器设备损坏，以及船上货物相互挤压、碰损破碎、混杂、渗漏、包装破裂或被水浸湿、冲走等。海运保险实务中，由于不同海域自然条件不同，保险人对"恶劣气候"一词并没有统一明确的定义。

Heavy weather generally refers to the jolting and tilting of the ship caused by hurricanes and high waves at sea, resulting in the breakage of the hull and damage to machinery and equipment; and the consequent crushing, breaking, mixing, leakage, breakage or wetting and washing away of the goods on board. In marine insurance practice, insurers do not have a uniform and clear definition of the term of "heavy weather" due to different natural conditions in different waters.

此外，英国 1982 年《协会货物条款》已不再使用"恶劣气候"这一概念，原因是"恶劣气候"所造成的船舶颠簸、晃动，进而导致的货物移位受损，往往与船方理舱不当造成的货物移位受损不易分清，而后者是保险人不保的损失。但在《协会货物条款》中，如果确实是直接由于恶劣气候而非理舱不当引起货物移位，造成货物受损或灭失，ICC（A）予以承保。

In addition, the concept of "heavy weather" is no longer used in the 1982 *Institute Cargo Clauses* as it is often difficult to distinguish between damage to shifted cargo caused by the jolting and rocking of the ship under "heavy weather", and damage to shifted cargo caused by improper stowage by the shipowner, the latter of which is a loss not insured by the insurer. However, ICC（A）will cover damage or loss of cargo if the shifting of the cargo is genuinely a direct result of heavy weather and not due to improper stowage.

2）雷电（Lightning）

海运货物保险所承保的雷电是指被保险货物在海上或陆上运输过程中被雷电击中所直接造成的损失，或者由于雷电引起的火灾造成的货物的灭失和损害，也包括船舶被雷电击中而破损致使海水进入船舱造成的货物损失等。

Lightning covered by marine cargo insurance is damage directly caused by lightning strikes on the insured cargo during transport at sea or on land, or loss of or damage to cargo due to fire caused by lightning, or loss of cargo due to seawater entering the hold of a ship damaged by lightning.

3）海啸（Tsunami）

海啸是指海底地震、火山活动、海岸地壳变异或特大海洋风暴等引起的海水强烈震动而产生巨大浪潮，因此导致船舶、货物被淹没、冲击或损毁。

A tsunami is a huge wave generated by the strong vibration of seawater caused by undersea earthquakes，volcanic activity，coastal crustal changes，or extreme ocean storms，resulting in the submersion，impact，or destruction of ships and cargo.

4）地震（Earthquake）

地震是指由于地壳发生急剧的自然变化，使地面发生震动、坍塌、地陷等造成船货的直接损失或由此引起的火灾、爆炸、淹没等损失。

Earthquake refers to the rapid natural changes in the earth's crust，causing the ground to vibrate，collapse，and sink，resulting in direct loss of cargo，or loss due to fire，explosion，and flooding.

5）火山爆发（Volcanic Eruption）

火山爆发是指由于火山爆发产生的地震及喷发出的火山岩灰造成的保险货物的损失。海底火山爆发还会引起海啸，从而导致航行中的船舶及装载的货物受损。

A volcanic eruption is a loss of insured cargo caused by the earthquake and the eruption of volcanic ash from a volcanic eruption. Submarine volcanic eruptions can also cause tsunamis，which can result in damage to ships and cargo on board.

6）洪水（Flood）

洪水是指因江河泛滥、山洪暴发、湖水上岸及倒灌、暴雨积水导致保险货物遭受浸泡、淹没、冲散、冲毁等损失。

Flood is the loss of insured goods by immersion，submergence，dispersion，and destruction caused by the overflowing of rivers，mountain torrents rushing down，lake uplift and inundation，or storm water accumulation.

7）浪击落海（Washing Overboard）

浪击落海是指存在舱面上的货物在运输过程中受海浪冲击落海而造成的损失，不包括在恶劣气候下船身晃动而造成货物落海的损失。我国现行保险条款基本险不保此项风险，而是在附加险的舱面险中承保。

Washing overboard refers to the loss of cargo stored on deck that falls overboard due to the impact of waves during transport，excluding the loss of cargo that falls overboard due to the rocking of the ship in bad weather. This risk is not covered by the basic insurance in the current insurance clauses of China，but is covered under on deck risk of additional insurance.

8）海水、湖水、河水进入船舶、驳船、运输工具、集装箱、大型海运箱或储存处所（Entry of Sea，Lake or River Water into Vessel Craft，Hold，Conveyance，Container，Liftvan or Place of Storage）

《协会货物条款》中自然灾害包括该风险。这种风险包括由于海水、湖水、河水进入船舶等运输工具或储存处所造成的保险货物的损失。对储存处所可以理解为包括陆上一切永久性的或临时性的有顶棚或露天的储存处所。

This risk is included in the *Institute Cargo Clauses* for natural calamities. This risk includes loss of the insured goods due to the entry of sea, lake, or river water into the means of transport such as ships, or into place of storage. Place of storage may be understood to include all permanent or temporary covered or open storage sites on land.

上述自然灾害中,洪水、地震、火山爆发以及海水、湖水、河水进入船舶、驳船、运输工具、集装箱、大型海运箱或储存处所的风险实际上并非真正发生在海上的风险,而是发生在内陆或海陆、海河以及海轮与驳船相连接之处的风险。但对海运货物来说,由于这些风险是随附海上运输而发生的,而且危害性往往很大,为了适应被保险人的实际需要,在海运货物保险业务的长期实践中,逐渐地也把它们列入海上保险的承保范围。

Among the above-mentioned natural calamities, risks such as floods, earthquakes, volcanic eruptions, and entry of sea, lake or river water into vessel craft, hold, conveyance, container, liftvan or place of storage are not really risks that occur at sea, but risks that occur inland or where land and sea, rivers and sea and ships and barges are connected. But for marine cargo, since these risks occur in connection with marine transportation and the hazard is often very large, in order to meet the actual needs of the insured, the risks are gradually included in the marine insurance coverage in the long-term practice of marine cargo insurance.

2. 意外事故(Fortuitous Accidents)

海上意外事故是指运输工具遭遇外来的、突然的、非意料之中的事故。例如,船舶搁浅、触礁、碰撞、沉没,船舶失踪,货物起火爆炸等。

Fortuitous accidents are external, sudden, and unanticipated accidents to the carrying conveyance. Examples include ship grounding, stranding, collision, sinking, missing, or fire and explosion of cargo, etc.

海洋货物运输保险承保的意外事故并不是泛指海上发生的所有意外事故。按照我国1981年1月1日修订的《海洋运输货物保险条款》的规定,意外事故是指运输工具遭受搁浅、触礁、沉没、互撞、与流冰或其他物体碰撞以及失火、爆炸等。根据英国伦敦保险协会1982年修订的《协会货物条款》,除了船舶、驳船的触礁、搁浅、沉没、倾覆、火灾、爆炸等属于意外事故外,陆上运输工具的倾覆或出轨也属意外事故的范畴。由此可以看出,海洋货物运输保险所承保的意外事故,也不仅指在海上发生的意外事故。

Accidents covered by marine cargo insurance do not generally include to all accidents occurring at sea. In accordance with the provisions of *Ocean Marine Cargo Clauses*, as revised on 1 January 1981, an accident is defined as grounding, stranding, sinking, collision with floating ice or other objects, fire, explosion, etc. of a carrying conveyance. According to *Institute Cargo Clauses* revised by Institute of London Underwriters (ILU) in 1982, overturning or derailment of land conveyance, in addition to stranding, grounding, sinking, capsizing, fire and explosion of vessel and craft, also falls under the category of accidents. It can be seen that accidents covered by marine cargo insurance are not only those that occur at sea.

海上保险业务中,各种意外事故都有其特定的含义。

Various accidents have specific meanings in marine insurance business.

1) 搁浅(Stranding)

搁浅是指船舶在航行中,由于意外原因与水下障碍物,如海滩、礁石及其他障碍物紧密接触,持续一段时间,如停航 12 小时以上,失去进退自由的状态。构成海上保险中的搁浅必须具备两个条件:①搁浅是意外发生的;②搁浅造成船底紧密搁置在障碍物上,持续一段时间处于静止状态,不能一擦而过。

Stranding is the state in which a ship loses its freedom of movement when it comes into close contact with underwater obstacles such as beaches, rocks, and other obstructions during its voyage for a period of time such as 12 hours or more. Two conditions must be present to constitute a stranding in marine insurance: ① the stranding occurred accidentally; ②the stranding caused the bottom of the vessel to rest closely on the obstruction, remaining stationary for a period of time, and not merely passing over the obstruction.

2) 触礁(Grounding)

触礁是指船舶擦过水中岩礁或其他障碍物而依然能够继续航行的一种状态。

Grounding is a condition in which a vessel is able to continue sailing even though it has scraped against rocks or other obstacles in the water.

3) 沉没(Sinking)

沉没是指船舶在航行中或停泊时,船体全部沉入水中而失去航行能力的状态,或虽未构成船体完全沉没,但已远超船舶吃水标准且船舶无法继续航行。如果船体的一部分浸入水中或海水虽不断浸入,但船舶仍具有航行能力,则不能认为是沉没事故。

Sinking refers to the state in which a ship is completely submerged while sailing or berthing and is incapable of navigation. Or, although the hull is not completely submerged, the draft of the ship has far exceeded the design standard and the ship is unable to continue its voyage. A ship is not considered to have sunk if the ship is capable of navigation despite part of its hull is submerged in water or there is continuous entrance of seawater.

4) 碰撞(Collision)

碰撞是指载货船舶与水以外的外界物体,如其他船舶、码头、浮冰、桥梁、冰山、河堤等发生直接的、猛烈的接触,因此造成船上货物的损失。但船舶同海水的接触以及船舶停泊在港口内与其他船舶并排停靠码头旁边,因为波动相互挤擦,均不能作为碰撞。

Collision refers to the direct and violent contact of vessel craft or conveyance with external objects other than water, such as other vessel, dock, floating ice, bridge, iceberg, and river bank, resulting in the loss of goods on board.

5) 失踪(Missing)

失踪是指船舶在海上航行,失去联络超过合理期限的一种情况。各个国家根据各自的情况，分别制定了一定的期限作为"合理期限"。在我国，这一期限为两个月。被保险船舶一旦宣告失踪，除非能证明失踪是因战争风险导致的，均由保险人当作海上风险损失负责赔偿。如果在保险人赔偿后船舶又重新出现，该船所有权归保险人。

Missing is a situation where a ship has been out of contact while at sea for more than a reasonable period of time. Each country has set a certain period of time as a "reasonable period" depending on its own circumstances. In the case of China，this period is two months. Once the insured ship has been declared lost，unless it can be proved that the missing was caused by a war risk，the insurer shall be liable for compensation as a loss of maritime risks. If the ship reappears after being indemnified by the insurer，the ownership of the ship shall be vested in the insurer.

6）倾覆（Capsizing）

倾覆是指船舶在航行中遭受自然灾害或意外事故，导致船体翻倒或倾斜，失去正常状态，非经施救或救助不能继续航行的情况。

Capsizing refers to the state in which a ship suffers a natural disaster or accident during its voyage，resulting in the ship overturning or tilting，losing its normal condition and being unable to continue its voyage without rescue or salvage.

7）火灾（Fire）

火灾是指由于意外、偶然发生的燃烧失去控制，蔓延扩大而造成的船、货的损失。海上货运保险中，无论是直接被火烧毁、烧焦、烧裂，还是间接被火熏黑、灼热或为救火而致损失，均属火灾风险。火灾是海上运输最严重的风险之一。海运货物通常由以下原因引起火灾：

（1）闪电、雷击；

（2）爆炸；

（3）船长、船员在航行中的过失；

（4）船舶遭遇海难后，在避难港修理，工作人员操作不当，如电焊。

凡由于上述原因及其他不明原因所致的火灾损失，保险人均负责赔偿。但是，由于货物固有瑕疵或在不适当的情况下运送引起的货物自燃，则不属于保险人的承保责任范围。

Fire refers to the loss of ship or cargo caused by accidental combustion that spreads out of control. In marine cargo insurance，the loss of cargo，whether directly destroyed，charred or cracked by fire，or indirectly blackened or heated by fire or for firefighting，belongs to the category of fire risk. Fire is one of the most serious risks of maritime transportation. Fire is usually caused by the following reasons in maritime transportation：

（1）Lightning，lightning strikes；

（2）Explosion，or explosion caused by fire；

（3）The negligence of the master and crew during navigation；

（4）Improper operation of staff after a shipwreck and the ship is repaired in the port of refuge，such as electric welding.

The insurer is liable to pay for any fire damage caused by the above mentioned causes and other unknown causes. However, spontaneous combustion of the cargo due to inherent defects or improper delivery of the cargo is not covered by the insurer's liability.

8）爆炸（Explosion）

爆炸是指物体内部发生急剧的分散或燃烧，迸发出大量气体和热量，致使物体本身及其周围的物体遭受猛烈破坏的现象。货物在海上运输过程中，因爆炸而受损的情况较多。如船舶锅炉爆炸致使货物受损，货物自身因气候、温度变化的影响产生化学作用引起爆炸而受损。

Explosion refers to the occurrence of rapid dispersion or combustion within an object, bursting out a large amount of gas and heat, resulting in violent destruction of the object itself and its surrounding objects. During maritime transport, cargo is more often damaged by explosions. For example, the cargo is damaged by the explosion of the ship's boiler; or the cargo itself is damaged by a chemical explosion caused by the effects of climatic temperature changes.

9）投弃（Jettison）

投弃是指当船舶及其承载的货物均处于紧急危险性情况下，船长为了船舶与货物的共同安全，故意将船上部分货物或设备抛弃海中所造成的损失。现行英国《协会货物条款》规定：凡因抛货造成的损失，保险人都给予赔偿，而不问其是否为共同海损行为所致。我国现行的《海洋运输货物保险条款》仅指共同海损的抛货。

Jettison refers to the loss caused by the captain intentionally abandoning part of the cargo or equipment to the sea for the common safety of the ship and the cargo when the ship and the cargo are in emergency. The current *Institute Cargo Clauses* stipulate that the insurer shall compensate for any loss caused by jettison, whether or not it is caused by a general average act. China's current *Ocean Marine Cargo Clauses* only refers to general average jettison.

10）吊索损害（Sling Loss）

吊索损害是指被保险货物在起运港、卸货港或转运港进行装卸时，从吊钩上摔下而造成的货物损失。对于此种风险，我国《海洋运输货物保险条款》的规定是："在装卸或转运时由于一件或数件整件货物落海造成的全部或部分损失。"而英国《协会货物条款》的规定是："货物在船舶或驳船装卸时落海或跌落造成任何整件的全损。"

Sling loss is damage caused by the insured goods falling from a sling hook while the insured goods are being loaded or unloaded at the port of shipment, discharge or transshipment. For this kind of risk, China's *Ocean Marine Cargo Clause* provide for "Partial or total loss consequent on falling of entire package or packages into sea during loading, transshipment or discharge". In contrast, *Institute Cargo Clause* states that "Total loss of any package lost overboard or dropped whilst loading on to, or unloading from, vessel or craft".

11）陆上运输工具倾覆（Overturning of Land Conveyance）

陆上运输工具倾覆是指海运保险货物从起运地指定的发货人仓库到港口装船以及在目的港从卸离海轮到指定的收货人仓库之间陆上载货工具因发生意外而翻倒、倾斜所导致的车祸损失事故。英国现行《协会货物条款》将此项风险损失包含在保险人的承保责任范围内。

Overturning of a land conveyance means damage caused by an accidental overturning or tilting of a land conveyance while the insured goods are being transported from the designated consignor's warehouse at the place of dispatch to the port of shipment, and on its way to the designated consignee's warehouse after being discharged from a vessel at the port of destination. This risk is included in the insurer's coverage under the current *Institute Cargo Clauses*.

12）海盗行为（Piracy）

海盗行为是指强盗为了个人目的无区别地对海运货物保险单所承保的保险标的进行劫掠所造成的损失，它区别于某些人为了政治目的而合法或非法地抢劫某一特定国家的财产的行为。

我国现行《海洋运输货物保险条款》中，海盗风险属于战争险的承保范围。英国《协会货物条款》将其定义为一般海上风险，而非战争风险，ICC（A）予以承保。

Piracy is the damage caused by the robbery of the subject matter insured covered by a marine cargo insurance policy by robbers for personal purposes without distinction, which is distinguished from the robbery of the property of a particular country by some people for political purposes, legally or illegally.

In China's current *Ocean Marine Cargo Clauses*, piracy risk is covered by war risks. In contrast, *Institute Cargo Clause* defines it as a general maritime peril, not a war risk, which is covered by ICC（A）.

13）船长和船员的恶意行为（Barratry of Master and Mariner）

船长和船员的恶意行为是指船长或船员背着船东或货主故意损害船东或货主利益的一种恶意行为，如丢弃船舶、纵火焚烧、凿漏船体、违法走私造成船舶被扣押或没收、故意违反航行规则而遭处罚等。海上保险承保此种风险的条件是：①船长或船员的恶意行为不是由于船东或租船人的纵容、共谋或授意所做出的；②他们的行为使船东、租船人或货主的利益受到了损害。

船长、船员的恶意行为是 S. G. Policy 中承保的一项海上风险，ICC 2009（A）也承保该项风险。在我国，此项风险属于海运货物罢工险的承保范围。

Barratry of master and mariner is a malicious act committed by the captain or crew behind the back of the shipowner or cargo owner to deliberately harm the interests of the shipowner or cargo owner, such as abandonment of ships, arson of ships and cargoes, cutting and leaking of hulls, illegal smuggling resulting in the seizure or confiscation of ships, and wilful violation of navigation rules resulting in penalties. Marine insurance covers such risks provided that: ① the master or crew acted in bad faith without the connivance, complicity, or authorization of the shipowner or charterer; ②They have acted to the detriment of the shipowner, charterer or cargo owner.

Barratry of master and mariner is one of the marine risks covered by S. G. Policy, ICC 2009(A) also covers this risk. In China, this risk is covered by cargo strike clause.

10.1.2　外来风险（Extraneous Risks）

外来风险是指海上风险以外的其他外来原因造成的风险。所谓外来原因,必须是意外的、偶然的、事先难以预料的,而不是必然发生的外来因素。国际海运货物保险业务中,保险人除了承保各种海上风险外,还承保外来风险所造成的损失。外来风险一般分为一般外来风险和特殊外来风险两类。

Extraneous risks are those that arise from external causes other than maritime perils. So-called external causes must be unexpected, accidental, and unforeseen in advance, rather than external factors that are bound to occur. In international marine cargo insurance business, the insurer covers not only various perils of the sea, but also losses caused by extraneous risks. Extraneous risks are generally classified as general extraneous risks and specific extraneous risks.

1. 一般外来风险（General Extraneous Risks）

我国海运保险业务中承保的一般外来风险有以下几种。

The general extraneous risks covered by marine insurance business in China are as follows.

1）偷窃（Theft，Pilferage）

偷窃是指整件货物或包装内一部分货物被人暗中窃取造成的损失,不包括公开的攻击性的劫夺行为造成的损失。

Theft and pilferage is a loss caused by the covert theft of the entire shipment or part of the package, excluding losses caused by overt and aggressive looting.

2）提货不着（Non-delivery）

提货不着是指货物在运输途中由于不明原因被遗失,造成货物未能运抵目的地,或运抵目的地发生整件短少,没能交付给收货人的损失。

Non-delivery refers to the loss of the goods in transit for unknown reasons, resulting in the goods not reaching their destination, or that they are not delivered to the consignee because of a shortage of the whole package upon arrival at the destination.

3）渗漏（Leakage）

渗漏是指盛在容器中的流质或半流质的货物在运输途中由于外来原因造成容器损坏而引起的损失。

Leakage is the loss caused by damage to the container due to external causes in transit when the fluid or semi-fluid goods are held in the container.

4）短量（Short Delivery）

短量是指被保险货物在运输途中或到达目的地被发现包装内货物数量短少或散装货物重量短缺。

Short delivery refers to the shortage of the quantity of goods in a package or the shortage of the weight of goods in bulk while the insured goods are in transit or arrive at their destination.

5）碰损（Clash）

碰损是指金属和金属制品等货物在运输途中因震动、颠簸、碰撞、受压等而造成凹陷、变形的损失。

Clash refers to the loss from denting and deformation of metal and metal products caused by vibration，jolt，collision，or pressure during transportation.

6）破碎（Breakage）

破碎是指易碎物品在运输中因搬运、装卸不慎或震动、颠簸、碰撞、受压等而造成的破碎和破裂。

Breakage refers to the breakage and rupture of fragile goods caused by careless handling，loading and unloading，vibration，bumping，collision and pressure.

7）钩损（Hook Damage）

钩损是指袋装、捆装货物在装卸、搬运过程中因使用手钩、吊钩操作不当而致货物的损失。

Hook damage is the loss of bagged and bundled goods due to improper handling of hand hooks and hooks in the process of loading，unloading and handling.

8）生锈（Rust）

生锈是指金属或金属制品的一种氧化过程。海洋运输货物保险中承保的生锈，是指货物在装运时无生锈现象，在保险期内生锈造成的货物损失。

Rusting is a process of oxidation of metal or metal products. Rust covered in marine cargo insurance refers to the loss of goods caused by rust during the period of insurance when the goods are not rusted at the time of shipment.

9）淡水雨淋（Fresh Water and Rain Damage）

淡水雨淋是指直接由于淡水、雨水以及冰雪融化造成货物的水渍损失。

Fresh water and rain damage is the loss of water stain damage to goods as a direct result of fresh water，rain，and melting snow and ice.

10）串味（Taint of Odor）

串味是指被保险货物受到其他带异味货物的影响，失去原味，丧失了原有的用途和价值。

Taint of odor means that the insured goods are affected by other goods with an odor，losing the original taste，and the original use and value.

11）玷污（Contamination）

玷污是指货物同其他物质接触而受污染，如布匹、纸张、食物、服装等被油类或带色的物质污染造成的损失。

Contamination is the defilement of goods by contact with other substances, such as damage caused by contamination of cloth, paper, food, or clothing with oil or coloured substances.

12) 受潮受热(Sweating and Heating)

受潮受热是指由于气温骤变或船上通风设备失灵而使船舱内水汽凝结,引起货物发潮或发热而导致货物霉烂等而造成的损失。

Sweating and heating refers to the damage caused by the sudden change of temperature or the failure of the ship's ventilation equipment to condense the water vapor in the cabin, which causes the cargo to be damp or hot, resulting in mold and rot of the cargo.

2. 特殊外来风险(Special Extraneous Risks)

特殊外来风险是指除一般外来风险以外的其他外来原因导致的风险,往往是与政治、军事、社会动荡、国家政策法令以及行政措施等的变化有关的风险。常见的特殊外来风险主要有战争风险、罢工风险、拒收风险、交货不到风险、进口关税损失风险等。

Special extraneous risks are those that arise from external causes other than general extraneous risks, often related to changes in political, military, social unrest, national policies and decrees, and administrative measures. Common special extraneous risks include war risks, strikes risks, rejection risks, failure to delivery risks, and import tariff loss risks.

1) 战争风险(War Risks)

战争风险是指由于战争或其他敌对行为而引起的对货物的捕获、拘留和各种战争武器直接造成的货物损失。

War risks refer to the capture or detention of goods caused by war or other hostile acts, as well as the loss of goods directly caused by various war weapons.

2) 罢工风险(Strikes Risks)

罢工风险是指由于罢工工人或参加工潮、暴动、民众斗争的人员的行动所造成的货物损失。

Strike risks refer to the loss of goods due to the actions of strikers or persons taking part in labour disturbances, riots or civil commotions.

3) 拒收风险(Rejection Risks)

拒收风险是指由于政府的相关法令,货物在进口港被进口国的有关当局拒绝进口或没收而造成货物的损失。比如,某些国家颁布新的政策或管制措施及国际组织颁布某些禁令,都可能导致货物无法出口或进口而造成损失。

Rejection risks refer to the loss of goods caused by the refusal or confiscation of goods by the relevant authorities of the importing country at the port of import due to the relevant laws and regulations of the government. For example, the enactment of new policies or controls in certain countries and the issuance of certain prohibitions by international organizations may prevent the goods from being exported or imported, resulting in losses.

4)交货不到风险(Failure to Delivery Risks)

交货不到风险是指由于政治、行政因素而非运输原因引起的货物在一定时期内无法运达原定目的地交货。例如,被保险货物由于禁运被迫在中途卸货而造成损失。

Failure to delivery risks refer to the situation when the goods cannot be delivered to the original destination within a certain period of time due to political and administrative factors rather than transportation reasons. For example, the insured goods are forced to unload midway due to the embargo, resulting in losses.

5)进口关税损失风险(Import Tariff Loss Risks)

进口关税损失风险是指有些国家对进口货物征收关税时,无论货物是否完好,一律按货物完好时的价值征收进口关税,使得货主遭受关税损失。

Import tariff loss risks refer to the tariff loss suffered by the cargo owner when some countries impose tariffs on imported goods according to the value of the goods when they are in good condition, regardless of whether the goods are in good condition.

10.2 海洋运输货物保险保障的损失
(Losses Covered by Marine Cargo Insurance)

船舶和货物在海上运输中由于海上灾害事故等造成的损害和灭失称为海上损失。按照国际保险市场的一般解释,凡与海上运输相关联的海陆连接的运输过程中发生的损害与灭失,也属于海上损失的范围。按照损失程度,海上损失可分为全部损失和部分损失。

The damage and loss of ships and cargoes in maritime transportation due to maritime calamities and accidents etc. is called maritime loss. In accordance with the general interpretation of the international insurance market, damage and loss occurring in connection with maritime carriage and in the course of carriage between land and sea also fall within the scope of maritime loss. Maritime loss can be divided into total lose and partial loss, depending on the extent of the loss.

10.2.1 全部损失(Total Loss)

全部损失简称全损,是指保险标的由于承保风险造成全部灭失或视同全部灭失的损害。海上保险业务中,全部损失可分为实际全损、推定全损、部分全损和协议全损。

Total loss is the damage caused by the insured risk resulting in the total or deemed total loss of the subject-matter insured. Total loss in marine insurance business can be divided into actual total loss, constructive total loss, total loss of part, and compromise total loss.

1. 实际全损(Actual Total Loss)

实际全损又称绝对全损,是指保险标的在实际上完全灭失或毁损。构成被保险货物实际全损有以下四种情况：①保险标的实体已经完全灭失；②保险标的遭到严重损害，完全失去原有的用途和价值；③保险标的不再归被保险人所有，即被保险人无可挽回地失去对保险标的的实际占有、使用、受益和处分等权利；④载货船舶失踪达到一定时期仍杳无音讯。

Actual total loss, also known as absolute total loss, means that the subject-matter insured is in fact completely lost or destroyed. The actual total loss of the insured goods may occur under the following four circumstances: ① the subject-matter insured has been completely destroyed; ② the subject-matter insured has been severely damaged, completely losing its original use and value; ③ the subject-matter insured no longer belongs to the insured, i. e. the insured has irretrievably lost the right to the actual possession, use, benefit and disposition of the subject-matter insured; ④ the ship carrying the cargo has been missing for a certain period of time without a trace.

2. 推定全损（Constructive Total Loss）

1）推定全损的概念和范围（Concept and Scope of Constructive Total Loss）

推定全损也称商业全损，指被保险货物在海上运输中遭遇承保风险后，虽未达到完全灭失的状态，但是可以预见到它们的全损将不可避免；或者为了避免全损，需要支付的抢救、修理费用与继续将货物运抵目的地的费用之和将超过保险价值。

判定货物推定全损有两个相互独立的标准：①实际全损不可避免；②为避免实际全损所需支付的费用和续运费用之和超过保险标的的价值。

构成推定全损的具体情况主要有以下几种：

（1）保险标的实际全损已经无法避免，或者是为了避免实际全损，需要花费的施救等费用，将超过获救后标的价值；

（2）保险标的发生保险事故后，被保险人失去标的所有权，而收回这一所有权所需花费的费用将超过收回后的标的价值；

（3）保险标的受损后，整理和续运到目的地的费用，超过货物到达目的地的价值；

（4）保险标的受损后，修理费用已超过其修复后的价值。

Constructive total loss, also known as commercial total loss, refers to the loss where an actual total loss appears to be unavoidable or the cost to be incurred in recovering or reconditioning the goods together with the forwarding cost to the destination named in the policy would exceed their value on arrival.

There are two independent criteria for determining the constructive total loss of the goods: ① the actual total loss is unavoidable; ② the sum of the costs of avoiding the actual total loss and the forwarding costs exceeds the value of the subject-matter insured.

The specific circumstances constituting a constructive total loss are mainly the following:

(1) The actual total loss of the subject-matter insured has become unavoidable or the costs of suing and laboring to avoid an actual total loss would exceed the value of the

subject matter to be rescued;

（2）The insured loses ownership of the subject-matter insured upon an insured event, and the cost of recovering that ownership would exceed the value of the subject-matter after recovery;

（3）In the case of damage to subject-matter insured, where the cost of repairing the damage and forwarding the goods to their destination would exceed their value on arrival;

（4）The cost of repairing the damage to the subject-matter insured would exceed its value when repaired.

2）推定全损的赔偿(Compensation for Constructive Total Loss)

在推定全损的情况下,对被保险人的赔偿有两种情况：①被保险人选择恢复和修理保险标的,按实际损失向保险人索赔部分损失；②被保险人按全部损失索赔,他必须无条件地把保险标的委付给保险人。

Where there is a constructive total loss, the assured is compensated in two ways：①the assured elects to restore and repair the subject-matter insured and claims partial loss from the insurer on the basis of the actual loss；②the assured treat the loss as if it were an actual total loss and unconditionally abandon the subject-matter insured to the insurer.

3）委付(Abandonment)

委付是指被保险人在保险标的处于推定全损状态时,向保险人声明愿意将保险标的的一切权限,包括财产权及一切由此产生的权利与义务转让给保险公司,而要求保险公司按全损给予赔偿的一种行为。

被保险人应以书面或口头方式向被保险人发出委付通知,且不得附带任何条件。保险人可以接受委付,也可以不接受委付,但应在合理的时间内将接受委付或者不接受委付的决定通知被保险人。保险人接受委付的,被保险人对委付财产的全部权利和义务转移给保险人。委付一经保险人接受便不能撤销,且保险人须承担由于所有权转移而相应产生的义务。

Abandonment is an act in which the insured declares to the insurer that he is willing to transfer all rights, including property rights and all rights and obligations arising therefrom, to the insurer when the subject-matter insured is in a state of constructive total loss, and requests the insurer to compensate the insured for the total loss.

The insured shall be given notice of abandonment in writing or orally and without any conditions. The insurer may or may not accept the abandonment, but shall inform the insured of the decision within a reasonable time. If the insurer accepts the abandonment, all rights and obligations of the insured to the abandoned property shall be transferred to the insurer. Once the abandonment is accepted by the insurer, it is irrevocable. The insurer must undertake the corresponding obligations arising from the transfer of ownership.

3. 部分全损（Total Loss of Part）

海上保险中的部分全损，是指货物中可以分割的某一部分发生全部损失。国际货运保险中，习惯上视为部分全损的情况包括：

（1）一批被保险货物在若干张保单下承保，其中一张保单所保货物的全部损失；

（2）一张保单上所保的分类货物的完全损失；

（3）装卸或转船时整件货物发生全损；

（4）使用驳船装运货物时，一条驳船所载货物的完全损失；

（5）一张保险单下包括多张提单，其中一张或几张提单货物的完全灭失。

Total loss of part in marine insurance is a total loss of any apportionable part of the goods. Circumstances customarily considered as partial total loss in international cargo insurance include：

（1）When a consignment of insured goods is covered under several policies，the total loss of the goods insured under one of the policies；

（2）Total loss of classified goods covered by a policy；

（3）Total loss of the whole package in loading，unloading，or transshipment；

（4）Total loss of the goods carried in a barge when a barge is used to load the goods；

（5）Total loss of the goods under one or more of the Bs/L，when there are several Bs/L under one insurance policy.

4. 协议全损（Compromise Total Loss）

某些情况下，保险标的所遭受的损失既不是实际全损，也没有达到推定全损的标准，但基于维护保险人与被保险人之间良好关系的目的，双方一致认为，如果以全损为基础进行赔偿，更有利于对保险合同规定的理解，有利于保险业务的开展。因此，保险人应被保险人的要求按照全损进行赔偿。

In some cases，the loss suffered by the subject-matter insured is neither an actual total loss nor a constructive total loss，but for the purpose of maintaining a good relationship between the insurer and the insured，both parties agree that it is more conducive to the understanding of the provisions of the insurance contract and the development of insurance business if compensation is based on total loss. Therefore，the insurer shall compensate the insured on the basis of total loss at the insured's request.

10.2.2　部分损失（Partial Loss）

部分损失简称分损，是指被保险货物的损失没有达到全部损失的程度。根据损失的性质，部分损失可以分为共同海损和单独海损。

Partial loss means that the damage to the insured goods does not reach the level of total loss. Depending on the nature of the loss，partial loss may be divided into general average and particular average.

1. 共同海损(General Average)

1) 共同海损的定义和内容(Definition and Content of General Average)

共同海损是指在同一海上航程中,船舶、货物和其他财产遭遇共同危险,为了共同安全,有意地、合理地采取措施所直接造成的特殊牺牲、支付的特殊费用。

共同海损的内容包括以下两个方面。

General average is any extraordinary sacrifice and expenditure paid as a direct result of voluntary and reasonable measures taken for the common safety of ships, cargo and other property encountering a common peril during the same voyage at sea.

The elements of general average include the following two aspects.

(1) 共同海损的牺牲。共同海损的牺牲是指共同海损行为导致的船舶、货物等本身的损失。其表现形式包括:抛弃货物;扑灭船上火灾;割弃残损物所造成的损失;有意搁浅所致的损害;机器和锅炉的损害;作为燃料而使用的货物、船用材料和物料;卸货过程中造成的损害等。

(1) General average sacrifice. General average sacrifice refers to the loss of the ship, cargo, etc. itself as a result of a general average act. It takes the form of: jettison; fighting of fires on board; damage caused by culling of wreckage; damage caused by intentional grounding; damage to machinery and boilers; cargo, ship's materials and supplies used as fuel; and damage caused during unloading, etc.

(2) 共同海损的费用。共同海损的费用是指为采取共同海损行为而支付的费用。其表现形式包括:救助报酬;搁浅船舶减载费用以及由此而受到的损害;避难港费用;驶往避难港和在避难港等地支付给船员的工资、伙食费及其他开支;修理费用;代替费用等。

(2) General average expenditure. General average expenditures refer to the expenses paid for taking general average acts. It takes the form of: salvage charges; expenses for the reduction of the load of a stranded ship and the consequent damage; expenses in port of refuge; wages, board and other expenses paid to the crew members for sailing to and at the port of refuge; repair costs; replacement costs, etc.

2) 构成共同海损的条件(Conditions Constituting a General Average)

根据共同海损的定义,共同海损的牺牲和费用必须符合下列条件。

(1) 导致共同海损的危险是真实存在的、危及船舶与货物共同安全的危险。例如,如果船舶在海上失去了螺旋桨,船舶和货物可能暂时还没有面临迫在眉睫的灾难性危险,但危险一定会到来。因此,船长命令船舶驶入附近港口修理而产生的港口费和修理费应属于共同海损。又如,船舶货舱起火,如不及时灭火,火势将蔓延,殃及全船,因此,灭火造成的船舶或货物损失应属于共同海损。

(2) 共同海损的措施是为了解除船货的共同危险,人为地、有意识地采取的合理的措施。例如,船舶搁浅导致船底被划破,货物进水受损,这是由意外事故直接造成的损失,修船费用和货物损失属于单独海损,分别由船方和货方承担。但是,如果为了使船舶浮起而丢弃货物以减少船舶载重量,则丢弃货物的损失是人为、有意造成的,属于共同海损,应由船方和货方共同分摊。

（3）共同海损的牺牲是特殊性质的，费用是额外支付的。例如，在船舶搁浅并处于危险中的情况下，如果为了共同安全而使船舶浮起，则因船舶机器的不正常和过度操作而造成的机器本身的损坏可包括在共同海损中。但是，在任何情况下，船舶在漂浮状态下使用推进器所造成的损害都不能作为共同海损予以赔偿。

（4）共同海损的损失是共同海损措施的直接、合理的后果。例如，如果船舶在航行中遇到共同海损事故，船底受损需要修理，为了修理船舶必须卸下舱内货物，卸货造成的货物损失是共同海损措施的直接后果，可以归入共同海损。但是，如果货物在避风港储存期间仓库起火，造成货物损失，则不是共同海损措施的直接后果，不能归入共同海损。

（5）造成共同海损损失的共同海损措施最终有效果。这里的最终有效是指在采取抢救措施后，船舶或货物的全部或部分安全抵达目的港，从而避免了船舶和货物一起灭失的情况。由于共同海损分摊将由各受益方分摊，而分摊又是由航程结束时船舶和货物的价值来确定的，如果全船失事，船舶和货物遭受全损，那么就没有获救财产，也就没有受益人，因而共同海损分摊就失去了根据，共同海损也就不成立了。

According to the definition of general average, general average sacrifice and expenditure must meet the following conditions.

(1) The danger leading to general average is real and endanger the common safety of ship and cargo. For example, if a ship loses its propeller while at sea, the ship and cargo may not be in imminent and catastrophic danger for the time being, but the danger is sure to come. So the port charges and repair costs incurred by the master in ordering the ship to sail into a nearby port for repairs shall be general average expenditures. Another example is that the ship's cargo hold is on fire, and if the fire is not put out in time, it will spread and affect the whole ship, so the loss of the ship or cargo caused by putting out the fire should be general average sacrifice.

(2) General average act is taken voluntarily, consciously, and reasonably for the purpose of preserving the ship and goods imperiled in the common adventure. For example, a ship running aground resulting in a cut in the bottom of the ship and water damage to the cargo is considered an accident; the cost of repairing the ship and the loss of cargo are particular average, which are borne by the shipowner and the cargo owner respectively. However, if the cargo is abandoned to reduce the ship's load for the purpose of floating the ship, the loss of the abandoned cargo is intentionally made and belongs to general average, which should be shared by the ship owner and the cargo owner.

(3) The general average sacrifice is exceptional and the expenditure is additional. For example, in the case of a ship running aground and in danger, if the ship is floated for common safety, damage to the machinery itself caused by abnormal and excessive operation of the ship's machinery may be included in general average. However, damage caused by the use of the propulsion machinery while the ship is afloat may not be

compensated as general average under any circumstances.

（4）The general average loss is the direct and reasonable consequence of a general average act. For example，if a ship encounters a general average accident during the voyage，the bottom of the ship is damaged and needs to be repaired，and the cargo in the hold must be unloaded in order to repair the ship，the loss of cargo caused by the unloading is a direct result of the general average measures and can be classified as a general average. However，if the goods catch fire in the warehouse during storage in the port of refuge，resulting in the loss of goods，it is not a direct consequence of the general average measures and cannot be classified as general average.

（5）The general average act that causes the general average loss is ultimately effective. The "ultimately effective" here means that after taking salvage measures，all or part of the ship or cargo arrived safely at the destination port of the voyage，thus avoiding a situation where the ship and cargo would have perished together. Because the general average will be apportioned by the beneficiary parties，and the apportionment is determined by the value of the ship and cargo at the end of the voyage，if the whole ship is wrecked，the ship and cargo suffered total loss，then there is no rescued property，and there will be no beneficiary parties，so the general average contribution will lose its basis，and the general average will not be established.

3）共同海损的分摊（Contribution to General Average）

共同海损成立后，为了船舶、货物等的共同安全所产生的共同海损的牺牲和费用必须由各受益方按照最后获救的价值按比例分摊，这种分摊称为共同海损的分摊。

After the establishment of general average，the general average sacrifice and expenses for the common safety of ships and goods must be apportioned among the beneficiaries in proportion to the value of the last rescued，and this apportionment is called general average contribution.

在海洋运输契约中，一般都订有共同海损理算条款，载明所依据的理算规则，以及理算地点等。国际上共同海损的理算一般按《约克-安特卫普规则》办理。《约克-安特卫普规则》虽不是强制性国际公约，但已为国际海运、贸易和保险界广泛接受。国际上大部分租船合同、海运提单、海洋船舶和货运险的保险单上都规定按此规则进行理算。

中国国际贸易促进委员会在总结我国共同海损理算工作经验的基础上，参照国际做法，制定了《中国国际贸易促进委员会共同海损理算暂行规则》（以下简称《北京理算规则》），并于 1975 年 1 月 1 日正式颁布施行。新版《中国国际贸易促进委员会共同海损理算规则》于 2022 年 9 月 1 日起正式实施，原《北京理算规则》同时废止。

In a contract of carriage by sea，there is generally a general average adjustment clause setting out the rules on which the adjustment is to be based and deciding the place of adjustment. The adjustment of general average in the world is generally governed by the *York-Antwerp Rules*. Although not a mandatory international convention，the *York-Antwerp Rules* have been widely accepted by the international shipping，trading and insurance circles. Most international charter parties, ocean bills of lading, marine ship and cargo transportation insurance policies provide for adjustment according to this rule.

On the basis of summing up China's general average adjustment experience and referring to international practices, the China Council for the Promotion of International trade (CCPIT) formulated the *Interim Rules for General Average Adjustment of the China Council for the Promotion of International Trade* (known as *Beijing Rules for Adjustment*, for short), which were officially promulgated and implemented on January 1, 1975. *Rules for General Average Adjustment of China Council for the Promotion of International Trade* came into effect from September 1, 2022, and the former *Beijing Rules for Adjustment* were repealed at the same time.

根据共同海损牺牲和费用的金额,在确定共同海损分摊价值后,可以计算出船舶、货物、运费及其他利益方的共同海损分摊价值。其计算方法如下:

共同海损分摊率＝共同海损损失(牺牲＋费用)总和/共同海损分摊价值总和

各方应承担的共同海损金额为

船方分摊金额＝船方分摊价值×共同海损分摊率
货方分摊金额＝货方分摊价值×共同海损分摊率
运费方分摊金额＝运费方分摊价值×共同海损分摊率

Base on the amount of general average sacrifice and expenditure, the contributory value of ship, cargo, freight and other interested parties can be calculated after the value of general average contribution is determined. The calculation method is as follows:

general average contribution rate = total general average loss (sacrifice + expenditure) / total general average contribution value

The general average amount to be borne by each party is as follows:

amount apportioned by the ship = contribution value of ship owner × general average contribution rate

amount apportioned by the shipper = contribution value of cargo owner × general average contribution rate

amount apportioned by the carrier (freight collecting party) = contribution value of carrier × general average contribution rate

2. 单独海损(Particular Average)

1) 单独海损的定义(Definition of Particular Average)

单独海损是指保险标的在海上遭受承保范围内的风险所造成的部分灭失或损害,即除共同海损以外的部分损失。单独海损是一种特定利益方的部分损失,它不涉及其他货主或船方,而只能由保险标的所有人单独负担。

示例 10.1　共同海损分摊的计算

Particular average loss is a partial loss of the subject-matter insured, caused by a peril insured against, and which is not a general average loss. Particular average is a kind of partial loss of a particular interest party, which does not involve other cargo owners or ship owners, but can only be borne by the owner of the subject-matter insured.

新的《协会货物条款》中已不再使用"单独海损"这个术语，但在海上保险实务中，它仍用来表示共同海损以外的一切意外损害。

The term "particular average" is no longer used in the new *Institute Cargo Clauses*, but it is still used to refer to all accidental damage other than general average in marine insurance practice.

2）构成单独海损的条件（Conditions Constituting Particular Average）

单独海损的构成必须符合下列三个条件：

（1）是意外的、偶然的和承保风险直接导致的保险标的本身受损；

（2）是船方、货方或其他利益方单方面所遭受的损失，而不涉及他方的损失；

（3）仅指保险标的本身的损失，而不包括由此而引起的费用损失。

The following three conditions must be met for a particular average:

（1）The damage to the subject-matter insured itself is the direct result of an accidental, fortuitous, insured risk;

（2）The loss is suffered unilaterally by the ship, cargo, or other interested parties and does not involve the loss of other parties;

（3）Only refers to the loss of the subject matter of the insurance itself and not the loss of the expenses incurred as a result.

3）单独海损的赔偿（Compensation for Particular Average）

保险人对于单独海损的赔偿，各国的做法不完全统一，通常有以下几种处理方式。

（1）单独海损绝对不予赔偿。这种规定通常适用于一些国家的海上船舶保险。

（2）除某些特定风险所造成的单独海损以外，单独海损不赔偿。我国平安险对单独海损的规定属于这种情况。

（3）单独海损赔偿，但单独海损未达到约定百分比的不赔，达到约定百分比的全部予以赔偿。

（4）单独海损赔偿，但只对超过约定金额或百分比的那部分单独海损予以赔偿。

（5）不加任何特别限制，凡是单独海损均予赔偿。

The insurer's approach to compensation for particular average is not entirely uniform from country to country and is usually dealt with in the following ways.

（1）Absolutely free from particular average. This provision is normally applicable to marine insurance for ships in some countries.

（2）Free from particular average except for those caused by certain particular risks. This is the case with provision on particular average in FPA(free of particular average).

（3）If the particular average does not reach the agreed percentage, no compensation shall be made; if the particular average reaches the agreed percentage, it shall be fully compensated.

（4）Compensation for particular average, but only for the part of particular average exceeding the agreed amount or percentage.

（5）Without any special limitation，compensation shall be made in respect of particular average.

3. 共同海损与单独海损的区别与联系（Distinction and Connection Between General Average and Particular Average）

从损失性质上看，共同海损和单独海损都属于部分损失，但二者在损失发生的原因和损失承担的方式上存在不同之处。

Both general average and particular average are partial losses in terms of the nature of the loss，but there are differences between them in terms of the cause of loss and the manner in which the loss is borne.

（1）造成损失的原因不同。单独海损是由海上风险直接造成的货物损失，没有人为因素在内，而共同海损则是在海上风险危及船货的共同安全时，因采取人为的、故意的措施而导致的损失。

（2）损失的责任承担不同。单独海损的损失由受损方自行承担，而共同海损的损失是由各受益方按获救财产价值的多少，按比例共同分摊。

（1）The causes of loss are different. Particular average is the loss of goods directly caused by the marine peril without human factors，while general average is the loss resulting from taking artificial and intentional measures when the maritime risk imperils the common safety of the ship and cargo.

（2）The liability for loss is different. The loss of particular average shall be borne by the injured party alone，while that of general average shall be shared by the beneficiaries in proportion to the value of the property rescued.

共同海损和单独海损之间有着密切的内在联系。一般而言，单独海损先发生，进而可能引起共同海损，在采取共同海损措施之前的部分海损一般可列为单独海损。

There is a close intrinsic link between general average and particular average. Generally speaking，particular average occurs first，which may give rise to a general average. The partial loss before general average measures are taken can be classified as a particular average.

扩展案例 10.1　共同海损与单独海损

10.3　海洋运输货物保险保障的费用
（Expenses Covered by Marine Cargo Insurance）

海上风险除了会造成被保险货物的损失，还有可能带来大量费用的支出。对于这些费用，保险人根据其性质的不同规定了不同的赔付原则。在海运保险中，保险人负责赔偿的费用主要有施救费用、救助费用、额外费用和特别费用等。

In addition to the loss of the insured goods，maritime risks may also entail substantial expenses. Depending on the nature of these expenses，the insurer has established different principles for payment. In marine insurance, the insurer is responsible for sue and labour charges, salvage charges, additional charges, and special charges, among others.

10.3.1 施救费用(Sue and Labour Charges)

1. 施救费用的概念(Concept of Sue and Labour Charges)

施救费用亦称诉讼及营救费用或损害防止费用,是指被保险货物在遭遇承保责任范围内的灾害事故时,被保险人或其代理人、雇用人员或受让人为了避免或减少货物损失,采取各种抢救与防护措施所支出的合理费用。

Sue and labour charges, also known as litigation and rescue charges or damage prevention charges, refer to the reasonable expenses incurred by the insured or its agents, employees, or assignees in taking all kinds of rescue and protective measures to avoid or reduce the loss when the insured goods encounter perils and accidents within the scope of insurance.

为鼓励被保险人对受损的保险标的积极地采取抢救措施,减小灾害对保险标的的损害,防止损失进一步扩大,减少保险赔款的支出,各国法律和保险条款一般都规定:保险人对被保险人所支付的施救费用应承担赔偿责任。

In order to encourage the insured to take active rescue measures against the damaged subject-matter insured, to reduce the damage caused by the calamity or accident to the subject-matter insured, and to prevent further loss and reduce the expenditure of insurance indemnity, the laws and insurance clauses of various countries generally provide that the insurer shall be liable to the insured for the sue and labor charges paid by the insured.

2. 施救费用构成的条件(Conditions for the Composition of Sue and Labour Charges)

施救费用构成的条件包括以下几个方面。

(1)施救费用的支出必须是必要的、合理的,否则保险人不予赔偿。

(2)施救费用必须是为防止或者减少承保风险造成的损失而采取的措施支出的费用;如果采取行动是为了避免或减少非承保风险的损失,保险人不承担赔偿责任。

(3)施救费用是由被保险人及其代理人、雇用人员或受让人采取措施而支出的费用。其不包括保险人或其他与被保险人无关的人支出的费用。

(4)施救费用的赔偿并不考虑措施是否成功。只要采取的施救措施得当,费用支出合理,即使没有抢救成功,保险人对施救费用仍然负责。

The conditions for the composition of sue and labour charges includes the following aspects.

(1) The sue and labour charge must be necessary and reasonable, otherwise the insurer will not compensate.

(2) The sue and labour charge must be the cost of measures taken to prevent or reduce the loss from a covered risk; the insurer is not liable for compensation if the

action was taken to avoid or reduce the loss from an uninsured risk.

（3）The sue and labour charge is the cost of measures taken by the insured and its agents, servants, or assignees. It does not include expenses incurred by the insurer or other persons unrelated to the insured.

（4）Compensation for the sue and labour charge does not take into account the success of the measures. As long as the rescue measures are appropriate and the charges are reasonable, even if the rescue is not successful, the insurer is still responsible for the charges.

3. 施救费用赔偿的限度（Limits of Compensation for Sue and Labour Charges）

施救费用条款是保险合同的补充性协议，因此，施救费用的补偿是在保险标的的损失赔偿之外另行支付的。施救费用的赔偿金额受保险金额的限制，最多不能超过保险金额，但其与保险标的的损失的赔偿额无关，按实际支付额单独在保险金额内予以赔偿，亦即保险人对保险标的损失的赔偿额与对施救费用的赔偿额两者之和不超过两个保险金额。在不足额保险的情况下，保险人按照保险金额与保险价值的比例支付施救费用，除非合同另有规定。

The clause of sue and labour charges is a supplementary agreement to the insurance contract, therefore, the compensation of sue and labour charges is paid separately in addition to the loss compensation of subject-matter insured. The amount of compensation for sue and labour charges is limited by the insured amount, which cannot exceed the insured amount at most, but it has nothing to do with the amount of compensation for the loss of the subject-matter insured, and shall be compensated separately within the limit of the insured amount according to the actual amount of expenditure. That is, the sum of the insurer's compensation for the loss of the subject-matter insured and the amount of compensation for the sue and labour charges shall not exceed two insurance amounts. In the case of insufficient insurance, the insurer shall pay the sue and labour charges in proportion to the insured amount and insurable value, unless otherwise specified in the contract.

10.3.2　救助费用（Salvage Charges）

1. 救助费用的含义（Meaning of Salvage Charges）

救助费用是指被保险货物在遭遇承保范围内的灾害事故时，由保险人和被保险人以外的第三者采取救助措施并获成功，由被救方付给救助人的一种报酬。救助费用往往发生在船货遭遇共同危难时，存在船舶、货物和运费等共同利益方，所以救助费用大多属于共同海损性质的费用支出。在各国保险法或保险公司的保险条款中，一般都列有保险人对救助费用负赔偿责任的规定。

Salvage charge refers to a remuneration paid by the salved party to the salvor when the insured goods encounter a peril insured against, and the insurer and a third party other than the insured take rescue measures and succeed. Salvage charges are often incurred when the ship and cargo are in common peril，so there are parties with common interest such as the ship，cargo and freight. As a result，salvage charges are mostly of the nature of general average expenses. In the insurance laws of various countries or the insurance policies of insurance companies，there are generally provisions on the liability of the insurer for salvage charges.

2. 救助费用产生的条件（Conditions for the Composition of Salvage Charges）

根据英国 1906 年《海上保险法》第 65 条的规定，救助费用的产生必须符合下列条件。

According to article 65 of *Marine Insurance Act* 1906，the salvage charges must meet the following conditions.

（1）救助人是海难中财产关系方的第三者。被保险人或其代理人、雇用人员（如船员、水手）所进行的救助不是救助行为，所支付的费用不可视为救助费用。

（1）The salvor is a third party other than a property-related party in the perils of the sea. Salvage charges do not include the expenses of services in the nature of salvage rendered by the assured or his agents，or any person employed for hire by them（e. g. crew，sailors），for the purpose of averting a peril insured against.

（2）救助行为是自愿的。救助人必须是自愿者，而不是由于事先与被救助方签订了合同，为了履行合同义务而对遇难船舶与货物进行救助。

（2）The salvage is voluntary. The salvor must be a volunteer who does not carry out the salvage of the ship and cargo in perils due to the contract signed with the salved party in advance.

（3）救助行为具有实际效果。这一条件并非要求救助必须完全成功，而是只要救助取得效果，救助方就有权获得相应的报酬。国际海上救助中普遍采用的救助合同是英国的以"无效果、无报酬"为原则的"劳合社救助合同标准格式"。《海商法》（1993 年）第 179 条明确采纳"无效果、无报酬"原则。交通运输部海事局 2024 年制定的《海上救助合同》是中国首次推出的官方推荐性海上救助合同范本，其中也体现了"无效果、无报酬"原则。

（3）The salvage is effective. This condition does not require that the salvage be completely successful，but rather that the salvor is entitled to be paid as long as the salvage is somewhat effective. The salvage contract commonly used in international maritime salvage is Lloyd's Open Form（LOF），which is based on the principle of "No Cure，No Pay". Article 179 of *Maritime Law*（1993）explicitly adopts the principle of "No Cure，No Pay". The *Maritime Salvage Contract* formulated by the Maritime Safety Administration，Ministry of Transport，PRC in 2024 was the first officially recommended model maritime salvage contract in China，which also embodied the principle of "No Cure，No Pay".

3. 救助费用的确定与取得（Determination and Acquisition of Salvage Charges）

救助费用是在救助完成之后，根据救助的效果、救助财产的价格、救助工作的难度和危险程度，以及救助工作时间和耗费的费用等，通过协商或仲裁来确定，但最多不能超过获救财产的价值。如果救助没有效果，便不能获得报酬。救助人为了保证其在救助之后获得报酬,一般都要求被救方提供担保,对未提供担保的被救财产,救助人享有留置权。但是,随着海上石油运输量不断增加,油轮遇难造成的海上污染十分严重。为保护海洋环境,防止或减少油污损失,根据有关方面要求,劳合社已在其 1980 年的救助合同格式中,对"无效果、无报酬"的原则做了一些例外的规定,如对于遇难油轮,救助人只要没有过失,即使救助无效,也可获得合理报酬。《海商法》还规定,救助人如取得防止或减轻污染损害效果,船舶所有人应当向救助方支付的特别补偿可以另行增加,增加的数额可以达到救助费用的 30%。

The salvage charge is determined by negotiation or arbitration after the completion of the salvage, depending on the effectiveness of the salvage, the price of the salved property, the difficulty and danger of the salvage, and the time and expense of the salvage acts, up to a maximum of the value of the salved property. If the salvage is ineffective, the salvor shall not be paid. The salvor generally requires the salved party to provide security in order to ensure that it will be paid after the salvage; the salvor has a lien on the salved property that is not secured. However, with the increasing volume of oil transportation by sea, marine pollution caused by tanker wrecks is very serious. In order to protect the marine environment and prevent or mitigate oil pollution losses, Lloyd's has made some exceptions to the principle of "No Cure, No Pay" in FOL in 1980 according to the requirements of relevant parties. For example, as long as the salvors are not at fault, even if the rescue is invalid, they can get reasonable remuneration. The *Maritime Law* also provides that if a salvor achieves the effect of preventing or mitigating pollution damage, the special compensation payable by the shipowner to the salvor may be increased by an amount up to 30% of the salvage costs.

4. 救助费用的分摊(Contribution of Salvage Charges)

如果被救助方只是船舶一方或其他财产一方,救助报酬应由被救助方独自承担,与共同海损无关。如果被救助方涉及船舶、货物与其他财产方,救助报酬应该作为共同海损来处理。习惯做法是被救助的各方支付救助报酬给救助方,之后及时将账单寄给海损理算师,作为共同海损费用处理。被救助各方对救助报酬分摊的原理与共同海损分摊一样,是根据被救助财产的价值来分摊的,只是分摊价值是以被救财产在救助完成地的实际净值作为分摊基础。

If the salved party is only the ship owner or the owner of other property, the salvage remuneration is to be borne by the rescued party alone and has nothing to do with general average. If the salved party is involved in the owner of ship, cargo, or other property, the salvage charges shall be treated as general average.

5. 施救费用与救助费用的区别(Difference Between Sue and Labour Charge and Salvage Charge)

(1) 采取行为的主体不同。施救是由被保险人及其代理人等采取的行为,而救助是保险人和被保险人之外的第三者采取的行为。

(2) 给付报酬的原则不同。施救费用是不论施救是否有效果,都给予赔偿,而救助则是"无效果、无报酬"。

（3）保险人的赔偿责任不同。施救费用可在保险货物本身的保险额以外再赔一个保额；而保险人对救助费用的赔偿责任是以不超过获救财产的价值为限，亦即救助费用与保险货物本身损失的赔偿金额二者相加不得超过货物的保额。

（4）救助行为一般与共同海损联系在一起，而施救行为并非如此。

（1）The subject of act is different. Suing and labouring are an act performed by the insured and his agent，etc.，whereas salvage is performed by a third party other than the insurer and the insured.

（2）The principle of payment is different. The sue and labour charges is to be compensated whether the rescue is effective or not，while the principle for salvage charges is "No Cure，No Pay";

（3）The liability of the insurer is different. Sue and labour charge may be paid in addition to the insured amount of the insured goods themselves，whereas the insurer's liability for the salvage charge is limited to the value of the property salved，i. e. the sum of the salvage charge and the amount of compensation for loss of the insured goods themselves shall not exceed the insured amount of the goods.

（4）The salvage act is generally associated with general average，which is not the case with suing and labouring.

10.3.3　额外费用（Additional Charges）

额外费用是指为了证明损失索赔的成立而支付的费用，如检验费用、查勘费用、海损理算师费等。一般只有在索赔成立时，保险人才对这些与索赔有关的费用负赔偿责任。但如果保险合同双方对某些额外费用事先另有约定，如公证、查勘等是由保险人授权进行的，不论有无损失发生，保险人都要负责赔偿。

Additional charges refer to the expenses paid to prove the establishment of a loss claim，such as inspection fees，survey fees，average adjuster fees，etc. Generally，only when the claim is established can the insurer be liable for the expenses related to the claim. However，if the parties to the insurance contract have agreed in advance to certain additional charges—for example，the notary or survey is authorized by the insurer—the insurer will be liable for compensation regardless of the occurrence of the loss.

10.3.4　特别费用（Special Charges）

特别费用是指运输工具在海上遭遇海难后，在中途港或避难港卸货、存放、重装及续运货物所产生的费用，其目的是防止或减小货物的损害。保险人对特别费用补偿可以单独负责，对续运费用的赔偿和对货物单独海损的赔偿总和以保险金额为限。

Special charges are the costs incurred in discharging，storing，reloading and forwarding the shipment at an intermediate port or port of refuge after the means of transport has suffered perils of the sea，the purpose of which is to prevent or mitigate damage to the cargo. The insurer may be separately liable for compensation for special charges，and the sum of compensation for forwarding of the shipment and compensation for particular average of the goods is limited to the insured amount.

Words and Expressions

即测即练

习题

第 11 章

Chapter 11

海洋运输货物保险条款
Marine Cargo Insurance Clauses

Learning Objectives:

1. Master the scope of cover, exclusions, period of insurance, duty of the insured, and time of validity of a claim of China's *Ocean Marine Cargo Clauses*;

2. Understand the contents of the general additional risks, special additional risks, and particular additional risks of China's *Ocean Marine Cargo Clauses*;

3. Understand the changes of the new clauses of *Institute Cargo Clauses* 1982;

4. Master the main contents of ICC(A), ICC(B) and ICC(C);

5. Understand the main contents of other insurance clauses of *Institute Cargo Clauses*.

引导案例

CIF 贸易术语下的险别

甲国某公司以 CIF 价格条件从乙国引进一套检测仪器,合同采用简式标准格式,保险条款仅简单规定"保险由卖方负责"。货物运到后,该公司发现其中一个部件变形影响仪器的正常使用。该公司向外商索赔,外商答复仪器出厂时经过了严格的检验,有质量合格证书,因此不是他们的责任。之后经过商品检验机构的检验,认为是运输途中部件受到震动、挤压而造成的。该公司于是向保险公司索赔,保险公司认为此种损失属于"碰损、破碎险"承保范围,但该公司提供的保单上只保了"协会货物条款"(C),碰损、破碎造成的损失不在其承保范围内,所以无法赔付。

公司业务人员想当然地以为合同规定卖方投保,卖方一定会投保"一切险"或 ICC(A),但按照国际商会 Incoterms® 2020 的解释,在 CIF 条件下,如果合同没有具体规定,卖方只需要投保最低责任范围的险别,即平安险或 ICC(C),即履行了义务。因此在进出口业务实践中应注意:①进口合同使用 CIF、CIP 等由卖方投保的价格术语时,应在合同中注明按发票金额的 110% 投保的具体险别及附加险;②进口合同应尽量选择 CFR、CPT 等价格术语,由买方在国内办理保险;③应根据货物的特点选择相应的险别和附加险。

资料来源:案例讨论及剖析 1 保险条款不明确导致纠纷案[EB/OL].(2018-12-22).https://max.book118.com/html/2018/1221/6153105142001240.shtm.

海上保险中,保险人可以承保的各种风险、损失和费用是国际货物运输中经常发生的,但对于投保人或被保险人而言,并不是在任何场合下都需要保险人全部予以承保。不同的投保人或被保险人,因其所托运的货物种类不同、载货船舶航行路线不同、停泊港口不同、运输季节不同等,货物在运输过程中可能遭遇的风险及造成的损失与费用支出往往是不同的,所以,需要保险人给予保障的范围也存在一定的差异。为了适应不同投保人或被保险人对保险的不同要求,各国保险组织或保险公司将其承保的风险按范围不同划分为不同的险别,并以条款的方式分别予以确定。投保人或被保险人在办理保险时,只需申明投保险别的名称,即可表明其所要获得的保险保障。同时,保险人也可按照相应的保险费率计收保险费,并履行相应的承保责任。

The various risks, losses and expenses that an insurer can cover under marine insurance are frequently incurred in the international carriage of goods, but the insurer is not required to cover all of them on all occasions for the policyholder or assured. Different policyholders or assureds may encounter different risks and suffer different losses and expenses in the course of transportation due to different types of cargo, different sailing routes of vessels, different ports of berth, different transportation seasons and other factors, as a result, there is some variation in the scope of coverage required from insurers. In order to meet the different insurance requirements of different policyholders or assureds, insurance organizations or insurance companies in various countries divide the risks they insure into different types of insurance according to their scope, and determine them separately by means of clauses. When applying for insurance, the policyholder or the insured only needs to state the name of the risk to be insured, which can indicate the insurance coverage he needs to obtain. The insurer may also charge premiums at the appropriate rate and perform the corresponding coverage obligations.

在我国进出口实务中,一般都采用中国保险条款,但在出口业务中有时应国外客户的要求,也可以采用国际上通用的《协会货物条款》或对方国家的条款。中国《海洋运输货物保险条款》和英国《协会货物条款》的主要险别如图 11-1 所示。

In China's import and export practice, China insurance clauses are generally adopted, but in the export business, sometimes at the request of foreign customers, it is also possible to adopt *Institute Cargo Clauses*, which is used universally or clauses of the counterpart country. Marine cargo insurance has more insurance types, which are customarily divided into three categories: basic risks, additional risks and specialized risks. The main coverage of China *Ocean Marine Cargo Clauses* and Britain *Institute Cargo Clauses* are shown in figure 11-1.

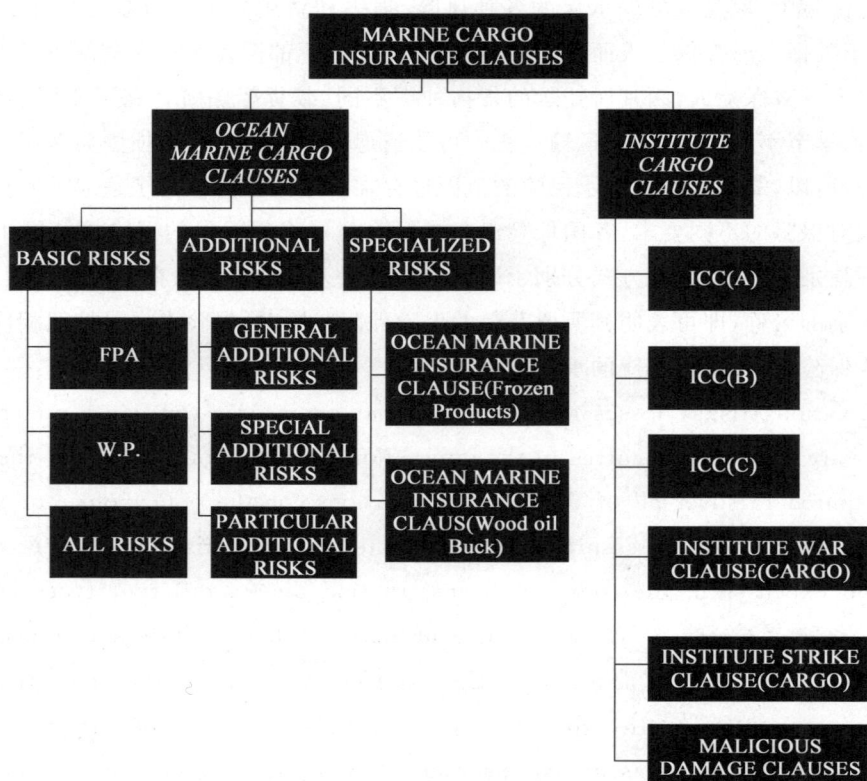

图 11-1　中国《海洋运输货物保险条款》和英国《协会货物条款》的主要险别

11.1　中国《海洋运输货物保险条款》
（China's *Ocean Marine Cargo Clauses*）

　　为了适应我国对外经济贸易不断发展的客观需要，中国人民保险公司根据中国保险业务的实际情况，并参照中国保险市场的习惯做法，陆续制定了各种涉外保险业务条款，总称为"中国保险条款"，货物运输保险条款是其中的重要组成部分。我国现行的《海洋运输货物保险条款》是中国人民保险公司于 1981 年 1 月 1 日修订并实施的，1994 年经中国保险监督管理委员会核准备案。条款中包括责任范围、除外责任、责任起讫、被保险人义务及索赔期限等内容。

　　In order to meet the objective needs of the continuous development of China's foreign economic and trade，the People's Insurance Company of China（PICC），in accordance with the actual situation of China's insurance business and with reference to the customary practice of the Chinese insurance market，has successfully formulated various foreign-related insurance terms and conditions，collectively called "China Insurance Clauses"，of which cargo transportation insurance clauses are an important part. China's current *Ocean Marine Cargo Clauses* was revised and implemented by PICC on January 1，1981，and approved for filing by the China Insurance Regulatory Commission（CIRC）in 1994. The clauses include scope of cover，exclusions，commencement to termination of cover，duty of the insured，and the time of validity of a claim，etc.

按照能否单独投保,中国海洋运输货物保险可分为基本险和附加险两类。

According to whether it can be insured separately，China's marine transportation insurance can be classified into basic risks and additional risks.

11.1.1　《海洋运输货物保险条款》基本险（**Basic Risks of *Ocean Marine Cargo Clause***）

基本险又称主险,是指可以独立投保,不必依附于其他险别项的险别。《海洋运输货物保险条款》的基本险分为平安险、水渍险和一切险三种。

Basic risks refer to the type of insurance that can be insured independently without being attached to other risks. The basic risks of *Ocean Marine Cargo Clauses* are classified into free from particular average(FPA)，with average(WA)，and all risks.

1. 基本险的责任范围（Scope of Cover of Basic Risks）

1）平安险的责任范围（Free From Particular Average）

"平安险"是我国保险业的习惯叫法,沿用已久,在三个基本险种中承保的责任范围最小。其原意是保险人只负责保险标的发生的全损,随着国际保险界对平安险条款的不断修订与补充,平安险的责任范围已远远超过全损险的责任范围。根据我国《海洋运输货物保险条款》,平安险的承保责任范围包括以下八个方面。

"FPA" has the smallest coverage among the three basic risks. Its original meaning is that the insurer is only responsible for the total loss of the subject-matter insured. With the continuous revision and supplement of the terms of FPA by the international insurance industry，the insurance coverage of FPA has far exceeded the scope of liability of the total loss insurance. According to China's *Ocean Marine Cargo Clauses*，the coverage of FPA includes the following eight aspects.

（1）自然灾害造成的全损。被保险货物在运输途中由于恶劣气候、雷电、地震、海啸、洪水等自然灾害造成整批货物的全损或推定全损。整批货物是指被保险货物的全部损失。

该条款中"整批货物"应包括以下几种情况：①一张保险单项下记载的全部货物；②一张保险单项下分类标明保险金额的某一类货物的全部；③一张保险单承保多份提单项下货物,某一份提单项下的全部货物；④被保险货物用驳船运往或远离海轮时,每一驳船所装运的全部货物。此外,该条款对推定全损的解释是：被保险货物的实际全损已经不可避免,或者恢复、修复受损货物以及运送货物到原定目的地的费用超过该目的地的货物价值。

（1）Total loss caused by natural calamities. Total or constructive total loss of the whole consignment hereby insured caused in the course of transit by natural calamities: heavy weather, lightning, tsunami, earthquake and flood.

The provision of the "whole consignment" shall include the following cases: ①all goods recorded under one insurance policy; ②all goods of a particular class for which the amount insured is separately stated under one insurance policy; ③an insurance policy covers goods under multiple bills of lading and all goods under a particular bill of lading; ④the entire cargo carried in each barge when the insured goods are transported by barge to or from a seagoing vessel. In addition, the clause interprets constructive total loss as: the loss where an actual total loss appears to be unavoidable or the cost to be incurred in recovering or reconditioning the goods together with the forwarding cost to the destination named in the policy would exceed their value on arrival.

（2）意外事故造成的全损或部分损失。由于运输工具遭受搁浅、触礁、沉没、互撞、与流冰或其他物体碰撞，以及失火、爆炸意外事故造成货物的全损或部分损失。

（2）Total loss or partial loss caused by accidents. Total loss or partial loss of goods due to accidents such as the carrying conveyance being grounded, stranded, sunk, in collision with floating ice or other objects, fire, or explosion.

本条款中"失火"与"爆炸"造成的损失，不仅仅限于在船上运输阶段，还包括陆运及储存阶段发生失火、爆炸所造成的货物损失，只要符合近因原则即可。

The loss caused by "fire" and "explosion" in this clause is not limited to the loss of goods caused by fire and explosion during the sea transportation, but also during the process of land transportation and storage, provided that the principle of proximate cause is met.

（3）在意外事故发生前后，自然灾害造成的部分损失。在运输工具已经发生搁浅、触礁、沉没、焚毁这四种意外事故的情况下，货物在此前后又在海上遭受恶劣气候、雷电、海啸等自然灾害所造成的部分损失。

（3）Partial loss caused by natural calamities before and after the accident. Partial loss of the insured goods attributable to heavy weather, lightning and/or tsunami, where the conveyance has been grounded, stranded, sunk or burnt, irrespective of whether the event or events took place or after such accidents.

保险人对单纯由于自然灾害造成的部分损失不负责赔偿，但当同一批货物在运输途中不仅因自然灾害受损，而且因上述四种意外事故而致损时，如果两者导致的货物损失无法分清，则保险人对损失应予赔偿。如果载货船舶在航行中发生上述意外事故，但货物并未受损，在摆脱意外事故后的航程中又遭遇自然灾害使货物受损，这种损失保险人不予赔偿。

The insurer shall not be liable for partial losses caused solely by natural calamities. However, when the same batch of goods is damaged not only by natural calamities but also by the above four kinds of accidents during transportation, if the loss of goods caused by the two cannot be distinguished, the insurer shall compensate for the loss. If the above accidents happen to the ship carrying the cargo，but the cargo is not damaged，and the cargo is damaged by natural disasters in the voyage after getting rid of the accidents，the insurer will not compensate for such losses.

（4）吊索损害。吊索损害指在装卸或转运时，由于一件或数件整件货物落海造成的全损或部分损失。

（4）Sling loss. It refers to the total loss or partial loss consequent on falling of entire package or packages into sea during loading，transshipment or discharge.

本条款规定仅对"落海"所致的损失予以赔偿，并不承保"跌落"，即落到岸上所造成的损失。此外，对于一件或数件整件货物的一部分散落在海里所造成的部分损失，保险人不负责赔偿。

This clause only provides for compensation for the loss caused by "falling overboard" and do not cover "drop"，that is，the loss caused by falling onto the shore. In addition，the insurer shall not be liable for any partial loss caused by the scattering of one or more pieces of the entire package or packages into the sea.

（5）施救费用。被保险人对遭受承保责任内危险的货物采取抢救、防止或减少货损的措施而支付的合理费用，但以该批被救货物的保险金额为限。

（5）Sue and labour charges. The reasonable cost paid by the insured on salvaging the goods or averting or minimizing a loss recoverable under the policy，provided that such cost shall not exceed the sum insured of the consignment so saved.

（6）避难港损失和费用。运输工具遭遇海难后，在避难港由于卸货所引起的损失，以及在中途港、避难港由于卸货、存仓和运送货物所产生的特别费用。

（6）Losses and expenses at port of refuge. Losses attributable to discharge of the insured goods at a port of distress following a sea peril as well as special charges arising from loading，warehousing and forwarding of the goods at an intermediate port of call or refuge.

本项规定中所说的海难是指海上固有的风险，而且仅指海上意外事故，如沉没、碰撞、触礁、飓风及其他偶发的灾害，而火灾、爆炸、战争、海盗、盗窃、抛弃以及船长和船员的不法行为等不属于海难。

The sea perils mentioned in this provision refer to the inherent risks at sea，and only refer to maritime accidents，such as sinking，collision，stranding，hurricane and other occasional disasters，while fire，explosion，war，piracy，theft，jettison，and barratry of the master and mariner are not sea perils.

（7）共同海损的牺牲、分摊和救助费用。对于共同海损牺牲的货物，由保险人作为单独海损先予赔偿。保险人享有向其他受益人要求分摊的权利，而被保险人也要参与分摊；对于被保险人应承担的共损费用的分摊，保险人并不先行赔偿，而是先理算，之后再承担相应的责任。通常，救助费用可列为共损费用，由保险人予以赔偿。

（7）Sacrifice in and contribution to general average and salvage charges. For the goods sacrificed in general average，the insurer shall compensate in advance as particular average. The insurer has the right to claim the contribution from other beneficiaries, and the insured shall also participate in the contribution; for the contribution of general average expenses that the insured shall bear, the insurer shall not make compensation first, but shall make adjustment first, and then bear the corresponding responsibilities. Generally, salvage charges can be classified as general average expenses, which are compensated by the insurer.

（8）货物根据运输合同条款偿还船方的损失。运输契约订有"船舶互撞责任"条款时，根据该条款规定应由货方偿还船方的损失。

(8) Such proportion of losses sustained by the shipowners as is to be reimbursed by the cargo owner under the contract of affreightment both to blame collision clause.

由于平安险的承保责任范围有限，其一般多适用于大宗、低值、粗糙的无包装货物，如废钢铁、木材、矿砂等的投保。

Due to the limited coverage of FPA, it is generally applicable to large quantity, low value, rough and unpacked goods, such as scrap steel, timber, and ore.

2）水渍险的责任范围［With Particular Average/ With Average （WPA/WA）］

水渍险也是我国保险业沿用已久的名称，其英文原文的含义是"负责单独海损"，也就是平安险不负责赔偿的部分损失，它予以赔偿。

根据《海洋运输货物保险条款》的规定，水渍险的责任范围包括：①平安险所承保的全部责任；②自然灾害造成的部分损失。被保险货物在运输途中由于恶劣气候、雷电、海啸、地震、洪水自然灾害所造成的部分损失。

水渍险的责任范围包括由于海上风险（自然灾害和意外事故）所造成的全部损失（实际全损或推定全损）和部分损失（单独海损或共同海损）。

需要注意的是，虽然水渍险对单独海损负责，但对被保险货物由于某些外部原因所导致的部分损失，如碰损、锈损、破碎等是不负责任的。因此，水渍险适用于不太可能发生碰损、锈损、破碎，或者容易生锈但不影响使用的货物，如五金类产品、钢管、散装金属原料、散装化肥及化工原料以及旧汽车、旧机械、旧设备等。

"Shuizixian" is also a long used name in Chinese insurance industry, and its original english name WPA （with particular average means） "responsible for particular average", that is, it pays for the partial losses that FPA is not responsible for.

According to *Ocean Marine Cargo Clauses*, the coverage of WPA is: ① all the liabilities covered by FPA; ② partial losses caused by natural disasters. WPA also covers partial losses of the insured goods caused by heavy weather, lightning, tsunami, earthquake and/or flood.

The scope of WPA covers total loss (actual total loss or constructive total loss) and partial loss (particular average or general average) caused by perils of the sea (natural calamities and accidents).

It should be noted that although WPA is responsible for particular average, it is not responsible for partial loss of the insured goods caused by some external reasons, such as collision，rust，and breakage．Therefore，WPA is applicable to goods that are unlikely to be bruised，rusted or broken，or are prone to rusting but do not affect their use，such as hardware products，steel pipes，bulk metal materials，bulk fertilizers and chemical materials，as well as old cars，old machinery and equipment．

3）一切险的责任范围（All Risks）

一切险是三种基本险中责任范围最广的险别。根据我国《海洋运输货物保险条款》的规定，一切险除包括平安险和水渍险的各项责任外，还负责被保险货物在运输途中由于外来原因所致的全部或部分损失。一切险承保的外来原因必须是意外的、事先难以预料的，不是必然发生的。一切险的责任范围涵盖了一般附加险别的责任，但不包括特别附加险别。

"All risks" has the largest scope of cover among the three basic risks．According to *Ocean Marine Cargo Clause*，aside from the risks covered under FPA and WA，this insurance also covers losses of or damage to the insured goods whether partial or total，arising from external causes in transit．The external causes covered by all risks must be accidental，unforeseen in advance，and not inevitable．The scope of liability of all risks covers the liability of the general additional risks，but not the special additional risks．

由于一切险提供的保障范围较为全面，所以在保险实务中，适用于各类货物，特别是价值较高、可能遭受损失因素较多的货物，如粮油食品、纺织品、工艺品、精密仪器等。

Due to the comprehensive coverage provided by all risks，it is applicable to all kinds of goods in insurance practice，especially those with higher value and more possible loss factors，such as cereals，oils and foodstuffs，textiles，handicrafts，precision instruments，etc．

扩展阅读 11.1　海上货运"一切险"保什么

2. 基本险的除外责任（Exclusions of Basic Risks）

除外责任是指保险人列明不负赔偿责任的风险范围。保险条款中规定除外责任，主要是为了分清保险人、被保险人、发货人和承运人等有关当事人对损失和费用应承担的责任，以使保险人的赔偿责任更加明确。

Exclusions refer to the scope of risks that the insurer shall not be liable for compensation．The exclusions stipulate in the insurance clause is mainly to distinguish the liability of the insurer，the insured，the consignor，and the carrier for the losses and expenses，so as to make the insurer's liability for compensation clearer．

1）被保险人的故意行为或过失造成的损失（Loss or Damage Caused by the Intentional Act or Fault of the Insured）

"被保险人"是指被保险人本人或其代表，并不包括其代理人或普通雇员。在海运保险中，保险单合法持有人即为被保险人。"故意行为"是指明知自己的行为可能造成损害后果，仍希望后果发生或放任后果发生。"过失"是指应当预见自己的行为可能产生损害结果，却因为疏忽大意而没有预见，或虽已经预见却轻信能够避免，以致产生损害结果。

"The insured" means the insured person himself or his representative，and does not include his agent or ordinary employee. In marine insurance, the legal holder of the insurance policy is the insured. "Intentional act" means an act done with the knowledge that it is likely to have damaging consequences and yet the act is done with the intent that such consequences occur or is allowed to occur. "Fault" means that one should have foreseen that one's conduct might have a damaging effect, but negligently failed to do so, or, having foreseen it, believed that it could have been avoided, which resulted in the occurrence of the damage.

2）属于发货人责任所引起的损失（Loss or Damage Falling Under the Liability of the Consignor）

属于发货人责任所引起的损失一般指发货人的故意行为或过失行为引起的货物损失。其具体表现为：发货人租用不适航船舶或是租用资信不良的承运人的船舶导致被保险货物损坏，或是在货损后无法向承运人追偿；发货人提供的货物包装不当，无法经受航程中通常的风险而致货损；货物标志不清或错误，导致货物错运、误运而产生灭失或损坏；在采用集装箱运输时，由发货人装箱引起的短装、积载不当、错装及所选用的集装箱不适货所造成的损失等。

It generally refers to the loss or damage caused by the intentional act or fault of the consignor. For example, damage to the insured cargo due to the consignor chartering an unseaworthy vessel or chartering a vessel of a carrier with poor creditworthiness, or inability to recover from the carrier after damage to the goods; damage to the goods due to improper packing of the goods provided by the consignor, which does not withstand the usual risks of the voyage; loss or damage arising from mis shipment of goods as a result of inadequate or incorrect marking of the goods; in the case of containerized transport, losses caused by short packing, improper stowage, wrong loading and improper selection of containers by the consignor.

3）在保险责任开始前，被保险货物已存在的品质不良或数量短缺所造成的损失（Loss or Damage Arising from the Inferior Quality or Shortage of the Insured Goods Prior to the Attachment of Insurance）

这种情况称为货物的原残，如易生锈的钢材、二手机械设备等货物常存在严重的原残。但在一般情况下，货物的损失是原残，还是在保险期限内由承保风险所造成的，会引起双方的争议。为避免这种情况的发生，最好在货物装船前进行检验。

This is called the original damage of the goods, such as rust-prone steel, second-hand machinery and other goods often have serious original damage. But in general, the loss of the goods is the original damage or caused by the insured risk within the insurance period will cause disputes between both parties. In order to avoid such a situation, it is best to inspect the goods before they are loaded on board.

4）被保险货物的自然损耗、本质缺陷、特性及市场跌落、运输延迟引起的损失与费用（Loss or Damage Arising from Normal Loss, Inherent Vice or Nature of the Insured Goods, Loss of Market and/or Delay in Transit and any Expenses Arising There From）

自然损耗是指在运输途中因货物自身特性而导致的水分蒸发、渗漏、扬尘、易碎品破碎、散装货短量等损失,保险人对此损失不予负责。

Normal loss refers to the loss caused by evaporation of water, leakage, dust, breakage of fragile goods, shortage of bulk cargo, etc. due to the characteristics of the goods themselves in transit, for which the insurer is not responsible.

货物的本质缺陷或特性引起的损失,是指一些特定货物因本质原因或本身属性而导致货物灭失或损坏,如煤炭因燃点低易自燃、粮食易产生虫蛀等。

Losses arising from inherent vice or nature of goods are losses of or damages to goods that result from the nature or inherent properties of some particular goods. For example, coal is prone to spontaneous combustion due to its low ignition point, and grain is susceptible to insect infestation.

市场跌落属于商业风险,是一种投机风险而不是直接物质损失,因此,该损失保险人不予负责。

Loss of market is a commercial risk, a speculative risk rather than a direct physical loss, and therefore the insurer is not liable for this loss.

运输延迟导致的损失或费用是指在运输途中由于种种原因,货物未能在规定时间到达目的地,由此而导致的季节性商品市价跌落,新鲜蔬菜、水果腐烂、变质等损失。

Losses or expenses caused by delay in transit refer to losses resulting from goods failing to reach their destination within the specified time due to various reasons. This includes market price declines of seasonal commodities and losses from the rotting, deterioration, or spoilage of fresh vegetables and fruits.

5)海洋运输货物战争险和罢工险规定的责任范围和除外责任[Risks and Liabilities Covered and Excluded by the Ocean Marine(Cargo)War Risks Clauses and Strike, Riot and Civil Commotion Clauses]

这两种保险属于特殊附加险,不在基本险责任范围之内,因此,只投保基本险时,保险人对该风险免责。

These two types of insurance are special additional risks and are not covered by the basic risks. Therefore, when only basic risks are taken out, the insurer is exempt from liability for this risk.

3. 基本险的责任起讫(Commencement to Termination of Cover for Basic Risks)

保险的责任起讫期间又称保险期间或保险期限,是指保险人承担责任的起讫时限。与国际市场的习惯做法一样,我国《海洋运输货物保险条款》基本险的保险期间以运输过程为限,在保险实务中通常被称为"仓至仓"原则。

Commencement to termination of cover, also known as the period of insurance, refers to the beginning and end of the period of liability of the insurer. In line with the customary practice in the international market, the period of insurance for basic risks in China's *Ocean Marine Cargo Clauses* is limited to the process of transportation, and is usually called the "warehouse to warehouse clause" in insurance practice.

"仓至仓"原则是海洋运输货物保险期间的基本原则,它规定了保险人承担责任的起讫地点,即保险人对保险货物的责任自被保险货物运离保险单载明的起运地发货人仓库或储存处所开始运输时生效,包括正常运输过程中的海上、陆上、内河和驳船运输在内,直到该项货物运抵保险单载明的目的地收货人的最后仓库或储存处所或被保险人用作分配、分派或非正常运输的其他储存处所。

"Warehouse to warehouse clause"(W/W clause) is the basic principle for the period of insurance of goods carried by sea, which defines the place where the insurer's liability begins and ends, i. e. the insurer's liability for the insured goods takes effect from the time the insured goods leave the warehouse or place of storage named in the policy for the commencement of the transit, and continues in force in the ordinary course of transit including sea, land, and inland waterway transits and transit in lighter, until the insured goods are delivered to the consignee's final warehouse or place of storage at the destination named in the policy, or to any other place used by the insured for allocation or distribution of the goods or for stories other than in the ordinary course of transit.

根据我国《海洋运输货物保险条款》"责任起讫"的规定,保险期间可分为正常运输和非正常运输两种情况。

According to the stipulation of "Commencement to Termination of Cover" in China's *Ocean Marine Cargo Clauses*, the insurance period can be divided into two situations: normal transportation and abnormal transportation.

1) 正常运输情况下的保险期间(Insurance Period Under Normal Transportation)

正常运输是指将货物从保险单载明的起运地发货人仓库或其储存处所运至目的地收货人的最后仓库或储存处所或被保险人用作分配、分派或非正常运输的其他储存处所,整个航程所需要的正常运输。其包括正常的运输工具(汽车、火车、内河船舶、海轮等)按正常的航线行驶并停靠港口以及途中正常的延迟和转船。

Normal transportation means the ordinary carriage required for the entire voyage from the warehouse or place of storage named in the policy to the consignee's final warehouse or place of storage at the destination named in the policy, or to any other place used by the insured for allocation and distribution of the goods, or for stories other than in the ordinary course of transit. This includes the ordinary course of traveling of conveyances (cars, trains, river vessels, seagoing vessels, etc.) on normal routes with port calls and normal delays and transshipments en route.

在正常运输情况下,保险期间是按"仓至仓"原则办理的,但在实际业务中,经常发生保险货物卸离海轮后,在运至保险单所载明的收货人仓库之前,需要在卸货港存放一段时间。为满足被保险人的需要,保险人对这段时间仍提供保险保障,但最长时间不能超过60天。若届满60天货物仍未进入收货人仓库,保险责任也将终止;若在60天内货物进入收货人仓库,保险责任在进入仓库时终止。其责任终止具体有以下几种情况。

In the case of normal transportation, the insurance period is handled on "warehouse to warehouse clause", the insurance shall, however, be limited to 60 days after completion of discharge of the insured goods from the seagoing vessel at the final port of discharge before they reach the above mentioned warehouse or place of stories. If prior to the expiration of the above mentioned 60 days period, the insured goods are to be forwarded to a destination other than that named in the policy, this insurance shall terminate at the commencement of such transit.

（1）以卸货港为目的地,被保险人提货后,运到自己的仓库时,保险责任即将终止。

（2）以卸货港为目的地,被保险人提货后并不将货物运往自己的仓库,而是对货物进行分配、分派或分散运转,保险责任从开始分配、分派或转运时终止。

（3）以内陆为目的地,从向船方提货后运到内陆目的地的被保险人仓库时,保险责任即行终止,此后如果被保险人将货物出售或分配,保险人不再承担责任。

（4）以内陆为目的地,如果保险货物在运抵内陆目的地时,先行存入某一仓库,然后又将该批货物分成几批再继续运往内陆目的地另外几个仓库,包括保险单所载目的地,在这种情况下,则以先行放入的某一仓库作为被保险人的最后仓库,保险责任在进入该仓库时即终止,而不管其中是否有部分货物最终运到了保险单所载明的内陆目的地仓库。

上述几种情况均以保险货物卸离海轮后 60 天为限,并以先发生者为准。

（1）If the destination is the port of discharge, the insurance liability will terminate when the insured takes delivery of the goods to his warehouse.

（2）If the port of discharge is the destination and the insured, after taking delivery of the goods, does not transport the goods to his own warehouse but allocates, distributes or disperses the goods, the insurance liability ceases from the commencement of the allocation, distribution or transshipment.

（3）If the destination is inland, the insurance liability shall cease when the insured has taken delivery of the goods from the vessel to a warehouse at the inland destination. Thereafter, if the insured sells or distributes the goods, the insurer is no longer liable.

（4）In the case of inland destination, if the insured goods are first deposited in a certain warehouse upon arrival at the inland destination, and then the goods are divided into several shipments and continue to be transported to several other warehouses at the inland destination, including the destination as stated in the insurance policy, the warehouse into which they were first deposited is taken as the final warehouse of the insured, and the insurance liability terminates upon entry into the warehouse, regardless of whether or not part of them are finally to the warehouse at the inland destination stated in the insurance policy.

All of the above are limited to 60 days after the insured goods have been discharged from the sea vessel. The rule is applied based on whichever situation occurs first.

2）非正常运输情况下的保险期间（Insurance Period Under Abnormal Transportation）

非正常运输是指被保险货物在运输中,由于被保险人无法控制的运输迟延、船舶绕道、被迫卸货、重新装载、转载或承运人行使运输合同赋予的权限所做的任何航海上的变更或终止运输合同,保险货物运抵非保险单所载明的目的地等非正常情况。

Abnormal transportation means an irregular situation in which the insured goods arrive at a destination other than the one stated in the insurance policy as a result of delay in transportation, deviation, forced discharge, reshipment or transshipment beyond the control of the insured, or any change or termination of the voyage arising from the exercise of the authority conferred on the carrier under the contract of carriage.

根据《海洋运输货物保险条款》的规定:由于被保险人无法控制的运输延迟、绕道、被迫卸货、重行装载、转载或承运人运用运输契约赋予的权限所做的任何航海上的变更或终止运输契约,被保险货物运到非保险单所载明目的地时,在被保险人及时将获知的情况通知保险人,并在必要时加缴保险费的情况下,保险仍继续有效,保险责任按下列规定终止。

(1)被保险货物如在非保险单所载明的目的地出售,保险责任至交货时为止,但不论任何情况,均以被保险货物在卸载港全部卸离海轮后满60天为止。

(2)被保险货物如在上述60天期限内继续运往保险单所载原目的地或其他目的地,保险责任仍按上述第(1)款的规定终止。

According to the provision of *Ocean Marine Cargo Clauses*: if, owing to delay, deviation, forced discharge, reshipment or transshipment beyond the control of the insured, or any change or termination of the voyage arising from the exercise of a liberty granted to the ship owners under the contract of affreightment, the insured goods arrive at a port or place other than that named in the policy, subject to immediate notice being given to the company by the insured and an additional premium being paid, repaired, the insurance shall remain in force and shall terminate as hereunder.

(1) If the insured goods are sold at port or place not named in the policy, this insurance shall terminate on delivery of the goods sold, but in no event shall this insurance extend beyond 60 days after completion of discharge of the insured goods from the carrying vessel at such port or place.

(2) If the insured goods are to be forwarded to the final destination named in the policy or any other destination, this insurance shall terminate in accordance with section (1) above.

4. 基本险的索赔期限(Time of Validity of a Claim)

《海洋运输货物保险条款》规定保险索赔时效为从被保险货物在最后全部卸离海轮后起算,最多不超过两年;但是《海商法》规定,向保险人要求保险赔偿的时效是从保险事故发生之日起两年。因此,中国人民保险公司在1995年将索赔期限的起算日改为保险事故发生之日,与《海商法》保持了一致。

Ocean Marine Cargo Clauses provides that the time of validity of a claim shall not exceed a period of two years counting from the time of completion of discharge of the insured goods from the seagoing vessel at the final port of discharge. However, *Maritime Law* provides that the limitation period for claiming insurance compensation from the insurer is two years from the date of the insurance accident. Therefore, PICC changed the starting date of the claim period to the date of the occurrence of the insurance accident in 1995, which is consistent with the *Maritime Law*.

值得注意的是,如果货损属于保险责任范围,又涉及向船方或其他第三者责任方索赔的情况,被保险人必须在相关法律法规或公约规定的、向有关责任方索赔的有效期限内办理索赔。否则,由于被保险人疏忽或其他原因逾期而丧失向有关责任方索赔的权益时,应由被保险人自行承担责任。例如,按照《海牙规则》或《海商法》的规定,收货人向承运人索赔的有效期限为交货之日起 1 年内。被保险人必须在这个期限到达之前向承运人提出索赔,或要求延长索赔时效,以便保险人在支付赔款之后向承运人行使代位追偿的权利。

此外,根据《海商法》的规定,被保险人向保险人索赔货物的共同海损分摊的诉讼请求时效为:从共同海损理算结束之日起 1 年。

It is worth noting that if the cargo damage is covered by the insurance and involves a claim against the ship or other responsible third party, the insured must handle the claim within the validity period of the claim against the responsible party as stipulated in the relevant laws and regulations or conventions. Otherwise, if the insured loses the right to claim compensation from the relevant responsible party due to negligence or other reasons, the insured shall be liable himself. For example, under the *Hague Rules* or the *Maritime Law*, the time limit for the consignee to claim against the carrier is one year from the date of delivery. The insured must file a claim with the carrier before this deadline or request an extension of the time limit for claims so that the insurer can exercise its right of subrogation against the carrier after payment of the claim.

In addition, according to the *Maritime Law*, the time limit for the claim of the insured against the insurer for the contribution of the goods to general average is one year from the date of the conclusion of the general average adjustment.

11.1.2 《海洋运输货物保险条款》附加险(**Additional Risks of *Ocean Marine Cargo Clause***)

国际贸易货物在运输过程中可能遭遇的风险和损失,除了前面基本险所承保的由于自然灾害与意外事故所造成的风险和损失外,往往还有其他外来原因所引起的风险和损失。为了满足投保人的需要,保险人在基本险条款之外又制定了各种附加险条款。附加险是基本险的扩大和补充,不能单独投保,必须在投保一种基本险的基础上加保。加保的附加险可以是一种或几种,由被保险人根据需要选择确定。附加险按照承保的风险不同,分为一般附加险、特别附加险和特殊附加险三类。

In addition to the risks and losses caused by natural calamities and accidents covered by the basic risks, there are often risks and losses caused by other external causes. In order to meet the needs of policyholders, insurers have developed various additional insurance clauses in addition to the basic insurance clauses. Additional risks are extension and supplement of the basic risks and cannot be insured separately, but must be added to one of the basic risks. Additional risks are divided into three categories according to the risks covered: general additional risks, special additional risks, and particular additional risks.

1. 一般附加险(General Additional Risks)

一般附加险负责赔偿一般外来风险所致的损失。由于一般附加险已包括在一切险中,所以若已投保一切险,则无须加保此险别。我国《海洋运输货物保险条款》规定的一般附加险有以下 11 种。

The general additional risks cover losses due to ordinary external risks. The following 11 types of general additional risks are provided in the *Ocean Marine Cargo Clauses* of China.

1) 偷窃、提货不着险(Theft, Pilferage and Non-delivery Clause, TPND)

这一险别主要承保在保险有效期内保险货物被偷走或窃取以及货物抵达目的地后整件未交的损失。“偷”一般是指货物整件被偷走;“窃”一般是指货物中的一部分被窃取。偷、窃都是指暗中的偷摸、窃取行为,不包括使用暴力手段的公开劫夺。提货不着是指货物的全部或整件未能在目的地交付给收货人。但本险别并非对任何原因所致的提货不着均负责,如保险货物在中途被当作危险品扣押,被保险人并不能据此险别获得赔偿。在这一险别下,为了便于确定责任,对于偷窃的损失,被保险人必须在及时提货后 10 天之内申请检验,而对于整件提货不着,被保险人必须向责任方、海关或有关当局取得证明,保险人才予赔偿。同时保险人享有代位追偿的权利。

It mainly covers theft or pilferage of the insured goods during the period of validity of the insurance and the loss of a whole shipment that is not delivered upon arrival at its destination. “Theft” generally means that the goods are stolen as a whole; “pilferage” generally means that a portion of the goods is stolen. “Theft” and “pilferage” both refer to covert acts of stealing, and do not include open robberies using violent means. “Non-delivery” means that the whole cargo or the whole package of goods has not been delivered to the consignee at the destination. However, this clause does not cover the insured against non-delivery for any reason whatsoever, e. g. if the insured goods are seized as dangerous goods in transit, the insured will not be indemnified under this clause. Under this clause, in order to facilitate the determination of liability, for the loss of theft, the insured must apply for inspection within 10 days after timely pick-up, while for the non-delivery of whole shipment, the insured must obtain proof from the responsible party, customs, or relevant authorities before the insurer will pay. At the same time, the insurer has the right of subrogation.

2) 淡水雨淋险[Fresh Water Rain Damage Clause (FWRD)]

淡水雨淋险承保被保险货物在运输途中由于淡水、雨水或冰雪融化等造成的损失,包括船上淡水舱、水管漏水以及舱汗所造成的货物损失。被保险人发现货物遭受淡水雨淋后,必须在提货后的 10 天内申请检验,并要以外包装痕迹或其他适当证明为依据,否则保险人不予赔偿。

It covers damage to the insured cargo in transit due to fresh water, rain, or melting snow and ice. The insured person must apply for inspection within 10 days of picking up the goods after discovering that they have been exposed to fresh water and rain, and must provide traces of the outer packaging or other appropriate proof as evidence, otherwise the insurer will not pay.

3）短量险（Shortage Clause）

短量险承保被保险货物在运输途中因包装破裂或散装货物散失而造成的数量短少或重量短缺。正常损耗不属于短量险的责任范围,必须事先扣除,因此双方往往在保险单中约定一个免赔额。对于包装货物的短少,被保险人应当提供外包装发生破裂现象的证明;对于散装货物,则以装船重量和卸船重量之间的差额作为计算短量的依据,同时还要扣除免赔额。

It covers shortage of quantity or shortage of weight of the insured goods due to package breakage or loss of bulk goods in transit. Natural loss is not covered by shortage clause and must be deducted in advance, so both parties often agree on a deductible in the insurance policy. For shortage of packaged goods, the insured should provide proof of rupture of the outer packaging; for bulk goods, the difference between the weight loaded on the ship and the weight unloaded from the ship is used as the basis for calculating the shortage, and the deductible is also deducted.

4）混杂玷污险（Intermixture and Contamination Clause）

混杂玷污险承保两类风险:一是保险货物在运输过程中,因混进杂质而致的损失;二是保险货物在运输途中受其他货物玷污所致的损失。如果因为船舱不洁而造成混杂、玷污,则属于承运方责任。

It covers two types of risks: the loss of the insured goods caused by the mixing of impurities and contamination by other goods in transit. Mixing and staining caused by uncleanliness of the ship's hold is the responsibility of the carrier.

5）渗漏险（Leakage Clause）

渗漏险承保两类损失:一是流质、半流质及油类货物在运输过程中,因容器损坏而引起的渗漏损失;二是用液体储藏的货物因液体的渗漏而引起的货物腐烂、变质等损失。对于渗漏出来的物质对其他货物或者船舶造成的损失保险人不予承保。

It covers two types of losses: firstly, it covers losses caused by leakage of fluid, semi-fluid, and oil cargoes due to damage of containers during transportation; secondly, it covers losses caused by decay and deterioration of cargoes due to leakage of liquids in storage. The insurer will not cover the loss caused by leakage to other cargoes or ships.

6）碰损、破碎险（Clash and Breakage Clause）

碰损、破碎险承保货物在运输过程中,因震动、碰撞、受压造成的碰损和破碎损失。碰损主要是指金属或金属制品,如机器、搪瓷制品等在运输过程中因震动、受压、碰击等造成的凹痕、脱漆、破裂等损失。破碎主要是指易碎货物,如玻璃、玻璃制品、陶瓷制品等,在运输过程中由于震动、挤压、撞击、颠簸等外来原因造成的损坏。

It covers clash and breakage caused by vibration, collision, and pressure of the goods during transportation. "Clash" mainly refers to the dent, paint removal, rupture and other losses of metal or metal product such as machines and enamel products, caused by vibration, pressure and collision during transportation. "Breakage" mainly refers to the damage of fragile goods, such as glass, glass products, ceramic products, etc., caused by vibration, extrusion, impact, bump and other external causes during transportation.

被保险货物在运输途中因遭遇自然灾害或意外事故而造成的碰损、破碎损失已经包含在平安险和水渍险的责任范围内,碰损、破碎险则扩展负责由于一般外来原因造成的碰损和破碎损失。

The insured goods are already covered by FPA or WPA against damage or breakage caused by natural disasters or accidents during transportation, while clash and breakage clause is extended to cover clash and breakage losses due to general external causes.

7) 串味险(Taint of Odor Clause)

串味险承保货物在运输过程中,因受其他异味货物的影响造成串味的损失。但如果串味损失是因承运人配载不当造成的,保险人在对被保险人赔付后,应向承运人追偿损失。

It covers the loss of goods tainted by other odorous goods in transit. However, if such loss is caused by the carrier's improper stowage, the insurer shall recover the loss from the carrier after paying the insured.

8) 受潮受热险(Sweat and Heating Clause)

受潮受热险承保货物在运输过程中,由于气温突然变化或船上通风设备失灵,船舱内的水汽凝结而引起货物发潮或发热所造成的霉烂、变质等损失。被保险人必须负举证之责,证明货物是由于外界原因而非本身缺陷致损的。

It covers losses caused by mildew and deterioration of cargo in transit due to sudden change in temperature or failure of ventilation equipment on board, resulting in condensation of water vapor in the ship's hold. It is the responsibility of the insured to provide evidence that the goods were damaged by external causes and not by their own defects.

9) 钩损险(Hook Damage Clause)

钩损险承保袋装、捆装货物在装卸或搬运过程中,由于装卸或搬运人员操作不当,使用钩子将包装钩坏或直接钩及货物而造成的损失。在实际业务中,袋装水泥、粮食及捆装货物、纸张等货物均可能遭受此类损失,一般应加保钩损险。

It covers the losses of bagged goods or bundled goods in the loading and unloading or handling process, due to improper operation of the loading and unloading personnel or handling personnel, thus using hooks to break the package or directly hook the goods. In actual business, bagged cement, grain and bundled goods, paper and other goods may suffer such losses, and generally should be insured against hook damage in addition to the basic risks.

10）包装破裂险（Breakage of Packing Clause）

包装破裂险承保货物在运输过程中，因装卸或搬运不慎，外包装破裂造成短少、玷污等导致的损失。对于在运输过程中，为了续运安全需要而产生的修补包装、更换包装所支付的费用，保险人也予负责。

It covers losses caused by the breakage of the outer packaging due to careless loading and unloading or handling of the goods in transit，resulting in shortage and staining. The insurer is also responsible for the costs incurred in repairing and replacing the packaging for the safety of subsequent transportation.

包装破裂险与钩损险的承保内容有重叠之处，但二者侧重点不同。本险仅适用于包装货物，且不限于货物在装卸过程中使用吊钩或手钩造成的损失。

There is an overlap between the coverage of breakage of packing clause and hook damage clause，but they have different emphases. This clause applies only to packaged goods and is not limited to losses caused by the use of hooks or hand hooks during the loading or unloading of goods.

11）锈损险（Rust Clause）

锈损险承保金属或金属制品在运输过程中，由于各种外来原因导致生锈造成的损失。由于有些裸装的金属板、块、条、管等货物以及习惯装在舱面的体积庞大的钢铁制品等在运输过程中难免发生锈损，而且与装运前的锈损难以分开，因而保险人对此类货物一般不愿接受锈损险的投保。

It covers damage caused by rusting of metal or metal products due to various external causes during transportation. As some bare metal plates，blocks，bars，tubes and other cargoes，as well as bulky iron and steel products that are customarily loaded on deck，are inevitably subject to rust damage during transportation，and it is difficult to separate from pre-shipment rust damage，the insurers are generally reluctant to accept rust clause for this type of cargo.

2. 特别附加险（Special Additional Risks）

特别附加险与一般附加险一样，不能独立投保，必须附属于基本险项。它与一般附加险的区别在于：特别附加险不包括在一切险的责任范围内，而一般附加险属于一切险的责任范畴。特别附加险所承保的风险，往往与政治、国家行政措施、政策法令、航运贸易习惯等因素相关。我国《海洋运输货物保险条款》中承保的特别附加险主要有以下六种。

Special additional risks，like general additional risks，cannot be insured independently. The risks covered by special additional risks are often related to politics，national administrative measures，policy decrees，shipping trade habits and other factors. The special additional risks in China's *Ocean Marine Cargo Clauses* mainly include the following 6 types.

1）交货不到险（Failure to Delivery Clause）

交货不到险承保货物装上船后，不论任何原因，从预定抵达目的地日期开始满 10 个月后仍未运到原定目的地交货的损失。"交货不到"与一般附加险中的"提货不着"不同，它并不是承运人运输上的原因，而是某些政治因素引起的。例如，由于运输途中被中途国政府当局禁运，保险货物被迫在中途卸货导致货主收不到货而造成损失。保险人在承保这种险别时，一般要求被保险人首先获得一切进口许可证件并办妥有关进口手续，以免日后由于无进口许可证等原因，被拒绝进口而造成交货不到。由于交货不到，保险货物很可能并未实际遭受全损，因此，保险人在按全损赔付时，都特别要求被保险人将保险货物的全部权益转移给保险人。

It covers losses resulting from goods not being delivered to the destination after 10 months from the scheduled date of arrival for any reason whatsoever after they have been loaded on board the ship. Unlike "non-delivery" in general additional risks, "failure to delivery" is not caused by the carrier's transportation, but by certain political factors. When insurers underwrite this type of insurance, they generally require the insured to first obtain all import licenses and complete the relevant import procedures, so as not to be denied import due to the lack of import licenses and other reasons in the future and result in non-delivery.

2）进口关税险（Import Duty Risk）

这个险别的设置是由于有些国家规定，不论进口货物有无损失，都要按照申报价值缴纳进口关税。如果货物发生全损或者丢失，根据一切险条款，进口商的货物损失可从保险公司得到补偿。但所纳关税属于间接损失，是一切险的除外责任，得不到补偿。收货人为取得这种在一切险责任以外的保障，需要向保险公司单独投保进口关税险。

This clause is set up because some countries require that import duties be paid on the declared value of the imported goods, regardless of whether there is any loss. In case of total loss of the goods, the importer will be compensated from the insurance company for the loss of the goods according to the terms of the all risks, but the customs duties paid are indirect losses, which are excluded from the all risks and therefore not compensated. The consignee needs to take out a separate import duty insurance policy with the insurance company in order to obtain this coverage outside the all risks liability.

进口关税险承保货物由于遭受保险事故损失，但被保险人仍需按完好货物价值缴纳进口关税所造成的损失。保险金额是单独的，与货物本身的保险金额分别载明在保险单内，是我国海运附加险中唯一需另行确定保险金额的险种。保险金额根据可能缴纳的关税来确定，通常由被保险人根据进口国进口关税的税率来制定。

Import duty risk covers losses arising from the payment of import duties by the insured on the value of the intact goods, notwithstanding that the goods have suffered an insured incidental loss. Its insurance amount and the insurance amount of the goods itself are separately stated in the insurance policy. It is the only type of insurance that needs to determine the insurance amount separately in China's marine additional insurances. The amount of insurance is determined on the basis of the customs duties that may be paid, and it is usually set by the insured on the basis of the rate of import duties in the importing country.

3）舱面险（On Deck Clause）

舱面险承保载于舱面上的货物,因遭受保险事故而致的损失以及抛弃和浪击落海的损失。海洋运输货物一般都是装在轮船舱内进行运输的,保险人在制定海洋运输货物保险的责任范围和费率时,都是以舱内运输作为考虑基础的,因此,对于货物装载舱面所发生的损失,保险人不负赔偿责任。但是,有些货物由于体积大、有毒性、有污染性或者易燃易爆等,根据航运习惯必须装载在舱面上。舱面险就是为了对这类货物的损失进行经济补偿而设立的附加险别。由于货物装载于舱面极易受损,遭受水浸雨淋等情况更是司空见惯,因此,保险人为避免责任过大,一般只接受在平安险、水渍险的基础上加保舱面险,不接受在一切险的基础上加保舱面险。集装箱货物视同舱内货物,不必加保本保险。

On deck clause covers loss of cargo loaded on the deck due to an insured accident as well as loss due to abandonment and washing overboard. Marine transportation cargoes are generally transported in the holds of the ship; therefore, when the insurer sets the scope of liability and rates of marine cargo insurance, it takes the hold transportation as the basis of consideration, and the insurer is not liable for the loss of the cargoes loaded on the deck. However, some cargoes must be loaded on the deck according to the shipping custom because they are too large, toxic, polluting, flammable or explosive, on deck clause is an additional insurance to compensate for the loss of such cargo. As cargo loaded on the deck is very easy to be damaged, and more common to sufler from water and/or rain damage. Therefore, in order to avoid excessive liability, the insurer generally only accepts on deck risk on the basis of FPA and WPA, and does not accept on deck risk on the basis of all risks. Container cargo is treated as hold cargo and does not need to be insured by this insurance.

4）黄曲霉素险（Aflatoxin Clause）

黄曲霉素险承保在保险责任有效期内,在进口港或进口地经当地卫生当局检验,证明黄曲霉素的含量超过进口国对该毒素的限制标准,因而被拒绝进口、没收或强制改变用途的损失。黄曲霉素是一种致癌毒素,发霉的粮食作物中一般都含有这种毒素。各国卫生当局对这种毒素的含量都有严格的限制标准。某种进口粮食作物的黄曲霉素含量如果超过限制标准,就会被拒绝进口,或者被没收,或者被强制改变用途。黄曲霉素险就是承保由此所造成的损失。

Aflatoxin clause covers losses caused by the refusal to import, confiscation, or compulsory change of use after the local health authorities have tested and proved that the aflatoxin content exceeds the limit standard of the importing country for the toxin at the port of import or at the place of import during the period of insurance liability. Aflatoxin is a carcinogenic toxin that is commonly found in moldy food crops. Health authorities in various countries have strict limits on the level of this toxin. If the level of aflatoxin in a certain imported food crop exceeds the limit, it will be rejected for import, or confiscated, or forced to change its use. Aflatoxin clause covers the resulting losses.

5)拒收险(Rejection Clause)

拒收险承保货物在进口时由于各种原因,被进口国政府和有关当局(如海关、动植物检疫局)拒绝进口或没收所造成的损失。被保险人在投保该险别时,必须持有必需的有效进口许可文件,而且货物的生产、质量、包装和商品检验符合产地国和进口国的有关规定。如果在保险货物起运后尚未抵达目的港,进口国宣布禁运或禁止,则保险人只负责赔偿将货物运回出口国或转口到其他目的地而增加的运费,但最多不能超过该批货物的保险价值。如果保险货物在起运前进口国即已宣布禁运或禁止,那么保险人不负任何赔偿责任。

Rejection clause covers losses caused by the refusal to import or confiscation of goods by the importing government and relevant authorities (e. g. customs, animal and plant quarantine bureau) due to various reasons at the time of import. The insured must have the necessary valid import license documents when taking out this insurance, and the production, quality, packaging and commodity inspection of the goods must comply with the relevant regulations of the country of origin and the country of import. If the insured goods have not yet arrived at the port of destination after shipment when the importing country declares an embargo or prohibition, the insurer is only responsible for compensating the increased freight costs for transporting the goods back to the exporting country or re-exporting them to other destinations, up to the insured value of the goods. The insurer is not liable for any compensation if the goods are embargoed or prohibited by the importing country before shipment.

6)出口货物到香港(包括九龙)或澳门存仓火险责任扩展条款(Fire Risk Extension Clause for Storage of Cargo at Destination Hong Kong, including Kowloon or Macao)

该险别专门适用于出口到港澳地区且在该地银行办理押汇的出口运输货物。它承保货物运抵香港或澳门卸离运输工具后,直接存放于保险单载明的过户银行指定的仓库时发生火灾造成的损失。

This insurance applies specifically to shipments exported to Hong Kong and Macau and settled foreign exchange in the bank there. It covers the loss caused by fire when the goods are unloaded from the means of transport in Hong Kong or Macau and stored directly in the warehouse designated by the transferring bank as stated in the insurance policy.

这一险别的保险期间,自被保险货物运入过户银行指定的仓库之时,直到过户银行收回货款解除货物权益,或者运输责任终止时起计算满30天。两者以先发生者为准。

The period of insurance for this coverage begins when the insured goods are delivered to the warehouse designated by the transferring bank and lasts until 30 days have elapsed from the time the transferring bank recovers payment for the goods and releases its interest in the goods or the transportation liability is terminated, whichever occurs first.

3. 特殊附加险（Particular Additional Risks）

特殊附加险与特别附加险一样，不能独立投保，只有在投保海洋运输货物保险基本险的基础上，才能加保。特殊附加险包括海运货物战争险、海运货物战争险的附加费用险和海洋运输货物运输罢工险。

Particular additional risks, like special additional risks, cannot be insured independently and can be added only on the basis of the basic risks of ocean marine cargo clause. Particular additional risks include ocean marine cargo war risks, additional expenses-ocean cargo war risks, and ocean marine cargo strike risks.

1）海运货物战争险（Ocean Marine Cargo War Risks）

海运货物战争险承保被保险货物由于战争、类似战争行为和敌对行为、武装冲突或海盗行为造成的直接损失。

Ocean marine cargo war risk covers direct loss of the insured cargo due to war, war-like acts and hostilities, armed conflict or piracy.

（1）责任范围。海运货物战争险的承保责任范围包括：

① 直接由于战争、类似战争行为和敌对行为、武装冲突或海盗劫掠等所造成运输货物的损失；

② 由于上述原因引起的捕获、拘留、扣留、禁制、扣押等所造成的运输货物的损失；

③ 各种常规武器，包括水雷、鱼雷、炸弹等所造成的运输货物的损失；

④ 由本险责任范围所引起的共同海损的牺牲、分摊和救助费用。

（1）Scope of cover. The scope of liability for ocean marine cargo war risk includes:

① Loss of transported goods directly caused by war, war-like and hostile acts, armed conflict, or piracy plunder;

② Loss of transported goods caused by capture, seizure, arrest, restraint, or detainment, etc. due to the above-mentioned reasons;

③ Loss of transported cargo caused by various conventional weapons, including mines, torpedoes, bombs, etc. ;

④ Sacrifice and contribution of general average and salvage charges arising from the liability of this insurance.

（2）除外责任。海运货物战争险对下列原因造成的损失不负赔偿责任：

① 由于敌对行为使用原子或热核制造的武器导致被保险货物的损失和费用；

② 由于执政者、当权者或其他武装集团的扣押、拘留引起的承保航程的丧失或挫折所致的损失。

（2）Exclusions. Ocean marine cargo war risk is not liable for losses caused by:

① Loss and expense of the insured cargo due to the use of atomic or thermonuclear weapons by hostile acts;

② Loss due to forfeit or frustration of a covered voyage caused by seizure or detention by the ruler, person in power, or other armed group.

（3）保险期间。海运货物战争险的保险期间同基本险有所不同,它承保责任的起讫不是"仓至仓",而是以"水上危险"为限,即从货物装上保险单所载明的起运港的海轮或驳船开始,到卸离保险单所载明的目的港的海轮或驳船为止。如果被保险货物不卸离海轮或驳船,保险责任期限以海轮到达目的港的当日午夜起算 15 天为止。如果货物需在中途港转船,不论货物是否卸载,保险责任均以海轮到达该港或卸货地点的当日午夜起算满 15 天为止。只有在此期限内装上续运海轮,保险责任才继续有效。

（3）Insurance Period. The period of ocean marine cargo war risk is different from the basic risks in that it is not "warehouse to warehouse", but "waterborne risk". That is, the insurance period commences from the cargo is loaded onto the oversea vessel or craft at the port of departure as stated in the insurance policy, until it is discharged from the oversea vessel or craft at the port of destination as stated in the insurance policy. If the insured cargo is not discharged from the vessel or craft, the period of liability shall be 15 days from midnight on the day of arrival of the vessel at the port of destination. If the cargo is to be trans-shipped at an intermediate port, the insurance liability shall continue for a period of 15 days from midnight of the day of arrival of the vessel at that port or place of discharge, regardless of whether the cargo is unloaded or not. The insurance liability shall continue only if the cargo is loaded onto the renewal vessel within this period.

2）海运货物战争险的附加费用险(Additional Expenses-Ocean Cargo War Risks)

这一险别是对战争险责任范围的扩展,主要承保由于战争险后果所引起的附加费用。其责任范围包括:发生战争险责任范围内的风险引起航程中断或挫折,以及由于承运人行使运输契约中有关战争险条款规定所赋予的权利,把货物卸在保险单规定以外的港口和地方,因而产生的应由被保险人负责的那部分附加的合理费用。这些费用包括卸货、上岸、存仓、转运、关税以及保险费等。

This insurance is an extension of the scope of liability of war risks and covers additional expenses arising from the consequences of war risks. The scope of liability covers additional reasonable expenses incurred by the insured due to the interruption or frustration of the voyage caused by the occurrence of risks covered by the war risks and the exercise of the carrier's right under the war risk provisions of the contract of carriage to unload the cargo at ports and places other than those specified in the insurance policy. These costs include unloading, disembarkation, warehousing, forwarding, customs duties and insurance premiums.

3）海洋运输货物运输罢工险(Ocean Marine Cargo Strike Risks)

罢工险是保险人承保被保险货物因罢工等人为活动造成损失的特殊附加险。我国的罢工险与《协会货物条款》基本相同,不同的是没有特别强调恐怖行为或政治目的行为损失。罢工险承保的风险包括罢工者、被迫停工工人或参加工潮暴动、民众斗争的人员的行动所造成的直接损失。

Strike risk is a special additional insurance in which the insurer covers the losses to the insured goods caused by man-made activities such as strikes. Strike risks in China is basically the same as the *Institute Cargo Clause*，except that there is no special emphasis on acts of terrorism or acts of political purpose losses. The risks covered by strike risks include direct losses caused by the actions of strikers，locked-out workmen or persons taking part in labour disturbances，riots or civil commotions.

罢工险只承保罢工行为所致的被保险货物的直接损失。如果因罢工造成劳动力不足或无法使用劳动力，而使货物无法正常运输、装卸以致损失，以及由此所造成的费用支出，保险人均不予以负责。

Strike risk covers only direct loss of the insured goods caused by the act of strike. The insurer is not responsible for loss of goods due to lack of labor or inability to use labor due to a strike，which prevents normal transportation，loading and unloading of goods，or for expenses incurred as a result.

罢工险对保险责任起讫的规定与战争险不同，而是与海运货物保险一样，采取"仓至仓"原则，即保险人对货物从卖方仓库到买方仓库的整个运输期间负责。

Unlike war risks，the insurance period of strike risks is based on the same "warehouse to warehouse" principle as marine cargo insurance，i. e. the insurer is responsible for the entire period of transportation of the goods from the seller's warehouse to the buyer's warehouse.

按照国际保险市场的习惯做法，被保险货物如已投保战争险，在加保罢工险时，一般不再加收保险费。中国人民保险公司也照此办理。

According to the customary practice in the international insurance market，if the insured cargo has been insured against war risk，no additional premium will be charged when the strike risk is added. The People's Insurance Company of China also follows this practice.

11. 1. 3 海运货物保险专门险（Ocean Marine Cargo Specialized Insurance）

海运货物保险专门险是根据海洋运输货物的特性而承保的专门险别，可以单独投保。目前，我国海运货物保险专门险主要有海洋运输冷藏货物保险和海洋运输散装桐油保险两种。

Specialized risks are special insurance underwritten according to the characteristics of marine transportation of goods，and can be insured separately. At present，the specialized risks of marine cargo insurance in China mainly include ocean marine insurance clause（frozen products）and ocean marine insurance clause（wood oil bulk）.

1. 海洋运输冷藏货物保险条款[Ocean Marine Insurance Clause（Frozen Products）]

海洋运输冷藏货物保险条款是根据冷藏货物的特性专门设立的。一些需要冷藏运输的鲜货，如鱼、虾、肉类、蔬菜及水果等，为了保持新鲜程度，需装入船舱冷藏舱内进行运输。但有时由于灾害事故和外来风险可能使冷藏设备失灵而造成鲜货腐烂，为此设立海洋运输冷藏货物保险。

Ocean marine insurance clause(frozen products)is specially established according to the characteristics of the refrigerated cargo. Some fresh goods that need to be transported in cold storage, such as fish, shrimp, meat, vegetables, and fruits, need to be transported in the refrigerated cabin in order to maintain the freshness. But sometimes disaster accidents and external risks may make the refrigeration equipment fail and cause fresh goods to rot; for this purpose, this insurance is established.

1) 海洋运输冷藏货物保险的险别[Types of Ocean Marine Insurance Clause(Frozen Products)]

(1) 冷藏险。冷藏险除负责由于冷藏机器停止工作连续 24 小时以上所造成的货物腐烂的损失外,其他赔偿责任与水渍险相同。此处的冷藏机器包括载运货物的冷藏车、冷藏集装箱及冷藏船上的制冷设备。

(1) Risks for shipment of frozen products. The scope of cover of risks for shipment of frozen products is the same as that of WPA except that it is responsible for the loss of goods due to decay caused by the stoppage of refrigerated machinery for more than 24 consecutive hours.

(2) 冷藏一切险。冷藏一切险与一切险的责任基本相同:除包括上列冷藏险的各项责任外,还负责被保险货物在运输途中由于外来原因所致的腐败或损失。

(2) All risks for shipment of frozen products. All risks for shipment of frozen products is basically the same as all risks insurance; in addition to the liabilities listed above for risks for shipment of frozen products, it is also responsible for corruption or loss of the insured goods due to external causes while in transit.

2) 除外责任(Exclusions)

海洋运输冷藏货物保险的除外责任,除海洋运输货物保险基本险的除外责任外,还针对冷藏货物保险的特点,增加了两点变化,对以下两点所造成的损失不负赔偿责任。

(1) 被保险货物在运输过程中的任何阶段,因未存放在有冷藏设备的仓库或运输工具中,或辅助工具没有隔温设备造成的货物腐败。

(2) 被保险货物在保险责任开始时因未保持良好状态,包括整理加工和包扎不妥,冷冻上的不合规定及肉食骨头变质所引起的鲜货腐烂和损失。

In addition to the exclusion of the basic risks, the exclusion of ocean marine insurance clause (frozen products) also adds two changes to the characteristics of refrigerated cargo insurance, and is not liable for the losses caused by the following situations.

(1) Corruption of the insured goods at any stage of transportation caused by not being stored in a warehouse or means of transportation with refrigeration equipment, or by the use of auxiliary means without thermal insulation equipment.

(2) Decay and loss of fresh goods caused by failure to keep the insured goods in good condition at the commencement of insurance liability, including improper finishing

and wrapping，non-compliant freezing operations and meat bone spoilage，etc.

3）保险期间（Insurance Period）

海洋运输冷藏货物保险的保险期间与海洋运输货物保险的保险期间基本相同，只是针对冷藏货物的特点，对有关时间进行了调整。

The insurance period of ocean marine insurance clause（frozen products）is basically the same as the insurance period of ocean marine cargo insurance，only that for the characteristics of refrigerated cargo，the relevant period has been adjusted.

（1）保险货物到达保险单载明的最后目的港后，必须在 30 天内卸离海轮，否则保险责任终止。

（2）保险货物全部卸离海轮并存入冷藏仓库，保险人负责保险货物卸离海轮后 10 天的风险。在上述期限内，保险货物一经移出冷藏仓库，保险责任即告终止。

（3）保险货物全部卸离海轮后不存入冷藏仓库，保险责任至卸离海轮即告终止。

（1）The insured cargo must be discharged from the vessel within 30 days after arriving at the last port of destination as stated in the insurance policy，otherwise the insurance liability will be terminated.

（2）If the insured cargo is completely discharged from the vessel and deposited in the refrigerated warehouse，the insurer is responsible for the risk for 10 days after the insured cargo is discharged from the vessel. Once the insured cargo is removed from the reefer warehouse within the above period，the insurance liability shall be terminated.

（3）If the insured cargo is not stored in the refrigerated warehouse after all of it is discharged from the vessel，the insurance liability will be terminated when it is discharged from the vessel.

关于被保险人的义务和索赔时效，海洋运输冷藏货物保险与《海洋运输货物保险条款》的规定相同。

Regarding the obligations of the insured and the statute of limitations for claims，the provisions of ocean marine insurance clause（frozen products）are the same as those of *Ocean Marine Cargo Clause*.

2. 海洋运输散装桐油保险条款[Ocean Marine Insurance Clause(Wood Oil Bulk)]

海洋运输散装桐油保险条款是根据散装桐油的特点而专门设立的，可以单独投保。桐油因自身的特性，在运输过程中容易受到污染、短少、渗漏、变质等损失，为此，它需要不同于一般货物保险的特殊保障。海洋运输散装桐油保险条款就是为了给桐油提供全面保障而制定的。

Ocean marine insurance clause（wood oil bulk）is specially established according to the characteristics of bulk wood oil，which can be insured separately. Because of its own characteristics，wood oil is vulnerable to pollution，shortage，leakage，deterioration and other losses during transportation，so it needs special protection different from general cargo insurance. Ocean marine insurance clause（wood oil bulk）is designed to provide comprehensive protection for wood oil.

1）承保风险(Scope of Cover)

除了货运险的责任外,它还包括以下内容。

（1）不论任何原因所致被保险桐油的短少、渗漏超过保险单规定的免赔率时的损失（以每个油轮作为计算单位）。

（2）不论任何原因所致被保险桐油的玷污或变质损失。

（3）被保险人对遭受承保责任危险的被保险桐油采取抢救、防止或减少货物损失的措施而支付的合理费用,但以该批被救桐油的保险金额为限。

In addition to the liability of the cargo insurance, it also covers the following contents.

（1）Loss of insured wood oil due to shortage or leakage from any cause in excess of the deductible specified in the insurance policy (calculated per tanker).

（2）Loss due to staining or deterioration of the insured wood oil for any reason whatsoever.

（3）The reasonable costs paid by the insured to salvage, prevent or reduce the loss of the insured wood oil suffering from the perils covered by the insurance, but to the extent of the insurance amount of the batch of rescued wood oil.

2）除外责任(Exclusions)

（1）被保险人的故意行为或过失所造成的损失。

（2）属于发货责任所引起的损失。

（3）在保险责任开始前,被保险桐油已存在的品质不良或数量短差所造成的损失。

（4）被保险桐油的市价跌落或运输延迟所引起的损失或费用。

（1）Loss caused by the willful act or negligence of the insured.

（2）Loss caused by the liability of delivery.

（3）Loss caused by poor quality or shortage of quantity of the insured wood oil that existed before the commencement of the insurance liability.

（4）Loss or expense caused by the decline of market price of the insured wood oil or the delay of transportation.

3）保险期间(Insurance Period)

海洋运输散装桐油保险的保险期间,与《海洋运输货物保险条款》基本险的保险期间基本一致,也是按"仓至仓"原则。其具体内容如下。

The insurance period of marine transportation bulk wood oil insurance is basically the same as that of basic risks of *Ocean Marine Cargo Clause*, also according to the principle of "warehouse to warehouse". The details are as follows.

（1）自被保险桐油运离保险单所载明的起运港的岸上油库或盛装容器开始运输时生效,在整个运输过程中继续有效,直至安全交至保险单所载明目的地的岸上油库。但若桐油不及时卸离海轮或未交至岸上油库,则最长保险期限以海轮到达目的港后15天为限。

（1）The insurance is effective from the time the insured wood oil leaves the oil depot or container on shore at the port of departure as stated in the policy and continues to be effective throughout the course of transit until it is safely delivered to the oil depot on shore at the destination as stated in the policy. However，if the wood oil is not discharged from the vessel in time or is not delivered to the shore depot, the maximum insurance period shall be limited to 15 days after the vessel arrives at the port of destination.

（2）在非正常运输情况下，被保险桐油运到非保险单所载明的目的港时，应在到达该港口 15 天内卸离海轮，在卸离海轮后满 15 天责任终止。如在 15 天内货物在该地出售，则保险责任以交货时为止。

（2）In the case of abnormal transportation，when the insured wood oil is transported to a port of destination other than that stated in the policy，it shall be discharged from the vessel within 15 days of arrival at that port，and the liability shall cease upon completion of 15 days after discharge from the vessel. If the goods are sold at the place within 15 days，the insurance liability shall end at the time of delivery.

（3）被保险桐油在上述非正常运输情况下，如在 15 天内继续运往保险单所载明的原目的地或其他目的地，保险责任则按上述条款的规定终止。

（3）If the insured wood oil continues to be transported to the original destination or other destinations as stated in the policy within 15 days under the above-mentioned abnormal transportation situation，the insurance liability will be terminated in accordance with the provisions of the above clause.

11.1.4　国际贸易货物其他保险条款（Other Insurance Clauses for Goods in International Trade）

1. 卖方利益险［Contingency Insurance Clause（Cover Seller's Interest Only）］

这种险别是在卖方没有投保货运基本险的情况下，为保障自身在货物运输中遇到事故时，买方不付款赎单而遭受的损失而设立的。它是一种独立险别，可单独投保。

This kind of insurance is established to protect the seller from the loss cansed by the buyer's failure to pay for the redemption of B/L in case of an accident in the transportation of goods，when the seller does not have the basic freight insurance. It's a stand-alone insurance that can be insured separately.

出口货物若采用付款交单、承兑交单或赊账等商业信用付款条件成交，进口商都是在取得货运单据时或其后甚至提取货物后才付款，使出口商承担了很大的商业信用风险。当合同中采用的是 FOB 或 CFR 贸易术语时，按照 Incoterms® 2020 的规定，由买方自行负责办理保险，一旦货物在运输途中遭受损失，如果买方不付款赎单，卖方既无法收回货款，又因为没有投保货运保险而不能向保险人索赔，不可避免会造成经济损失。为避免这种情况发生，使卖方的损失得到及时补偿，中国保险公司设立了卖方利益险。

When using D/P，D/A or O/A and other commercial credit payment terms to export，importers usually pay at the time of obtaining the shipping documents or later，or even after picking up the goods，which makes the exporters bear a large commercial credit risk. When FOB or CFR trade terms are used in the contract，according to the provisions of Incoterms®2020，the buyer is responsible for their own insurance. Once the goods suffer losses in transit，if the buyer does not pay to obtain the shipping document，the seller can neither recover the payment for the goods nor claim from the insurer because it does not take out cargo insurance，which will inevitably cause financial losses. To avoid this situation and to enable the seller to be promptly compensated for losses，China's insurance companies have established contingency insurance clause（cover seller's interest only）.

根据卖方利益险条款的规定，该险别负责赔偿货物遭受保险单上载明的货运险条款责任范围内的卖方损失，但仅在买方不支付该项受损货物部分的货款时才予赔偿，且赔偿的仅是遭遇货运保险事故的那部分货物的损失，对于因买方拒绝提货而使卖方遭受的其他损失和费用，保险人不承担赔偿责任。

According to the terms of this clause，it is responsible for compensating the seller for the loss of goods suffered by the seller within the scope of responsibility of the freight insurance provisions contained in the insurance policy，but only when the buyer does not pay for the damaged part of the goods，and the compensation is only the loss of the part of the goods that suffered a freight insurance accident，the insurer is not liable for other losses and expenses suffered by the seller due to the buyer's refusal to pick up the goods.

卖方利益险的费率为货运险费率的 25%。卖方利益险条款还规定被保险人应将其向第三方或买方追偿的权利转让给保险人。由于买方不付款赎单的行为违反了贸易合同，应当承担违约责任，保险人取得代位追偿权后可向买方追偿。

The rate for contingency insurance clause（cover seller's interest only）is 25% of the freight insurance premium rate. The clause also provides that the insured shall assign its right to recover from a third party or the buyer to the insurer. As the buyer's non-payment is a breach of the trade contract，it should be liable for breach of contract，and the insurer can recover from the buyer after obtaining the right of subrogation.

2. 产品责任险（Product Liability Insurance）

产品责任险承保因生产商和销售商或修理商生产、销售或修理的产品存在缺陷，致使用户或消费者在使用过程中发生意外事故，而遭受人身伤害或财产损失，依法应由产品的生产商、销售商或修理商承担的经济赔偿责任。

Product liability insurance covers the economic liability which should be borne by the manufacturer，seller，or repairer of the product according to law due to defects in the production，sale or repair of the product，resulting in an accident in the course of use by the user or consumer，who suffers personal injury or property damage.

生产商、出口商、进口商、批发商、零售商及修理商等一切可能因产品事故造成损害而负有赔偿责任的人都可以投保产品责任保险。根据具体情况，可以由他们中的任何一人投保，也可以由他们中间的几个人或全体联名投保。产品责任险的保险期限通常为 1 年，期满可以续保。

Manufacturers，exporters，importers，wholesalers，retailers and repairers，all of whom may be liable for damages caused by product accidents，can take out product liability insurance. Depending on the circumstances，any one of them can be insured，or several of them or all of them can be insured jointly. Product liability insurance is usually provided for a period of one year and is renewable at the end of that period.

3. 出口信用保险（Export Credit Insurance）

出口信用保险是指以出口贸易中国外买方按期支付的信用作为保险标的的保险，由债权人（出口商或贷款银行）为了保障自己的债权利益向保险公司投保，保险人对被保险人因国外买方或借款人到期不能履行清偿债务的义务而造成的相关损失负经济赔偿责任。出口信用保险属于政策性保险，开办的目的是鼓励和促进本国出口贸易的发展而不是盈利。

Export credit insurance is an insurance that takes the credit paid by the foreign buyer in the export trade as the subject of insurance，and is taken out by the creditor (exporter or lending bank) with the insurance company in order to protect the interests of their claims，and the insurer is financially liable for the losses caused by the insured due to the foreign buyer or borrower's failure to fulfill their obligations to settle their debts when due. Export credit insurance is a policy-based insurance，and its purpose is to encourage and promote the development of domestic export trade rather than profit.

出口信用保险承保的是出口商的收汇风险，造成出口商不能安全收汇的风险主要有政治风险和商业风险。政治风险包括买方所在国家实行外汇管制、进口管制及发生战争、暴动或其他非常事件等；商业风险通常包括：买方无力偿还债务或买方破产，买方收货后拖延支付货款以及货物出运后买方违约拒绝收货或拒绝付款等。

Export credit insurance covers the exporter's risk of collecting foreign exchange. The main risks that cause exporters to fail to collect foreign exchange safely are political risk and commercial risk. Political risks include foreign exchange control，import control，war，riots or other extraordinary events in the buyer's country；commercial risks usually include buyer's insolvency or bankruptcy，delay in payment after receipt of goods by the buyer，refusal of receipt or refusal of payment by the buyer for breach of contract after the goods are shipped，etc.

11.2 《协会货物条款》（*Institute Cargo Clauses*）

作为近代海上保险的中心，英国在国际海上贸易航运和保险业中具有重要地位。它所制定的各种保险规章制度对世界各国有着深远影响。世界上很多国家在海上保险业务中直接采用了英国伦敦保险协会所制定的货物条款（简称《协会货物条款》），或者在制定本国保险条款时参考或部分采用了上述条款。

As the center of modern marine insurance，Britain has an important position in the international maritime trade shipping and insurance industry. The various insurance rules and regulations it established have had a profound impact on countries around the world. Many countries around the world have directly adopted the *Institute Cargo Clause* (ICC) formulated by Institute of London Underwriters in their marine insurance business, or have referred to or partially adopted the above clause when developing their own insurance clauses.

11.2.1 《协会货物条款》的发展(Development of *Institute Cargo Clauses*)

1.《协会货物条款》简介(Introduction to *Institute Cargo Clauses*)

英国劳合社的"船、货保险单"于1779年投入伦敦市场上使用;1795年,它取代了所有其他形式的海上保险单,成为船舶与货物运输的标准保单。1906年,英国议会通过了《海上保险法》,该法把劳合社的"船、货保险单"正式列为第一附则,使其成为英国法定的海上保险单,并逐渐成为国际海上保险单的范本。1912年,伦敦保险协会的技术与条款委员会制定了《协会货物条款》,对沿用已久、内容陈旧的S.G.保险单的内容进行了修改和补充,以加贴的形式附于保险单背面。后经过多次修改,于1963年形成了一套完整的海上运输货物保险标准条款,即ICC旧条款,也即以前的平安险条款、水渍险条款和一切险条款,并仍与S.G.保险单配合使用。为了适应不同时期贸易、航运、法律、判例等方面的变化和发展,《协会货物条款》进行了多次修订和补充。1981年,英国对ICC进行了修订,并于1982年1月1日起在伦敦市场使用,旧的《协会货物条款》和劳合社S.G.保险单于1983年3月31日起在伦敦保险市场停止使用,从1983年4月1日起,强制性要求改用新的海上保险单格式和新的《协会货物条款》。新保险单本身不能单独使用,必须与新条款同时使用才能构成一份完整的保险合同。

The Lloyd's "Ship and Goods Policy" was introduced into the London market in 1779; by 1795, it had replaced all other forms of marine insurance policies as the standard policy for the ships and carriage of cargo. In 1906, the British Parliament passed the *Marine Insurance Act*, which officially listed Lloyd's "S. G. Policy" as the first appendix, making it a statutory marine insurance policy in Britain, and gradually becoming the model of international marine insurance policy. In 1912, the Technical and Clause Committee of Institute of London Underwriters formulated the *Institute Cargo Clause*, which modified and supplemented the content of the long-standing and obsolete S. G. Policy by attaching to the back of the policy. After several revisions, a complete set of standard clauses for marine cargo insurance was formed in 1963, that is, ICC old clauses, which includes the former FPA clause, WPA clause and all risks clause, is still used in conjunction with the S. G. policy. In order to adapt to the changes and development of trade, shipping, law and jurisprudence in different periods, *Institute Cargo Clause* has been revised and supplemented several times. The ICC was revised in the UK in 1981 and used in the London market from January 1, 1982, and the old

Institute Cargo Clauses and Lloyd's S. G. policy was discontinued in the London insurance market on March 31, 1983. From April 1, 1983, it was mandatory to switch to the New Marine Policy Form (or The Lloyd's Marine Policy) and the new *Institute Cargo Clauses*. The new policy itself cannot be used alone, but must be used in conjunction with the new clauses to form a complete insurance contract.

2009 年,伦敦保险协会又对 1982 年条款重新进行了一些完善和改进,虽然和 1982 年那场革命性的修改无法相比,但却作出了一些对被保险人更加有利的规定,同时也进行了一些文字上的修改,使条款更加符合时代的要求,含义也更加清晰。

In 2009, Institute of London Underwriters made some further refinements and improvements to the 1982 clause, which, while not comparable to the revolutionary changes made in 1982, made some provisions more favorable to the insured and also made some textual changes to make the clause more up-to-date and clearer in meaning.

新的海上保险单格式比较简单、清晰。其内容除包括前言和签字外,还包括一张表格供记载以下内容:①保险单号码;②被保险人名称及船舶名称;③保险航程或保险期间;④保险标的及其约定价值(若有约定的话);⑤保险金额;⑥保险费;⑦附加条款及批单;⑧其他特约条件或担保。

The new marine policy form is more simple and clearer. In addition to the preamble and signing, it also includes a form to record the following contents: ① the policy number; ② the names of the assured and the vessel; ③ the voyage or period of insurance; ④ the subject-matter insured and its agreed value-if any; ⑤ the amount insured; ⑥the premium; ⑦clauses and endorsements to be attached; ⑧a "catch all" of special conditions and warranties.

2. ICC 1982 的主要特点(Main Characteristics of ICC 1982)

1982 年《协会货物条款》具有下列特点。

The 1982 *Institute Cargo Clauses* has the following characteristics.

1) 条款结构统一,体系完整,语言简练(Uniform Structure, Complete System, Concise Language)

1982 年《协会货物条款》各种险别条款的条文均按问题的性质做了统一的分类排列,体系完整,语言简练。各种险别条款除了作为附加险的"恶意损害险条款"之外,均包括八项内容,即承保范围、除外责任、保险期间、索赔、保险利益、减少损失、防止迟延及法律惯例。在上述八项内容中,除了前三项之外,其他五项在新条款的 ICC(A)、ICC(B)、ICC(C)以及战争险和罢工险中都是完全相同的。由于战争险和罢工险也完整地包括上述八项内容,因而也可以独立投保,无须作为特殊附加险加保于基本险中。与 1963 年的《协会货物条款》相比,其增加了保险利益条款、续运费用条款、增值条款、放弃条款和英国法律与惯例条款,内容更加全面,体系更加完整。

The provisions of the 1982 *Institute Cargo Clauses* are arranged in a uniform classification according to the nature of the problem, with a systematic structure and concise language. Except for the "malicious damage clause", which is an additional insurance, all the clauses include eight items, namely, risks covered, exclusions, duration, claims, benefit of insurance, minimising losses, avoidance of delay, and law and practice. Of the eight items listed above, all but the first three are identical in ICC (A), ICC(B), ICC(C), as well as war and strike insurance of the new clauses. Since war and strike insurance also cover the above eight items, they can also be insured independently without being added to the basic risks as a particular additional risk. Compared with *Institute Cargo Clauses* of 1963, provisions on benefit of insurance, forwarding charges, increased value, as well as waiver and law and practice have been added, making the content more comprehensive and the system more complete.

2）主要险别条款的名称改用英文字母表示（The Name of the Main Insurance Clause is Changed to English Letters）

新条款取消了旧条款"单独海损不赔""负责单独海损"及"一切险"的名称，而替换为"协会货物条款 A""协会货物条款 B""协会货物条款 C"。这一改变克服了旧条款的名称与内容不一致，易使人们产生误解的弊端。另外，新条款 A、B、C 都取消了免赔额（率）的规定。

The new clause cancels the names of the old clauses "free from particular average", "with particular average" and "all risks" and replaces them with "institute cargo clause A" [ICC(A)], "institute cargo clause B" [ICC(B)] and "institute cargo clause C" [ICC(C)], which overcomes the disadvantages of inconsistency between the names and contents of the old clauses that can easily lead to misunderstanding. In addition, the new clauses A, B, and C all eliminate the provisions on deductibles (rates).

3）承保责任采用"列明风险"和"一切风险减除外责任"两种方式（Scope of Coverage is Stipulated in Two Ways: "List the Risks" and "All Risks Except Exclusions"）

除了个别险以外，新条款均采用"列明风险"和"一切风险减除外责任"的方式表示保险人的承保责任。例如，新条款 A 就是采用"一切风险减除外责任"的方式，即除了"除外责任"项下所列风险保险人不予负责外，其他风险均予负责。新条款 B、C 以及战争险与罢工险则采用"列明风险"的方式，即在条款的开头就把保险人所承保的风险一一列出。

Except for individual insurance, the new provisions use the "list the risks" and "all risks except exclusions" approach to express the insurer's coverage responsibilities. For example, ICC(A) uses the "all risks except exclusions" approach, which means that the insurer is responsible for all risks except for those listed under "exclusions". ICC(B), ICC(C), and war clause (cargo) and strike clause (cargo) use "list the risks" approach, i. e., the risks covered by the insurer are listed at the beginning of the clause.

4）取消了"全部损失"与"部分损失"的划分（The Distinction Between "Total Loss" and "Partial Loss" Has Been Eliminated）

自 1982 年起，ICC 条款对保险人承保的风险损失，不再做全部损失与部分损失的划分。按照 ICC 条款，凡属承保责任范围内的损失，无论是全部损失还是部分损失，保险人均负赔偿责任；相反，凡不属承保责任范围内的损失，保险人不予负责。这一改变简化了对保险人承保责任的规定,使各种险别的承保责任范围比较明确,减少了不同险别的承保责任范围交叉重复的现象。

Since 1982, the ICC no longer makes a distinction between total and partial losses for risks covered by insurers. According to ICC, the insurer is liable for all losses within the scope of coverage, regardless of whether they are total or partial losses; conversely, the insurer is not responsible for any losses that are not within the scope of coverage. This change has simplified the provisions on insurers' coverage, made the coverage of various risks clearer, and reduced the phenomenon of overlapping coverage of different risks.

5) 险别的差距扩大,险别的划分容易(The Gap Between the Scope of Coverage of Various Risks Has Widened, Which Makes it Easier to Classify Insurance)

旧条款中"单独海损不赔"与"负责单独海损"的差距较小,极易混淆;而新条款中的ICC(A)、ICC(B)及 ICC(C)险别的差距较大,且容易划分。

In the old clause, the difference between "free from particular average" and "with particular average " is relatively small and easy to confuse; while in the new clause, the difference between ICC(A), ICC(B) and ICC(C) is large and easy to divide.

《协会货物条款》的基本条款主要有五种:协会货物条款(A)、协会货物条款(B)、协会货物条款(C)、协会战争险条款(货物)和协会罢工险条款(货物)。恶意损害险条款(货物)为附加险,不能单独投保,只能在基本险的基础上加保。

There are five main types of basic clauses of *Institute Cargo Clauses*: institute cargo clause A, institute cargo clause B, institute cargo clause C, institute war clause-cargo, and institute strike clause-cargo. malicious damage clause (cargo) is an additional risk that cannot be taken out separately, but only in addition to the basic risks.

3. ICC 2009 的主要变化[①](Main Changes of ICC 2009)

1) 普遍性的改变(Universal Changes)

ICC 1982 的除外责任条款下分别列有副标题,如除外责任 4 的副标题为"一般除外责任",除外责任 5 的副标题为"不适航或不适货除外责任"等。ICC 2009 的除外责任条款删除了副标题,直接表示为除外责任 4、5、6、7。这是因为副标题并不能完全准确地表述出副标题下所有具体列明的事项,容易产生歧义与误解。

此外,ICC 2009 对 ICC 1982 中的部分词汇进行了更换,从而使意思表达更加准确,具体包括:将所用"雇员"一词由"servant"更换为"employee",将"货物"更换为"保险标的",将"承保人"更换为"保险人"等。

---

① 此处参考了:丁元平.2009 英国协会货物保险 A 条款的新发展及对我国的借鉴意义[D].大连:大连海事大学,2013;王莹.2009 年伦敦协会货运险条款较 1982 年版的变化[J].上海保险,2009(7):9-13,17;姚新超.英国协会货物条款(ICC2009)『除外责任』的新变化[J].对外经贸实务,2012(8):47-50.

The exclusions clause of ICC 1982 are subtitled. For example，the subheading of exclusions 4 is "general exclusions clause"，the subheading of exclusions 5 is "unseaworthiness and unfitness exclusion clause"，etc. The subtitle of the exclusion clause in ICC 2009 has been deleted and directly expressed as exclusions 4，5，6 and 7，because the subtitle does not fully and accurately express all the matters specified under it and is prone to ambiguity and misunderstanding.

In addition，ICC 2009 has replaced some of the words in ICC 1982 to make the meaning more accurate，including replacing "servant" with "employee"，"goods or cargo" with "subject-matter insured"，and "underwriters" with "insurers"，etc.

2）表述更加清晰（Clearer Expression）

ICC 1982 的一些表达存在晦涩、拗口的问题，如船舶互有责任碰撞条款，2009 年版对其表述进行了修改，使其表达更为清楚、易于理解。

Some expressions of ICC 1982 are obscure and awkward，the 2009 edition has modified its expression to make it clearer and easier to understand.

3）对除外责任条款进行了较大的修改（Significant Changes to the Exclusions Clause）

（1）条款 4.3 对保险标的包装不固或包装不当或配载不当作出了更为细致的规定。首先，明确了该除外条款仅适用于下述两种情况：一是保险标的的包装或配载是由被保险人或其雇员完成的；二是保险标的的包装或配载是在保单责任开始前完成的。很明显，该规定缩小了关于包装的除外责任，更有利于被保险人。其次，明确了"不固"或"不当"的标准是"无法抵挡运输途中发生的通常事故"。再次，2009 年版删除了"托盘"，因为"托盘"从法律角度或贸易角度都无法达成一个统一的定义。此外，该条款表明了独立承包商不属于被保险人的受雇人。

（1）Clause 4.3 provides more detailed provisions on the subject-matter insured being insufficiently or unsuitably packed or loaded. Firstly，it is made clear that the exclusion only applies to the following two situations：①such packing or preparation is carried out by the assured or their employees；②such packing or preparation is carried out prior to the attachment of this insurance. Obviously，this provision narrows the exclusion of packaging，which is more beneficial to the insured. Secondly，it clarifies that the standard of "insufficiency" or "unsuitability" is "to withstand the ordinary incidents of the insured transit". Thirdly，the term "liftvan" was deleted from the ICC 2009 because it was not possible to arrive at an agreed definition of "liftvan" from either a legal or a trade perspective. In addition，the clause indicates that independent contractors are not employees of the insured.

（2）条款 4.5 关于"延迟除外"的规定中，删除了"直接由延迟引起"中"直接"一词。如果发生运输延迟的事实，则属于 ICC 2009（A）规定的除外责任范围，无须再区分该损失或费用是否直接或间接由延迟引起。对保险人而言，这样的修改简化了理赔程序。

（2）In clause 4.5 on "exclusion for delay", the word "proximately" has been deleted from the phrase "proximately caused by delay". That is, if the fact of delay in transit occurs, it falls within the scope of the exclusion under ICC 2009(A), and it is no longer necessary to distinguish whether the loss or expense is directly or indirectly caused by the delay. This change simplifies the claims process for insurers.

（3）条款 4.6 对"经营人破产或不履行债务"的规定作出了相应的修改。一是对保险人引用该除外条款作出时间限制，即被保险人不能获得赔偿的免责只适用于"保险标的装上船舶时"。换言之，若保险标的已装上船舶，再发生因承运人或船东经营破产或不履行债务而导致保险标的的损失或费用，则不属于除外责任。显然这更有利于被保险人。二是作出了被保险人无主观过错限制。只有在被保险人知道或参与该业务时应该知道，在该航次中会发生船东或承运人破产或经营陷入困境，由此可能导致该航程被取消时，保险人才能对由此产生的损失或费用不予赔偿。

（3）Clause 4.6 on "insolvency or financial default of the operator" has been amended accordingly. Firstly, it imposes a time limit on the insurer to invoke this exclusion clause, i.e. the exclusion of the insured's inability to obtain compensation only applies "at the time of loading of the subject-matter insured on board the vessel". In other words, if the subject-matter insured has been loaded onto the vessel, the loss or expense of the subject-matter insured caused by insolvency or default of the carrier or the shipowner will not be an exclusion. Obviously, this is more favorable to the insured. Secondly, a limitation of no subjective fault of the insured is made. Only if the insured knew or should have known, at the time of engaging in the business, that the shipowner or carrier would become insolvent or in difficulty during the voyage, which might result in the cancellation of the voyage, can the insurer not compensate for the loss or expense incurred as a result.

（4）条款 4.7"核战争武器除外"的规定有两点显著的变化：一是用"直接或间接造成的损失或费用"代替了 1982 年条款的"造成的损失或费用"，明确认定导致损失的原因无论是直接的还是间接的都属于除外责任。二是用"任何武器或装置"代替了"战争武器"一词，扩大了武器除外责任的范围，除外的情况既包括战争武器也包括其他非战争武器，既包括武器也包括普通设备。这一修订将恐怖主义行为导致保险标的的损失和费用也排除在保险人赔偿的范围之外，明显扩大了保险人的免责范围。

（4）There are two notable changes in the provision of article 4.7 "exclusion for nuclear weapon of war", The first is the substitution of "Loss damage or expense directly or indirectly caused by or arising from" for "Loss damage or expense arising from" in article 1982, which clearly recognizes that the causes of loss, whether direct or indirect, are excluded. The second is to replace "any weapon of war" with "any weapon or device", thus expanding the scope of the weapons exclusion. The exclusion covers both weapons of war and other non-war weapons, as well as weapons and ordinary equipment. The amendment also excludes loss and expense of the subject-matter insured resulting from terrorist acts from the scope of indemnification by the insurer，which obviously expands the scope of exemption of liability of the insurer.

（5）条款 5 关于"不适航和不适货除外责任"的规定有以下主要变化：①删除了"大型海运箱"的规定；"受雇人"由"servant"更换为"employee"。②强调了集装箱或运输工具不适货而导致除外责任的情况仅适用于：装货在本保险生效前已经开始操作，或被保险人或其雇员在货物装船时已经知道上述情况。③明确若收货人根据本保险向保险人提出索赔，不适航或不适货除外规定就不再适用。可以将其理解为，作为善意的第三方收货人，保险人不得引用不适航或不适货进行抗辩。④1982 年版条款 5.2 是附条件的弃权，即保险人放弃船舶适航和适货的默示保证，前提条件就是被保险人或其雇员不知该情况；2009 年版条款 5.3 是不附任何条件的弃权，即保险人放弃船舶适航和适货的默示保证，无论被保险人或其雇员知道或不知道该情况。由此可见，2009 年版条款 5 对保险人引用该除外条款作出了很大的条件限制，提高了对善意保单受让人的保护程度，也使保险人以此条款抗辩的难度增加。

（5）There are the following major changes in the provisions of clause 5 on the "unseaworthiness and unfitness exclusion"：① The provision of "liftvan" has been deleted；"servant" has been replaced by "employee". ② It was emphasized that the exclusion due to the unfitness of the container or conveyance applied only when：loading is carried out prior to attachment of this insurance or by the assured or their employees and they are privy to such unfitness at the time of loading. ③ It clarifies that the unseaworthiness or unfitness exclusion no longer applies if the consignee makes a claim against the insurer under this insurance. It is to be understood that，as a bona fide third party consignee，the insurer may not invoke the unseaworthiness or unfitness exclusion as a defense. ④ Clause 5.2 of the 1982 version is a conditional waiver，i. e.，the insurer's waiver of the implied warranty of seaworthiness and fitness of the ship is conditional on the assured or their servants are privy to such unseaworthiness or unfitness；clause 5.3 of the 2009 edition is an unconditional waiver，i. e. the insurer waives the implied warranty of seaworthiness and fitness for carriage of the ship，whether the assured or their employees knew or did not know of the condition. It can be seen that clause 5 of the 2009 edition has made great restrictions on the conditions for insurers to invoke this exclusion clause，which has increased the protection for bona fide policy assignees，and also makes it more difficult for insurers to defend themselves against this clause.

（6）条款 7 关于"罢工和恐怖主义除外"的规定有两点显著变化：其一，将"恐怖主义行为"范围扩大，即包括"恐怖主义行为，或与恐怖主义行为相联系，任何组织通过暴力直接实施的旨在推翻或影响法律上承认的或非法律上承认的政府的行为"；其二，将"任何人出于信仰或宗教目的实施的行为"也纳入除外责任。因此，该除外责任条款的范围有所扩大。

（6）There are two significant changes in article 7 on the "strikes and terrorism exclusion"：first，the scope of "acts of terrorism" is expanded to "any act of terrorism being an act of·any person acting on behalf of，or in connection with，any organization which carries out activities directed towards the overthrowing or influencing，by force or violence，of any government whether or not legally constituted"；second，the exclusion also includes "any person acting from a political，ideological or religious motive". Thus，the scope of the exclusion has been expanded.

4）扩展了保险责任的起讫期限（Extended the Period of Commencement and Termination of Insurance Liability）

从保险责任起点来看，2009 年条款关于保险责任期间的改变首先体现在承保风险开始时间的前移，将 1982 年条款中"本保险责任开始于货物运离保险单载明的仓库或储存处所开始运输之时……"的规定，修改为："除下文第 11 条另有规定外，本保险责任开始于保险标的首次从（保险合同注明地点的）仓库或储存地点，为了开始运输而立即装入或装上运输车辆或其他运输工具而移动之时……"；将承保期间扩展到包括起运出库的装货、运输过程和到达入库的卸货过程。

从保险责任期间来说，包括正常运输过程，2009 年版与 1982 年版的规定一致，没有变化。

从保险责任终点来说，1982 年版列明有三个可能的终点，2009 年版列明有四个可能的终点，都是以最先发生者作为保险责任的实际终点。对于各自列明的前两个终点，1982 年版强调的是"运到"，2009 年版强调的是"完成卸货"，显然 2009 年版扩展了 1982 年版的终点，对被保险人更为有利。此外，2009 年版多出来的一个终点是"被保险人或其雇员在正常运输过程之外选择任何运输车辆或其他运输工具或集装箱储存货物"，这是限制被保险人或其雇员在非正常运送过程中的临时仓储问题。

In terms of the commencement of insurance liability，the change in ICC 2009 regarding the period covered by the insurance is firstly reflected in the forward shift of the start time of coverage，amending the provision of " This insurance attaches from the time the goods leave the warehouse or place of storage at the place named herein for the commencement of the transit…" in ICC 1982 to："Subject to Clause 11 below，this insurance attaches from the time the subject-matter insured is first moved in the warehouse or at the place of storage（at the place named in the contract of insurance）for the purpose of the immediate loading into or onto the carrying vehicle or other conveyance for the commencement of transit…"，i. e. extending the period of coverage to include the loading process at the time of departure from the warehouse，the course of transit，and the unloading process at the time of arrival at the warehouse.

The 2009 edition is unchanged from the 1982 edition with respect to the provision of period of insurance liability，including the ordinary course of transit.

In terms of the endpoints of insurance liability，the 1982 edition lists three possible endpoints and the 2009 edition lists four possible endpoints，with the first to occur being the actual endpoint of insurance liability. For the first two respective endpoints，the

1982 edition emphasizes "terminate" and the 2009 edition emphasizes "completion of unloading". It is clear that the 2009 version is more favorable to the insured by expanding the endpoints of liability in the 1982 version. In addition，one of the additional endpoints of the 2009 version is "the Assured or their employees elect to use any carrying vehicle or other conveyance or any container for storage other than in the ordinary course of transit"，which restricts the issue of temporary storage of goods by the insured or its employees during unusual course of transit.

5）"航程变更"的变化(Changes in "Change of Voyage")

条款 10 关于"航程变更"的规定有两点变化：一是考虑了发生航程变更后的实际操作问题，对"仍然有效"作出了一些限制。有可能被保险人虽然已经通知保险人变更情况，但确实还没有和保险人就变更后的条件最终达成一致就发生保险事故的情况。这种情况下，只有保险费率和保险条件符合合理的市场行情，保单才会仍然有效。二是规定在被保险人或其雇员不知道运输保险标的的船舶驶向非保单载明的另一目的地时，保单仍然被视为在本保险合同规定的航程开始时生效。此项规定增加了对善意被保险人利益的保护。

There are two changes to the "change of voyage" in clause 10：firstly, it takes into account the practical operation after the change of voyage，and places some restrictions on "held covered". It is possible that although the insured has notified the insurer of the change，the insurance accident occurred before the insurer and the insurer finally reached an agreement on the conditions after the change. In this case，the policy will remain valid only if the premium rates and conditions are in line with reasonable market conditions. Secondly，it is provided that in the event that the insured or its employees do not know that the vessel transporting the subject-matter insured is sailing to another destination other than that stated in the policy，the policy is still deemed to be in force at the commencement of the voyage specified in this insurance contract.

6）扩大了被保险人的范围(Expanding the Scope of the Insured)

ICC 2009 的条款 15"保险利益"与 ICC 1982 的条款 15 相比，将被保险人的范围扩大到包括收货人。

扩展阅读 11.2
2009 年伦敦协会货运险条款较 1982 年版的变化

Clause 15 "benefit of insurance" of ICC 2009 extends the scope of the insured to include the consignee as compared to clause 15 of ICC 1982.

11.2.2 《协会货物条款》的主要内容(**Main Contents of _Institute Cargo Clauses_**)

《协会货物条款》的基本险条款分为 A、B、C 三个条款。

The basic risks of _Institute Cargo Clause_ are divided into clause A，B and C.

1. ICC 2009(A)条款的主要内容[Main Contents of ICC 2009(A)]

1) 承保风险(Risks Covered)

该部分的内容包括三个条款,即风险条款、共同海损条款和船舶互有责任碰撞条款。

The content of this part consists of three clauses, namely risks clause, general average clause, and both to blame collision clause.

(1) 风险条款。在风险条款中,A 条款仍与 ICC 1982(A)相同,采用"一切风险减除外责任"的方式,承保除外责任以外的保险标的灭失或损害的一切风险。对约定和法定的除外事项,在"除外责任"部分全部予以列明,对于未列入除外责任项下的损失,保险人均予负责。

(1) Risks clause. In the risks clause, ICC 2009(A) remains the same as ICC 1982 (A), using the "all risks except exclusions" approach to cover all risks of loss of or damage to the subject-matter insured except as provided in Exclusions Clauses. All agreed and statutory exclusions are listed in the "Exclusions" section, and the insurer is responsible for any loss not listed under the exclusions.

(2) 共同海损条款。共同海损条款是对英国 1906 年《海上保险法》有关共同海损和救助费用规定的补充,明确了共同海损理算或救助费用确定应该适用的法律。在 ICC (A)、ICC(B)和 ICC(C)中,除了"除外责任"或其他条款的不保责任外,对共同海损的牺牲和救助费用予以赔偿。根据该条款,保险人不仅赔偿保险货物本身遭受的共同海损牺牲,还包括保险货物应承担救助费用以及共同海损的分摊。

(2) General average clause. General average clause is a supplement to the provisions of the *Marine Insurance Act* 1906 of UK regarding general average and salvage charges, which specifies the law that shall apply to the adjustment of general average or the determination of salvage charges. In ICC(A), ICC(B) and ICC(C), in addition to the exclusions clauses or other provisions of the exclusion, the sacrifice of general average and salvage charges are compensated. Under this clause the insurer shall indemnify the insured not only for general average sacrifice suffered by the insured goods but also for their contribution in salvage charges and in general average.

(3) 互有责任碰撞条款。本保险对被保险人根据运输契约的船舶互有责任碰撞条款,由被保险人就承保风险应承担的责任予以赔偿。若承运人向被保险人提起索赔,被保险人同意通知保险人,保险人有权自负费用为被保险人就此项索赔抗辩。

(3) Both to blame collision clause. This insurance indemnifies the assured, in respect of any risk insured against liability incurred under any both to blame collision clause in the contract of carriage. In the event of any claim by carriers under the said clause, the assured agree to notify the insurers who shall have the right, at their own cost and expense, to defend the assured against such claim.

2) 除外责任(Exclusions)

(1) 第 4 条一般除外责任的内容与含义。

在任何情况下,ICC(A)不承保以下风险。

① 可归因于被保险人的恶意行为引起的灭失、损害或费用。值得注意的是,ICC 2009(A)中仅规定保险人对被保险人的恶意行为所致损失或费用不负赔偿责任,而没有规定归因于被保险人以外的其他人的恶意行为所致损失或费用不予负责。这就意味着在 ICC(A)条款下,类似船长、船员等的恶意行为,如沉船、纵火或任何形式的破坏所致的损失,保险人均需负责。ICC(A)的承保风险包括"恶意损害险"所承保的风险。

② 保险标的的自然渗漏、重量或容量的自然损耗或自然磨损。这些损失是由货物本质原因引起的,是意料之中的,因此列为除外责任,保险人不予赔偿。需要注意的是,对于原料或新制造产品的"自然磨损",保险人仍需负责;相反,二手货的"自然磨损"属除外责任范围。

③ 由于保险标的的包装或配装不足或不当引起的无法承受运输途中发生的通常的事故而产生的灭失、损害或费用。此种情况适用于:该包装或配装是由被保险人或其雇员完成的,或该包装或配装是在本保险责任开始前完成的。(本条所称的"包装",包括集装箱内的积载;本条所称的"雇员",不包括独立合同人。)

④ 保险标的的固有缺陷或特性导致的灭失、损害或费用。所谓固有缺陷或特性是指保险标的本身蕴藏或存在的瑕疵或本性,这种瑕疵或本性极易导致标的的受损。如保险货物为易燃品或易爆品,其本身在适当条件下极易引起损失。此类损失属于货物固有缺陷或特性而引起的,不属于保险承保范围。

⑤ 迟延引起的灭失、损害或费用,即该迟延由于承保风险所引起[但按照条款2(共同海损条款)的规定可以赔付的费用除外]。例如船舶由于搁浅而引起迟延,因迟延又引起货物品质受损,即使货物的损失起因于船舶搁浅,而搁浅属于承保风险范围,保险人对货物的损失及费用仍不负赔偿责任。如果迟延是非被保险人所能控制的原因而引起的,根据运输条款的规定,保险合同仍然有效,只是被保险人就该迟延造成的损失和费用不能请求保险人赔偿。但若因共同海损或救助而引起迟延,被保险人可请求保险人补偿在迟延期间其所分摊的任何费用。

⑥ 因船舶所有人、经理人、租船人或经营人破产或不履行债务导致的灭失、损害或费用。这一除外责任的目的在于防止或减少被保险人将货物交给有财务困难的承运人。与1982年条款相比,该款除外责任对保险人的免责有所限制,即保险人的免责情况仅适用于在保险标的装上船舶之时,被保险人知道或被保险人在正常业务经营中应当知道,此种破产或不履行债务会导致该航程被取消。此外,该款明确规定:本条除外条款不适用于当保险合同已经转让给另一方,即另一方已经善意购买或同意购买保险标的且受保险合同约束的情况。

⑦ 因使用任何原子或核子裂变和(或)聚变或其他类似反应或放射性力量或物质的武器或设备直接或间接导致的灭失、损害或费用。在 ICC 2009(A)下,保险人不仅对由于"敌对行为"使用原子或热核武器或设备等所致的损失和费用不负赔偿责任,而且对由于任何其他原因(包括实验)遭受原子或热核武器或设备等的袭击所致损失或费用也不负赔偿责任。此外,明确指出无论造成损失的原因是直接的还是间接的,都属于除外责任。

(1) The content and meaning of article 4 of the exclusions(general exclusions clause).

In no case shall ICC(A) cover the following risks.

①Loss, damage or expense attributable to willful misconduct of the assured. It is note worthy that ICC 2009(A) only excludes the insurer's liability for loss or expense arising out of the insured's malicious act, and does not provide for exclusion of liability for loss or expense arising out of a malicious act attributable to a person other than the insured. This means that under ICC(A), the insurer is liable for losses caused by malicious acts such as shipwreck, arson, or any form of sabotage by the captain or crew. In other words, the risks covered by ICC(A) include the risks covered by "malicious damage clause".

② Ordinary leakage, ordinary loss in weight or volume, or ordinary wear and tear of the subject-matter insured. These losses are caused by the essential causes of the goods, are expected and therefore classified as exclusions and not compensated by the insurer. It should be noted that the insurer is still liable for "ordinary wear and tear" of raw materials or newly manufactured products, whereas "ordinary wear and tear" of second-hand goods is the scope of exclusion.

③ Loss, damage or expense caused by insufficiency or unsuitability of packing or preparation of the subject-matter insured to withstand the ordinary incidents of the insured transit where such packing or preparation is carried out by the assured or their employees or prior to the attachment of this insurance (for the purpose of these clauses "packing" shall be deemed to include stowage in a container and "employees" shall not include independent contractors).

④ Loss, damage or expense caused by inherent vice or nature of the subject-matter insured. The so-called inherent vice or nature refers to a defect or characteristics inherent or present in the subject-matter insured itself, which is highly likely to cause damage to the subject matter. For example, if the insured goods are inflammable or explosive products, which are themselves highly likely to cause losses under appropriate conditions, such losses are caused by the inherent vice or nature of the goods themselves, and are not covered by the insurance.

⑤ Loss, damage or expense caused by delay, i. e. delay caused by a risk insured against (except expenses payable under general average clause above). For example, if a ship is delayed due to grounding, and the delay causes damage to the cargo, the insurer will not be liable for the loss of the cargo and its expenses, even if the loss of the cargo is caused by the grounding of the ship and the grounding is an insured risk. If the delay occurs for reasons beyond the control of the insured, the insurance contract remains in force under the terms of the transportation clause, except that the insured cannot claim indemnification from the insurer for losses and expenses caused by the delay. However, in the event of delay arising from general average or salvage, the insured may claim reimbursement from the insurer for its share of any costs incurred during the period of delay.

⑥ Loss，damage or expense caused by insolvency or financial default of the owners managers charterers or operators of the vessel. The purpose of this exclusion is to prevent or reduce the insured handing over the goods to a carrier in financial difficulty. In contrast to the 1982 version，this clause limits the insurer's exclusion to cases where，at the time the subject-matter insured was loaded on board the vessel，the insured knew，or the insured in the ordinary course of business should have known，that such insolvency or default would result in the cancellation of the voyage. In addition，the clause explicitly states："This exclusion shall not apply where the contract of insurance has been assigned to the party claiming hereunder who has bought or agreed to buy the subject-matter insured in good faith under a binding contract. "

⑦ Loss，damage or expense directly or indirectly caused by or arising from the use of any weapon or device employing atomic or nuclear fission and/or fusion or other like reaction or radioactive force or matter. Under ICC 2009(A)，the insurer is not liable not only for losses and expenses resulting from the use of atomic or thermonuclear weapons or device etc. as a result of a "hostile act"，but also for losses or expenses resulting from an attack on atomic or thermonuclear weapons or device，etc. for any other reason，including experimentation. In addition，it is made clear that the exclusion applies regardless of whether the cause of the loss is direct or indirect.

（2）第 5 条不适航和不适货除外责任的内容与含义。

第 5 条是关于"不适航与不适货"的除外责任规定。其内容是："5.1　本保险在任何情况下均不承保由于下述原因所致的灭失、损害或费用：被保险人在保险标的装船时已经知道船舶或驳船的不适航，及船舶或驳船不适合安全运输保险标的；在本保险合同生效前，装载已开始或已完成，或被保险人或其受雇人在装载时已经知道集装箱或运输工具不适合安全运输保险标的。5.2　上述第 1 款所述的除外条款不适用于：当保险合同已经善意转让给另一方，即另一方已经购买或同意购买保险标的且受合同约束。5.3　保险人放弃运载保险标的至目的地的船舶违反适航和船舶适货的任何默示保证。"

（2）The content and meaning of article 5 of the exclusions(unseaworthiness and unfitness exclusion clause).

Article 5 is on the "unseaworthy and unfitness of vessel or craft" exclusion. It reads："5.1 In no case shall this insurance cover loss damage or expense arising from：unseaworthiness of vessel or craft，or unfitness of vessel or craft for the safe carriage of the subject-matter insured，where the assured are privy to such unseaworthiness or unfitness，at the time the subject-matter insured is loaded therein；unfitness of container or conveyance for the safe carriage of the subject-matter insured，where loading therein or thereon is carried out prior to attachment of this insurance or by the assured or their employees and they are privy to such unfitness at the time of loading. 5.2 Exclusion above shall not apply where the contract of insurance has been assigned to the party claiming hereunder who has bought or agreed to buy the subject-matter insured in good faith under a binding contract. 5. 3 The insurers waive any breach of the implied warranties of seaworthiness of the ship and fitness of the ship to carry the subject-matter insured to destination. "

对于本条除外责任的理解应注意以下几项。

The following shall be noted in the understanding of this exclusion clause.

对条款 5.1 的理解：①ICC 2009 规定船舶与驳船、运输工具或集装箱都必须具有适航性和适货性，因此，对于因集装箱欠缺适货性所导致的货损，保险人同样可以拒绝赔偿。②与 ICC 1982 相比，ICC 2009 对于船舶或驳船的不适航只局限在被保险人的货方知情，而不再包括其受雇人(指直接受被保险人指挥的人)的知情。对于集装箱安全运载货物问题，在以下两种情况下的货损，保险人可拒赔：一是在运输开始前，发货人或卖方自己在仓库或工厂将货物装入集装箱，若其此时发现集装箱不适货但仍继续装货；二是由被保险人的受雇人负责装箱，并且对于集装箱的不适货知情。

Understanding of article 5. 1：① ICC 2009 stipulates that vessel and craft, conveyance, and containers must be seaworthy and cargo worthy, therefore, the insurer can also refuse to indemnify for cargo damage caused by unfitness of the container. ②In contrast to ICC 1982, ICC 2009 limits the unseaworthiness of a vessel or craft to the knowledge of the cargo party as the insured and no longer includes the knowledge of its employees (persons under the direct command of the insured). With regard to the safe carriage of goods in containers, the insurer may refuse to pay compensation for cargo damage under the following two circumstances：one is that the consignor or seller himself loads the goods into a container in a warehouse or factory before the commencement of the transportation, who then discovers that the container is not fit but continues to load the goods；the second is that the insured's employee is responsible for the loading of the container and has knowledge of the container's unfitness.

对条款 5.2 的理解：第 1 款除外责任不影响善意的第三者受让保险合同，即表明无辜的提单持有人，同时也是保单持有人不受影响。

Understanding of article 5. 2：the exclusion in article 5. 1 does not affect the assignment of the insurance contract to a bona fide third party, i. e. it shows that the innocent holder of the bill of lading, who is also the holder of the policy, is not affected.

对条款 5.3 的理解：与 ICC 1982 相比，ICC 2009 规定的保险人放弃运载保险标的至目的地的船舶违反适航和船舶适货的默示保证只局限在被保险人的货方知情，而不再包括其受雇人的知情，并且对不适航或不适货的知情只是针对装货的时候。

Understanding of clause 5. 3：compared with ICC 1982, the implied warranty of the insurer to waive the breach of seaworthiness and the fitness of the ship carrying the subject-matter insured to the place of destination under ICC 2009 is limited to the knowledge of the insured, and no longer includes the knowledge of its employees. And the knowledge of unseaworthiness or unfitness for cargo is only for the time of loading.

（3）第 6 条战争除外责任的内容与含义。

第 6 条是关于战争除外责任的规定，其内容是："本保险在任何情况下均不承保由于下述原因所致的灭失、损害或费用：6.1　战争、内战、革命、叛乱、暴乱，或由此引起的内乱，或来自交战方或针对交战方的任何敌对行为；6.2　捕获、扣押、扣留、管制或拘押（海盗除外），以及由此引起的后果或任何企图、威胁；6.3　丢弃的水雷、鱼雷、炸弹或其他被遗弃的战争武器。"根据本条款，海盗行为被排除在战争除外责任之外，也就是说投保 ICC（A）时，保险人对由于海盗行为造成的货物损失或费用支出负责赔偿。

（3）The content and meaning of article 6 of the exclusion (war exclusion clause).

Article 6，which deals with the war exclusion，reads："In no case shall this insurance cover loss, damage or expense caused by: 6.1 War, civil war, revolution, rebellion, insurrection, or civil strife arising therefrom, or any hostile act by or against a belligerent power; 6.2 Capture, seizure, arrest, restraint, or detainment (piracy excepted), and the consequences thereof or any attempt threat; 6.3 Derelict mines, torpedoes, bombs or other derelict weapons of war." Under this clause, piracy is excluded from the exclusion of war, which means that the insurer is responsible for compensation for loss or expense of goods due to piracy when the ICC(A) is insured.

（4）第 7 条罢工除外责任的内容与含义。

第 7 条是关于罢工除外责任的规定，其内容包括："本保险在任何情况下均不承保下述灭失、损害或费用：7.1　由罢工者、被迫停工工人或参与工潮、暴动或民众骚乱人员引起的；7.2　由罢工、被迫停工、工潮、暴动或民众骚乱结果引起的；7.3　由任何恐怖主义行为，或与恐怖主义行为相联系，任何组织通过暴力直接实施的旨在推翻或影响法律上承认的或非法律上承认的政府的行为引起的；7.4　由任何人出于政治、信仰或宗教目的实施的行为引起的。"

（4）The content and meaning of article 7 of the exclusion (strikes exclusion clause).

Article 7 is a strike exclusion which reads，" In no case shall this insurance cover loss, damage or expense：7.1 Caused by strikers, locked-out workmen, or persons taking part in labour disturbances, riots or civil commotions; 7.2 Resulting from strikes, lock-outs, labour disturbances, riots or civil commotions; 7.3 Caused by any act of terrorism being an act of any person acting on behalf of, or in connection with, any organization which carries out activities directed towards the overthrowing or influencing, by force or violence, of any government whether or not legally constituted; 7.4 Caused by any person acting from a political, ideological, or religious motive."

条款 7.1 和 7.2 适用近因原则，即货物灭失、损害或费用是直接由于罢工、停工等原因引起的才属于除外责任。条款 7.3 同样适用近因原则，该条款的目的在于将"反政府行为"的任何人所引起的灭失、损害或费用排除在承保范围之外。此外，该项规定所排除的不限于使用爆炸物，即使因恐怖主义者强占货物所导致的灭失、损害或费用也列为除外责任。条款 7.4 是 ICC 2009 新增加的规定，因此，该除外责任条款的范围比 ICC 1982 有所扩大。

Clauses 7. 1 and 7. 2 apply the principle of proximate cause, i. e. loss of, damage to, or expense of the goods is excluded only if it is directly caused by a strike, lockout, etc. The same principle of proximate cause applies to clause 7. 3, which is designed to exclude the loss, damage or expense caused by any person who commits an "anti-government act" from coverage. In addition, the exclusion from this provision is not limited to the use of explosives, as any loss, damage or expense resulting from the seizure of the goods by terrorists is excluded. Clause 7. 4 is a new addition to ICC 2009 and, as such, the scope of this exclusion has been expanded from ICC 1982.

3) 保险期间(Duration)

ICC 2009 对保险期间的规定包括三个条款,分别是运输条款、运输合同终止条款和航程变更条款。

扩展阅读 11.3　英国协会货物条款-ICC 2009 除外责任的新变化

The ICC 2009 regulation of the insurance period includes three clauses, namely transit clause, termination of contract of carriage clause, and change of voyage clause.

(1) 运输条款。运输条款规定的是保险责任的开始、持续和终止的条件。它和我国的《海洋运输货物保险条款》基本一致,均以"仓至仓"为限。根据该条款,保险责任的开始和终止有以下几种情况。

(1) Transit clause. The transit clause stipulates the conditions for the commencement, continuation and termination of insurance liability. It is basically the same with China's *Ocean Marine Cargo Clauses*, which is limited to "warehouse to warehouse". According to this clause, there are several conditions for the commencement and termination of insurance liability.

保险责任自保险标的在仓库或储存地(本保险合同载明的地点)首次移动,以便立即搬运至运输车辆或其他运输工具开始运输之时起生效,包括正常运输过程,直至运到下述地点时终止:①在本保险合同载明的目的地最后仓库或储存处所,从运输车辆或其他运输工具完成卸货;②在本保险合同载明的目的地任何其他仓库或储存处所,或在中途任何其他仓库或储存处所,从运输车辆或其他运输工具完成卸货,上述任何其他仓库或储存处所是由被保险人或其受雇人选择,用于在正常运送过程之外储存货物,或分配货物,或分派货物;③被保险人或其受雇人在正常运输过程之外选择任何运输车辆或其他运输工具或任何集装箱储存货物;④保险标的在最后卸货港卸离海轮满 60 天为止。上述情况以先发生者为准。其中,终点③是 ICC 2009 新增的,目的是限制被保险人或其受雇人在非正常运输过程中的临时仓储。

This insurance attaches from the time the subject-matter insured is first moved in the warehouse or at the place of storage (at the place named in the contract of insurance) for the purpose of the immediate loading into or onto the carrying vehicle or other conveyance for the commencement of transit, continues during the ordinary course of transit and terminates either: ①on completion of unloading from the carrying vehicle or other conveyance in or at the final warehouse or place of storage at the destination named in the contract of insurance；②on completion of unloading from the carrying vehicle or other conveyance in or at any other warehouse or place of storage，whether prior to or at the destination named in the contract of insurance，which the assured or their employees elect to use either for storage other than in the ordinary course of transit or for allocation or distribution；③when the assured or their employees elect to use any carrying vehicle or other conveyance or any container for storage other than in the ordinary course of transit；④on the expiry of 60 days after completion of discharge overside of the subject-matter insured from the oversea vessel at the final port of discharge，whichever shall first occur. Among them，endpoint ③ was added by ICC 2009 to restrict the use of temporary storage by the insured or its employees in the course of abnormal transportation.

如果保险标的在最后卸货港卸离海轮后，但本保险责任终止前，需被转运至非保单载明的其他目的地，该保险在依然受上述四项有关终止规定制约的同时，截止于该项保险标的为向该其他目的地转运而开始搬移之时。

If，after discharge overside from the oversea vessel at the final port of discharge，but prior to termination of this insurance，the subject-matter insured is to be forwarded to a destination other than that to which it is insured，this insurance，whilst remaining subject to termination as provided in the above clauses，shall not extend beyond the time the subject-matter insured is first moved for the purpose of the commencement of transit to such other destination.

此外，本条款规定：在被保险人无法控制任何运输迟延、任何绕航、被迫卸货、重新装载、转运以及承运人运用运输合同授予的权力所做的任何航海上的变更的情况下，保险单仍然有效。这一点和我国《海洋运输货物保险条款》不同，我国的条款规定，如果出现上述情况，被保险人应该立即通知保险人，并在必要时加缴保险费。

This insurance shall remain in force during delay beyond the control of the assured，and in the case of any deviation，forced discharge，reshipment or transhipment and during any variation of the adventure arising from the exercise of a liberty granted to carriers under the contract of carriage. This is different from the terms of China's *Ocean Marine Cargo Clauses*，which stipulates that in case of the above-mentioned situation，the insured should immediately notify the insurer and pay additional premium if necessary.

（2）运输合同终止条款。本条规定，如果因被保险人不能控制的情况，运输合同在保险单载明的目的地以外的港口或地点终止，或运输在保险标的按照上述运输条款规定卸载前而终止，则本保险也将终止，除非被保险人于获悉后立即通知保险人，请求延长保险责任期间，并在必要时加缴保险费，保险责任在下列情况下继续有效：①直至保险标的在该港口或地点出售，或除非另有约定，在保险标的抵达该港口或地点后满 60 天，两者以先发生者为准；②若保险标的在上述 60 天（或任何约定的延长期限）内，继续运往保险合同载明的目的地或任何其他目的地，则保险责任仍按上述运输条款的规定终止。

该条款的规定与我国《海洋运输货物保险条款》的规定是一致的。

（2）Termination of contract of carriage clause. This clause provides that if owing to circumstances beyond the control of the assured either the contract of carriage is terminated at a port or place other than the destination named therein or the transit is otherwise terminated before unloading of the subject-matter insured as provided for in the above clause, then this insurance shall also terminate unless prompt notice is given to the insurers and continuation of cover is requested when this insurance shall remain in force, subject to an additional premium if required by the insurers, either: ①until the subject-matter insured is sold and delivered at such port or place, or, unless otherwise specially agreed, until the expiry of 60 days after arrival of the subject-matter insured at such port or place, whichever shall first occur; ② if the subject-matter insured is forwarded within the said period of 60 days（or any agreed extension thereof）to the destination named in the contract of insurance or to any other destination, until terminated in accordance with the provisions of the above clause.

The provisions of this clause are consistent with the provisions of China's *Ocean Marine Cargo Clauses*.

（3）航程变更条款。航程变更条款规定,保险责任开始后,被保险人变更目的地,必须立即通知保险人,并另行商定保险费率和条件。在此费率和条件达成一致前,若发生保险事故,在保险费率和保险条件符合合理的商业市场行情情况下,保险仍然有效。

（3）Change of voyage clause. This clause provides that after attachment of this insurance, if the destination is changed by the assured, this must be notified promptly to insurers for rates and terms to be agreed. Should a loss occur prior to such agreement being obtained cover may be provided but only if cover would have been available at a reasonable commercial market rate on reasonable market terms.

当保险标的按照保险合同的航程规定开始航行时,被保险人或其受雇人对该船舶驶向另一目的地不知情,则仍然被视为在保险合同规定的航程开始时生效。

Where the subject-matter insured commences the transit contemplated by this insurance, but, without the knowledge of the assured or their employees the ship sails for another destination, this insurance will nevertheless be deemed to have attached at commencement of such transit.

可以看出,该条款允许被保险人在及时通知保险人并另行缴费的前提下变更目的地。而我国《海洋运输货物保险条款》规定,若航程有所变更,被保险人应在获悉后立即通知保险人,并在必要时加缴保险费,保险合同继续有效。显然,这一规定与 ICC(A) 是有区别的。

It can be seen that the clause allows the insured to change the destination with timely notification to the insurer and separate payment of premium. In contrast, China's *Ocean Marine Cargo Clauses* provide that if the voyage is changed, the insured shall notify the insurer immediately upon learning of the change and pay additional premium if necessary, and the insurance contract shall remain in force. Obviously, there is a difference between this provision and ICC（A）.

4）索赔（Claims）

现行《协会货物条款》中，有关索赔的规定主要反映在"可保利益""续运费""推定全损"和"增值"等条款中。

In the current *Institute Cargo Clause*, the claims provisions are mainly reflected in the "Insurable Interest""Forwarding Charges""Constructive Total Loss" and "Increased Value" clauses.

（1）可保利益条款。ICC 2009 第 11 条关于可保利益的规定是："11.1　在保险标的发生损失时，被保险人必须对保险标的具有可保利益，才能获得本保险的赔偿。11.2　被保险人有权按照上款的规定，对本保险期间内发生的承保范围内的损失获得赔偿，即使损失发生在本保险合同订立之前，但在保险合同订立时被保险人已经知道损失发生，而保险人并不知晓者除外。"

（1）Insurable interest clause. Article 11 of ICC 2009 on insurable interest provides："11.1 In order to recover under this insurance the assured must have an insurable interest in the subject-matter insured at the time of the loss. 11.2 Subject to clause 11.1 above, the assured shall be entitled to recover for insured loss occurring during the period covered by this insurance, notwithstanding that the loss occurred before the contract of insurance was concluded, unless the assured were aware of the loss and the insurers were not."

根据本条款的规定，被保险人在订立保险合同时对保险标的（货物）可以没有可保利益，但在货物发生损失时则必须具有可保利益，才能获得保险赔偿。同时，若在保险合同订立之前，保险标的已经发生损失，但在订立保险合同时被保险人对此并不知情，仍然与保险人订立保险合同，在这种情况下，被保险人仍可获得赔偿。

According to the provisions of this clause, the insured may have no insurable interest in the subject-matter insured（the goods）at the time of the conclusion of the insurance contract, but must have an insurable interest in the event of loss of the goods in order to obtain insurance compensation. At the same time, if the loss of the subject-matter insured has already occurred before the conclusion of the insurance contract, but the insured did not know about it at the time of the conclusion of the contract and still concluded it with the insurer, in this case, the insured can still receive compensation.

（2）续运费条款。该条款规定："由于本保险承保的风险，致使保险运输在非保险单载明的港口或处所终止，保险人应偿付被保险人在卸货、存仓和续运保险标的物至保险单载明的目的地时适当而合理产生的任何额外费用。"同时该条款还规定，本条不适用共同海损和救助费，须受上述第 4、5、6 和 7 条款所包含的除外责任的约束，但不包括因被保险人或其雇员的过失、疏忽、破产或不履行债务而引起的费用。

（2）Forwarding charges clause. This clause provides that："As a result of the operation of a risk covered by this insurance, the insured transit is terminated at a port or place other than that to which the subject-matter insured is covered under this insurance, the insurers will reimburse the assured for any extra charges properly and reasonably incurred in unloading storing and forwarding the subject-matter insured to the destination to which it is insured. " It is also provided that this clause does not apply to general average and salvage charges，shall be subject to the exclusions contained in clauses 4，5，6 and 7 above，and shall not include charges arising from the fault negligence insolvency or financial default of the assured or their employees.

（3）推定全损条款。本条款规定："本保险不负推定全损责任，除非保险标的的实际全损看起来不可避免，或恢复、修复和续运保险标的至保险目的地的费用将超过其抵达时保险标的本身的价值，经对保险标的的合理委付的情况下，可按推定全损赔偿。"

（3）Constructive total loss clause. This clause states that："No claim for constructive total loss shall be recoverable hereunder unless the subject-matter insured is reasonably abandoned either on account of its actual total loss appearing to be unavoidable or because the cost of recovering，reconditioning and forwarding the subject-matter insured to the destination to which it is insured would exceed its value on arrival. "

（4）增值条款。增值条款是货物在投保增值保险的情况下对有关赔偿问题的规定。所谓增值保险是指买方估计所买进的货物在到达目的地时的完好价值将比卖方投保原始保险的金额要高，而将两者之间的估计差额另行投保（一般在原保险单基础上按原保险条件投保）的保险。为此，ICC 2009 第 14 条规定，若被保险人对保险标的的办理了增值保险，保险标的的约定价值应视为原保险金额和增值部分的保险金额两者之和。当保险标的发生损失时，若为全损，保险人将赔偿两者之和；若为部分损失，保险人按其保险金额占总保险金额的比例承担赔偿责任。该条款还规定，在增值保险下，若被保险人提出索赔，则应向保险人提供所有其他保险的所保金额的证据。

（4）Increased value clause. The increased value clause is a provision for compensation in the event that the goods are insured for increased value insurance. Increased value insurance is an insurance policy in which the buyer estimates that the value of the purchased goods intact at the time of arrival at destination will be higher than the amount insured by the seller under the original insurance，and the estimated difference between the two is insured separately (generally on the basis of the original policy and under the original terms of insurance). To this end，article 14 of ICC 2009 provides that if any increased value insurance is effected by the assured on the cargo insured，the agreed value of the cargo shall be deemed to be increased to the total amount insured under this insurance，and all increased value insurance covering the loss and liability under this insurance shall be in such proportion as the sum insured bears to such total amount insured. When a loss occurs to the subject-matter insured，the insurer will pay the sum of the two if it is a total loss; if it is a partial loss，the insurer will be liable for the proportion of its insured amount to the total insured amount. The clause also states that in the event of claim，the assured shall provide the underwriters with evidence of the amount insured under all other insurances.

5）保险利益（Benefit of Insurance）

ICC 2009（A）第15条规定："本保险保障被保险人，包括根据本保险合同提出索赔的人或收货人；除非有特别说明，承运人或其他受托人不得享受本保险的利益。"该条第1款是新增加的，将被保险人的范围扩大到包括收货人。第2款是保留的旧条款，目的是避免承运人或其他受托人因有保险存在而享有保险利益并因此来摆脱对货损、货差或延迟交货的责任，从而使保险人丧失代位追偿权。

Article 15 of ICC 2009（A）states："This insurance covers the assured which includes the person claiming indemnity either as the person by or on whose behalf the contract of insurance was effected or as an assignee, shall not extend to or otherwise benefit the carrier or other bailee." Sub-clause 1 of this clause is a new addition, extending the scope of the insured to include the consignee. Sub-clause 2 is an old clause retained to prevent the carrier or other bailee from enjoying the benefit of insurance by virtue of the existence of the insurance and thereby freeing itself from liability for loss, difference or delay in delivery of the goods, thereby depriving the insurer of its right of subrogation.

6）减少损失（Minimising Losses）

ICC 2009第16条"减少损失"中规定了"被保险人义务"条款和"弃权"条款。

Article 16 of ICC 2009,"Minimising Losses", provides for "duty of assured" clause and "waiver" clause.

"被保险人义务"规定：当保险标的发生承保范围内的损失时，被保险人、其受雇人和代理人有下述义务：采取为避免或减少此种损失的合理措施，并且确保对承运人、受托人或其他第三方追偿的所有权利被适当维护和行使。保险人将在赔偿承保责任范围内的任何损失外，还负责赔偿被保险人履行上述义务所产生的任何适当与合理的费用。

"Duty of assured" provides：it is the duty of the assured and their employees and agents in respect of loss recoverable hereunder to take such measures as may be reasonable for the purpose of averting or minimizing such loss, and to ensure that all rights against carriers, bailees or other third parties are properly preserved and exercised and the insurers will, in addition to any loss recoverable hereunder, reimburse the assured for any charges properly and reasonably incurred in pursuance of these duties.

ICC 2009在第17条制定了"弃权"条款。该条款规定：被保险人或保险人为了施救、保护或恢复保险标的所采取的措施，不应视为放弃或接受委付的表示，或视为影响任何一方的权益。本条款的目的一方面是鼓励被保险人积极施救，另一方面是不得将施救措施视作放弃或接受委付。

ICC 2009 has a "waiver" clause in article 17. This provision states that：measures taken by the assured or the insurers with the object of saving, protecting or recovering the subject-matter insured shall not be considered as a waiver or acceptance of abandonment or otherwise prejudice the rights of either party.

7）防止迟延（Avoidance of Delay）

本条是为了提醒被保险人履行其义务，因此规定被保险人应在所有其控制的情况下，采取合理迅速的措施加以处理。

This clause is intended to remind the assured of its obligations and therefore provides that the assured shall act with reasonable dispatch in all circumstances within their control.

8）法律与惯例（Law and Practice）

本条款规定本保险受英国法律和惯例约束。其目的是以英国法律作为 ICC 的准据法。但应注意，保险合同究竟应以哪国法律为准据法，则以保险单规定为优先考虑。

This clause provides that this insurance is subject to English law and practice. It is intended that English law shall be the governing law of ICC. It should be noted，however，that the law of the country in which the insurance contract is to be governed should take precedence over the provisions of the insurance policy.

2. ICC 2009（B）条款的主要内容[Main Contents of ICC 2009（B）]

1）承保风险（Risks Covered）

ICC（B）承保的责任范围比 ICC（A）小，它采用列明风险的方式，将所承保的风险逐一列明。其对下述原因所导致的保险标的的损失和损害负责赔偿：

（1）火灾或爆炸；

（2）船舶或驳船触礁、搁浅、沉没或倾覆；

（3）陆上运输工具倾覆或出轨；

（4）船舶、驳船或运输工具同水以外的其他任何外界物体碰撞或触碰；

（5）在避难港卸货；

（6）地震、火山爆发或雷电。

ICC（B） covers a smaller scope of liability than ICC（A），and it uses a "list the risks" approach to specify each of the risks it covers. This insurance covers loss of or damage to the subject-matter insured reasonable attributable to：

（1）Fire or explosion；

（2）Vessel or craft being stranded，grounded，sunk or capsized；

（3）Overturning or derailment of land conveyance；

（4）Collision or contact of vessel craft or conveyance with any external object other than water；

（5）Discharge of cargo at a port of distress；

（6）Earthquake，volcanic eruption or lightning。

它还承保由于下列原因造成的保险标的损失：

（1）共同海损牺牲；

（2）投弃（或抛货）或浪击落海；

（3）海水、湖水或河水进入船舶、驳船、运输工具、集装箱或储存处所；

（4）货物在装卸船舶或驳船时落海或跌落造成的整件全损。

It also covers loss of or damage to the subject-matter insured caused by：

（1）General average sacrifice；

（2）Jettison or washing overboard；

（3）Entry of sea lake or river water into vessel craft hold，conveyance，container，liftvan or place of storage；

（4）Total loss of any package lost overboard or dropped whilst loading on to，or unloading from，vessel or craft.

此外,保险人还承保共同海损分摊和救助费用。英国 1906 年《海上保险法》规定,保险人仅对保险事故所引起的共同海损负赔偿责任；ICC(A)、ICC(B)、ICC(C)进一步规定保险人对所有共同海损的分摊额均应负责,但属于除外责任者不在此限。

This insurance covers general average contribution and salvage charges. The UK *Marine Insurance Act* 1906 provides that the insurer is liable only for general average arising out of an insured accident；ICC(A)，ICC(B) and ICC(C) further provide that the insurer is liable for all contribution of general average，except for those falling within the exclusions.

由此可见,ICC(B)主要承保自然灾害和意外事故所致的损失,以及共同海损的牺牲、分摊和救助费用。与我国《海洋运输货物保险条款》中的水渍险相比,首先,ICC(B)明确将承保风险扩大到陆上,对发生在保险期内的陆上运输工具的意外倾覆、出轨予以负责。其次,凡海水、湖水或河水进入船舱、驳船、集装箱、运输工具或储存处所而造成的货物损失均在承保范围内。而且,只要有海水等进入船舱等而导致货物损失的事实,不论其是否因保险事故所致,保险人都予以赔偿。此外,ICC(B)承保货物在装卸船舶或驳船时落海或跌落造成的整件全损,这与水渍险的规定有所区别。

It can be seen that ICC(B) mainly covers losses caused by natural calamities and accidents，as well as the sacrifice，contribution of general average and salvage charges. Compared with WPA in China's *Ocean Marine Cargo Clauses*，firstly，ICC (B) explicitly extends the scope of cover to land and is responsible for accidental overturning and derailment of land conveyance occurring during the insurance period. Secondly，any loss of cargo caused by entry of sea lake or river water into vessel craft hold，conveyance，container，liftvan or place of storage is covered. In addition，ICC(B) covers a total loss of the entire package lost overboard or dropped while being loaded on to or unloaded from a ship or craft，which is different from the provisions of WPA.

2）除外责任(Exclusions)

ICC(B)的除外责任和 ICC(A)大致相同,但有两点区别。

（1）ICC(A)的除外责任规定,保险人仅对被保险人的故意不法行为所致损失和费用不负赔偿责任,而 ICC(B)增加了"由于任何个人或数个人的不法行为故意损坏或故意破坏保险标的或其任何部分"的规定,这意味着在 ICC(B)下,保险人不但对被保险人的蓄意不法行为所致的损失不负责任,对任何其他人的故意非法行为所致损失也不负责任。因此,在 ICC(B)下,要获得此种风险的保障,则需加保"恶意损害险"。

（2）ICC（B）的"战争除外责任"中没有像 ICC（A）那样明确将海盗风险从除外责任中剔除，但也未将其列入承保风险。由于 ICC（B）采取列明风险的方法确定承保风险，因而，"海盗行为"属于其除外责任。

The exclusions clause of ICC(B) is substantially the same as ICC(A), but with two differences.

（1）The exclusions of ICC (A) provides that the insurer is not liable only for loss, damage or expense attributable to wilful misconduct of the assured, while ICC (B) adds the provision of "Deliberate damage to or deliberate destruction of the subject-matter insured or any part thereof by the wrongful act of any person or persons", which means that under ICC(B), the insurer is not liable not only for loss caused by the intentional wrongful act of the insured, but also for loss caused by the intentional unlawful act of any other person. Therefore, in order to be covered under ICC(B) for such risks, it is necessary to add "malicious damage clause".

（2）The "war exclusion clause" in ICC(B) does not explicitly exclude the risk of piracy from the exclusion as it does in ICC(A), but it does not include it as a covered risk either. Since ICC (B) takes a risk-based approach to determining the risks covered, "piracy" falls under its exclusion.

3）其他内容（Other Contents）

ICC（B）关于保险期间、索赔、保险利益、减少损失等条款的规定和其他内容在字面上与 ICC（A）相同。

The provisions of ICC (B) regarding duration, claims, benefit of insurance, minimizing losses and other elements are literally the same as ICC (A).

3. ICC 2009（C）条款的主要内容[Main Contents of ICC 2009（C）]

ICC（C）条款是《协会货物条款》中保险人责任范围最小的条款，其承保范围也是采取逐一列明的方式。

ICC(C) is the clause with the smallest scope of insurer's liability in *Institute Cargo Clause*, and its coverage is also on an itemized basis.

1）承保风险（Risks Covered）

保险人对下列原因造成的保险标的的损失负责：

（1）火灾或爆炸；

（2）船舶或驳船触礁、搁浅、沉没或倾覆；

（3）陆上运输工具倾覆或出轨；

（4）船舶、驳船或运输工具同水以外的其他任何外界物体碰撞或触碰；

（5）在避难港卸货；

（6）共同海损牺牲；

（7）投弃（或抛货）。

此外，保险人对非除外风险所致的共同海损的分摊和救助费用负责赔偿。

The insurer is responsible for damage to the subject-matter insured caused by:

（1）Fire or explosion；

（2）Vessel or craft being stranded grounded sunk or capsized；

（3）Overturning or derailment of land conveyance；

（4）Collision or contact of vessel craft or conveyance with any external object other than water；

（5）Discharge of cargo at a port of distress；

（6）General average sacrifice；

（7）Jettison.

可见 ICC（C）的承保范围比 ICC（B）更小，主要承保"重大意外事故"所致的损失以及共同海损和救助费用。ICC（C）未将地震、火山爆发、雷电列入承保风险范围，说明对自然灾害造成的损失全部不予负责。原则上不承保海水进入船舶所造成货物的损失，因而海水进入船舶不在承保范围，但下列情况除外：①载货船舶或驳船因搁浅、触礁、沉没或倾覆而进水，导致货物损失，其间有合理归因关系；②货物损失可合理归因于船舶、驳船与外界物体碰撞或接触而发生的进水；③货物直接因共同海损或投弃而造成的损失。此外，ICC（C）对于浪击落海与吊索损害也不予赔偿。

与我国《海洋运输货物保险条款》中的平安险相比，ICC（C）的承保风险范围显然较小。

It can be seen that ICC（C）has a smaller coverage than ICC（B），mainly covering losses caused by "major accidents" as well as general average and salvage charges. ICC（C）does not include earthquakes，volcanic eruptions，or lightning in its coverage，indicating that it is not responsible for all losses caused by natural calamities. Loss of cargo caused by entry of sea water into vessel is not covered in principle，except in the following cases：① the entry of water into a laden ship or craft due to stranding，grounding，sinking or capsizing，resulting in loss of cargo，for which there is a reasonable relationship of attribution；②the loss of cargo is reasonably attributable to water intake resulting from a collision or contact between a ship or barge and other object；③loss of goods as a direct result of general average or jettison. In addition，ICC（C）does not provide compensation for washing overboard and sling loss.

Compared with FPA of *Ocean Marine Cargo Clause*，the scope of cover of ICC（C）is obviously smaller.

扩展阅读11.4　伦敦保险协会货物保险条款

2）其他内容（Other Contents）

ICC（C）关于除外责任、保险期间、索赔、减少损失等条款的规定和其他内容在文字上与 ICC（B）完全一致。

The provisions of ICC（C）regarding exclusions，duration，claims，minimizing losses and other elements are textually identical to ICC（B）.

11.2.3　《协会货物条款》其他保险条款（Other Insurance Clauses of *Institute Cargo Clauses*）

1. 协会海运货物战争险条款［Institute War Clause（Cargo）］

协会海运货物战争险条款由八项组成，除"承保风险""除外责任"和"保险期间"三项外,其他五项都与 A、B、C 条款内容完全相同。因其具有完整的结构体系,所以可以独立投保。

Institute war clause (cargo) consists of eight items, except for three items, namely "risks covered", "exclusions" and "duration", the other five items are exactly the same as the content of clauses A, B and C. Since it has a complete structure, it can be insured independently.

1) 承保风险(Risks Covered)

协会海运货物战争险条款主要承保由下列原因造成的保险标的损失或损害:

(1) 战争、内战、革命、叛乱、造反或由此引起的内乱,或交战方之间的任何敌对行为;

(2) 由上述承保风险引起的捕获、拘留、扣留、禁制或羁押及其后果,或任何进行此种行为的企图;

(3) 被遗弃的水雷、鱼雷、炸弹或其他被遗弃的战争武器;

(4) 上述原因导致的共同海损和救助费用。

上述承保风险中不包括海盗行为所造成的损失,这一点与中国现行海运货物战争险条款的规定不同。

This insurance covers loss of or damage to the subject-matter insured caused by:

(1) War, civil war, revolution, rebellion, insurrection, or civil strife arising therefrom, or any hostile act by or against a belligerent power;

(2) Capture, seizure, arrest, restraint, or detainment, arising from above covered risks, and the consequences thereof or any attempt threat;

(3) Derelict mines torpedoes bombs or other derelict weapons of war;

(4) General average and salvage charges resulting from the above causes.

Losses caused by acts of piracy are not included in the above covered risks, which is different from the provisions of China's current ocean marine cargo war risk.

2) 除外责任(Exclusions)

在除外责任方面,战争险与 A 条款的第 4 条和第 5 条的规定基本相同,但在第 4 条中增加了一个"航程挫折"条款,规定由于战争原因造成航程中止,货物未能到达保险单所载明的目的地而引起的间接损失,保险人不负赔偿责任。此外,战争险除外责任还规定:由于敌对行为使用原子或热核武器所致灭失或损害不负赔偿责任。也就是说,协会海运货物战争险承保原子或热核武器的非敌对性使用(如试验)而造成的保险标的的损失。

In terms of exclusions, war clause is basically the same as clause 4 and 5 of ICC (A). However, a "voyage frustration" clause has been added to clause 4, which provides that the insurer shall not be liable for consequential loss caused by the suspension of the voyage due to war and the failure of the goods to reach the destination stated in the insurance policy. In addition, exclusions of war clause provide that this insurance does not cover loss, damage or expense arising from any hostile use of any weapon of war employing atomic or nuclear fission and/or fusion or other like reaction or radioactive force or matter. In other words, institute war clause covers loss of the subject-matter insured resulting from the non-hostile use (e. g. , testing) of atomic or thermonuclear weapons.

3）保险期间（Duration）

协会战争险的保险期间涉及“运输条款”和“航程变更条款”。其中，航程变更条款的内容与协会货物 A、B、C 保险条款是一致的，而运输条款内容有较大变化。协会战争险关于保险期间的规定主要包括以下几个方面。

Duration clause of institute war clause involves "transit clause" and "change of voyage clause". The contents of the "change of voyage clause" are the same as ICC(A), ICC(B) and ICC(C) while the contents of the "transit clause" have changed significantly. The provisions on the period of insurance of institute war clause mainly include the following aspects.

（1）保险期限以“水上危险”为限，而不采取“仓至仓”原则，亦即保险责任自货物装上海轮时开始，直到卸离海轮时为止，如果载货海轮到达最后港口或卸货港口当日午夜算起满 15 天仍未从海轮卸下货物，保险责任亦告终止。

（1）The insurance period is limited to "waterborne risk", instead of "warehouse to warehouse" principle, that is, the insurance liability starts from the time the goods are loaded onto the oversea vessel until the time they are discharged from the vessel, and the insurance liability will be terminated if the goods have not been discharged from the vessel for 15 days from the midnight of the day when the vessel arrives at the last port or the port of discharge.

（2）当保险责任中途终止时，如果货物继续运往保险单载明的目的地，通过支付保险人所要求的额外保险费，自续运开始后，保险单可以重新恢复效力。

（2）When the insurance liability is terminated in transit, the policy may be reinstated from the commencement of the renewal if the goods continue to be transported to the destination stated in the insurance policy, by paying the additional premium required by the insurer.

（3）对于在装货港码头与海轮之间以及在海轮与卸货港码头之间需经驳船转运的货物，保险人仅对已装载驳船上的、由于驳船触及水雷或遗弃鱼雷而致损失的货物负赔偿责任。同时，除非另有协议，保险人对从海轮上卸入驳船的货物的承保期限为 60 天。

（3）The insurer is only liable for the loss of cargo loaded on the barge due to the barge hitting a mine or abandoning torpedo between the loading port terminal and the oversea vessel and between the oversea vessel and the unloading port terminal via barge. Also, unless otherwise agreed, the insurer's liability for cargo discharged from the seagoing vessel to the barge is limited to 60 days.

协会的该条规定同我国海运货物战争险的规定有很大不同。按照我国条款的规定，保险人在海运战争险中对装在驳船上驳运货物所承担的保险责任及保险期间同装在海轮上的货物所承担的保险责任及保险期间是相同的。

This provision of ICC is very different from the provision of China's ocean marine cargo war risks. According to the provisions of China, the insurer's liability and insurance period for cargoes loaded on barges in ocean marine cargo war risk is the same as the liability and insurance period for cargoes loaded on seagoing vessels.

扩展阅读 11.5　英国保险协会战争险（货物）保险合同条款

2. 协会海运货物罢工险条款〔Institute Strike Clause（Cargo）〕

1）承保风险（Risks Covered）

协会海运货物罢工险的承保风险同我国海运货物罢工险一样，也仅负责由于罢工等风险所直接造成的保险标的的物质损失，而不负责由于罢工等风险所产生的费用或间接损失。协会海运货物罢工险的承保风险包括：

（1）罢工者、被迫停工工人，或参与工潮、暴动或民变的人员所造成的保险标的的灭失或损害；

（2）恐怖分子或出于政治动机而行为的人员引起的保险标的的灭失或损害；

（3）根据运输合同、准据法和惯例理算或确定的共同海损和救助费用，其产生是为了避免任何原因造成的损失或与避免任何原因造成的损失有关。

Institute strike clause covers the same risks as China's ocean marine cargo strike clause, and is only responsible for the physical loss of the subject-matter insured directly caused by the strike risk, but not for the costs or consequential losses arising from the strike risk. This insurance covers loss of or damage to the subject-matter insured caused by：

（1）strikers, locked-out workmen, or persons taking part in labour disturbances, riots or civil commotions；

（2）any terrorist or any person action from a political motive；

（3）general average and salvage charges, adjusted or determined according to the contract of affreightment and/or the governing law and practice, incurred to avoid or in connection with the avoidance of loss from a risk covered under these clauses.

从上述承保风险可以看出，协会海运货物罢工险的承保风险大大超出了罢工的范围。它除了负责罢工风险损失外，对于工潮、民变以及恐怖主义者或出于政治目的采取行动的人所致风险损失也予以负责。

As can be seen from the risks covered above, institute strike clause covers risks that go well beyond strikes. It is responsible for losses from strike risks, but also for losses from labor unrest, civil commotion, and risks caused by terrorists or persons acting for political purposes.

2）除外责任（Exclusions）

罢工险的除外责任也与 A 条款的第 4 条和第 5 条的规定基本相同。但由于罢工险只负责由于承保风险直接造成的损失，因此，下列损失和费用保险人不负责赔偿：

（1）由于罢工、停工、工潮、暴动或民变造成的各种劳动力缺乏、短少或扣押引起的损失、损害或费用；

（2）由于航程挫折而引起的损失；

（3）由于战争、内战、革命、叛乱或由此引起的内乱，或交战国或针对交战国的任何敌对行为所造成的损失或费用。

The exclusions of strike clause are also essentially the same as those provided in clauses 4 and 5 of ICC(A). However, since strike clause is only responsible for losses directly caused by a covered risk, the insurer is not responsible for the following losses and expenses.

（1）loss damage or expense arising from the absence, shortage or withholding of labour of any description whatsoever resulting from any strike, lockout, labour disturbance, riot or civil commotion；

（2）any claim based upon loss of or frustration of the voyage or adventure；

（3）loss, damage or expense caused by war, civil war, revolution, rebellion insurrection, or civil strife arising therefrom, or any hostile act by or against a belligerent power.

扩展阅读 11.6
INSTITUTE-
STRIKE-CLAUSE-
(CARGO)

3）保险期间（Duration）

协会海运货物罢工险的保险期间与 A、B、C 条款一样，采用"仓至仓"原则，即保险人对货物从卖方仓库到买方仓库的整个运输期间负保险责任。

The insurance period of the institute strike clause is the same as that of ICC(A), ICC(B) and ICC(C), using the "warehouse to warehouse" principle, i. e. the insurer is liable for the entire period of transportation of the goods from the seller's warehouse to the buyer's warehouse.

11.2.4 协会货物附加险条款（Additional Insurance Clause of *Institute Cargo Clause*）

1. 协会货物恶意损害险（Institute Malicious Damage Clause）

协会货物恶意损害险条款作为补充性的条款，于 1983 年 8 月 1 日开始使用。由于没有完整的结构，其不能单独投保，只能在基本险基础上加保使用。

Institute malicious damage clause was introduced as a supplementary clause on August 1, 1983. Since there is no complete structure, it cannot be insured separately and can only be used in addition to the basic insurance.

协会货物恶意损害险承保的是被保险人以外的其他人（如船长、船员等）的故意破坏行为所致被保险货物的灭失或损害。出于政治动机的人的行为造成的损失不属于本险别的承保风险，但可以在罢工险条款中得到保障。

Institute malicious damage clause covers loss of or damage to the insured cargo caused by the intentional act of sabotage by someone other than the insured (e. g. captain, crew, etc.). However, losses caused by the actions of politically motivated persons are not a covered risk under this clause but may be covered under the strike clause.

恶意损害的风险,除了在 ICC(A)中被列为承保风险外,在 ICC(B)和 ICC(C)中均列为除外责任。因此,在投保 ICC(B)和 ICC(C)时,如果被保险人需要对这种风险取得保险保障,则需另行加保"恶意损害险"。

The risk of malicious damage, in addition to being a covered risk under ICC(A), is excluded under ICC(B) and ICC(C). Therefore, if the insured needs to obtain insurance coverage for this risk under ICC(B) and ICC(C), he/she will need to take out a separate "malicious damage clause".

2. 偷窃、提货不着险(Institute Theft, Pilferage and Non-delivery Clause)

偷窃、提货不着险与协会货物恶意损害险一样,在投保 ICC(A)时无须加保。本条款承保两类风险:一是偷窃,二是提货不着。所谓"偷"是指海上袭击性偷窃,须伴有暴力或暴力威胁,不包括暗中的小偷小摸。而"窃"指暗中进行的小偷小摸。提货不着指由于任何不明原因造成整件货物不知去向,或者误交给不知姓名的其他提货人而无法追回。交货时货物短量或件数不足不属于"提货不着"的范畴。此外,如果提货不着的原因和货物所在处所是知道的,那么也不属于此范畴。

As with institute malicious damage clause, theft, pilferage and non-delivery clause is not required when ICC(A) is taken out. This clause covers two types of risk, one is theft and pilferage, the other is non-delivery of the goods. "Theft" means theft by assault at sea, accompanied by violence or threat of violence, and does not include theft by stealth. "Pilferage" refers to theft by stealth, while "non-delivery" refers to the unrecoverable loss of the entire shipment due to any unknown cause, or the misdelivery of the shipment to another unnamed consignee. Delivery of goods in short quantity or in insufficient pieces does not fall under the category of "non-delivery". In addition, if the reason for non-delivery and the location of the goods are known, then such loss does not fall into this category either.

此外,伦敦保险协会在协会货物条款 A、B、C 的基础上,对特种货物的海运保险制定了适应该种货物特别需要的保险条款,包括协会冷冻食品保险条款、协会散装油类保险条款、协会商品贸易保险、协会木材贸易联合会条款等。

In addition, Institute of London Underwriters, on the basis of "Institute Cargo Clause" A, B and C, has developed insurance clauses adapted to the special needs of maritime transportation for specialized cargoes, including institute frozen food clauses, institute bulk oil clause, institute timer trade federation clause, etc.

Words and Expressions

即测即练

习题

第 12 章

Chapter 12
其他运输方式货物保险
Cargo Insurance for Other Modes of Transport

Learning Objectives：

1. Master the scope of cover（risks covered），exclusions，period of insurance，time of validity of a claim，etc. of overland transportation cargo clauses；
2. Master the main contents of air transport cargo insurance in China and institute cargo insurance for air transport；
3. Understand the main contents of parcel carrier cargo insurance.

引导案例

我国最大国际航空运输事故损害赔偿纠纷案

2000 年 3 月，中国化工建设大连公司（以下简称"大连化建"）在购买 80 桶 8-羟基喹啉后，将其出售给一家印度公司，委托马来西亚航空公司（以下简称"马航公司"）承运。大通公司作为马航公司的货运代理人，办理了该批货物的报关手续，海关、商检等部门签发了报关单并审验、放行。大通公司将货物交给地服公司包装、装机，在地服公司的要求下，大通公司提供了所需单证，其提供的由迪捷姆公司出具的《鉴定书》的鉴定结论是货物为8-羟基喹啉，按普通货物装卸、运输。虽然迪捷姆公司以检验人的身份参与，但其没有对货物进行样品检验，而是直接变更以前《鉴定书》的运单号得出上述鉴定结论。地服公司根据《鉴定书》的鉴定结论，按照普通货物运输标准将该批货物装入飞机。当飞机抵达马来西亚进行中转卸货时，马航公司发现该批货物发生泄漏，货物不是 8-羟基喹啉，而是强酸性腐蚀化学品，属危险品货物的草酰氯。大连化建承认货物真正名称为草酰氯。

经鉴定评估，各保险人和再保险人认为飞机修理成本大大超过飞机全额保险金 9 500 万美元的 75%，据此推定飞机全损，各保险人和再保险人向马航公司支付了全额 9 500 万美元的保险赔偿金，并取得了保险代位追偿权。

合议庭经审理认为，大连化建对此案事故及损害发生存在过错或者过失行为，并存在直接因果关系，构成对各原告的侵权行为，应对此承担赔偿责任。迪捷姆公司也存在一定过错行为，且与此案事故及损害的发生具有因果关系，构成对各原告的侵权行为，应对此承担相应的赔偿责任。最终判决：大连化建赔偿各保险人损失 6 500 余万美元，其中 91.5% 的赔偿金 5 900 余万美元直接偿付给各再保险人；迪捷姆公司对大连化建不足以赔偿上述判决款项部分，承担不超过人民币 200 万元的赔偿责任。

资料来源：索赔标的额最大的国际航空货物运输保险损害赔偿纠纷案［EB/OL］. (2020-09-03).
https://www.shenlanbao.com/zhishi/10-86305.

随着各国之间的经济联系日益密切，国际贸易快速发展，货物运输除了主要采用海运方式外，以陆上、航空、邮包、集装箱以及多式联运等方式运输的数量在国际贸易货运量中的比重也呈现明显的上升趋势，这些运输方式的货物保险在保险业务中的重要性也日益提高。

With the increasingly close economic ties between countries and the rapid development of international trade, in addition to the main use of sea transport, the proportion of goods transported by land, air, parcel, container, multimodal transport and other modes of transport in international trade freight volume has also shown a significant upward trend, and the importance of these modes of transport of cargo insurance in the insurance business is also increasing.

12.1 陆上运输货物保险（Overland Transport Cargo Insurance）

陆上运输主要包括以火车和汽车为运输工具的铁路运输和公路运输两种方式，包括我国在内的各国保险公司现行的陆上运输货物险条款通常明确规定以火车、汽车为限。

Overland transport mainly includes rail transport and highway transport with trains and automobiles as the vehicles respectively. The current cargo insurance clauses for overland transport in various countries, including China, usually stipulate that their insurance services of overland transport are limited to trains and automobiles only.

陆上货物运输的风险有其自身的特点，有些与海上货物运输的风险不同，如车辆碰撞、倾覆或出轨、铁路坍塌、道路损坏、桥梁折断、山体滑坡和泥石流等；有些与海上运输中的风险相同，如偷窃、短量、破损等一般外来风险以及战争、罢工等特殊外来风险，在陆上运输中也是一样存在的。因此，陆上运输货物保险与海上运输货物保险有一定的相似之处，但也有所不同。

The risks of overland freight transport have their own characteristics, some of which are different from those of maritime transport, such as vehicle collision, overturning or derailment, railway collapse, road damage, bridge fracture, landslide and debris flow; some of which are the same as those in marine transport, for example, general extraneous risks such as theft, shortage and damage, and special extraneous risks such as war and strike also exist in land transport. Therefore, the overland transport cargo insurance and the marine cargo insurance have some similarities and differences as well.

根据中国人民保险公司 1981 年修订的《陆上运输货物保险条款》，我国陆上运输货物保险的基本险别有陆运险和陆运一切险两种。此外，还有适用于陆运冷藏货物的专门保险——陆上运输冷藏货物险，其性质也是基本险。

According to the *Overland Transportation Cargo Clauses* amended by the People's Insurance Company of China in 1981, the basic risks of China's overland transportation cargo insurance are overland transportation risks and overland transportation all risks. In addition, there is a special kind of insurance applicable to refrigerated goods transported by land: overland transportation insurance of frozen products which is also a basic risk.

12.1.1 陆运险与陆运一切险(Overland Transportation Risks and Overland Transportation All Risks)

1. 承保责任范围(Scope of Cover)

陆运险的承保责任范围与《海洋运输货物保险条款》中的"水渍险"或《协会货物条款》中的 B 条款相似。保险人对下列损失承担赔偿责任：第一,因被保险货物在运输途中遭受暴风、雷电、洪水、地震等自然灾害或由于运输工具遭受碰撞、倾覆、出轨或在驳运过程中因驳运工具遭受搁浅、触礁、沉没、碰撞,或由于遭受隧道坍塌、崖崩或失火、爆炸等意外事故造成的全部或部分损失；第二,被保险人对遭受承保责任内危险的货物采取抢救、防止或减少货损的措施而支付的合理费用,但以不超过该批被救货物的保险金额为限。

The coverage of overland transportation risks is similar to WPA in the *Ocean Marine Cargo Clauses* or clause "B" in the *Institute Cargo Clauses*. The insurer shall be liable for the following losses: first, total or partial loss caused by natural disasters such as storms, lightning, floods, earthquakes, etc. suffered by the insured goods in transit or by accidental accidents such as collision, overturning, derailment of the means of transportation or by stranding, reefing, sinking or collision of the means of barging during the barging process, or by collapse of the tunnel, cliff collapse, or fire or explosion; second, the reasonable costs incurred by the insured in rescuing, preventing or reducing damage to the goods subject to the perils covered by the insurance, up to the insured amount of the rescued goods.

陆运一切险的承保责任范围与《海洋运输货物保险条款》中的"一切险"或《协会货物条款》中的 A 条款类似。保险公司除承担陆运险的赔偿责任外,还负责被保险货物在运输途中由于一般外来原因所造成的全损或部分损失。

The coverage of overland transportation all risks is similar to "all risks" in *Ocean Marine Cargo Clauses* or clause A in *Institute Cargo Clauses*. In addition to the liability of overland transportation risks, the insurance company is also responsible for the total or partial loss of the insured goods caused by general extraneous reasons in transit.

陆运险和陆运一切险的除外责任与海洋运输货物险的除外责任基本相同。

The exclusions of overland transportation risks and overland transportation all risks are basically the same as those of marine cargo insurance.

2. 责任起讫（Commencement and Termination of Cover）

陆上运输货物险的责任起讫也采用"仓至仓"责任条款,保险责任从被保险货物运离保险单载明的起运地仓库或储存处所开始运输时生效,包括正常运输过程中的陆上和与其有关的水上驳运在内,直到该货物运到保险单上所载明的目的地收货人的仓库或被保险人用以分配、分派的其他储存处所。如未运抵上述仓库或储存处所,则以被保险货物运抵最后卸载的车站满60天为止。

The "warehouse to warehouse" clause is also adopted for the commencement and termination of the liability for the overland transportation risks. The insurance liability takes effect from the time when the insured goods are transported from the warehouse or storage place at the place of departure specified in the insurance policy, including land and related water barging in the normal transportation process, until the goods are delivered to the consignee's warehouse at the destination stated in the policy or to other storage premises used by the insured for distribution or assignment. If the goods are not delivered to the above warehouse or storage premises, the insurance liability shall be effective for 60 days after the insured goods arrive at the last unloading station.

3. 索赔时效（Time of Validity of a Claim）

陆上运输货物保险的索赔时效为：从被保险货物在最后目的地车站全部卸离车辆后起算,最多不超过2年。

The validity time of a claim for overland transport cargo insurance shall be no more than 2 years from the date when the insured cargo is discharged from the vehicle at the station of final destination.

从上述内容中可以看出,陆运货物保险的两种基本险与海运货物的基本险有以下不同。

It can be seen from the above that the two basic risks of overland cargo insurance are different from the basic risks of marine cargo as follows.

（1）陆运货物保险的承保风险中,不包括流冰、海啸等海上运输中的自然灾害,而增加了倾覆、出轨、隧道坍塌、崖崩等陆上运输中所特有的意外事故。

（1）The risks covered by overland cargo insurance do not include natural disasters in marine transportation such as drift ice and tsunami, but include accidents unique to land transportation such as overturning, derailment, tunnel collapse and cliff avalanche.

（2）陆上运输一般不涉及海上运输时可能产生的共同海损问题,因此,其承保风险中没有共同海损牺牲、分摊以及救助费用。

（2）Land transport generally does not involve the issue of general average that may arise when transporting by sea, and therefore there is no general average sacrifice, contribution and salvage charges in its underwriting risk.

（3）陆上运输货物保险业务通常不区分全部损失和部分损失,只要承保责任内风险所导致的损失,一般都予以赔偿。

（3）Land transport cargo insurance business usually does not distinguish between total loss and partial loss. Losses are generally covered as long as they are caused by a covered risk.

12.1.2　陆上运输冷藏货物险（Overland Transportation Insurance of Frozen Products）

陆上运输冷藏货物险属于陆上运输货物险中的一种专门保险，它是专门针对冷藏货物的基本险。

Overland transportation insurance of frozen products is a kind of special insurance in land transportation cargo insurance，which is a basic insurance particularly for refrigerated goods.

1. 承保责任范围（Scope of Cover）

（1）陆运险所列举的自然灾害和意外事故所造成的全部或部分损失。

（1）Total or partial losses caused by natural disasters and accidents listed in overland transportation risks.

（2）由于冷藏机器或隔温设备在运输途中损坏所造成的被保险货物解冻融化而腐烂造成的损失。

（2）Losses caused by thawing and decay of the insured goods caused by damage to refrigerated machinery or insulation equipment in transit.

（3）被保险人对遭受承保责任范围内危险的货物采取抢救、防止或减少货损的措施而支付的合理费用，但以不超过该批被救货物的保险金额为限。

（3）The reasonable fees incurred by the insured for rescuing，preventing or reducing the damage to the goods under the insurance liability，but not exceeding the insured amount of the salvaged goods.

2. 除外责任（Exclusion Clause）

本保险对下列损失不负赔偿责任。

This insurance is not liable for the following losses.

（1）被保险人的故意行为或过失所造成的损失，以及属于发货人责任所引起的损失。

（1）Loss or damage caused by the intentional act or fault of the insured，and loss or damage falling under the liability of the consignor.

（2）被保险货物在运输过程中的任何阶段，因未存放在有冷藏设备的仓库或运输工具中，或辅助运输工具没有隔温设备或没有在车厢内贮存足够的冰块所致的货物腐烂。

（2）Decay of the insured goods caused by not being stored in a warehouse or conveyance with refrigeration equipment，or by the auxiliary conveyance not having insulation or not having sufficient ice stored in the compartment at any stage of transportation.

（3）被保险货物在保险责任开始时因未保持良好状态，包括整理加工、包扎不妥或冷冻不合规格所造成的货物腐败和损失。

（3）The decay and loss of the insured goods due to the failure to maintain them in good condition at the beginning of the insurance liability, including improper finishing and wrapping or freezing out of specification.

（4）被保险货物的自然损耗、本质缺陷、特性及市价跌落、运输延迟所引起的损失和费用。

（4）Loss or damage arising from normal loss, inherent vice or nature of the insured goods, loss of market and/or delay in transit and any expenses arising there from.

3. 责任起讫（Commencement to Termination of Cover）

陆上运输冷藏货物险的保险责任自被保险货物运离保险单所载明的起运地点的冷藏仓库装入运输工具开始运输时生效，把正常的陆运和与其有关的驳运包括在内，直至货物到达保险单所载明的目的地收货人的仓库。但最长保险责任的有效期以被保险货物到达目的地车站后 10 天为限。

The insurance liability of overland transportation insurance of frozen products shall take effect from the time when the insured goods are transported from the refrigerated warehouse at the place of departure specified in the insurance policy and loaded into the means of transport, including normal land transportation and related barge transport, until the goods reach the warehouse of the consignee at the destination specified in the insurance policy. However, the maximum term of validity of the insurance liability shall be 10 days after the arrival of the insured goods at the station of destination.

4. 索赔时效（Time of Validity of a Claim）

陆上运输冷藏货物险的索赔时效与陆运险和陆运一切险的索赔时效规定完全一样，从被保险货物在最后目的地全部卸离车辆后起算，最多不超过 2 年。

The statute of limitations for claims under overland transportation insurance of frozen products is exactly the same as that for overland transportation risks and overland transportation all risks, starting from the time the insured cargo is fully unloaded from the vehicle at its final destination, up to a maximum of 2 years.

12.1.3 陆上运输货物战争险（Overland Transportation Cargo War Risks）

陆上运输货物战争险是陆上运输货物险的一种附加险。只有在投保了陆运险或陆运一切险的基础上经过投保人与保险人协商，方可加保战争险。这种陆运战争险，国外私营保险公司大都是不承保的，中国人民保险公司为适应外贸业务需要，接受加保战争险，但目前仅限于火车运输，若使用汽车运输，则不能加保战争险。加保陆上运输货物战争险须另缴付保险费。

Overland transportation cargo war risks are an additional risk of overland cargo transportation insurance. Only on the basis of overland transport risks or overland transport all risks, can war risks be covered after negotiation between the applicant and the insurer. Most foreign private insurance companies do not cover this kind of overland war risk, while People's Insurance Company of China accepts war risks in order to adapt to the needs of foreign trade business. But at present, this insurance is limited to train transportation，and if motor transportation is used，war risk cannot be covered unless additional premium is paid.

1. 责任范围（Scope of Cover）

保险公司负责赔偿在火车运输途中由于战争、类似战争行为和敌对行为、武装冲突所致的损失，以及各种常规武器包括地雷、炸弹所致的损失。

Insurance companies are responsible for the compensation of losses caused by war，warlike acts and hostile acts，armed conflicts，as well as losses caused by conventional weapons，including mines and bombs，while in transit by train.

但是，由于敌对行为使用原子或热核武器所致的损失和费用，以及根据执政者、当权者或其他武装集团的扣押、拘留引起的承保运程的丧失和挫折而造成的损失，保险公司不负赔偿责任。

However，the insurance company shall not be liable for losses and expenses arising from the use of atomic or thermonuclear weapons in hostile acts，as well as loss or frustration of a covered voyage caused by seizure or detention by the ruler，person in power，or other armed group.

2. 责任起讫（Commencement and Termination of Cover）

与海运战争险相似，陆运战争险以货物置于运输工具时为限，即自被保险货物装上保险单所载起运地的火车时开始到卸离保险单项所载目的地火车时。如果被保险货物不卸离火车，则从火车到达目的地的当日午夜起计算，满 48 小时为止；如在运输中途转车，不论货物在当地卸载与否，保险责任都从火车到达该中途站的当日午夜起计算，满 10 天为止。如货物在此期限内重新装车续运，仍恢复有效。

Similar to marine war risks，liability of war risks here is subject to the time the goods are placed in the means of transport. That is，from the time when the insured goods are loaded onto the train at the place of departure specified in the policy to the time when they are unloaded from the train at the destination of the policy. If the insured goods are not discharged from the train，it shall be counted from midnight on the day of the train's arrival at the destination，and shall expire in 48 hours. In the event of transshipment，whether or not the goods are unloaded locally，the insurance coverage shall be calculated for a period of 10 days from midnight on the day the train arrives at the intermediate station. If the goods are reloaded and continue to be transported within this period，the insurance will be reinstated.

但需要指出的是，如运输契约在保险单所载目的地以外的地点终止，该地即视作本保险单所载目的地，保险责任在货物卸离该地火车时为止。如不卸离火车，则保险责任从火车到达该地当日午夜起计算，满 48 小时为止。

It is important to note，however，that if the contract of carriage terminates at a place other than the destination stated in the policy，that place shall be deemed to be the destination stated in the policy and the liability shall remain until the goods are discharged from the train there. If the goods are not unloaded from the train，the insurance liability will terminate after 48 hours from midnight of the day the train arrives at that place.

同海洋运输货物保险一样,陆上运输货物可以在投保战争险的基础上加保罢工险。加保罢工险不另收费,但如单独要求加保罢工险,则按战争险费率收费。陆上运输罢工险的承保责任范围与海洋运输货物罢工险的承保责任范围相同。

As with marine transportation cargo insurance, land transportation cargo can be insured against strike risk in addition to war risk. There is no additional charge for strike risk on top of war risk, but if strike risk is taken out separately, it will be charged at war risk rate. The coverage of overland transportation strike risk is the same as that of marine cargo strike risk.

12.2 航空运输货物保险(Air Transport Cargo Insurance)

航空货物运输是 20 世纪才出现的运输方式,随着国际贸易的迅猛发展,通过航空进行运输的货物逐渐增多,对航空运输货物保险的需求也相应增长。但由于航空运输方式较复杂且航空运输货物保险起步较晚,航空运输货物保险迄今尚未成为一个完整、独立的体系。

Air cargo transportation is a mode of transport that appeared in the 20th century. With the rapid development of international trade, the amount of goods transported by air increases gradually, and the demand for air cargo insurance also increases. However, due to the complexity of air transport mode and the late start of air cargo insurance, air cargo insurance has not yet become a complete and independent system.

伦敦保险协会在 1965 年制定了用于航空运输的保险条款,并在 1982 年进行了修订,现为协会货物险条款(航空)(邮包除外),此外还制定了协会战争险条款(航空货物)(邮包除外)和协会罢工险条款(航空货物)。

Institute of London Underwriters established insurance clauses for air transport in 1965 and revised them in 1982 as institute cargo clauses (air) (excluding sending by post), in addition to institute war clauses (air cargo) (excluding sending by post) and institute strike clauses (air cargo).

我国现行的航空运输货物保险条款的险别及承保责任范围是参考国际市场通行做法特别是伦敦保险协会的上述条款内容制定的。现行的中国航空运输货物保险包括"航空运输险"和"航空运输一切险"两种基本险条款及"航空运输货物战争险"的附加险条款。

The existing clauses of air cargo insurance in China are formulated with reference to the prevailing international market practice, especially the above-mentioned clauses of the Institute of London Underwriters. The current air transport cargo insurance in China includes two basic clauses of "air transportation risks" and "air transportation all risks", as well as the additional clauses of "air transportation cargo war risks".

12.2.1　中国航空运输货物保险(Air Transport Cargo Insurance in China)

1. 航空运输险和航空运输一切险(Air Transportation Risks and Air Transportation All Risks)

1) 承保责任范围(Scope of Cover)

航空运输险与海运保险中水渍险及陆运险的承保责任大致相同,承保被保险货物在运输途中遭受雷电、火灾、爆炸或由于飞机遭受恶劣气候或其他危难事故而被抛弃,或者由于飞机遭受碰撞、倾覆、坠落、失踪等意外事故所造成的全部或部分损失。

The coverage of air transportation risks is basically the same as that of marine WPA and overland transport risks. It covers the total or partial loss of the insured cargo caused by lightning, fire, explosion, or abandonment due to heavy weather or other perils, or due to collision, overturning, crashing, or disappearance of the aircraft during transportation.

不同的是,航空运输险排除了流冰、海啸、地震、洪水等自然灾害和运输工具搁浅、触礁、沉没、与流冰互撞等不可能发生的意外事故以及共同海损的牺牲、分摊和救助费用,并针对航空运输的特点增加了飞机倾覆、坠落或失踪等风险。

The difference is that air transportation risks exclude natural disasters such as floating ice, tsunami, earthquake, flood and other unlikely accidents such as grounding, stranding sinking, colliding with drift ice, as well as general average sacrifice, contribution and salvage charges, and adds risks such as aircraft capsizing, crashing or missing for the characteristics of air transport.

航空运输一切险的承保责任与海运一切险及陆运一切险责任基本一致,除了包括航空运输险的各项责任外,还负责被保险货物由于一般外来原因所致的全部或部分损失。

The insurance liability of air transportation all risks is basically the same as that of marine transport all risks and overland transport all risks. In addition to the responsibilities of air transportation risks, it is also responsible for all or part of the loss of the insured goods due to general extraneous reasons.

上述两种基本险的除外责任与海洋运输货物险的除外责任基本相同。

The exclusions of the above two basic risks are basically the same as those of marine cargo insurance.

2) 责任起讫(Commencement and Termination of Cover)

航空运输货物两种基本险的保险责任也采用"仓至仓"原则,但与海洋运输险的"仓至仓"责任条款不同。

The "warehouse to warehouse" principle is also used for the two basic risks of air transport cargo, but it differs from the "warehouse to warehouse" clause of marine transport insurance.

(1) 如货物运达保险单所载明的目的地,但未运抵保险单所载明的收货人仓库或储存处所,则以被保险货物在最后卸载地卸离飞机后满 30 天保险责任终止。如在上述 30

天内被保险货物需转送到非保险单所载明的目的地，则以该项货物开始转运时终止。

（1）If the goods arrive at the destination named in the policy but fail to reach the consignee's warehouse or storage premises named in the policy, the insurance shall terminate 30 days after the insured goods are discharged from the aircraft at the final place of discharge. If the insured goods need to be transferred to a destination other than that specified in the policy within 30 days, the insurance liability of the insured goods shall be terminated upon transshipment.

（2）如果被保险人无法控制的运输延迟、绕道、被迫卸货、重新装载、转载或承运人运用运输契约赋予的权限所做的任何航行上的变更或终止运输契约，致使被保险货物运到非保险单上所载的目的地，在被保险人及时将情况通知保险人，并在必要时加缴保险费的情况下，航空运输货物保险合同继续有效，保险责任的终止按照下列具体规定：①如被保险货物在非保险单所载目的地出售，保险责任至交货时为止。但不论任何情况，均以被保险货物在卸载地卸离飞机后满 30 天为止。②被保险货物如在 30 天期限内继续运往保险单所载原目的地或其他目的地，保险责任仍按上述（1）的规定，即货物运到保险单所载目的地或其他目的地卸离飞机满 30 天时保险责任终止。

（2）If, due to delay, detour, forced unloading, reloading, transshipment, or any carriage contract alteration or termination by the carrier under the authority of the contract of carriage, the insured goods are transported to a destination other than those listed in the insurance policy, when the insured promptly notify the insurer of the situation and pay additional premiums if necessary, the air cargo insurance contract will remain effective. The termination of the insurance liability is effected under the following circumstances：①If the insured goods are sold at a place other than the destination stated in the policy, the insurance shall continue until delivery of the goods. However, in any event, the coverage shall expire 30 days after the insured goods are discharged from the aircraft at the place of discharge. ②If the insured goods continue to be shipped to the original destination or other destinations stated in the policy within 30 days, the insurance liability shall continue in accordance with the provisions of（1）above, that is, the insurance liability ends when the cargo is delivered to the destination stated in the policy, or when it is unloaded from the aircraft at another destination for 30 days.

2. 航空运输货物战争险（Air Transportation Cargo War Risks）

航空运输货物战争险是航空运输险的一种附加险。投保人只有投保了航空运输险或航空运输一切险后，才能够加保航空运输货物战争险。

Air transportation cargo war risks is an additional risk to air transportation risks. Only after the insured has taken out air transportation risks or air transportation all risks, can air transportation cargo war risks be covered.

1）责任范围（Coverage）

在航空运输货物战争险项下，保险人负责承担在航空运输途中由于战争、类似战争行为和敌对行为、武装冲突所致的损失，以及由于上述原因引起的捕获、拘留、扣留、禁制、扣押所造成的损失和各种常规武器包括炸弹所致的货物损失。与其他方式下的战争险一样,它也把使用原子或热核武器所造成的损失作为除外责任。

Under air transportation cargo war risks, the insurer is responsible for losses caused by war, war-like acts and hostilities, armed conflict while in transit by air, as well as losses caused by capture, seizure, arrest, restraint, or detainment and loss of cargo caused by conventional weapons of all kinds, including bombs, as a result of the above. As with other forms of war risk, losses resulting from the use of atomic or thermonuclear weapons are also excluded.

2) 责任起讫(Commencement and Termination of Cover)

航空运输货物战争险的保险责任是自被保险货物装上保险单所载明的起运地的飞机开始生效,直到在保险单载明的目的地卸离飞机时为止。如被保险货物没卸离飞机,则从飞机到达目的地当日午夜起计算,满 15 天为止;如被保险货物需在中途转运,则保险责任从飞机到达转运地的当日午夜起计算,满 15 天为止,待装上续运的飞机,保险单再恢复有效。

The liability for war risks for air cargo is effective from the time the insured cargo is loaded onto the aircraft at the place of origin stated in the policy to the time it is unloaded from the aircraft at the destination stated in the policy. If the insured cargo is not unloaded from the aircraft, the period of insurance shall be counted as 15 days from midnight of the day the aircraft arrives at the destination; if the insured cargo is in transit, the period of insurance shall be counted as 15 days from midnight of the day the aircraft arrives at the place of transit, and the insurance policy shall be reinstated once it is loaded on the renewed aircraft.

与其他运输方式下的做法相同,投保人在投保战争险后,如欲加保罢工险,不需另行缴纳保费;如仅要求加保罢工险,则按照战争险的费率缴纳保费。航空运输罢工险的责任范围与海洋运输罢工险的责任范围相同。

As with other modes of transportation, the policyholder is not required to pay a separate premium if he/she wishes to add strike risks after taking out war risks; if only strike coverage is required, the premium is paid at the war risks rate. The scope of liability for air transport strike risks is the same as that for marine transport strike risks.

12.2.2　协会航空运输货物保险(Institute Cargo Insurance for Air Transportation)

1. 协会货物险条款(航空)(邮包除外)〔Institute Cargo Clause(Air) (Excluding Sending By Post)〕

1) 承保责任范围(Coverage)

该条款的承保责任范围较广,对承保风险的规定与 ICC(A)条款一样,是采用一切风险减除外责任的方法。在本保险条款中被特别规定的除外责任是一般除外责任、战争除外责任和罢工除外责任。与 ICC(A)条款不同之处是,其缺少不适航、不适货除外责任,这是考虑到飞机运输的特殊性而采取的一种措施。即使没有规定,承担货物运输的飞机起飞时均应具备适航性,用于航空运输的特殊集装箱也必须适合于货物的安全运输。

This clause has a broader scope of coverage and uses the same "all risks except exclusions" approach as the ICC(A) for covered risks. The exclusions specified in this clause are general exclusions, war exclusions and strikes exclusions. The difference with ICC(A) is the lack of "unseaworthy and unfitness of vessel or craft" exclusion, which is a measure to take into account the special nature of aircraft transportation. Even without the relevant provisions, aircraft undertaking cargo transportation should have airworthiness when taking off, and special containers used for air transportation must be suitable for the safe transportation of goods.

此外,在"承保风险"中,该条款与 ICC(A)条款相比,没有共同海损条款和船舶互有过失碰撞责任条款,而只有风险条款。这是因为航空运输有其特殊性,一旦发生事故,其发生全损的可能性最大。

In addition, in the "risks covered" clause, compared with ICC (A), there is no general average clause nor both to blame collision clause, but only risks clause. This is because air transportation has its own special characteristics, and in the event of an accident, the possibility of total loss is the greatest.

2) 责任起讫(Commencement and Termination of Cover)

协会货物险条款(航空)的保险期限亦采用"仓至仓"条款。与我国航空运输险和航空运输一切险的规定相同,保险期限是在最终卸货地货物从飞机上卸下以后 30 天。如在上述 30 天内被保险货物运到非保险单所载明的目的地,则以该货物开始转运时保险责任终止。该条款的其他内容均与海运 ICC(A)条款的各有关内容相同。

The "warehouse to warehouse" clause is also used for the insurance period of ICC (air). Same as China air transportation risks and air transportation all risks, the insurance period is 30 days after the cargo is unloaded from the aircraft at the final discharge place. If the insured cargo is delivered to a destination other than the one stated in the insurance policy within the above 30 days, the insurance liability shall terminate when the cargo transshipment starts. All other contents of this clause are the same as the relevant contents of the marine ICC (A).

2. 协会战争险条款(航空货物)(邮包除外)[Institute War Clauses (Air Cargo) (Excluding Sending By Post)]

投保协会战争险(航空货物),保险公司承担赔偿在航空货物运输途中因战争、内乱、革命、叛乱、动乱及由此而发生的国内斗争或由交战国采取的或对交战国采取的一切敌对行为引起的捕获、扣留、禁制、拘留而造成的保险标的的损失,其中也包括废弃水雷、鱼雷、炸弹以及其他废弃武器造成的损失。可见,该条款不包括因使用原子武器所造成的损失。此外,在一般除外责任中还包括专门针对航空运输的飞机与集装箱等不合格的除外责任。

For institute war clauses (air cargo), the insurance company undertakes compensation for the loss of the subject-matter insured caused by war, civil strife, revolution, rebellion, turmoil and the internal struggle arising therefrom, or the capture, detention, prohibition and detention caused by the belligerent state or all hostile acts taken by the belligerent country, including abandoned mines and torpedo damages caused by mines, bombs and other abandoned weapons. It can be seen that the article does not include losses caused by the use of atomic weapons. In addition, the general exclusions also include the exception of unqualified aircraft and containers for air transportation.

协会战争险(航空货物)的保险期限是自保险标的或其一部分因开始运输而被装上飞机时开始,直到在最终卸货地卸离飞机时为止。如保险标的不卸离飞机,则从飞机到达最终卸货地当天午夜起计算,满 15 天为止;如保险标的在中途转运,在转运地的承保期限是 15 天,待装上续运飞机,保险责任再恢复有效。由此可见,如同海上运输的战争险适用"水上危险"一样,航空运输战争险适用的是"空中危险"。

The insurance period of institute war clauses (air cargo) begins when the subject-matter insured or a part thereof is loaded onto the aircraft for transport and continues until it is unloaded from the aircraft at the point of final discharge. If the subject-matter insured is not discharged from the aircraft, the period will last 15 days from midnight on the day when the aircraft arrives at the final place of discharge; if the subject-matter insured is transshipped midway, the period of coverage at the place of transshipment shall be 15 days and the liability shall be reinstated upon loading on the aircraft carrying the cargo. Thus, just as war risk for maritime transportation applies to "waterborne", war risk for air transportation applies to "airborne".

该条款中的其他内容,诸如索赔、保险利益、减少损失等条款均与海运货物保险 ICC (A)条款相同。这些条款的存在使该险别具有独立性及完整性,因而也可以单独投保。

Other elements of this clause, such as claims, insurable interest clause, and minimising losses, are the same as the ICC (A) for maritime cargo insurance. The existence of these clauses gives independence and completeness to the coverage, and thus makes it possible to insure separately.

3. 协会罢工险条款(航空货物)[Institute Strikes Clauses (Air Cargo)]

投保协会罢工险(航空货物),保险公司负责赔偿在航空货物运输途中因罢工、关厂、劳资纠纷、暴动、骚乱或出于恐怖主义与政治动机而采取的行动所引起的保险标的的损失。

By insuring the institute strikes clauses (air cargo), the insurer is responsible for the loss of the subject-matter insured caused by strikes, lockouts, labor disputes, riots, unrest or actions taken for terrorist and political motives while the air cargo is in transit.

该险别的保险期限与协会货物险条款(航空)一致,采用的是"仓至仓"原则,货物卸离飞机后的承保期限是 30 天。该险别的其他条款与协会战争险条款(航空货物)一样,具有独立性和完整性,可单独投保。

The duration of this risk is in accordance with the institute cargo clauses (air) and is covered on a "warehouse to warehouse" basis for a period of 30 days after discharge of the cargo from the aircraft. The other clauses of this coverage have the same independence and integrity as the institute war risk clauses (air cargo) and can be insured separately.

12.3　邮包运输货物保险(Parcel Carrier Cargo Insurance)

在国际贸易中,小件货品的运输或买卖双方寄送样品经常会采用邮政包裹的形式,因此,根据具体需要,也就出现了邮包运输货物保险。由于邮包运输可能同时涉及海、陆、空三种运输方式,因此保险人在确定承保责任范围时,必须同时考虑这三种运输方式可能出险的因素。

In international trade, the form of postal parcel transportation is often used when transporting small goods or when sending samples between buyers and sellers, therefore, according to specific needs, insurance of goods transported in parcels has also emerged. Since parcel transportation may involve three modes of transportation at the same time—sea, land and air, the insurer, in determining the scope of its liability, must take into account the factors that may cause risk in all three modes of transportation.

各国保险人针对邮包运输而制定的保险条款不尽相同,比较常见的是沿袭了海洋运输货物险的"平安险""水渍险"与"一切险"的险别名称,但具体条款内容有所区别。中国人民保险公司参照国际通行做法,在 1981 年 1 月 1 日修订并公布了一套比较完备的邮包运输保险条款,包括邮包险、邮包一切险和邮包战争险。

The insurance clauses formulated by insurers in various countries for the transportation of postal parcels are not the same, and the more common ones follow the names of "FPA""WPA" and "all risks" of marine cargo insurance, but the contents of the specific clauses are different. Referring to the international practice, the People's Insurance Company of China amended and published a set of relatively complete parcel transport insurance clauses on January 1, 1981, including parcel post risks, parcel post all risks, and parcel post war risks.

12.3.1　邮包险和邮包一切险(Parcel Post Risks and Parcel Post All Risks)

邮包险的承保责任范围是负责赔偿被保险邮包在运输途中由于恶劣气候、雷电、海啸、地震、洪水等自然灾害或运输工具搁浅、触礁、沉没、碰撞、出轨、倾覆、坠落、失踪,或是失火和爆炸意外事故造成的全部或部分损失;另外,还负责被保险人对遭受承保责任内风险的货物采取抢救、防止或减少货损的措施而支付的合理费用,但以不超过该批被救货物的保险金额为限。

The scope of liability of parcel post risks is to indemnify the insured for all or part of the loss of parcels in transit due to natural calamities such as heavy weather, lightning, tsunami, earthquake, and flood, or due to stranding, grounding, sinking, collision, derailment, capsizing, falling, missing of the means of transportation, or due to accidents caused by fire and explosion; in addition, it is responsible for the reasonable costs incurred by the insured in taking measures to salvage, prevent or minimize damage to the goods exposed to the covered risks, up to the insured amount for the salvaged goods.

邮包一切险的承保责任范围除了包括邮包险的全部责任外,还包括被保险邮包在运输途中由于外来原因所致的全部或部分损失。

In addition to the full liability of the parcel post risks, parcel post all risks also covers total or partial loss of the insured post parcels in transit due to extraneous reasons.

邮包险和邮包一切险对下列损失不负赔偿责任:

(1) 被保险人的故意行为和过失所造成的损失;

(2) 属于发货人责任所造成的损失;

(3) 在保险责任开始时,被保险邮包已经存在的品质不良或数量短差所造成的损失;

(4) 被保险邮包的自然损耗、本质缺陷、特性及市价跌落、运输延迟所引起的损失;

(5) 邮包战争险条款和货物运输罢工险条款规定的责任范围和除外责任。

The following losses are not covered by parcel post risks or parcel post all risks:

(1) Loss or damage caused by the intentional act or fault of the insured;

(2) Loss or damage falling under the liability of the consignor;

(3) Loss or damage arising from the inferior quality or shortage of the insured parcels prior to the attachment of insurance;

(4) Loss or damage arising from normal loss, inherent vice or nature of the insured parcels, loss of market and/or delay in transit and any expenses arising there from;

(5) Risks and liabilities covered and excluded by the parcel post war risks clauses and strike risks clauses.

保险责任自被保险邮包离开保险单所载起运地点寄件人的住所运往邮局时开始生效,直至被保险邮包运达保险单所载明的目的地邮局,从邮局签发到货通知书给收件人当日午夜起算,满 15 天为止,但在此期限内,邮包一经递交至收件人的住所,保险责任即行终止。

The insurance liability shall take effect from the time the insured parcel leaves the sender's residence at the place of departure named in the insurance policy and is transported to the post office, until the insured parcel is delivered to the post office at the destination specified in the policy. The insurance liability shall be terminated within 15 days from midnight on the day when the post office issues the notice of arrival to the addressee; however, the insurance liability ends as soon as the parcel is delivered to the addressee's residence within this period.

保险的索赔时效,从被保险邮包递交收件人时起算,最多不超过 2 年。

The time of validity of a claim shall not exceed two years from the time the insured parcel is delivered to the addressee.

12.3.2　邮包战争险(Parcel Post War Risks)

邮包战争险是邮政包裹保险的一种特殊附加险,只有在投保了基本险之后,增加支付保费，方可加保。

Parcel post war risk is a special additional risk of parcel post insurance. It can be covered only after the basic risk is insured and the additional premium is paid.

邮包战争险中，保险人负责赔偿在航运途中由于战争、类似战争行为、敌对行为或武装冲突、海盗行为，以及常规武器包括水雷、鱼雷、炸弹等所造成货物的损失。另外，对于被保险人对遭受承保责任范围内风险的物品采取抢救、防止或减少损失的措施支付的合理费用，也予以负责。但同样，保险人不负责因使用原子或热核制造的武器所造成的损失。

As for the parcel post war risks, the insurer is responsible for the losses of goods caused by war，acts similar to war，hostile or armed conflict，piracy，and losses by conventional weapons，including mines，torpedoes and bombs. In addition，the insurer shall also be responsible for the reasonable expenses paid for rescuing，preventing or reducing the loss of the articles within the scope of insurance liability. But again，the insurer is not responsible for damage caused by the use of weapons made of atoms or thermonuclear materials.

邮包战争险的保险责任从被保险邮包经邮政机构收讫后自储存处所开始运送时生效，直到该邮包运达保险单所载明的目的地邮政机构送交收货人为止。

The insurance liability shall take effect from the time when the insured postal parcel is received and sent by the post office to the time when the parcel reaches the destination specified in the insurance policy and is delivered to the consignee by the postal agency.

Words and Expressions

即测即练

习题

第 13 章

Chapter 13

国际运输货物保险实务
Practice of International Transportation Cargo Insurance

Learning Objectives：

1. Understand the factors that should be considered when choosing the insurance coverage in the international cargo transportation insurance practice；
2. Master the calculation method of insurance amount；
3. Master the preparation of the insurance policy and considerations；
4. Understand the insurance method of imported goods；
5. Master the insurance terms under different trade terms；
6. Master the types，preparation methods，amendment，and transfer of insurance policies；
7. Understand the insurance claims and claim settlement procedures and content.

引导案例

外贸公司因"提货不着"索赔案

某外贸公司与保险公司于 2022 年 8 月 3 日签订了海上货物运输保险合同,被保险人为该外贸公司,保险标的物为布料,保险金额为 48.1 万美元,投保险别为一切险和战争险,航程为青岛至莫斯科。该批货物于 8 月 12 日装船,承运人签发了青岛至莫斯科的全程提单。提单载明:托运人为外贸公司,收货人为买方达卡公司。货物由青岛船运至俄罗斯东方港,再由东方港改为铁路运输,10 月初抵达目的地,之后买方持铁路运单要求提货。因买方是单据上的收货人,承运人便在未收回全程正本提单的情况下放货,买方办理完清关手续后将货物提走。外贸公司见买方迟迟未支付货款,便派人持正本提单至莫斯科提货,并在提不着货物后向保险公司索赔。保险公司认为,本案货物已经运抵目的地并被收货人提走,去向是明确的,不存在"提货不着"的问题,因此,保险公司拒绝承担赔偿责任。外贸公司遂起诉至海事法院。

法院经审理认为:"提货不着"是本案保险合同中约定的一种风险,但并不是所有的"提货不着"都应当由保险公司承担保险责任。海上货物运输保险合同中的风险一般是指货物在运输过程中由于外来原因造成的风险,既包括自然因素造成的风险,也包括人为因素造成的风险。但是,保险合同所指的风险都应当具备不可预见性的特征。本案是因承运人无单放货造成持有正本提单的外贸公司"提货不着",但这种"提货不着"是可预见的,不具有海上货物运输保险的风险特征,故不属于保险合同约定的承保风险。实际上,当承运人故意违约无单放货时,外贸公司就应当根据海上货物运输合同的约定,向这个确定的责任人追究违约责任。外贸公司不去追究承运人的违约责任,却以"提货不着是约定的风险"为由,要求保险公司赔偿,遭拒后向法院起诉,可以说是告错了对象,其诉讼请求混淆了海上货物运输合同与海上货物运输保险合同之间的法律关系与责任界定。

资料来源:根据货物运输保险案例解析[EB/OL].(2017-04-08).https://max.book118.com/html/2017/0324/96732318.shtm.改编。

国际运输货物保险操作实务在不同时期有不同的做法,但究其根本,保险实务就是将保险原理运用到实际业务中。对被保险人来说,掌握货物的投保基数,熟悉保险单的种类、制作、修改及转让手续,在被保险货物发生损失时懂得如何办理索赔手续,是国际运输货物保险实务的必要条件。

The practice of international transportation cargo insurance has different approaches at different times, but at its root, insurance practice is the application of insurance principles to actual business. Knowledge of the insured amount of goods, familiarization with the types, making out, amending and transferring procedures of insurance policies, as well as knowledge of how to make a claim in the event of a loss of the insured goods, are the necessary conditions for the insured to carry out the practical operation of the insurance of internationally transported goods.

13.1　国际运输货物保险投保实务(Insuring Practice of International Transportation Cargo Insurance)

国际贸易运输中,货物会面临各种风险,遭受各种损失,因此,通常都需办理运输保险。应由卖方还是买方向保险人办理保险,主要取决于贸易合同中采用的贸易术语。如我国出口贸易中,如果选用 FOB、FCA 或 CFR、CPT 等贸易术语,由国外买方办理保险;如果选择 CIF、CIP 等贸易术语,则由国内卖方办理保险。无论由何方投保,都会涉及选择投保险别、确定保险金额及办理投保手续等问题。

In the international trade transportation, the goods will face various risks and suffer various losses. Therefore, transportation insurance is usually required. Whether the seller or the buyer should take out insurance from the insurer mainly depends on the trade terms used in the trade contract. In export trade, if the trade terms of FOB, FCA, CFR, or CPT are chosen, the insurance is handled by the foreign buyer; if the trade terms of CIF or CIP are chosen, the insurance is handled by the domestic seller. Regardless of the party taking out an insurance policy, it involves issues such as choosing the type of insurance, determining the amount insured, and going through the insurance procedures.

13.1.1　选择投保险别（**Choice of Coverage**）

买卖双方根据贸易术语确定由何方办理运输保险，并选择适当的投保险别。保险人承担的保险责任是以险别为依据的，不同的险别所承保的责任范围不同，其保险费率也不相同。我国海运货物基本险中，平安险的责任范围最小，水渍险次之，一切险最大。与此相对应，平安险的费率最低，水渍险次之，一切险最高。

The buyer and the seller shall, according to the trade terms, determine who shall handle the transportation insurance and select the appropriate insurance coverage. The insurance liability assumed by the insurer is based on the type of insurance, and the scope of liability covered by different types of insurance varies, as do the premium rates. Among the basic marine cargo insurance types in China, the coverage of FPA is the smallest, followed by WPA and all risks. Correspondingly, the rate of FPA is the lowest, followed by WPA and all risks.

投保人在选择险别时应根据货物运输的实际情况予以全面衡量，既要使货物得到充分的保障，又要尽量节约保险费的支出，降低成本，提高效益。在国际货物运输保险实务中，选择何种险别，一般应综合考虑多种因素。

The insured should make a comprehensive assessment of the actual situation of cargo transportation when choosing the type of insurance, not only to enable the goods to be fully protected, but also to try to save the insurance premiums, reduce costs and improve efficiency. In the practice of international cargo transportation insurance, generally a variety of factors should be taken into account to determine the type of insurance.

1. 货物的性质和特点（**Nature and Characteristics of Goods**）

不同种类的货物，由于其性质和特点不同，在运输时即使遭遇同一风险事故，所致的损失后果也往往并不相同。因此，投保人在投保时应充分考虑货物的性质和特点，选择适当的险别。例如，粮谷类食物的特点是含水分，经过长途运输水分蒸发，可能造成短量；在运输途中如果通风设备不良，还易发汗、发热或者发霉。对于此类货物，一般可以在投保水渍险的基础上加保短量险和受潮受热险，或者投保一切险。又如油脂类商品，在运输途中常因容器破裂而渗漏或沾染杂质，造成玷污损失；如果是散装，会因油脂本身沾在舱壁或者在装卸过程中消耗而造成短量。因此，对于此类货物，可以在水渍险的基础上加保短量险和混杂玷污险。对于家用电器及相机等商品，由于在运输中易受碰损和被窃，一般应在水渍险或平安险的基础上加保碰损险或偷窃、提货不着险。

Due to the different nature and characteristics of different types of goods, the consequences of loss during transportation are often not the same even if they are exposed to the same risk. Therefore, the policyholder should take full account of the nature and characteristics of the goods and choose the appropriate type of insurance when taking out an insurance. For example, grain and cereals are characterized by moisture content, and after long-distance transportation the moisture is evaporated, which may result in a short amount; if the ventilation equipment is poor during transportation, it is also prone to sweating, heat or mold. Therefore, for this type of cargo, shortage clause and sweating and heating clause can be added to WPA, or all risks can be taken out. Another example is oil and grease commodities, which are often tainted by leakage or contamination due to rupture of containers during transportation; if they are in bulk, shortages may be caused by the oil itself staining the bulkheads or being consumed during loading and unloading. Therefore, for this type of cargo, shortage clause and intermixture and contamination clause can be added to WPA. For household appliances, cameras and other goods, because they are easy to be damaged and stolen in transportation, the risk of clash and breakage or TPND should be covered on the basis of WPA, or FPA.

2. 货物的包装(Packaging of Goods)

货物的包装对货物的安全运输具有重要作用,在有些货物运输过程及装卸转运过程中,常因包装破损而造成质量或数量上的损失。因此,在办理投保和选择险别时,对货物包装在运输过程中可能发生的损坏以及对货物可能造成的损害也应加以考虑。但需注意,由于包装不良或包装不适应国际货物运输的一般要求而致货物遭受损失,保险人一般不需负责,因为包装不良或不当属于装运前发货人的责任。

The packaging of goods plays an important role in the safe transportation of goods. In the process of transportation, loading, and unloading, the quality or quantity loss is often caused by package damage. Therefore, when determining the type of insurance, the possible damage to the packaging of goods and the possible damage to the goods should also be considered. It should be noted, however, that the insurer is generally not liable for loss of goods due to poor packaging or packaging that is not adapted to the general requirements of international carriage of goods, since poor or improper packaging is the responsibility of the consignor prior to shipment.

3. 货物用途与价值(Use and Value of Goods)

货物的用途与投保的险别也有关系。例如,食品、化妆品以及药品等与人的身体、生命息息相关的货物,由于其用途的特殊性,一旦发生污染以及变质损失,就会丧失全部使用价值。因此,在投保时应尽量考虑使货物得到充分、全面的保障。例如,茶叶在运输过程中一旦被海水浸湿或吸收异味即无法饮用,失去使用价值,应当投保一切险。

The use of goods is also relevant to the type of insurance. For example, food, cosmetics and pharmaceuticals, which are closely related to human bodies and lives, will lose their full value in the event of contamination and deterioration due to the special nature of their use. Therefore, when taking out insurance, consideration should be given to ensuring that the goods are fully and comprehensively covered. For example, once tea is soaked by seawater or absorbs odors during transportation, it becomes undrinkable and loses its value, so it should be insured against all risks.

货物价值的高低对投保险别也有影响。对于古玩、金银、珠宝以及贵重工艺品之类的货物,由于其价值高昂,一旦损坏,对其价值影响较大,所以应投保一切险,以获得全部的保障。对于砂石、矿砂等大宗货物,因其价值低廉,也不易受损,所以一般仅需在平安险的基础上加保短量险即可,陆上运输则可投保陆运险并加保短量险。

The value of the goods also has an influence on the choice of insurance coverage. For antiques, gold, silver, jewelry and precious crafts and other goods, due to their high value, once damaged, the value will be greatly affected, so such goods should be insured all risks to obtain full coverage. For bulk goods such as sand and ore, because their value is low and not easy to be damaged, generally only need to add shortage clause on the basis of FPA insurance, while for goods transported by land, shortage clause can be covered in addition to overland transportation risks.

4. 运输方式和运输工具(Mode of Transport and Means of Transport)

货物采用不同的运输方式和运输工具进行运输,途中可能遭遇的风险并不相同,可供选择的险别因此也各不相同。投保人或被保险人应根据不同的运输方式或运输工具选择适用的险别。

When goods are transported by different modes and means of transportation, the risks that may be encountered en route are not the same, and the types of insurance available are therefore different. The policyholder or the insured should choose the applicable insurance according to the different modes or means of transportation.

此外,随着运输技术的发展,国际多式联运作为新的运输方式,越来越多地被采用,但国际上并无专门的承保国际多式联运的保险条款,因而需要根据多式联运过程具体采用的运输方式,分段投保相应的险别。

In addition, with the development of transportation technology, international multimodal transport is increasingly being adopted as a new mode of transportation, however, there are no specialized insurance clauses to cover international multimodal transport, and therefore it is necessary to take out insurance coverage in segments according to the specific mode of transport used in the multimodal transport process.

5. 运输路线及船舶停靠港口(Transportation Routes and Ports of Call)

一般而言,运输路线越长,所需的运输时间越长,货物在运输过程中可能遭遇的风险越多。另外,在运输路途中经过的区域的地理位置、气候情况以及政治局势等也会对货物的安全运输产生影响。在政局动荡不定或已经发生战争的海域航行,货物遭受意外损失的可能性会增大。

In general, the longer the transportation route, the longer the transportation time required and the more risks the goods may encounter during transportation. In addition, the geographic location, climatic conditions and political situation of the regions passing through on the way will also have an impact on the safety of cargo transportation. The possibility of accidental loss of cargo increases when sailing in politically volatile or war-torn waters.

同时，由于不同停靠港口在设备、装卸能力以及安全设施、管理水平、治安状况等方面有很大差异，进出口货物在港口卸货时发生货损、货差的情况也就不同。投保人在投保时，应事先了解装卸地区及中转地港口的情况，根据需要选择适当的险别。

At the same time, due to the great differences in equipment, loading and unloading capacity as well as safety facilities, management level and security situation of different ports of call, the situation of cargo loss and cargo discrepancy when imported and exported goods are unloaded at ports is also different. When taking out an insurance policy, the insured should know in advance the situation of the loading and unloading areas and ports of call, and choose the appropriate type of insurance according to the needs.

6. 运输季节（Transportation Season）

运输季节不同，也会给货物带来不同的风险和损失。例如，载货船舶在北纬 60 度以北航行，极易发生与移动冰山相撞的风险；夏季运送粮食、果品，极易发生腐败变质或生虫的现象；而冬季运送橡胶制品，极可能出现冻裂损伤。因此，投保人应根据不同季节的气候特点选择险别。

Different transportation seasons also pose different risks and losses to cargo. For example, a cargo-carrying ship sailing north of 60 degrees north latitude is highly susceptible to the risk of collision with a moving iceberg; the transportation of grain and fruit products in summer is highly susceptible to spoilage or insect infestation; and the transportation of rubber products in winter is highly likely to suffer from frostbite damage. Therefore, the insured should choose the type of insurance according to the climatic characteristics of different seasons.

13. 1. 2 确定保险金额（Determination of Amount Insured）

保险金额是被保险人对保险标的的实际投保金额，是保险人承担保险责任的标准和计收保险费的基础。在被保险货物发生保险责任范围内的损失时，保险金额就是保险人赔偿的最高限额。因此，投保人投保运输货物保险时，一般应按保险价值向保险人申报保险金额。

The amount insured is the actual insurance amount of the subject-matter insured, which is the standard for the insurer to undertake the insurance responsibility and the basis for charging the insurance premium. In the event of loss of the insured goods within the scope of insurance liability, the amount insured is the maximum limit of the insurer's compensation. Therefore, the insured should generally declare the amount insured to the insurer according to the value insured when taking out transportation cargo insurance.

1. 保险金额的构成要素（Elements of Amount Insured）

在国际货运保险中，保险金额一般是以 CIF 或 CIP 的发票价格为基础加成确定的，加成率通常为 10%。保险金额中除包括商品的价值、运费和保险费外，还应包括被保险人在贸易过程中支付的经营费用,如开证费、电报费、借款利息、税款等,此外还应包括在正常情况下可以获得的预期利润。

In terms of international freight insurance, the insurance amount is generally determined on the basis of CIF or CIP invoice price, and the mark-on percentage is usually 10%. In addition to the value of the goods, freight and insurance premium, the insurance amount shall also include the operating expenses paid by the insured in the course of trade, such as L/C fees, telegraph fees, interest on loans, taxes, etc., in addition to the expected profits that can be made under normal circumstances.

关于保险加成率,《跟单信用证统一惯例》和 2020 年《国际贸易术语解释通则》中均规定,最低保险金额应为货物的 CIF 或 CIP 价格加 10%。但是,保险人同投保人可以根据不同的货物、不同地区进口价格与当地市价之间的差价、不同的经营费用和预期利润水平,约定不同的加成率。在我国出口业务中,保险金额一般按货物的 CIF 或 CIP 价格加 10% 计算。如果买方要求较高的加成率计算投保金额,在保险公司同意的情况下我方可以接受,但是保费差额部分应由买方负担。

As for the insurance markup rate, it is stipulated in the *Uniform Customs and Practice for Documentary Credits* (UCP600) and Incoterms[®] 2020 that the minimum insurance amount shall be the CIF or CIP price of the goods plus 10%. However, the insurer and the applicant may agree on different markup rates according to different goods, the difference between the import price and the local market price in different regions, different operating expenses, and expected profit levels. In China's export business, the amount insured is generally calculated according to the CIF or CIP price of the goods plus 10%. If the buyer requires a higher markup percentage to calculate the amount insured, we can accept it with the consent of the insurance company, but the increased premium shall be borne by the buyer.

2. 保险金额的计算(Calculation of Amount Insured)

保险金额的计算公式为

$$保险金额=CIF(CIP)价×(1+保险加成率)$$

如果以 CFR 或 CPT 成交,则

$$CIF(CIP)价=CFR(CPT)价/[1-(1+保险加成率)×保险费率]$$

$$保险金额=CIF(CIP)价×(1+保险加成率)$$
$$=CFR(CPT)价×(1+保险加成率)/[1-(1+保险加成率)×保险费率]$$

The formula for calculating the amount insured is

$$amount\ insured=CIF(CIP)×(1+markup\ rate)$$

If the business is transacted under the CFR or CPT, then

$$CIF(CIP)=CFR(CPT)/[1-(1+markup\ rate)×premium\ rate]$$

$$amount\ insured=CIF(CIP)×(1+markup\ rate)$$
$$=CFR(CPT)×(1+markup\ rate)/[1-(1+markup\ rate)×premium\ rate]$$

中国各进出口公司的出口货物保险是逐笔投保的，保险金额按上述方法确定。而对于进口货物保险，则是根据中国人民保险公司所签订的预约保险合同办理。保险金额以进口货物的 CIF 价格为准，一般不再加成，即保险金额等于 CIF 进口货价，如按 CFR(CPT)或 FOB(FCA)条件进口，则按特约保险费率和平均运费率直接计算保险金额。

The exported goods of China's import and export companies is insured on a case-by-case basis, and the amount insured is determined according to the above method. For insurance of imported goods, it is handled according to the open insurance contract signed by the People's Insurance Company of China. The amount insured shall be subject to the CIF price of the imported goods, and there is no mark-on percentage generally, that is, the sum insured is equal to the CIF import price. If the import is made under CFR (CPT) or FOB (FCA) terms, the amount insured shall be calculated directly according to the special premium rate and average freight rate.

按 CFR(CPT)进口时：

$$保险金额＝CFR(CPT)价格×(1＋特约保险费率)$$

When import on CRF (CPT) basis：

$$amount\ insured＝CFR\ (CPT)×(1＋special\ premium\ rate)$$

按 FOB(FCA)进口时：

$$保险金额＝FOB(FCA)价格×(1＋平均运费率＋特约保险费率)$$

When import on FOB (FCA) basis：

$$amount\ insured＝FOB(FCA)×(1＋average\ freight\ rate＋special\ premium\ rate)$$

13.1.3 办理投保手续（Apply for Insurance）

确定了保险人和险别之后，投保人应办理具体的投保手续。投保人向保险人投保是一种签订合同的法律行为。按照保险的一般原则，投保人必须对保险标的拥有保险利益，保险合同才有效，这是办理投保的前提条件。但在国际贸易运输货物保险中，一般并不要求投保人在投保时必须拥有可保利益，只要求在保险货物发生损失、被保险人要求损害赔偿时具有可保利益，即拥有预期的可保利益即可办理保险。在我国，投保货物运输保险时，投保人通常以书面方式作出投保要约，即填写货物运输保险投保单，经保险人在投保单上签章承诺，或是出立保险单，保险双方即确立合同关系。

After determining the insurer and the type of insurance, the applicant should go through the specific insurance procedures. It is a kind of legal act to sign a contract for the applicant to insure with the insurer. According to the general principles of insurance, the insurance contract is valid only if the applicant has an insurable interest in the subject-matter insured, which is a prerequisite for insurance. However, as for the international cargo transportation insurance, it is generally not required that the insured must have insurable interests at the time of insurance, but only requires that the insured have the insurable interest when the insured claims for damages in case of loss of the insured goods, that is, the insurance can be handled with the expected insurable interests. In China, when taking out cargo transportation insurance, the applicant usually makes an offer in writing, that is, filling in the application form for insurance, and after the insurer signs and accepts all terms on the application form, or issues the insurance policy, the insurance parties then have established a contractual relationship.

1. 出口货物的投保（Insuring for Exported Goods）

按 FOB、CFR 或 FCA、CPT 条件成交时，买方承担运输途中的风险，并由买方自行办理保险。但卖方在交货之前一段时间内，仍承担货物可能遭受意外损失的风险，需自行安排这段时间内的保险事宜，投保相应险别。

When the transaction is made on FOB, CFR or FCA, CPT terms, the buyer shall bear the risks in transit and shall take out insurance by himself. However, the seller still bears the risk of accidental loss of the goods for a period of time before the delivery of the goods, so he needs to arrange the corresponding insurance for this period of time.

当出口合同采用 CIF 和 CIP 条件时，虽然运输途中的风险仍由买方承担，但保险由卖方办理，因此，出口企业一般应在出口货物从装运地仓库运往交货地之前办妥投保手续。根据买卖合同和信用证的规定，在备妥货物并确定装运日期和运输工具后，按规定格式逐笔填制投保单，送交保险公司投保，并交付保险费，保险公司凭此出具保险单或保险凭证。实际业务中，对于长期顾客，保险公司也可同意投保人用发票副本替代投保单，但应在发票副本上将投保单所规定的内容补齐。

When the export contract adopts CIF and CIP terms, although the risk during transportation is still borne by the buyer, the insurance is handled by the seller, therefore, the exporter should generally complete the insurance procedures before the exported goods are transported from the warehouse of the place of shipment to the place of delivery. According to the provisions of the contract of sale and letter of credit, after preparing the goods and determining the date of shipment and means of transportation, the seller shall fill in the application form according to the prescribed format, and send it to the insurance company to insure and pay the insurance premiums, and the insurance company will issue the insurance policy or the insurance certificate based on it. In practice, for long-term customers, the insurance company may also agree to replace the policy with a copy of the invoice, provided that the copy of the invoice is completed with the contents specified in the policy.

各国保险公司投保单的格式虽有不同，但内容基本一致，一般都包括被保险人名称、被保险货物名称、数量、包装及标志、保险金额、起讫地点、运输工具名称、起航日期、投保险别、赔偿地点等。

Although the format of insurance application forms in different countries is different, the contents are basically the same, generally including the name of the insured, the name of the insured goods, quantity, packaging and mark, amount insured, place of origin and destination, name of means of transport, date of departure, type of insurance, place of indemnity, etc.

1）投保单的缮制（Preparation of Insurance Application Form）

投保单是投保人在投保时对保险标的及有关事实的告知和陈述，也是保险人签发保险单和确定保险费的依据。投保单的法律效力表现在保险合同生效后，投保单将作为保险合同不可分割的组成部分。因此，投保单的填写必须真实、准确。中国人民保险公司的进出口货物运输保险投保单的具体内容包括以下几个方面。

The application form is the applicant's notification and statement of the subject-matter insured and the relevant facts when applying for insurance, and it is also the basis for the insurer to issue the policy and determine the insurance premium. The legal effect of the application form is manifested in that after the insurance contract comes into effect, it will be an integral part of the insurance contract, so the filling in of the application policy must be true and accurate. The specific contents of the application form of the People's Insurance Company of China for imported and exported cargo include the following aspects.

（1）被保险人。被保险人是享受保险单权益的人。当货物以 CIF 或 CIP 条件出口时，应由出口方以投保人的身份办理保险，出口方应以本人作为被保险人。当货物在装运港装上船或交付承运人之前发生损失时，风险应由出口方承担，出口方可以向保险人索赔。一旦货物装上船或交予承运人，出口方根据信用证或贸易合同的要求在保险单上签章背书，即可将保险单转让给进口商或指定的第三方（如银行）。

（1）The insured. The insured is the person who has the rights and benefits under the insurance policy. When the goods are exported under CIF or CIP terms, the insurance shall be taken out by the exporter as the policyholder, and the exporter shall take himself as the insured. When a loss occurs before the goods are loaded onto a ship or delivered to the carrier at the port of shipment, the risk shall be borne by the exporter, who may claim compensation from the insurer. Once the goods are loaded on board the vessel or delivered to the carrier, the exporter can assign the insurance policy to the importer or a designated third party (e. g. a bank) by signing and endorsing the insurance policy in accordance with the requirements of the letter of credit or trade contract.

当货物以 FOB、FCA 或 CFR、CPT 等条件出口时，应由进口方自行办理运输货物保险，投保人与被保险人一般均为进口方。出口方承担的货物在起运港装上船或货交承运人之前的风险可通过投保国内短途货运险予以保障。

When the goods are exported under FOB, FCA, CFR, CPT or other terms, the importer should handle the transportation insurance by himself and the applicant and the insured are generally the importer. The risks borne by the exporter before the goods are loaded on board at the port of departure or delivered to the carrier can be covered by insurance against domestic short-haul freight.

（2）发票号码和合同号码。为了便于在发生索赔时进行核对，投保人应在投保单上填写出口货物的发票号码和贸易合同号码。

（2）Invoice No. and contract No. In order to facilitate verification in the event of a claim，the applicant should fill in the invoice number and trade contract number of the export goods on the application form.

（3）标记。投保单上的标记应与提单上所载的标记相一致，特别要同刷在货物外包装上的实际标记相同，以免在发生理赔时引起检验、核赔、确定责任上的混乱。

（3）Marks. The marks on the application form should be consistent with those on the B/L，especially the same as the actual marks on the outer package of the goods，so as to avoid confusion in inspection，claim verification and liability determination in case of claim settlement.

（4）包装及数量。此栏需写明包装方式，如捆、箱、袋、桶等，以及包装的数量。如果一次投保有数种不同包装，可以"件"为单位。散装货应填写散装重量。采用集装箱运输时，应予注明"装集装箱"。

（4）Packing and quantity. The column of packing and quantity should be filled in with the modes of packaging like bundles，cases，bags，or drums，and the number of packages. Should there be many different types of packages for one insurance application，the "packages" can be taken as units. For cargo in bulk，"…M/T in bulk" needs to be filled into the form and carriage by container should be indicated as "in container".

（5）货物名称。应填写保险货物的具体类别、名称，如棉布、茶叶、小麦等，以便保险人确定适当的保险费率。一般不应笼统地填写货物大类，如纺织品、食品等。

（5）Name of the goods. The specific category and name of the insured goods shall be filled in，such as cotton，tea，and wheat，in order to facilitate the insurer to determine the appropriate insurance rate. General categories of goods such as textiles and food should not be filled in.

（6）保险金额。保险金额应按照发票的 CIF 或 CIP 价格加上合同所规定的保险加成计算得出的数值填写。保险金额的货币名称要与信用证、发票一致。

（6）Insurance amount. The insurance amount shall be filled in according to the value calculated by the CIF or CIP prices of the invoice plus the markup rate stipulated in the contract. The currency name of the insurance amount shall be consistent with the L/C and invoice.

（7）装载运输工具。如果采用班轮运输，应写明船名，如果中途需转船，已知第二程船时应填写船名，若第二程船名未知，则只需填写"转船"字样；集装箱运输应写明"集装箱运输"；如果采用火车或航空运输，最好注明火车班次和班机航次；如果采用多式联运，应写明联运方式，如注明海空或陆海联运。

（7）Means of transportation. If liner transportation is adopted，the name of the ship shall be indicated. If transshipment is required during the voyage，the name of the second ship shall be filled in; if the name of the second route is unknown, only the words "with transshipment" shall be filled in. For container transport, "by container" shall be indicated. If train or air transport is adopted, it is best to indicate the train number and flight number. If multimodal transport is adopted, the mode of multimodal transport shall be specified, such as air-sea or land-sea transport.

（8）航次、航班。若采用班机或班轮，应注明飞机或船舶航行的航班、航次。

（8）Voyage/ flight. If a liner or flight is used, the flight and voyage number of the aircraft or ship shall be indicated.

（9）开航日期。一般应注明"按照提单"，或注明船舶的大致开航日期。

（9）Date of departure. It should generally be stated "as per B/L" or the approximate date of departure of the vessel.

（10）提单或运单号码。此处应清楚地填写提单或运单的号码，以备保险公司核对。

（10）Number of B/L or number of waybill. The number of B/L or waybill should be clearly stated for the insurer's verification.

（11）运输路线。填写起始地和目的地名称。中途如需转运则应注明转运地。到目的地后若需转运内陆，应注明内陆地名称。如果到达目的地的路线不止一条，要填写经过的中途港（站）的名称。

（11）Transport route. The names of the departure and destination should be filled in the application form. And the name of transshipment place is also demanded if transshipment is needed. If inland transfer is necessary after the goods arrive at the destination, the names of the inland places shall be indicated. If there is more than one route to the destination, the name of the intermediate ports (stations) should be filled in.

（12）承保险别。填写投保何种险别，包括基本险和附加险，还应注明采用何种条款。投保人如果对保险条款有特殊要求也应注明，以便保险人考虑是否接受。

（12）Insurance coverage. The types of coverage, including basic risks and additional risks, should be filled in the form and the corresponding insurance terms should be stated as well. Any special requirements of the policyholder regarding the terms and conditions of the insurance should also be indicated so that the insurer can consider whether to accept them or not.

（13）赔付地点。一般都是在保险目的地支付赔款。如果被保险人要求在目的地以外的地方给付赔款，应予注明。

（13）Indemnity location. The indemnity is generally paid at the destination of the insurance. If the insured claims to be paid at a place other than the destination, it should be indicated.

（14）投保人签章及企业名称、电话和地址。填写投保人的名称、地址等具体信息。

（14）The applicant signature, name, telephone and address. The name, telephone number, address and signature of the applicant are required to be filled in the form.

（15）投保日期。出口方投保时，投保日期应在船舶开航日期或货物起运日期之前。根据 UCP600 的规定，银行有权拒收保险单日期迟于货物装船或发运日期的保险单。

（15）Date of application. When the exporter takes out an insurance, the date of the policy should be before the date of departure of the ship or the date of shipment of the goods. According to UCP600, the bank has the right to reject the insurance policy if the date of the policy is later than the date of loading or shipment of the goods.

2）填写投保单应注意的事项（Matters to Note When Completing an Application Form）

单据13.1　投保单

填写投保单应注意的事项主要包括以下几个方面。

Matters to be noted for filling out the application form mainly include the following aspects.

（1）投保单所申报的内容必须属实。保险是建立在最大诚信原则基础上的合同关系，投保人必须履行如实告知的义务。保险人是否承保以及保险费率的确定主要是依据投保人所申报的情况。因此，投保人在办理投保时，应当将有关被保险货物的重要事项向保险人做真实的申报。如申报不实或故意隐瞒事实，保险人有权解除合同或不负赔偿责任，且不必退还保险费。如果投保人因过失而未如实申报重要事实，保险人可以酌情作出解除保险合同或加收保费的决定。

（1）The contents declared in the application form must be real and true. Insurance is a contractual relationship based on the principle of utmost good faith, and the applicant must fulfill the obligation of truthful disclosure. Whether the insurer underwrites the insurance and the determination of the premium rate are mainly based on the information declared by the applicant. Therefore, when applying for insurance, the applicant should make a true declaration to the insurer concerning the important matters of the insured goods. In case of inaccurate declaration or intentional concealment of facts, the insurer has the right to terminate the contract or not to be liable for compensation, and is not obliged to refund the insurance premium. If the policyholder fails to truthfully declare material facts due to negligence, the insurer may, at its discretion, decide to terminate the insurance contract or increase the premium.

（2）投保单的内容必须同买卖合同及信用证上的有关规定相一致。保险单是依据投保单的内容签发的，因此，如果投保人不按照贸易合同的规定填写投保单，保险人据此出具的保险单就会与贸易合同的规定不符，收货人可拒绝接受该种保险单。信用证支付方式下，投保单的内容还应符合信用证的有关规定，否则保险人据此签发的保险单会因"单证不符"而遭到银行的拒付。

（2）The contents of the insurance policy must be consistent with the relevant provisions of the sales contract and the letter of credit. The insurance policy is issued on the basis of the content of the application form; therefore, if the policyholder does not fill in the form in accordance with the provisions of the trade contract, the insurance policy issued by the insurer will not be consistent with the provisions of the trade contract，and the consignee may refuse to accept the policy. Under the letter of credit payment，the contents of the policy should also comply with the relevant provisions of the L/C，otherwise the insurance policy issued by the insurer will be refused by the bank due to "non-conformity of the documents with the L/C".

（3）尽可能投保到内陆目的地。若国际货物运输的目的地在内陆,在投保时应将保险期限的终止地指定为内陆的目的地,尤其采用海运方式时,不能只投保到目的港,应保证货物的全部运输过程都得到保险保障。这是因为在实际业务中,货物的损失往往在货物运抵目的地仓库经检验后才能发现,若只保到目的港,就会对损失责任的确定造成困难。

（3）Insure to inland destinations whenever possible. If the destination is inland，the termination place of the insurance period should be designated as the inland destination. When the goods are transported by sea，the insurance can not be insured only to the port of destination，but the whole transportation process of the goods should also be covered. Because in the actual business，the loss of goods is often found after the goods are transported to the warehouse of destination and inspected. If the goods are only insured to the port of destination，it will be difficult to determine the responsibility for loss.

（4）特殊要求应事先征得保险公司同意。采用 CIF 或 CIP 等贸易术语出口时,如果进口方对保险提出特殊的要求,如加保某项特殊险,或要求过高的保险加成等,出口方应征得保险公司同意后再接受进口方的要求。

（4）Special requirements shall be approved by the insurance company in advance. When exporting using CIF or CIP trade terms，if the importer puts forward special requirements for insurance，such as insuring an additional special insurance，or asking for too high mark-on percentage of insurance，the exporter should seek the consent of the insurance company before accepting the importer's requirements.

（5）投保后发现投保项目有错漏,要及时向保险公司申请批改,如保险目的地变动、船名错误或保险金额增减等。

（5）If any errors or omissions are found in the insured items after taking out the policy，the policyholder should apply to the insurance company for approval in time，such as change of the insured destination，wrong name of the vessel，or the increase or decrease of the insured amount.

2. 进口货物的投保(Insuring for Imported Goods)

采用 FOB、CFR 或 FCA、CPT 贸易术语进口时,货物的运输保险由国内买方办理,投保方式有以下两种。

When FOB，CFR or FCA，CPT trade terms are used for import，the transportation insurance of the goods is handled by the domestic buyer，and there are two following ways to insure the goods.

1) 订立预约保险合同(Conclusion of Open Insurance Contract)

在我国实际保险业务中,专营进口业务的企业可通过订立预约保险合同的方式为进口货物办理保险,这样既简化了保险手续,又能够防止进口货物在国外装运后因信息传送不及时而发生漏保或来不及办理投保等情况。

In China, enterprises specializing in import business can handle insurance for imported goods by signing open insurance contracts, which not only simplifies the insurance procedures, but also prevents the imported goods from missing insurance or being insured too late due to the delay in information transmission after shipment abroad.

预约保险合同规定,该公司从国外进口的全部货物,凡贸易条件规定由买方办理保险的,保险公司都负有自动承保的责任,但投保人应向保险公司办理投保手续并支付保险费。同保险公司签订预约保险合同的进口公司,对每批进口货物无须填制投保单,只需在获悉所投保货物在国外起运时,将装运情况通知保险人即可。我国通常的做法是:投保人填写"国际运输预约保险起运通知书",保险公司通常以上述起运通知书作为投保人投保依据,签章后退回一份给投保人,作为承保依据,代替保险单。

The open insurance contract stipulates that the insurance company has an automatic responsibility to underwrite all goods imported by the company from abroad where the trade terms stipulate that the buyer should handle the insurance. However, the applicant shall go through the insurance procedures with the insurance company and pay the premium. An importing company that has signed an open insurance contract with an insurance company does not need to fill out an application form for each shipment of imported goods, but only needs to notify the insurer of the shipment when it learns that the insured goods are being shipped abroad. The usual practice in China is that the policyholder fills in the "Notice of Shipment for International Transportation Open Insurance", and the insurance company usually takes the said notice of shipment as the basis for the policyholder to take out the insurance, and returns a copy of the notice of shipment to the policyholder after signing, as the basis for underwriting the insurance, instead of the insurance policy.

2) 逐笔办理投保(Specific Deal Cover)

此种方式适用于不经常有货物进口的企业。采用这种投保方式时,进口方在接到国外发货通知后立即填写投保单,向保险公司办理投保手续,缴纳保险费。保险公司根据投保单签发保险单。

单据13.2　预约保险起运通知书

This method is applicable to enterprises that do not often import goods. When this type of insurance is adopted, the importer fills in the application form immediately after receiving the notice of shipment from abroad, goes through the insurance procedures with the insurance company and pays the insurance premium. Then the insurance company issues an insurance policy based on the application form.

13.2 国际贸易合同中的保险条款(Insurance Terms in International Trade Contracts)

保险条款是国际贸易合同中必不可缺的内容,进出口方在签订买卖合同时,必须明确规定保险由谁办理、保险费由谁承担、依照什么保险条款、投保何种险别、保险金额如何确定等内容,明确买卖双方各自的责任,避免因责任不清引起纠纷。如果其中一方有特殊要求,也应事先在合同中约定。

Insurance terms are indispensable in international trade contracts. When signing sales contracts, importers and exporters must clearly specify who will handle the insurance, who will bear the insurance premium, what insurance clauses to follow, what kind of risks to be insured and how to determine the insurance amount, so as to clarify their respective responsibilities and avoid disputes caused thereafter. Any specific requirements, if any, shall also be agreed upon and stated in the contract in advance.

13.2.1 FOB、CFR、FCA、CPT 贸易术语项下的保险条款(Insurance Terms Under FOB, CFR, FCA, CPT Trade Terms)

(1) 以这些贸易术语成交时,大多数情况下,保险由买方自行办理,买卖合同中保险条款可订为"保险由买方负责"。

(1) When the transaction is concluded under these trade terms, in most cases, the insurance is handled by the buyer, and the insurance clause in the contract of sale usually reads like "Insurance: To be covered by the Buyer".

(2) 如经买卖双方商定由卖方代办保险,保险条款可订为:"保险由买方委托卖方按发票金额 110% 代为投保海运一切险,按中国人民保险公司《海洋运输货物保险条款》负责,保险费由买方负责。"

(2) If the buyer and the seller agree that the insurance will be carried out by the seller, the insurance clause may be as follows: " To be effected by the Seller on behalf of Buyer for 110% of total invoice value against All Risks, as per and subject to *Ocean Marine Cargo Clauses* of the People's Insurance Company of China, and the premium shall be borne by the Buyer. "

13.2.2 CIF、CIP 贸易术语项下的保险条款(Insurance Terms Under CIF and CIP Trade Terms)

按照 Incoterms® 2020 的规定,当价格条件为 CIF、CIP 时,保险应由卖方办理。买卖双方在合同中应明确何方办理保险、投保的险别、保险金额与保险加成、采用何种保险条款等。如果买方对保险有特殊要求,如加保拒收险等特殊险别,应将该种要求写明并明确由此增加的保险费由何方承担。保险条款举例如下。

According to Incoterms® 2020, for the transactions on the basis of CIF or CIP, the insurance shall be handled by the seller. The buyer and seller should specify in the contract who will handle the insurance, the type of insurance to be taken out, the amount of insurance and the insurance premium, and the type of insurance clauses to be adopted. If the buyer has special requirements for insurance, such as handling the additional rejection clause and other special risks, such requirements should be clearly stated and it should be made clear who will be responsible for the increase in insurance premiums. Examples of insurance clauses are as follows.

（1）投保海运平安险/水渍险，加保战争险，保险条款可订为："保险由卖方按发票金额的 110％投保平安险/水渍险和战争险，以中国人民保险公司 2009 年 1 月 1 日《海洋运输货物保险条款》为准。"

（1）To cover marine FPA/WPA, plus war risk, on the terms as follows："To be covered by the seller for 110% of total invoice value against Free from Particular Average/With Particular Average and War Risks as per *Ocean Marine Cargo Clauses* of People's Insurance Company of China, dated 1/1/2009."

（2）投保陆运一切险，保险条款可订为："保险由卖方按发票金额的 110％投保陆运一切险，以中国人民保险公司 1981 年 1 月 1 日《陆上运输货物保险条款》为准。"

（2）To insure against overland transportation all risks, the terms of insurance may be as follows："To be covered by the seller for 110% of total invoice value against Overland Transportation All Risks as per *Overland Transportation Cargo Clauses* of People's Insurance Company of China, dated 1/1/1981."

（3）要求保险责任延长到内陆最后目的地，保险条款可订为："保险由卖方按发票金额的 110％投保空运一切险，保险责任延伸到纽约收货人仓库，以中国人民保险公司 1981 年 1 月 1 日《航空运输货物保险条款》为准。"

（3）If the insurance liability is required to be extended to the final inland destination, the insurance terms can be："To be covered by the seller for 110% of total invoice value against Air Transportation All Risks, insurance liability extends to the consignee's warehouse in New York, as per *Air Transportation Cargo Clauses* of People's Insurance Company of China, dated 1/1/1981."

（4）要求延长保险期限，保险条款可订为："保险由卖方按发票金额的 110％投保一切险，包括目的港 90 天期限，以中国人民保险公司 2009 年 1 月 1 日《海洋运输货物保险条款》为准。"

（4）If the buyer requests an extension of the insurance period, the insurance clause may be concluded as follows："To be covered by the seller for 110% of total invoice value against All Risks, the insurance period is extended to 90 days after the arrival of the goods at the port of destination, as per *Ocean Marine Cargo Clauses* of People's Insurance Company of China, dated 1/1/2009."

（5）保险规定免赔率的，保险条款可订为："保险由卖方按发票金额的 110％投保一切险，免赔率为 1％，以中国人民保险公司 2009 年 1 月 1 日《海洋运输货物保险条款》

为准。"

（5）In case of being insured with deductible，insurance terms can be："To be covered by the seller for 110% of total invoice value against All Risks with deductible of 1%，as per *Ocean Marine Cargo Clauses* of People's Insurance Company of China，dated 1/1/2009."

（6）要求按国外条款承保，保险条款可订为："保险由卖方按发票金额的 110% 投保海运保险，按 2009 年 1 月 1 日协会货物保险条款 A 负责。"

（6）When foreign insurance clauses are required，the insurance terms may be set as follows："To be effected by seller for 110% of invoice value covering marine risks，as per Institute Cargo Clause（A），dated 1/1/2009."

13.3 国际运输货物保险承保实务（Underwriting Practice of International Transportation Cargo Insurance）

国际运输货物保险的承保过程通常是保险人收到投保人的投保申请后，根据投保人的投保意向，按照规定的风险标准和操作程序对投保申请进行严格的筛选，并提出相应的保险条件，对符合条件的投保单予以承保，签发保险单，即保险双方协商一致后，签订保险合同。

The underwriting process of international cargo transportation insurance is usually that after receiving the policyholder's application for insurance，the insurer，based on the policyholder's intention to insure，conducts a rigorous screening of the application in accordance with the prescribed risk criteria and operational procedures，then puts forward the corresponding insurance conditions，underwrites the qualified application form，and issues the insurance policy. In a word，after the insurance parties reach an agreement through consultation，the insurance contract is then concluded.

13.3.1 保险单的种类（Types of Insurance Policy）

保险单是保险人接受被保险人的申请，并在其交纳保险费后而订立的保险契约，是保险人和被保险人之间权利与义务的说明，是当事人处理理赔和索赔的重要依据，也是出口商在 CIF 条件下向银行办理结汇所必须提交的单据。

Insurance policy is an insurance contract concluded after the insurer accepts the application of the insured and pays the insurance premium，which is a statement of the rights and obligations between the insurer and the insured，an important basis for the parties to deal with settlements and claims，and a document that exporters are required to submit to the bank to handle the settlement of foreign exchange under the CIF conditions.

保险单是保险公司根据投保人所提交的投保单的内容制作的，因此，其内容应与投保单一致，以满足投保人对保险的要求。在保险单的正面，是特定的一笔保险交易，同时，该笔保险交易的当事人、保险标的、保险金额、险别、费率等应一一列出。在保险单的背面，详细地列出了投保人、保险人、保险受益人的权利、义务以及各自的免责条款。

The insurance policy is made by the insurer according to the application form presented by the insured, therefore, discrepancies are not allowed between the policy and the application. On the front of the policy, the specific insurance transaction is clearly stated with the indication of the insurance parties, the subject-matter insured, the insured amount, type of insurance, premium, etc. On the back of the policy, the rights and obligations of the policyholder, insurer, and insurance beneficiary, as well as their respective exemptions, are set out in detail.

海上运输保险单可以从不同的角度划分为以下不同的类型。

Marine transport insurance policies can be categorized into different types as the following.

1. 按保险标的的不同划分（Classification According to the Subject-matter Insured）

1）船舶保险单［Ship Policy（Hull Policy）］

它是以船舶为保险标的的保险单据。船舶保险单与货物保险单格式类似，只是在保险单上附有船舶保险的相关条款。船舶保险单又分为定期保险单和航次保单。

Ship policy is an insurance document with the ship as the subject-matter insured. The format of ship policy is similar to that of cargo policy, except that the relevant clauses of ship insurance are attached to the policy. Ship policy is divided into time policy and voyage policy.

2）货物保险单［Goods Policy（Cargo Policy）］

它所承保的是具有商品性质的货物，这种货物一般以装在船舱里为限，舱面货物和活动物一般不在承保范围内，但事先特别声明并商定费率后，保险人也可承保。

It covers commercial goods which are generally limited to those loaded in the hold of the ship, while deck cargo and live animals are generally excluded from the scope of coverage, but may be covered by the insurer after a special declaration and agreement on rates in advance.

3）运费保险单（Freight Policy）

它与船舶保险单和货物保险单不同，后两者的保险标的都是有形物体，而运费保险单所承保的是一种无形的利益。船东为了保障收取运费的安全，可向保险人办理运费保险。

Freight policy is different from ship policy and cargo policy. The subject matter of the latter two is tangible, while the freight policy covers an intangible interest. In order to ensure the certainty of freight collection, the shipowner can apply for freight insurance from the insurer.

2. 按保险价值是否确定划分（Classification According to the Certainty of the Insurance Value）

1）定值保险单（Valued Policy）

定值保险单是在保险单上载明保险人与被保险人约定保险标的的价值的保险单。定值保险情况下，发生保险责任内的损失时，不论保险标的在损失当时、当地的实际价值（市价)是多少,保险人都按照保险单上约定的保险金额计算赔款。全部损失按保险金额全部赔偿,部分损失按保险金额乘以损失比例赔偿。海洋运输货物保险和船舶保险一般采用定值保险的方式。

Valued policy is an insurance policy in which the insurer and the insured agree on the value of the subject-matter insured. In the case of valued insurance, in the event of a loss within the scope of insurance liability, the insurer calculates the compensation in accordance with the insurance amount agreed in the policy, regardless of the actual value of the subject-matter insured at the time of the loss and in the local area (market value). The total loss is compensated according to the insurance amount, and the partial loss is compensated according to the insurance amount multiplied by the percentage of loss. Marine transportation cargo insurance and ship insurance generally adopt the method of fixed-value insurance.

2)不定值保险单(Unvalued Policy)

不定值保险单是在保险单上不载明保险标的价值,而留待损失发生后再具体核实的保险单。在不定值保险情况下,若发生保险责任范围内的损失,按照《海商法》的规定,保险价值依照保险责任开始时货物在起运地的发票价格及运费和保险费的总和计算。若计算出的保险价值等于保险金额(足额保险),按实际损失计算保险赔款;若低于保险金额(超额保险),赔款最高不超过保险价值;若高于保险金额(不足额保险),赔款按保险金额与保险价值的比例计算,最高不超过保险价值。不定值保险单大多运用于海运货物保险和船舶保险以外的财产保险或责任保险。

Unvalued policy is an insurance policy in which the value of the subject-matter insured is not stated, but is left to be specifically verified after the loss has occurred. In the case of unvalued insurance, in the event of a loss covered by insurance, the insured value is calculated in accordance with the provisions of the *Maritime Law* on the basis of the invoice price of the goods at the place of shipment at the time of the commencement of the insurance liability, as well as the sum of the freight charges and the insurance premium. If the calculated insurance value is equal to the amount insured (insurance to value), the insurance compensation will be calculated according to the actual loss; if it is lower than the insurance amount (excess insurance), the compensation will not exceed the insurance value at the maximum; if it is higher than the insurance amount (under insurance), the compensation will be calculated according to the ratio of the amount insured to the insurance value, and the maximum will not exceed the insurance value. Unvalued policies are mostly used for property or liability insurance other than marine cargo and ship insurance.

3. 按保险期限划分(Classification by Insurance Period)

1)航程保险单(Voyage Policy)

航程保险单是指承保规定航程内保险标的所遭受损失的保险单,即以航程为保险期限的保险单。对航程的规定是:不载货船舶的起讫时间自起运港解缆或起锚时开始,至目的港抛锚或系缆完毕时终止；载货船舶的起讫时间自起运港装货时开始，至目的港卸货完毕时终止。但自船舶抵达目的港当日午夜起，最多不得超过 30 天。

被保险人对于其拥有的船舶或货物都可以向保险人投保航程险。但在一般情况下航程保险单主要用于海洋货物运输保险，有时也可用于接受新船及其他特殊情况。我国进出口货物大多采用航程保险形式。

Voyage policy refers to the insurance policy that covers the losses suffered by the subject-matter insured within the specified voyage, that is, the insurance policy with the voyage as the insurance period. The provisions on voyage are: the duration of an unladen ship starts from the time of untying or anchoring at the port of shipment to the time of completion of anchoring or tying at the port of destination; the duration of a laden ship starts from the time of loading at the port of shipment to the time of completion of unloading at the port of destination. However, the maximum period shall not exceed 30 days from midnight on the day the ship arrives at the port of destination.

An insured may take out a voyage policy with an insurer for any ship or cargo owned by him. However, in general the voyage policy is mainly used for marine cargo transportation insurance, and sometimes it can also be used for accepting new ships and other special cases. In China, most of imported and exported cargoes adopt the form of voyage insurance.

2）定期保险单（Time Policy）

定期保险单是对保险标的在某一规定时间予以保险的一种保险单，即保险单在某一特定时间有效。这种保险单很少用于进出口贸易，而经常用于船舶保险。

Time policy is an insurance policy that insures the subject-matter insured for a specified period of time, i.e., the policy is in effect during a specific time period. This policy is rarely used in import and export trade, but is often used for ship insurance.

3）混合保险单（Mixed Policy）

混合保险单是兼有航程和定期性质的保险单。在这种保险单下，保险人既承保保险标的的特定航程，又在某一段固定时间内对其负责。如中国海运货物保险中普遍采用"仓至仓"条款的保险单，一方面规定保险责任在航程范围内有效，另一方面又规定以货物卸离海轮后 60 天为限，就属于此类性质的保险单。

Mixed policy is an insurance policy with both voyage and time policies. Under this type of policy, the insurer both covers the subject-matter insured for a specific voyage and is liable for a fixed period of time. For example, the "warehouse to warehouse" clause is widely used in China's marine cargo insurance. On the one hand, it stipulates that the insurance liability is valid within the scope of the voyage, and on the other hand, it stipulates that the insurance liability is limited to 60 days after the goods are discharged from the vessel.

4. 按船名是否确定划分(Classification According to Whether the Name of the Ship is Determined or Not)

1) 船名已定保险单(Specified-ship Policy)

船名已定保险单是指被保险人投保时载货船舶已经确定,并在保险单上注明船名及开航日期的保险单。一般保险单都属于此类。

Specified-ship policy is one in which the vessel carrying the cargo has been identified at the time the insured takes out the policy, and the name of the vessel and the date of sailing are stated in the policy. Insurance policies generally fall into this category.

2) 船名未定保险单(Unspecified-ship Policy)

这类保险单是在投保时无法确定载货船舶名称,需以后确定的保险单。属于此类保险单的主要有流动保险单、预约保险单和总括保险单三种。

It refers to the policy issued without indicating the specific vessel, which has to be decided in the future when necessary. This policy can further be categorized into three types: floating policy, open policy and blanket policy.

(1)流动保险单(统保单)。流动保险单是一种连续有效的保险单,适用于长期有相同类型货物需要陆续分批装运的场合。这种保险单一般只载明保险的一般条件,而将载货船舶的名称及其他细节留待以后每次装货时由被保险人分批申报。流动保险单内规定一个总保险金额,被保险人在每次装运货物后将投保金额通知保险人,保险人即从总保险金额中逐笔扣除,直至总保险金额被扣完,流动保险单的效力即告终止。

(1) Floating policy. Floating policy is a continuously valid insurance policy for long periods of time when the same type of goods are to be shipped in successive batches. Such policies generally contain only the general conditions of insurance, leaving the name of the vessel carrying the cargo and other details to be declared by the insured in subsequent installments on each loading. Floating policy provides for a total amount insured, which is deducted from the total sum insured by the insurer by notifying the insurer of the sum insured after each shipment until the total sum insured is deducted and the validity of the mobile insurance policy is terminated.

(2)预约保险单。预约保险单同流动保险单一样,也是经常有相同类型货物需陆续分批装运时所采用的一种保险单。严格来讲,它是一种没有总保险金额限制的预约保险合同,是保险人对被保险人将要装运的属于约定范围的一切货物自动承保的总合同。预约保险单上载明保险货物的范围、险别、保险费率、每批运输货物的最高保险金额以及保险费的结付、赔款处理等项目。凡属于此保险单范围内的进出口货物,一经起运,即自动按保险单所列条件承保。但被保险人在获悉每批保险货物起运时,应立即将货物装船详细情况包括货物名称、数量、保险金额、运输工具种类和名称、航程起讫地点、开船日期等情况通知保险公司和进口商。被保险人的申报如有遗漏或差错,即使货物已经发生损失,只要是出于善意的,仍可更正或补报,保险人仍按规定负责赔偿。

(2) Open policy/Open cover. An open policy, like a floating policy, is often used when the same type of goods need to be shipped in batches. Strictly speaking, it is an

open cover contract with no limit on the total amount insured. It is a general contract in which the insurer automatically underwrites all the goods that the insured will ship within the agreed scope. The open policy shall specify the scope，type，premium rate of the insured goods，the maximum amount insured of each batch of transported goods，the settlement of insurance premium，compensation treatment and other items. All imported and exported goods falling within the scope of this insurance policy shall be automatically insured according to the conditions set out in the insurance policy upon shipment. However，when the insured learns the departure of each batch of insured goods，he shall immediately notify the insurance company and importer of the details of the shipment of the goods，including the name of the goods，quantity，insured amount，type and name of means of transport，place of departure and destination，date of departure，etc. If there is any omission or error in the declaration of the insured，even if the goods have been lost，it can be corrected or supplemented as long as the error is in good faith，and the insurer is still responsible for compensation according to the regulations.

（3）总括保险单。总括保险单又称闭口保险单，是保险人在约定的保险期限内对一定保险标的的总承包单。采用这种保险方式，被保险人只要与保险公司商定一个承保范围，明确保险标的、保险总额、航程、险别等，支付一笔总保险费，双方约定一个保险期，在期限内凡属保险范围内的货物全部承保。每批货物出运时被保险人不必通知保险人，保险人也不为每批货物计算保险费。发生赔款即在保险总额内扣除，总额扣完，保险责任即终止。被保险人如果希望继续得到保险保障，可加贴"恢复条款"，按比例加缴保险费后，即可恢复原保险责任。

此类保险单多用于整批成交、分批多次出运、运输距离短、每次出运的种类及价值相似的货物。它对于保险人与投保人来说，都具有简化保险手续、节约时间的优点。

（3）Blanket policy. Also known as closed policy，it is a general contract issued by the insurer for a certain subject-matter insured within the agreed insurance period. With this type of insurance，the insured only needs to agree with the insurance company on a scope of coverage，specify the subject-matter insured，the total amount of insurance，the voyage，type of insurance，etc. ，pay a total premium，and both parties should agree on a period of insurance，within which all the goods within the scope of the insurance are fully insured. The insured is not required to notify the insurer of each shipment and the insurer does not calculate the premium for each shipment. Any claims incurred will be deducted from the total amount of the insurance，and the insurance liability will be terminated when the total amount is deducted. If the insured wishes to continue to be covered by the insurance，a "reinstatement clause" can be affixed，and the original insurance liability can be reinstated with a proportionate increase in premium.

This kind of insurance policy is mostly used for goods that are sold in a whole batch but shipped in several batches，with short transportation distance，and of similar type and value in each shipment. It has the advantages of simplifying insurance procedures and saving time for both the insurer and the policyholder.

5. 按保险单形式划分(Classification by Form of Insurance Policy)

1)保险单(Insurance Policy)

保险单俗称大保单,是被保险人与保险人之间订立的正式保险合同,除载明被保险人(投保人)的名称、被保险货物(标的物)的名称、数量或重量、唛头、运输工具、保险的起讫地点、承保险别、保险金额、出单日期等项目外,其背面还列有保险人的责任范围,以及保险人与被保险人各自的权利、义务等方面的详细条款,它是最完整的保险单据。保险单可由被保险人背书,随物权的转移而转让,它是一份独立的保险单据。

海运货物保险中,这种保险单是由保险人根据投保人逐笔投保、逐笔签发的,承保保险单内指定的、经由指定船舶和航次承运的货物在运输途中的风险,货物安全抵达目的地,保险单效力即告终止。保险单是被保险人在保险标的遭受承保范围内风险而发生损失时向保险人索赔的主要凭证,同时也是保险人向被保险人索赔的主要依据。

Insurance policy, also known as the major policy, is a formal insurance contract concluded between the insured and the insurer, in addition to the name of the insured (the policyholder), the name of the insured goods (the subject matter), quantity or weight, shipping marks, means of transportation, the place of origin and destination of the insurance, the type of insurance covered, the insurance amount, the date of issuance of the policy, etc., but also the scope of the insurer's liability is listed in the back of the policy, as well as the detailed terms and conditions regarding the respective rights and obligations of the insurer and the insured, which is the most complete insurance documents. An insurance policy may be endorsed by the insured and transferred with the transfer of property rights, it is an independent insurance document.

In marine cargo insurance, this type of policy is issued by the insurer in accordance with the policyholder's application form on a case-by-case basis and covers the risks during transportation of the goods specified in the policy and transported on the designated vessel and voyage. The policy is the main document for the insured to claim compensation from the insurer when the subject-matter insured suffers a loss due to a risk covered by the insurance, and it is also the main basis for the insurer to claim compensation from the insured.

2)保险凭证(Insurance Certificate)

保险凭证俗称小保单,是保险人签发给被保险人的、用以证明保险合同业已生效的文件。它有保险单正面的基本内容,但没有保险单反面的保险条款,是一种简化的保险合同,它同保险单具有相同的作用和效力。信用证中大多规定保险单或保险凭证均可接受。在采用预约保险和流动保险的情况下经常采用保险凭证。

The insurance certificate is a document issued by the insurer to the insured to prove that the insurance contract has come into effect. It has the basic content of the front side of the insurance policy, but without the insurance terms on the reverse side of the policy, it is a simplified insurance contract, which has the same function and effect as the insurance policy. Most letters of credit generally provide for the acceptance of either insurance policies or insurance certificates. Insurance certificates are often used where open and floating insurance are used.

3）联合保险凭证（Combined Insurance Certificate）

联合保险凭证俗称承保证明，它是我国保险公司特别使用的一种更为简化的保险单据，由保险公司在出口公司提交的发票上加上保险编号、承保险别、保险金额、装载船只、开船日期等，并加盖保险公司印章，这种单据不能转让。

The combined insurance certificate，commonly known as the risk note，is a more simplified insurance document especially used by the Chinese insurance company. The insurance company will add the insurance number，insurance coverage，insurance amount，loading vessel，sailing date，etc.，to the invoice submitted by the export company and stamp the seal of the insurance company on it，and this kind of document is not transferable.

4）暂保单（Cover Note，Binder）

暂保单是一种临时性的保险单，是投保人在不了解保险货物装载船名和起航日期的情况下，先行办理投保时，保险人签发的一种非正式的保险单，待投保人获得船名及起航日期信息后再通知保险人，换取正式保险单，或者用批单方式加贴在暂保单上。暂保单作为一种临时性保险单，在其规定的有效期内（一般是 30 天），其效力同正式保险单相同。

Cover note is a kind of temporary insurance policy，which is an informal insurance policy issued by the insurer when the policyholder first applies for the insurance without knowing the name of the ship on which the insurance goods are loaded and the date of sailing. When the policyholder obtains the information of the ship's name and sailing date，he will notify the insurer and exchange it for a formal insurance policy or affix an endorsement on the cover note. As a temporary insurance policy，a cover note has the same effect as a formal insurance policy for its stated period of validity （usually 30 days）.

13.3.2　保险单的缮制（Preparation of Insurance Policies）

保险单是保险公司根据投保人所提供的投保单的内容制作的，因此，保险人在接受投保后，所缮制的保险单的内容应与投保单一致，以满足投保人对保险的要求。

The policy is made by the insurance company according to the application form made out by the applicant. Therefore，the contents of the policy shall be consistent with the insurance application form to meet the requirements of the applicant.

保险单通常应包括下列事项。

Usually，policy making involves the following.

（1）保险公司名称（name of insurance company）。保险单最上方均事先印就保险公司的名称。投保人应根据信用证和合同要求到相应的保险公司去办理保险单据，尤其在信用证支付方式下，如规定"insurance policy in duplicate by PICC"，PICC 即中国人民保险公司，信用证要求出具由中国人民保险公司出具的保险单。

（2）保险单据名称。如海运货物保险单的名称为"货物运输保险单"（cargo transportation insurance policy）。此栏按照信用证和合同填制，如来证规定"insurance policy in duplicate"，即要求出具保险单而非保险凭证（insurance certificate）等。

（3）发票号码（invoice No.）。此栏填写投保货物商业发票的号码。

（4）保险单号（No.）。此栏为保险公司按出单顺序编排的保险单号码。

（5）被保险人（insured）。被保险人俗称"抬头"，应按投保单中的内容填写。如信用证规定被保险人为某公司或某银行，保险单抬头应直接打上该公司或该银行的名称。在CIF、CIP术语下，如信用证无特别规定，此栏一般填信用证的受益人，即出口公司名称。

（6）保险货物项目（description of goods）。此栏填制货物的名称，一般按投保单填制，应与发票及其他单据上名称相符。

（7）包装及数量（quantity）。此栏按投保单填制。包装货物应标明包装方式及数量，如"100箱""200包"等，有两种或两种以上包装方式时，应标明"包装件数"（如500 packages），散装货物需标明，并注明重量，如"…M/T in bulk"。

（8）保险金额（amount insured）。应按照投保单金额填写，小数点后的尾数一律进为整数。保额的加成比例严格按照信用证或合同的规定，如信用证和合同无明确规定，一般都以CIF或CIP发票金额的110%填写。

（9）承保险别（conditions）。此栏应根据投保单的要求填制，具体载明保险公司承担的保险责任，要求全面、详细和准确。

（10）标记（marks and notes）。此栏应填制发票上所标的唛头，也可采取填写"as per invoice No. ×××"的做法。这是因为保险索赔时必须提供发票，保险单与发票可以相互参照。

（11）总保险金额（amount insured in capital）。这一栏只需将（8）中的保险金额以大写的形式填入，计价货币也应以全称形式填入。注意：保险金额使用的货币单位应与信用证中的一致，如应填say U. S. dollars one thousand two hundred and fifty-five only。

（12）保费（premium）。此栏一般只打"按照约定"（as arranged），除非信用证另有规定，如"insurance policy endorsed in blank full invoice value plus 10% marked premium paid"，此栏就填入"paid"字样。若信用证要求标明保费和费率，则应打上具体保费金额和保险费率。

（13）装载运输工具（per conveyance S. S）。如采用海运，按照投保单和提单上的记载填写船名和航次。若船名未知，则填写"to be declared"；如需转船，则在第一程船名后加注第二程船名。如采用铁路运输，此栏填写by railway或加注车号；如采用航空运输，此栏填写by air；如采用邮包运输，此栏填写by parcel post。

（14）开航日期（sailing on or about 或 date of commencement）。此栏一般填写"按所附提单"（as per B/L），表明以提单为准，或填写具体日期或大致日期（about 1 SEP. 2023）。

（15）、（16）运输起讫地点（from…to…）。此栏按照投保单和提单填制货物实际装运的起运港口和目的港口名称，货物如转船，也应把转船地点填上，如 From Ningbo, China to New York,USA via HongKong(or W/T HongKong)。

注：有时信用证中未明确列明具体的起运港口和目的地港口，如 any Chinese port 或 any Japanese port，填制时应根据货物实际装运选定一个具体的港口，如 Shanghai 或 Osaka 等。

（17）赔款偿付地点(claim payable at/in...)。一般以目的地为赔款偿付地，不能把国家名称作为赔付地点。如果投保人要求在目的地以外的某一具体地点付款，如属于贸易需要或正当要求，一般应予接受。

若信用证规定赔付的货币名称，本栏填写：at...（目的地）in...（货币名称），如 Claim payable at New York in USD。

（18）出单日期与地点(issuing date...at...)。保险单的签发日期应不迟于运输单据的日期，因为银行不接受迟于运输单据的保险单。实务中一般以投保单上的日期作为保单签发日期。

（19）保险公司在目的地的检验、理赔代理人名称及详细地址、电话号码等内容(survey by...)。检验代理人和理赔代理人可能是同一个人，也可能不是同一个人，应在保险单中注明。若最后目的地没有保险公司检验代理人，应规定可由当地合格的代理人检验(Survey to be carried out by a local competent surveyor)。

（20）保险公司代表签名(authorized signature)。保险单需经保险公司授权的人签章才能生效。

中国人民保险公司出具的保险单一式四份，由两份正本和两份副本构成。保险公司和出口商各留一份副本，其余两份正本由出口商提交给银行进行结汇。

The policy issued by the people's Insurance Company of China is in quadruplicate，consisting of two originals and two copies．The insurance company and the exporter shall keep one copy respectively，and the other two originals shall be submitted by the exporter to the bank for foreign exchange settlement.

单据 13.3　保险单

13.3.3　保险单的批改和转让(Policy's Amendment and Transfer)

1. 保险单的批改(Amendment of Policy)

保险单签发后，在保险单有效期内，其内容一般不宜修改，但在实际业务中，由于种种原因，投保人在向保险公司申报时，陈述错误或遗漏是难以完全避免的。在此情况下，如不及时变更或修改，被保险人的利益极有可能受到影响，甚至导致保险合同失效。此外，保险货物在运输过程中，也可能遇到某种意外情况，如承运人根据运输合同所赋予的权利改变航行路线、更改目的地、临时挂靠非预定港口或转船等。这些新变化也要求对原保险单内容及时进行变更或修改，以便保险标的获得与新的情况相适合的保险保障。

After the issuance of an insurance policy, it is generally inappropriate to amend its contents during the validity period of the policy. However, in actual business, due to various reasons, it is difficult to completely avoid mistakes or omissions in the statements made by the policyholder when declaring to the insurance company. In this case, if the policy is not changed or modified in time, the interests of the insured are likely to be affected, and even lead to the invalidation of the insurance contract. In addition, the insured goods may also encounter certain unforeseen circumstances in the course of transportation, such as the carrier's change of sailing route, change of destination, and temporary attachment to a non-scheduled port or transfer of vessel, in accordance with the rights conferred by the contract of carriage. These new changes also require that the contents of the original policy be changed or modified in a timely manner so that the subject-matter insured is covered by insurance appropriate to the new circumstances.

保险单内容的变更和修改,往往会影响保险人的承保责任范围以及承担的风险。投保人或被保险人如果需要对保险单内容进行变更或修改,应以书面形式向保险人申请批改。通常只要不超过保险条款规定允许的内容,保险人都会接受。如果涉及扩大承保责任或增加保险金额,一般也是可以的,但是必须在被保险人不知有损失事故发生的情况下,在抵达目的地之前申请办理,并需追加一定的保险费。

Changes and modifications to the contents of policies often affect the insurer's coverage and risks assumed. If the contents of the policy needs to be changed or modified, the applicant or the insured shall apply to the insurer for approval in writing. Normally, the insurer will accept the insurance as long as it does not exceed what is permitted under the insurance clause. If it involves expanding the liability or increasing the amount of insurance, it is generally acceptable, but it must be applied for before the arrival of the subject-matter insured at its destination without the insured's knowledge of the occurrence of the loss, and a certain amount of additional insurance premium is required.

批改保险单一般采用签发批单的方式。此项工作可由保险人自己办理,也可由保险人授权设在国外港口的代理人办理。保险人或其代理人所签发的批单,一般应贴在原保险单上,构成原保险单的一个组成部分,对双方当事人均有约束力。

The amendment of policy is generally done by way of issuing an endorsement. This may be done by the insurer himself or by an agent authorized by the insurer to be located in a foreign port. The endorsement issued by the insurer or his agent should generally be affixed to the original policy, constituting an integral part of the original policy and binding on both parties.

2. 保险单的转让(Assignment of Policy)

保险单的转让是指持有保险单的人将保险单所赋予的要求损失赔偿的权利以及相应的诉讼权转让给受让人,因此,保险单的转让即保险单权利的转让。这种权利的转让与保险货物本身所有权的转让是两种不同的法律行为,买卖双方交接货物,转移货物所有权,并不能自动转移保险单的权利。

The transfer of policy means that the holder of the policy transfers the right to claim compensation for losses and the corresponding litigation right to the assignee, so the transfer of policy is the transfer of the right to the policy. The transfer of such rights and the transfer of ownership of the insured goods themselves are two different legal acts，and the handing over of the goods by the buyer and the seller and the transfer of ownership of the goods do not automatically transfer the rights under the policy.

保险单的转让通常采取由被保险人背书或其他习惯方式进行。根据国际保险业的习惯做法，保险单经被保险人背书后，即随同被保险货物权利的转移而自动转让给受让人，事先事后都不需通知保险人。保险单的背书需在正本保险单上进行，背书的方式分为记名背书和空白背书两种。除非信用证另有规定，保险单多为空白背书，即在正本保险单的背面注明被保险人的名称。

The transfer of policy is usually carried out by the insurer's endorsement or by other customary means. According to the customary practice in the international insurance industry，policy，once endorsed by the insured，is automatically transferred to the assignee with the transfer of the rights to the insured goods，without prior or subsequent notice to the insurer. The endorsement of the policy must be made on the original policy，and the endorsement is divided into two types：full endorsement (named endorsement) and blank endorsement. Unless otherwise stipulated in the letter of credit，the policy is mostly endorsed in blank，i. e.，the name of the insured (name of the insurance company and signature of the agent) is indicated on the back of the original policy.

13.4　保险的索赔与理赔实务(Insurance Claim and Settlement Practice)

13.4.1　保险索赔实务(Insurance Claim Practice)

保险索赔是指被保险货物遭受损失后，被保险人应按规定办理索赔手续，向保险人要求赔偿。办理国际货运保险索赔时，被保险人对保险标的必须具有保险利益，以海运为例，若以 CIF 条件成交，货物的损失若是发生在起运港货物装上船之前的运输途中，应由卖方向保险公司索赔；如果货物损失发生在装上船之后，根据保险利益原则，应由买方向保险公司索赔。保险索赔程序包括以下步骤。

Insurance claim refers to that after the insured good have suffered losses, the insured shall go through the claim procedures according to the regulations and claim for compensation from the insurer. When handling an international cargo insurance claim, the insured must have an insurable interest in the subject-matter insured. Taking marine transportation as an example，if the transaction is concluded on CIF terms, the seller shall claim compensation from the insurance company if the loss of the goods occurs in transit before the goods are loaded on board; if the loss of the goods occurs after loading on board，the buyer shall claim from the insurance company according to the principle of insurance interests. The insurance claim procedure includes the following steps.

1. 损失通知，申请检验(Informing the Insurer of the Loss and Applying for Inspection)

被保险人一经获悉或发现保险标的遭受损失，应立即向保险人或其指定的代理人发出损失通知，同时申请对货物损失进行检验。保险人在接到损失通知后，一方面对货物提出施救意见并及时对货物进行施救，避免损失扩大；另一方面尽快对货物损失进行检验，核定损失原因，确定损失责任，查核发货人或承运人的责任等。

As soon as the insured learns of or discovers the loss of the subject-matter insured, he shall immediately send a notice of loss to the insurer or the designated agent and apply for inspection of the loss of the goods. After receiving the notice of loss, the insurer shall, on the one hand, put forward rescue advice on the goods and rescue the goods in time to avoid the expansion of losses; on the other hand, inspect the loss of the goods as soon as possible, verify the cause of the loss, determine the liability for the loss, and check the liability of the consignor or carrier.

保险人对货物的损失通知和检验申请都有严格的时间限制，中国的保险公司一般要求申请检验的时间最迟不能超过保险责任终止后 10 天。若被保险人延迟通知，耽误了保险公司核查工作，保险人有权拒绝理赔。

The insurer has strict time limit on the notice of loss and application for inspection. Chinese insurance companies generally require that the time for applying for inspection shall not exceed 10 days after the termination of insurance liability. If the insured delays the notification and the verification work of the insurance company as well, the insurer has the right to refuse to settle the claim.

我国对受损货物进行损失检验一般采取联合检验的方式，即凡与受损货物有关的各方，包括收货人、保险人、承运人或其代理及商检部门等共同对货物损失进行检验和鉴定。

In China, joint inspection is generally adopted for the damage inspection of damaged goods; that is, all parties related to the damaged goods, including the consignee, the insurer, the carrier or its agent and the commodity inspection department, shall jointly inspect and identify the loss of the goods.

2. 向承运人等有关方面提出索赔(Lodging Claims Against the Carriers and the Other Parties Concerned)

被保险人或其代理人在提货时若发现货物包装有明显残损痕迹，或者整件短少等情况，还应立即向承运方、受托人及海关、港务当局等索取货损货差证明。当这些货损货差涉及承运人、受托方、码头或装卸公司等的责任时，应立即以书面形式向他们提出索赔并保留追偿权利。因为按照运输契约等相关规定，若不在当时提出索赔，等于收货人承认提货时货物完好，这可能会影响后续的索赔工作。保险公司对丧失追偿权利部分的损失可以拒绝赔偿。因此，及时向责任方进行追偿、维护保险人的代位追偿权是被保险人应履行的重要义务。

When taking delivery of the goods, if the insured or his agent finds obvious traces of damage to the package of the goods, or the whole package of goods is short, the insured or his agent shall immediately request the carrier，the trustee，the customs and port authorities，etc.，for proof of damage and deficiency of the goods. When such cargo damage and deficiency involves the responsibility of the carrier，the agent，the terminal or the stevedoring company，etc.，the insured shall immediately file a claim in writing to them and reserve the right to recover. Because according to the relevant provisions of the contract of carriage，if the claim is not made at the time，it is equivalent to the consignee admitting that the goods are in good condition when the goods are taken，which may affect the subsequent claim work. The insurance company may refuse to pay for the loss for which the right of recovery has been lost. Therefore，it is an important obligation for the insured to seek compensation from the responsible party in time and maintain the insurer's right of subrogation.

3. 对受损货物采取合理的施救措施（Taking Reasonable Rescue Measures for Damaged Goods）

保险货物受损后，被保险人应对受损货物采取必要的施救、整理措施，以免损失扩大。在我国，根据《海商法》的规定，进口货物受损后，被保险人应根据保险人的通知，对受损货物进行施救与整理，若违反规定造成货物损失的扩大，保险人对该扩大的损失部分不负赔偿责任。

After the insured goods are damaged，the insured shall take necessary rescue and sorting measures for the damaged goods，so as to avoid extra loss. In China，according to the *Maritime Law*，after the imported goods are damaged，the insured shall rescue and sort out the damaged goods according to the notice of the insurer. If the loss of the goods is enlarged due to violation of the regulations，the insurer shall not be liable for the extended loss.

4. 提交索赔单据（Submitting Documents for Claim）

保险货物的损失经过检验，向承运人等第三者的追偿手续办妥之后，被保险人可向保险公司或其代理人提请赔偿。索赔时应提交必需的各种单证，包括保险单正本、运输单据、发票、装箱单、货损货差证明、检验报告、海事报告、索赔清单等。

After the loss of the insured goods has been inspected and the procedures for recovery from the carrier and other third parties have been completed，the insured may claim compensation from the insurance company or its agent. When claiming for compensation，all kinds of necessary documents should be submitted，including original insurance policy，transportation document，invoice，packing list，certificate of cargo damage and shortage，inspection report，maritime report，claim list，etc.

13.4.2　保险理赔实务（Claim Settlement Practice）

保险理赔是指保险人接到被保险人的货物损失通知后，对损失进行检验和调查，确定损失的近因和损失的程度，并对责任归属进行确定，最后计算保险赔偿金额并支付赔款的一系列过程。国际货运保险中的理赔包括以下内容。

Insurance claim settlement refers to a series of processes in which the insurer, after receiving the insured's notice of loss of goods, examines and investigates the loss, determines the proximate cause of the loss and the extent of the loss, and determines the attribution of liability, and finally calculates the amount of insurance compensation and pays out the indemnity. Claims in international freight insurance include the following.

1. 确定损失的近因(Determining the Proximate Cause of the Loss)

对货物损失进行检验时,很重要的一项任务就是确定损失的原因。根据保险的近因原则,保险人只对近因属于承保风险而导致的损失予以负责。实际事故中,货物损失的情况多种多样,原因也复杂不一,因此,必须从若干致损原因中找出损失的近因,才能确定损失是否属于保险责任。

When inspecting the loss of goods, a very important task is to determine the cause of the loss. Under the proximate cause principle of insurance, the insurer is only liable for the losses caused by a proximate cause that counts as insured risk. In actual accidents, the loss of goods occurs in a variety of situations and for a variety of complex reasons. Therefore, it is necessary to identify the proximate cause of the loss from several causes of damage to determine whether the loss is covered under the insurance liability.

2. 确定责任归属(Ascertaining Liability Attribution)

损失原因确定后,保险人应根据保险条款中的险别及保险期限等规定,确定损失是否属于保险责任。同时,根据保险的最大诚信原则,审定被保险人是否履行了保险合同中规定的告知、保证义务。如未履行,保险人有权拒赔甚至解除保险合同。如果涉及第三者责任,保险人还要审定被保险人是否及时向责任方进行追偿,获取有关证明,有效地维护保险人代位追偿权的行使。如果被保险人放弃了向第三者要求赔偿的权利,或因被保险人的过错而使保险人丧失代位追偿权,保险人可以扣减保险赔款甚至拒付赔款。

After the cause of the loss is determined, the insurer shall determine whether the loss is covered by the insurance according to the insurance coverage and the insurance period specified in the insurance clause. At the same time, according to the principle of utmost good faith of insurance, it is determined whether the insured has fulfilled the obligation of notification and warranty stipulated in the insurance contract. If this is not done, the insurer has the right to refuse to pay compensation or even to terminate the insurance contract. If the liability of a third party is involved, the insurer will also have to determine whether the insured has made a timely recovery from the liable party, obtain relevant proofs and effectively safeguard the exercise of the insurer's right of subrogation. If the insured waives the right to claim compensation from a third party, or the insurer loses the right of subrogation due to the fault of the insured, the insurer can deduct the insurance compensation or even refuse to pay the compensation.

3. 计算赔偿金额（Calculating the Compensation Amount）

1）货物损失的赔偿（Compensation for Loss of Goods）

（1）对全损的赔偿。进出口货物运输保险通常都是定值保险,保险货物遭受全部损失,包括实际全损和推定全损,均以保险单载明的保险金额为准,全额赔付。如一份保险单按货物或品种分别列明保险金额,其中一种货物或一个品种遭受全损,也按其保险金额赔付。

（1）Compensation for total loss. Insurance for the transportation of imported and exported goods is usually fixed-value insurance, in which all losses of the insured goods, including actual total loss and constructive total loss, are paid in full according to the insurance amount stated in the policy. If policy specifies the amount of insurance according to the goods or varieties, and one of the goods or a variety suffers a total loss, it will also be paid according to its insurance amount.

（2）单独海损的赔偿。

（2）Compensation for particular average loss.

① 数量（重量）损失的赔偿。保险货物中部分货物灭失或数量（重量）短少,以灭失或损失的数量（重量）占保险货物总量之比乘以保险金额计算赔款。其计算公式为

$$赔款金额 = 保险金额 \times [损失数量（重量）/保险货物总量]$$

① Compensation for quantity or weight loss. If part of the insured goods is lost or the quantity（weight）of the insured goods is short, the compensation is calculated by multiplying the ratio of the quantity（weight）of the lost or damaged goods to the total amount of the insured goods by the insurance amount. The calculation formula is:

$$compensation\ amount = insurance\ amount \times [(quantity\ or\ weight\ lost)/$$
$$total\ quantity\ or\ weight]$$

② 质量损失的赔偿。保险货物遭受质量损失时,应先确定货物完好的价值和受损的价值,计算出贬值率,以此乘以保险金额,计算出赔款金额。完好价值和受损价值一般以货物抵达目的地时的市场价格为准。若受损货物在中途处理,不再运往目的地,则可按处理地的市场价格为准。其计算公式为

$$赔款金额 = 保险金额 \times [（货物完好价值 - 受损后价值）/货物完好价值]$$

实际业务中,若当地市价一时难以确定,经协议也可按发票价值计算,则计算公式为

$$赔款金额 = 保险金额 \times （按发票价值计算的损失额/发票价值）$$

② Compensation for quality loss. When the insured goods suffer quality loss, the value of intact and damaged goods should be determined first, and the depreciation rate should be calculated, which should be multiplied by the insurance amount to calculate the amount of compensation. The intact and damaged values are generally based on the market price of the goods at the time they arrive at the destination. If the damaged goods are disposed of in transit and are no longer transported to the destination, the market price at the place of disposal may prevail. The calculation formula is:

$$\text{compensation amount} = \text{insurance amount} \times [(\text{the intact value} - \text{the damaged value})/\text{the intact value}]$$

In real business, if it's difficult to determine the local market price, through agreement, the compensation amount can be calculated according to the invoice value. Then the calculation formula is:

$$\text{compensation amount} = \text{insurance amount} \times (\text{amount of loss reckoned on the invoice value}/\text{the invoice value})$$

③ 规定有绝对/相对免赔率的货物损失赔偿。对易碎、易损、易耗货物的保险,保险人往往规定有免赔率。免赔率的高低由保险人根据商品种类的不同而定,中国各保险公司采用的是绝对免赔额,即无论货物损失程度如何,对于免赔额度内的损失,保险人不予赔偿。

③ Compensation for loss of goods for which a deductible/franchise is provided. For insurance of fragile, perishable and consumable goods, insurers often provide for a deductible or franchise. The deductible/franchise is determined by the insurer according to the different types of commodities. Chinese insurance companies adopt absolute deductible, i. e. , regardless of the degree of loss of the goods, the insurer will not compensate for the loss within the deductible.

2) 有关费用损失的赔偿(Compensation for Loss of Related Expenses)

一旦发生保险事故,除了货物的损失,往往还导致费用的支付。这些费用包括施救费用、救助费用、续运费用、检验费用、出售费用以及理算费用等。对于这些费用的支出,保险人赔付的原则是,若货物损失属于保险责任,则对费用的支出予以赔付。

In the event of an insured accident, in addition to the loss of goods, it often results in the payment of expenses. These costs include rescue costs, salvage costs, renewal costs, inspection costs, selling costs and adjustment costs. The principle of the insurer's compensation for these expenses is that if the loss of the goods is covered by the insurance, the expenses will be paid.

3) 共同海损牺牲和分摊的赔偿(Compensation for Sacrifice and Contribution of General Average)

保险人承保的三种基本险(平安险、水渍险和一切险)对共同海损的损失,包括共同海损的牺牲和共同海损的分摊都负责赔偿。根据《海商法》第二百零三条的规定,共同海损理算适用合同约定的理算规则(如《约克-安特卫普规则》《中国国际贸易促进委员会共同海损理算规则》等),若合同没有约定,适用《海商法》第十章关于共同海损的相关规定。

The three basic risks (FPA, WA, all risks) insured by the insurer are liable to pay for the loss of general average, including the sacrifice and contribution of general average. According to article 203 of *Maritime Law*, the adjustment of general average shall be governed by the adjustment rules agreed upon in the contract (e. g. , the *York-Antwerp Rules*, the *Rules for General Average Adjustment of China Council for the Promotion of International Trade*, etc.), and if there is no such agreement in the contract，the relevant provisions of Chapter Ⅹ of *Maritime Law* on general average shall apply.

Words and Expressions

即测即练

习题

参 考 文 献

[1]　姚新超.国际贸易运输与保险[M].5 版.北京:对外经济贸易大学出版社,2020.

[2]　李勤昌.国际货物运输[M].6 版.大连:东北财经大学出版社,2022.

[3]　梁瑞,修媛媛,杨山峰,等.国际货物运输与保险[M].北京:清华大学出版社,2020.

[4]　黄海东,孙玉红.国际货物运输保险[M].4 版.北京:清华大学出版社,2021.

[5]　孟恬.国际货物运输与保险[M].北京:对外经济贸易大学出版社,2008.

[6]　潘永,李宝奕,廖佳.国际贸易运输与保险[M].大连:东北财经大学出版社,2020.

[7]　姚新超.国际贸易保险[M].4 版.北京:对外经济贸易大学出版社,2019.

[8]　顾寒梅,张华.国际货物运输保险理论与实务[M].北京:中国财富出版社,2005.

[9]　李贺.国际货物运输与保险 理论·实务·案例·实训[M].2 版.上海:上海财经大学出版社,2016.

[10]　崔玮.进出口业务模拟实训[M].北京:清华大学出版社,2011.

[11]　丁元平.2009 英国协会货物保险 A 条款的新发展及对我国的借鉴意义[D].大连:大连海事大学,2013.

[12]　王莹.2009 年伦敦协会货运险条款较 1982 年版的变化[J].上海保险,2009(7):9-13,17.

[13]　姚新超.英国协会货物条款(ICC2009)除外责任的新变化[J].对外经贸实务,2012(8):47-50.

[14]　张荣忠.世界能源运输线的咽喉要道——中国进口能源的运输风险与应对[J].港口经济,2004(5):35-38.

[15]　林子涵,唐雅晴.巴拿马运河水位"新低"冲击国际贸易[N].人民日报海外版,2023-07-18(10).

[16]　陈凯,陈继红.班轮公会的前世今生[J].中国远洋航务,2010(4):66-68.

[17]　董璐宇.从历史发展角度再论海运提单的法律性质[J].东南大学学报(哲学社会科学版),2021(6):112-116.

[18]　陈苾.由一则案例引发的海运提单抬头的写法思考[J].对外经贸,2020(10):22-25.

[19]　李艳利.分析海运提单的风险及防范措施[J].现代经济信息,2016(4):156-157.

[20]　孙佳佳,赵婷婷.海上货运"一切险"保什么[J].中国外汇,2016(1):68-69.

教师服务

　　感谢您选用清华大学出版社的教材！为了更好地服务教学，我们为授课教师提供本书的教学辅助资源，以及本学科重点教材信息。请您扫码获取。

≫ 教辅获取

本书教辅资源，授课教师扫码获取

≫ 样书赠送

国际经济与贸易类重点教材，教师扫码获取样书

清华大学出版社

E-mail: tupfuwu@163.com
电话：010-83470332 / 83470142
地址：北京市海淀区双清路学研大厦 B 座 509

网址：https://www.tup.com.cn/
传真：8610-83470107
邮编：100084